# Antique Boxes, Tea Caddies, & Society

## 1700—1880

### Antigone Clarke & Joseph O'Kelly

2nd Edition

Schiffer Publishing Ltd

4880 Lower Valley Road • Atglen, PA 19310

Copyright © 2018 by Antigone Clarke & Joseph O'Kelly

Library of Congress Control Number: 2018937431

Designed by RoS
Cover design by Justin Watkinson
Type set in Manuale

ISBN: 978-0-7643-5621-6
Printed in China

Published by Schiffer Publishing, Ltd.
4880 Lower Valley Road
Atglen, PA 19310
Phone: (610) 593-1777; Fax: (610) 593-2002
E-mail: Info@schifferbooks.com
Web: www.schifferbooks.com

For our complete selection of fine books on this and related subjects, please visit our website at www.schifferbooks.com. You may also write for a free catalog.

Schiffer Publishing's titles are available at special discounts for bulk purchases for sales promotions or premiums. Special editions, including personalized covers, corporate imprints, and excerpts, can be created in large quantities for special needs. For more information, contact the publisher.

We are always looking for people to write books on new and related subjects. If you have an idea for a book, please contact us at proposals@schifferbooks.com.

*To Pandora*

# *Acknowledgments*

Many people and institutions have helped, supported, and encouraged us throughout this project. Without them the work would have been more arduous and certainly poorer.

We extend our thanks to everyone who has contributed to the book in any way, especially John Bell for sharing his Scottish knowledge and heritage; Yasha Beresiner of InterCol, London, for his advice about playing cards; David Dyke, of Luthiers Supplies, East Sussex, UK, for advice on timbers; Don Jameson for photographic equipment and encouragement; Sylvia Long for sharing her library; Neil McLennan for help with Chinese calligraphy; and Gillian Nott and Andrew Renton for sharing their knowledge of straw work.

Our very special thanks to Guy Groen for translating old Dutch for us; also to David Tomsett for putting his extensive knowledge of Chinese history and culture at our disposal, and for his translations of Chinese texts and poetry. Unfortunately, lack of space does not permit inclusion of all his work.

We would also like to thank the librarians and staff of the British Library, the Patent Library, and Hackney Public Libraries for sourcing hard to find out-of-print material for us.

Collections in museums and stately homes have been indispensable. Particular mention should be made of the Victoria and Albert Museum, the Museum of Childhood, the Geffrye Museum, the Museum of London, Sir John Soane's Museum, and the British Museum in London.

Thanks to Rebekka Deighton, Collections Administrator and Access Coordinator of the Science Museum, London, for giving us access to Marc Isambard Brunel's Polygraph.

The straw marquetry collections of the Guildhall Museum, Rochester Kent, and of the Peterborough Museum & Art Gallery, Cambridgeshire, also deserve mention.

Heartfelt thanks to Ann Jameson for patiently and diligently proofreading the text.

Grateful thanks to everybody who lent us their boxes for illustration or provided us with photographs, including all the collectors who chose to remain anonymous.

Special thanks to the Bielstein Collection, Anne Brooks, Cathy A. Crim, K. R. Chin, the Christodoulides Family Collection, Betsy Dorminy, Robert A. Erlandson, Mrs. I. Finn, Mylissa Fitzsimmons-Grieve, Elizabeth Fuller, T. M. Golodetz, Ian Gouldsbrough, Christopher and Katharine Hughes, Ann Jameson, Joan Kiernan, Kevin R. Kiernan, Lana McLain, Dr. Joseph Martin, Samantha Millar, Berry and Marcia Morton, Charleen Plumly Pollard, Mary Harris Russell, Alan and Joanne Tausz, David Tomsett, Janice Walls Interiors, and Susan Webster.

We want to thank Graham Fowler, Christina Tattum, and Vincent Freeman Antiques for allowing us to photograph boxes from their stock and collections.

Our editors Donna Baker and Sandra Korinchak deserve a really heartfelt thank you for guiding us through the book-building process with transatlantic phone calls and email.

Our cats, who kept vigil throughout the work, sitting when and where required (or not required), meow mention.

# CONTENTS

# Introduction

Figure 1. Pandora opens her box! Penwork detail ca. 1810–1820: see figure 21.

The box is the great temptation. "Open me," it says. The human cannot resist it; its charm is overwhelming. Boxes have followed man through history—a useful, beautiful, fascinating companion.

Trying to deal with the complete history of the box is no less of a task than trying to deal with the history of humanity in one single book. The reason we have chosen the eighteenth and nineteenth centuries is because this particular period is a significant point in time in terms of the aesthetic and social history in the development of the box.

During the sixteenth and seventeenth centuries, the movement of trade brought awareness of diverse foreign cultures to a small European elite. As the eighteenth century progressed, the idea of unified design, which had been pioneered during the seventeenth century by Inigo Jones, began to take root. The momentum of knowledge had accumulated enough force to shape the aesthetic consciousness of a hitherto slow-changing and complacent clientele. At this time of increased appreciation of the potential expansiveness of design, widespread wealth made it possible to commission more pieces and thus drive forward such eclectic crafts as the making of boxes.

England was at the forefront of this movement, partly because of its aggressive trading practices and partly because of its progress into industrialization. After the loss of America, there was a concerted effort to increase development and wealth in new directions. Engineering progress made travel possible for more people and sailing on the high seas easier for merchants. Travel increased awareness, need, and demand.

In his latter years, a bewildered Dr. Johnson (1709—1784) summed up the age: "The age is running mad after innovation." By 1791, Sir Samuel Bentham, a naval officer and engineer, had patented his first woodworking machine. Bentham patented machines for planing, molding, rebating, grooving, mortising, and sawing. By the middle of the nineteenth century, many processes had been refined and simplified. Such innovations made it possible to set up complex professional workshops and produce well-constructed objects that were financially accessible to more people.

This book tries to deal with boxes not merely as lifeless objects, but as participants in a vibrant culture, which was responsible for their creation, and which, in their turn, they enhanced. For this reason we have constructed this work in three parts. The first chapters deal with the history and the influences that channeled the aesthetic direction of the times. The second group of chapters deals with specific work, which was sometimes encouraged on account of regional conditions or availability of materials. The last chapters deal with boxes selected by their use.

As space is not infinite, hard decisions had to be made in the selection of images. Sometimes we have used macro details without an overall picture of the box. Some boxes have been shown by using more than one image to give the reader a good understanding of period form, decoration, and finish.

## Second Edition

In this edition, we have replaced a few illustrations with examples that provide a better visual representation of the type of box in discussion. We have also added a few outstandingly rare and special boxes that we have been able to trace since the first edition of the book.

The temptation for collectors of only one type of box will be to skip all chapters except the one dealing with their particular interest. Please resist turning the pages too hastily. Much of the information in the early chapters applies to all types of boxes, and a deep understanding of the subject requires this background knowledge. By dealing with the material in this way, we have avoided the necessity of constant repetition.

Finally, we must beg the indulgence of the reader for our fascination with the gossip of the times; to our mind this is what breathes life into the boxes and makes them such personal chronicles of history.

# Price Guide

The price given is the price expected at specialized collection auctions, or special shows and retail establishments.

In the first edition, the prices were mostly relevant to the US market. Since the advent of the internet, prices have become more global, with other countries catching up with the US. The prices are still a good guide, although now that a level has been established we expect a more even rise worldwide. Certain sections, such as lacquer, are showing increased interest, and special rare examples in all sections can achieve unpredictably high prices at good auctions. It is best to buy with your heart and not trust examples that have been refinished or enhanced.

Prices for antiques are not strictly consistent, since different people value different elements according to their own preferences. Our most important consideration is that an object has survived with its integrity. Conservation and sensitive restoration are acceptable. Recent, brutal refinishing is detrimental, especially for boxes dating from the pre-Victorian period. Unless a Georgian box is extremely rare, a refinished example should be bought for less than half the lower listed figure.

Boxes that command a premium are:

Boxes that are in good original condition with rich patination.
Boxes with cultural content or historical significance.
Boxes that are exceptionally good examples of a genre.
Boxes that demonstrate an individualistic interpretation of a style.

I have omitted giving prices for some boxes. This is because they are very rare or special examples and, as such, the price they could fetch at auction is unpredictable. It is not unusual for collectors to contest pieces that do not appear often on the market for more than ten times the auctioneer's estimated price.

I have also not given prices for tea chests with silver containers. The quality and the maker of the silver are of paramount importance in such pieces, and, as such, an expert in antique silver would be a better person to consult as to the price.

### Ivory

Since the first edition of this book, the laws governing ivory sales have changed. Boxes incorporating or made of ivory are subject to CITES regulations that are enforced differently by different countries. This makes it difficult to offer universal values or advice (see https://cites.org/eng).

Currently (2018), the United Kingdom permits sales of "worked" ivory, which is pre-1947. Exports must be accompanied by pre-convention certificates. Auction prices have remained high, especially for important boxes and objects. Unfortunately, in the United States ivory sales have been almost totally forbidden. This is not stopping sales of ivory in the United States. Fraudulent descriptions such as "cow bone" are being used to try to get around the regulations. We advise against involvement in such transactions (see www.fws.gov/international/travel-and-trade/ivory-ban-questions-and-answers.html).

It is our sincere hope that effective measures can be put in place to stop the illegal slaughter of elephants. Destroying our cultural heritage with ineffectual laws put in place for populist political expediency has resulted only in devious fraudulent practices. We all wish for the survival and welfare of these magnificent animals. It would be very sad if the lazy laws to protect endangered species led to the destruction of antiques that represent cultural history and have often only *de minimis* or small amounts of ivory, such as an escutcheon.

any boxes made in the first half of the eighteenth century are practically indistinguishable from boxes that date from the latter part of the previous century. Boxes in solid carved wood and early chinoiserie-decorated boxes are impossible to date precisely. Stylistic development was slow at the time, especially since boxes were made in very limited numbers and mostly for specific patrons. Box making as such had not yet developed as a separate applied art form, with the result that it was treated as an extension of the work of the furniture maker. In stately homes, boxes were made by resident carpenters.

The first tentative attempts at producing boxes as art objects took place at the town of Spa in the Low Countries and, a little later, at Tunbridge Wells in England. The curative waters of these locations attracted both the invalids and the hypochondriacs of the time. Because indulging in hypochondria is a costly pastime, such health spots soon became magnets for society and fashion. Local crafts acquired a new impetus and developed along sophisticated aesthetic directions.

During the early part of the eighteenth century, the few boxes that were made by cabinetmakers or carpenters featured structural and decorative elements found on the furniture of the period. The forms of the boxes were simple, mostly rectangular, with protruding flat lids. Walnut, oak, and later mahogany

veneers were used to cover the structure of the box, which was usually made in oak.

After about 1730, the lids were mostly constructed with some depth, a form that has survived to this day.

The respect for the quality of the wood was evident in the careful way that juxtapositions of veneers, inlays, marquetry, and parquetry designs were executed. The grain, color, and figure of the timbers were skillfully combined in order to achieve rich, yet subtle effects. The arts of inlay and marquetry were held in high regard and gained in popularity as the century progressed. The partnership of William Ince and John Mayhew (1758—1804), one of the most significant cabinetmaking firms of the eighteenth century, contributed to the development of the art of inlay, in "remarkable fine-colored woods." Their work can still be seen in many stately homes. One feature that this major workshop pioneered was the successful combination of earlier panels of floral marquetry with new work.

This reuse of panels was not surprising, given the skill that was necessary in crafting such complex and costly work. If, for example, a piece of furniture was destroyed by fire, parts that were worth preserving were salvaged and reused. Incorporating earlier marquetry into the design of a box proved very effective, since it enabled important surviving work to be given

Figure 2. Veneered in burr wood, probably mulberry, and mounted in silver, this Dutch made box is characteristic of late-seventeenth- to early-eighteenth-century work. 6.5" wide. $3,500–5,000.

Figure 3. Juxtaposed light oak and mahogany on a "country"-made striking box. 9.5" wide. Second half eighteenth century. $1,400–2,000.

prominence within a smaller framework. Furthermore, the earlier work did not feature "engraving" on the wood but had an altogether graver appearance, which harmonized well with some of the early-eighteenth-century venerable interiors.

After the middle of the eighteenth century, increased mobility encouraged the production of more boxes. By this time, boxes began to acquire a more assertive identity. They were designed within the stylistic concepts of the period, and they were considered as necessary accessories. At about the same time, cabinetmaking was beginning to demand recognition as a craft on a par with other professional disciplines.

*Of all the Arts which are either improved or ornamented by Architecture, that of Cabinet-Making is not only the most useful and ornamental, but capable of receiving as great assistance from it as any whatever. I have therefore prefixed to the following designs a short explanation of the five Orders. Without an acquaintance with this science and some knowledge of the rules of Perspective, the Cabinet-maker cannot make the designs of his work intelligible, not show in a little compass, the whole conduct and effect of the piece. These, therefore, ought to be carefully studied by everyone who would excel in this branch, since they are the very soul and basis of his Art.*

Figure 4. Flat top and side carving typical of seventeenth- and early-eighteenth-century work. *Courtesy of Ann Jameson*. $1,200–1,500.

*Above and left:*
Figure 5. This box illustrates both the artistic and the technical virtuosity of the maker. It is veneered in laburnum oysters, the patterns separated by fruitwood lines. The book-matched veneers are orchestrated in circular patterns that follow the swirl of the color variation and line of the wood. The inverted semicircular design that frames the central flower-suggesting circle throws the roundness into a spiky, exploding relief. This is work that truly uses wood as an art medium. Boxes of this large, flat form are referred to as "lace boxes." They would have been used to store small precious pieces of lace accessories. Such boxes were made for a very short period of time from the end of the seventeenth century to the first years of the eighteenth. 19" wide. Ca. 1700. $4,000–5,000.

Figure 6. Book-matched yew wood veneer banded in rosewood. Note how the robust figure is utilized to a striking and yet unfussy effect. 10" wide. Ca. 1790. $1,000–1,500.

Figure 7. A box veneered in very striking veneers of ash and ice birch made in simple lines of well-balanced and pleasing proportions. 8" wide. Ca. 1780. $1,200–1,800.

These are the words of Thomas Chippendale in his preface to his *Gentleman and Cabinet-Maker's Director*, three editions of which were published between 1754 and 1762. This is the first time that several boxes appeared in a serious work of cabinet design, and boxes bearing the characteristics of the illustrated examples are often referred to as in the "Chippendale style." This is not to say that Chippendale promoted only these particular styles. He, in fact, gave substance to many ideas and cooperated with other giants of design, such as Robert Adam, on important cabinetmaking projects.

Chippendale's most important contribution, however, was his insistence that the cabinetmaker's approach to his work must be utterly professional, adhering to scientific and aesthetic principles and having complete mastery of his materials.

Trade cards of the earlier part of the century describe woodworkers as "joiners." By the time Chippendale was writing, he referred to his fellow workers as cabinetmakers and emphasized the need to treat their work as equally valid as the work of architects. It is interesting that Thomas Chippendale's own father, John, referred to himself as a joiner. On the other hand, his son, who continued Thomas's work, was a "cabinet maker."

Chippendale himself was a master of his art. He contributed to the evolution of box style not only through his specific box drawings, but also through his furniture. His contribution to chinoiserie cannot be overstated. He also made extensive use of classical motifs and structures. In his furniture work, he used woods and techniques identical to those found on boxes. His carved ornament and feet were translated into gadrooning, reeded and radiating carving, and turned and carved feet, all

of which feature on late-eighteenth- and early-nineteenth-century boxes.

However, although Chippendale's contribution enhanced every style of the period, it is his designs for chest-shaped tea caddies that have given such boxes their "Chippendale style" label. Some of the designs have both rococo and earlier baroque elements, and some feature the straight lines of neoclassicism. In the first edition of the *Director*, there is blind fretting in the Chinese taste shown on boxes. These designs are omitted from the third edition, which paradoxically contains furniture decorated in this fashion. (See figure 316.)

Any box structured in the form of a chest, usually with a handle on the top and standing on metal feet or wooden brackets, is usually referred to as "Chippendale." These boxes vary in quality and were made by many makers, some of whom worked before Chippendale. It is important to remember that Chippendale did not initiate style. He worked within the confines of the aesthetics of his period, interpreting the "Chinese, Gothic, Rococo, and Modern Taste" in the most "elegant" way. His art was to give life to the concepts that were engendered by the intellectual curiosity of the time, and translate them into works that combined usefulness and beauty. In this he set standards that inspired many a box maker.

From about 1780 onward, the "Chippendale" style in boxes was superseded by the vogue for neoclassical design. At the same time, chinoiserie and japanning, which had been practiced throughout the eighteenth century, also became a favorite form of decoration on boxes. These two diverse fashions coexisted for the next fifty years, and sometimes they fused on rare, single items.

*Above and left:*
Figure 8. A rare example of a box dating from the second half of the century, incorporating a panel of arabesque foliage marquetry of an earlier date. The sides are made of earlier panels of floral marquetry in woods and ivory, framed by walnut veneer. The design on the side panels is more abruptly cut than the top panel, which is impeccably matched. 15.5" wide. Ca. 1750, with late-seventeenth- to early-eighteenth-century panels. $?

*Above and right:*
Figure 9. A Chippendale-style tea chest veneered in walnut. The sides show part of an earlier star design marquetry panel. 9.75" wide. Ca. 1760. $3,000–4,000.

Figure 10. A late-eighteenth-century box veneered in richly colored mahogany and edged with a band of very fine lines forming a geometric design. Ca. 1790–1800. *Courtesy of Janice Walls Interiors.* $800–1,000.

Figure 11. This is a piece of its time. The box is made of maple and is edged in fine lines of boxwood and green wood. An oval central cartouche in the neoclassical style is defined by typical neoclassical leaf-and-dot design. The proportions of the box are again typical of early neoclassical form. The surface of the box is decorated in penwork. The border is foliated and the center is worked with a chinoiserie scene. The two major trends of the century uncharacteristically fused on one item. 11.5" wide. Ca. 1790. $1,600–2,000.

Figure 12. A box covered in leather with cut-steel and cloth decoration in fern patterns. This is a piece that shows late-eighteenth-century decorative techniques. By this time, box making was beginning to establish a separate identity, allowing for more idiosyncratic and delightfully fine decoration. 6.5" wide. Ca. 1790. $1,200–1,500.

Before abandoning this period, a word must be said about the finishes on these early boxes. Most cabinetmakers had their own recipes for varnishing, or simply waxing, their boxes. Francis Thompson, who advertised knife boxes and other boxes among his wares, also offered "Ready Money for Bees Wax" on his 1750 trade card. Beeswax was a major ingredient for most finishes. In his *Cabinet Dictionary* of 1803, Sheraton gives a "receipt for a polishing wax" that entails melting turpentine with beeswax and, while still on the fire, adding a small quantity of finely ground red lead and fine Oxford ochre. When the mixture was taken off the fire, a little copal varnish was added, mixed in well, and worked in water into a ball. This was to be applied with a brush. Copal is a hard resin obtained from tropical trees.

Linseed, nut, and poppy oil combined with beeswax, as well as other resins in addition to copal, were also used. As with japanned finishes, there was no standard rule. It is very rare to find boxes with these original idiosyncratic finishes. It is very important not to refinish these pieces, since they are often unique and have mellowed into warm, glowing surfaces, which are just not possible to reproduce. In their original condition, they are a complete record of their time.

Figure 13. A box covered in silk and decorated with silver leaf-and-dot patterns. The whole is under glass. The glass is embellished with mirrored designs. This piece oozes stylish decadence. Its decoration is reminiscent of "patches" that were part and parcel of eighteenth-century makeup. A special commission by a spirited "macaroni"? 10.25" wide. Third quarter eighteenth century. $?

The term "neoclassicism" is often equated with the brothers Adam, especially Robert. The neoclassical style, however, is broader than the style expounded by the Adams, although "in the Adam style" is often used loosely when describing certain eighteenth-century boxes. Robert Adam (1728—1792) was born in Scotland and spent the years 1750—1758 in Italy. He then came to England, where he established himself as the most distinguished exponent of the neoclassical style. Adam influenced the design of objects primarily by advocating unity of style in architecture, which demanded that interiors were in harmony with the overall design of a building. It therefore followed that boxes destined for neoclassical interiors were designed to contribute to the aesthetic unity of the overall decorative scheme.

Adam was neither the inventor nor the first architect-designer to design in the neoclassical tradition; this distinction must be accorded to James "Athenian" Stuart, who on his return from Greece designed the first neoclassical interiors at Spencer House in London between 1756 and 1765. Arguably, however, Adam was the most finite exponent of the style. Nothing before his designs was so stylistically precise, and nothing after was so rigidly prescribed. Adam defined and drew his ideas within a recognized concept, which made his brand of neoclassicism very distinct.

Before Adam, designs primarily followed the Italian Renaissance interpretations of antiquity. After Adam, neoclassicism developed beyond Greece and Rome to include the ancient styles of the Middle East. However, during the last two decades of the eighteenth century, his influence on box design was so strong that it is no wonder that his name is used as a generic term for describing neoclassical style boxes.

The eighteenth century positively palpitated with classical thought and form. The early decades saw the rise of a ponderous classicism, which favored heavy ornamentation, often verging on the baroque. Very few boxes were made during this period, and even fewer that can be described as of a definite style.

The more widespread influence of classicism was sparked off by the excavations in Herculaneum in 1738 and Pompeii ten years later. The story goes that a peasant tripped up and the lava-covered city was thus accidentally discovered. Whatever the truth of the discovery, it captivated the imagination of the world and, for a time, became the idealized aesthetic prototype.

Somewhere deeply embedded in the psyche of the eighteenth-century person was a belief that moral and aesthetic harmonies were inextricably interlinked. The philosophical formulation of the century's thought was expounded by many

Figure 14. A mahogany tea caddy inlaid with a swag of laurel in the style of classical ornament. The contrast of the wood is very subtle, and the components that make up the leaves and berries are delicately cut and arranged in a continuous yet uncluttered garland. The top is inlaid in the four corners with sprigs of laurel and the center with an elongated wreath. Most of the inlaid pieces are cut from end-grain wood, which has contracted differently from the main veneer. This has resulted in exceptionally fine patination. 6.75" wide. Ca. 1780. $?

Figure 15. A deceptively simple box veneered with bands of different woods, which offer variety without strong contrasts. The outer band is in burr walnut, then burr yew, then a thinner line of rosewood, and then elm. The different woods are separated with boxwood stringing. The sides are veneered in two types of wood, walnut and yew. The top and the sides are inlaid with ebony with a stylized motif in symmetrical mirror image. The perfect proportions, straight lines, and symmetry of decoration place this piece within the neoclassical tradition. 11" wide. Ca. 1790. $2,000–2,500.

Figure 16. A sycamore-veneered box painted with classical figures having a picnic under a tree draped with a red cloth. The figures seem to be sitting comfortably on luxurious cushions and their wine (?) amphora is of considerable size. The scene is rooted in a more romantic style of neoclassicism and is reminiscent of classical wall paintings, such as *Lovers on a Couch* from Herculaneum. The concave border of the box is decorated with a classical, continuous palmette motif. The sides are painted with naturalistic flowers in another concession to romanticism. 10.75" wide. Ca. 1815. $4,000–6,000.

Figure 17. An oval caddy veneered in mahogany and fruitwood, with a good central patera design. The patera motif, in its various forms, was an abstraction of a shallow dish used in the classical world for offering libations. Ca. 1790. *Courtesy of a private collection.* $3,500–4,500.

thinkers and found many followers. Archibald Alison's *Essays on the Nature and Principles of Taste* ran into six editions between 1790 and 1825. He even justified the Chinese style on account of its Eastern significance and splendor and the Gothic style by reason of its recollection of manners and adventure. Everything needed a grand past. A few decades later, classicism acquired a glow of romanticism. In his *Ode on a Grecian Urn* (1819), John Keats summarized the final phase:

*Beauty is truth—truth beauty,—that is all*
*Ye know on earth and all ye, need to know.*

The pursuit of aesthetic excellence as a manifestation of moral integrity may have been a self-deluding veneer for the expense spent on an ever-increasing number of luxurious objects, which were deemed necessary for a genteel style of living. This new thinking recognized the need for the infusion of new ideas into the stagnating mores of the time, and visual impact was an accessible method of ushering in the new philosophy.

Johann Joachim Winckelmann (1717–1768) is credited as the trail blazer of neoclassical thought. He was one of a handful of archaeologists who at an early stage examined the remains of Herculaneum, Pompeii, and Paestum. He also worked as the librarian to antiquarian Cardinal Albani. In 1763, he became the superintendent of antiquities in Rome. In 1755, he produced his first influential opus, *Reflections on the Imitation of Greek Works in Painting and Sculpture*. He published his epoch-shaking work, *Geschichte der Kunst des Alterthums*, in 1764. This work brought to his readers more than two hundred

engravings of firsthand observations of the ancient world, and it was translated both into English and French. His *Monumenti Antichi Inediti*, which included prints of line drawings, followed in 1766. These works extinguished the last whiff of rococo for the remainder of the century and paved the way for the more practical exponents of the neoclassical style.

Purity of form and mind was espoused in England by the Society of Antiquaries and the Society of Dilettanti. The Dilettanti society was founded in 1732 and consisted of a group of architects and patrons who favored classical design. Most of these men had traveled to some of the sites of the ancient world and had pretensions to intellectual superiority. In 1769, the society sponsored the first publication of *Ionian Antiquities*. Four more volumes followed.

By the 1760s, there was already an eager and willing clientele for objects and interiors in the neoclassical fashion. The Grand Tour, which was a journey to Italy via other European countries and to which every young man of social standing embarked on in the hope of completing his education, was already well established. Travel accounts and drawings were in circulation early on in the century. Many Europeans set up their quarters in the city of Rome and frequented establishments such as the *Caffe degli Inglesi* to rub shoulders with artists, scholars, dealers, and would-be connoisseurs. Only the very determined went as far as Greece, the Middle East, or North Africa.

Many youths, or other persons aspiring to classical credentials, did not make the grade and became the butt of such caricatures as Thomas Patch's *The Golden Asses*, painted in 1761, or Joshua Reynolds's 1751 parody of the *School of Athens*. Despite

*Above and right:*
Figure 18. A painted box that encapsulates the spirit of the late eighteenth century. The center is painted with two classical figures draped in diaphanous clothes, flanking a classical urn. They hold tools emblematic of the arts of painting and sculpture. The frame depicts naturalistically painted native flowers. The front and sides have further symbolic representations of art and nature. Note the beehive on the front, symbolizing industry in nature, and the harp, symbolizing music. The box has a shallow drawer on the side, which is released by a spring mechanism. The top is partitioned. An early example of a paint box. 14.5" wide. Ca. 1780. $6,000–8,000.

Figure 19. Two boxes framed in stringings and inlays with centrally placed prints of the same classical scene. A cutout pasted inside one tells us that it is Minerva quitting Telemachus. 4" and 6.5" wide. Ca. 1800–1810. $700–1,000.

the fact that the majority of those who embarked on the Grand Tour did not have the aptitude to absorb much culture, nor the potential for intellectual effort, they did adopt neoclassicism as a lifestyle. The travelers had the money to buy artifacts and also to get their portrait painted by enterprising artists such as Pompeo Batoni (1708—1787), who specialized in painting gentlemen posing against classical ruins and objects. Some even dressed themselves in togas! Others opted for group paintings among ancient art treasures. The channels of knowledge were sometimes superficial, but all the same, the moneyed young men acquired a taste for the classical, even if they did not quite understand it. Many matured into important patrons of the cabinetmakers and architects, who fortunately had a good grasp of the principles of the newly adopted style.

Not to be outdone by the traveled gentlemen, the ladies also had their portraits painted, dressed as Greek goddesses or mythological queens. Emma, Lady Hamilton, was painted in many a classical guise, including all of the three muses in a single picture! In her self-portraits, Angelica Kauffmann chose to portray herself as a figure of antiquity.

*Above and right:*
Figure 20. Writing slope with sewing drawer. Painted in the manner of Angelica Kauffmann. The central panel depicts an idealized classical figure draped in floating robes, attended by a putto. The background of the painting is gessoed and the whole is varnished, resulting in the texture and color suggestive of a fresco. The sides are swagged with garlands. 13.5" wide. Ca. 1790–1800. $15,000–20,000.

As well as sitting for their portraits, the ladies also showed their love of classicism in considerably more down-to-earth ways. They took the posing a step further, adopting it as an after-dinner aesthetic relaxation for the gentlemen. They transformed themselves into living sculptures by dressing in figure-revealing classical robes and draping their bodies in quasi-antique poses. The crowned queen of this suggestive activity was once again Emma, Lady Hamilton.

After the Battle of the Nile in 1798, Lord Nelson went to Italy, where he was fêted as the hero who kept the French at bay. In the elevated circles where he circulated, he met and fell in love with Emma Hamilton. Emma—a girl with a past—had the good fortune to captivate and marry an older, rich man and classical scholar, Lord Hamilton. This raised her to the stratosphere of aristocracy. Under the pretext of paying homage to antiquity, she displayed her charms dressed in demi-diaphanous garments, striking classical poses. Emma was an old hand at this game. It was rumored that as early as 1781, when she was still Emma Lyon, she posed as the Greek goddess of health in Dr. Graham's clinic, where the celebrated quack offered—among his other cures—a "celestial bed" for the conception of perfect infants!

It was an age of elaborate social games, and, after the arduous work of war, Lord Nelson was ready to be captivated. So were other gentlemen who could not resist the seductive way ladies draped themselves in the pursuit of Olympian credentials. In a way, this infusion of humanity into the stricter code of neoclassicism was in the true ancient Greek spirit. After all, Dionysus and Aphrodite were just as strongly archetypal as Athena—not to mention the dalliances of Zeus!

Robert Adam commissioned Angelica Kauffmann and her husband, Antonio Zucchi, to paint panels on furniture he designed during the 1770s. Usually the central panels depicted idealized classical figures and allegories, and the surrounds were framed with festoons and garlands. When Kauffmann left England for Italy, plates of her work were published and copied. Other artists, too, worked on furniture decoration, the most notable being Cipriani and William Hamilton. Their work was also copied. It is difficult to attribute work accurately, since decorative painting was within the same genre. Original painting has a delicacy of execution that distinguishes it from late attempts at enhancing old pieces. This must be remembered when judging the authenticity of painted decoration on boxes of this period.

Throughout the eighteenth century, avid British connoisseurs collected fragments, statues, ceramics, bronzes, and any other tangible evidence of the ancients that they could find. In 1743, Horace Walpole, who set off for a visit to the ancient world with the poet Thomas Gray, wrote to the classical scholar Conyers Middleton that he had "a bust of Vespasian ... I have a dozen smaller busts ..." Collecting became the most eclectic of pastimes. Sir William Hamilton, who is remembered more as the husband of Emma, was a serious collector of Etruscan ceramics. Etruscan art, which was characterized by its distinctive black-and-red color, became a branch of neoclassicism espoused by many, including Josiah Wedgwood and Henry Clay.

One of the most serious collectors, whose treasure trove can still be seen in London, was the architect Sir John Soane (1753–1837). His collection of prints, sculpture, and fragments is a veritable visual grammar of classical ornament and structural

*This whole page:*

Figure 21. A complete classical repertory on a tea chest. Both the carefully balanced composition and the scenes on this box are rooted in the classical tradition. Mythical scenes, creatures, and figures suggest a thorough knowledge of the ancient world. There are Pegasus, Apollo, Cupid, Themis with her scales of justice, and, appropriately, Pandora opening her box. The top is fascinating. On one side there is a chariot driven by Athena and a warrior, symbolizing the art of war. On the other side, a naked Dionysus drives with Persephone in a celebration of life and peace, on an oxen-driven cart. This idea of balanced forces is further emphasized by two figures standing on columns on each side: one symbolic of war, the other of peace. The two sides are separated by an Egyptian-inspired arrangement. This is defined by two pillars, the bases of which are formed by the leaves of the papyrus plant. These support a triangular pediment. Under the pediment there is an elaborate symmetrical arrangement centered by the torso of what appears to be an Egyptian high priestess. This suggests the arcane level of classicism, the priestess standing in the center of balance. A touch of mystical exoticism among the Greco-Roman figures. The whole is executed with great assuredness and precision. Two doves floating on the top hold two strips on their beaks. One reads H.W.; the other, 1820. H.W. must be the initials of the owner or maker. Could it have a connection with the Wise family of Tunbridge ware makers, who also produced penwork? A very cerebral piece. 14" wide. Ca. 1810–20. $?

Figure 22. A caddy, unusually veneered in beech, that combines several neoclassical decorative elements. Note the fine multiple stringing, the directly inlaid pattern of laurel leaf and berry around the yew oval medallion, and the inlay of fluted patterns in the canted corners. The fluting was inspired and was meant to represent carved classical columns. 4.5" wide. Ca. 1800. $4,000–5,000.

proportion. The British Museum and other public institutions, as well as many private libraries, housed ancient statues and fragments, which educated both the vision and the mind. Whole rooms were covered with prints of classical ruins. This was erudite as well as economical, since it was one way of avoiding the heavy duty on imported wallpapers—truly in accordance with the classical *dulce et utile*!

Prints of architectural drawings were available from the early 1700s onward, although the first comprehensive work was not published until 1755. After extensive study of the ruins of Italy and Greece, James Stuart and Nicholas Revett produced their *The Antiquities of Athens*, which aimed at depicting the ancient finds with accuracy and precision. In 1764, another publication appeared that aimed to capture a less educated audience with its simplified version of the ancient world. Stephen Riou's *The Grecian Orders* was not for scholars but must have played an important part in spreading the influence of the new style. Other books, prints, and articles of various degrees of authenticity soon followed.

During the time the Adam brothers were in Italy, their public was being prepared for the reception of their designs. While in Italy, the brothers met Piranesi, whose idealized drawings of ancient ruins have influenced generations of designers, sculptors, and artists. Arguably, these prints set the fashion for the "ruin rooms," where ladies and gentlemen could play at being gods, or shepherds and shepherdesses in some bucolic Greek poem. The Adams did not go to Greece but concentrated their research in the direct study of imperial Roman architecture—not Palladio's sixteenth-century interpretation of it, which was the model for early-eighteenth-century classicism. In particular, the brothers were impressed by the ruins of the

*Above and right:*
Figure 23. Although silver-plated handles were used mostly on tea chests, a box was sometimes also given this feature. The mahogany veneer is exceptionally well figured and is used so as to form a symmetrical pattern with the central handle. This is within the neoclassical tradition of subtle understatement. The box opens up to a surprise of a parquetry pattern lining the inside of the lid. 10.5" wide. Ca. 1790. *Courtesy of Samantha Millar*. $1,400–1,600.

palace of Emperor Diocletian at Spalatro, an account of which they published in 1764.

In 1773, the Adams published their *Works in Architecture*, which defined the direction of the Adam thinking and set the fashion for architects and cabinetmakers for the next two decades. Eager to prove themselves on par with professionals, cabinetmakers made a point of designing within prescribed rules. Many subscribed to publications such as George Richardson's *Treatise on the Four Orders of Architecture*, which was published in 1787. The earlier Palladian classical structures and decorations were considerably lightened. Rococo, with its spikes and whimsical asymmetrical curves, was deleted from the annals of good taste. What the Adam style dictated was simple, linear form with no protruding ornaments or structures.

Ornament was to be graceful and delicate and, most importantly, in keeping with the interior of the whole room. When Robert Adam died, the *Gentleman's Magazine* eulogized on his achievement in transforming the style of the age with grace, lightness, and humor.

Boxes dating from this period are painstakingly made, often with extremely fine bandings, inlays, and stringing. Yet, to the inexperienced eye they look deceptively simple.

Decorating manuals and pattern books giving guidance as to neoclassical geometry and dimensions were avidly followed both by professionals and amateurs. In 1775, P. Columbani published *A New Book of Ornament*. The new ornaments could be copied on furniture, walls, fabrics, and, of course, boxes.

Briefly, the Adam style (neoclassical decoration) followed the rules of symmetry. A box would be edged, strung, or inlaid—sometimes all three—by using very fine lines of contrasting woods. The stringing and edging formed a frame to the centrally positioned marquetry medallion. Sometimes, especially in tea chests, the inlay would be replaced by a centrally positioned silver (Sheffield plated) handle on an oval or rectangular backplate. Whether inlay or handle, the composition would be completely balanced.

Another way of inlaying was directly into the wood, using stylized motifs such as festoons of husks, acanthus leaves, palmettes, anthemions, grotesques, ribbons, musical instruments, drapery, swags of flora, Greek key patterns, and other classical designs. These were used either around a central panel or symmetrically arranged in other patterns. Inlays dating from this period were often enhanced with engraved lines worked in penwork, which emphasized the detail and gave more vitality to the design (penwork is a term that describes decoration of line drawing in ink). Bills describing work in Nostell Priory and Harewood House by Thomas Chippendale describe the work as "curiously Inlaid with various fine woods." In the Harewood bill for the Lascelles family there is mention of "fine Antique Ornaments . . . Curiously inlaid and Engraved."

The main woods used for boxes were mahogany, satinwood, harewood, partridgewood, yew, and fruitwoods. The stringings were mostly in boxwood and ebony; the inlays, in various woods, either in their natural or enhanced colors. Oak and holly sometimes yielded natural greens, which were the result of a fungal attack. Light woods were treated with natural dyes and oxidization, which changed their color or created stronger contrasts. Shading on the marquetry was achieved by burning the light wood in sand or lead. This gave a gradual darkening effect and looked more natural than dyeing.

The inlays were not always made by the cabinetmakers who made the boxes. More-ambitious work was often executed by

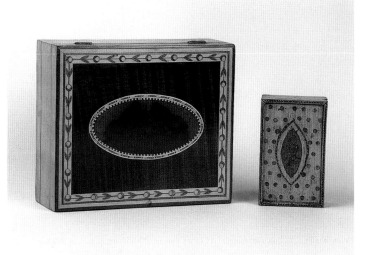

Figure 24. Two examples of fine small boxes with typical neoclassical decoration. The larger 6" wide. Ca. 1800–1810. $500–700.

Figure 25. A box edged, strung, and decorated with a centrally positioned oval marquetry shell, a typical neoclassical arrangement. This particular shell is further enhanced with inlaid ebony dots. 7" wide. Ca. 1790. $800–1,000.

Figure 26. Shells, reminiscent of Britannia's rule of the waves, were ideal motifs for oval medallions. They were delicately cut and shaded using the hot-sand technique.

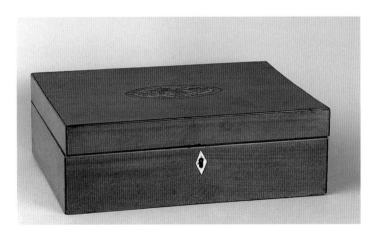

Figure 27. A satinwood box with a marquetry medallion of flowers. 10" wide. Ca. 1790–1800. $700–800.

masters of marquetry. The oval medallions of marquetry were usually brought in from specialist craftsmen. For example, Joseph Binns worked in London, and on his trade card dating from the last decade of the eighteenth century, he described himself as "Oval Shell & Stringing Maker, Dyed Woods of Different Colors." Other prevalent neoclassical motifs of the 1770s, 1780s, and 1790s were fans or paterae, medallions, stylized urns and vases, or simply ovals of wood framed by fine stringing.

A form of decoration that gave excellent neoclassical effects was a frame or border of inlay, penwork, or both, with a central hand-colored print of a classical mythological or allegorical scene. This method of decoration was favored by Tunbridge ware makers and continued well into the nineteenth century.

Before abandoning Robert Adam for other influential figures in the neoclassical movement, a mention must be made of a different box shape that he was the first to use. This was the urn-shaped knife box, an extension of the classical ceramic and bronze urn design. This was the only exception to his rule of straightening rather than curving the basic

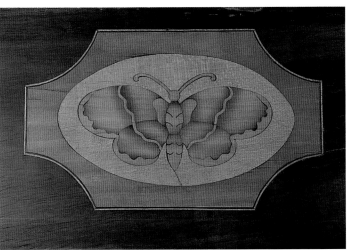

Figure 28. Details of typical marquetry medallions.

structural line; the knife urns were considerably more curvilinear than the knife boxes, although they were immaculately symmetrical.

The other name often used to describe neoclassical design is that of George Hepplewhite. Hepplewhite's *The Cabinet-Maker and Upholsterer's Guide* was published two years after his death in 1788 by his widow. The designs are very much in the neoclassical tradition, but their elegance is imbued with robustness reminiscent of earlier classicism, and even baroque. For example, he offers two designs for tea chests in bombe shapes. Although his inlays and decorations are still within the neoclassical tradition, some of his designs show vitality both in their execution and in the introduction of more-naturalistic motifs, such as shells and sunflowers.

One of Hepplewhite's motifs, that of the Prince of Wales's Feathers, became *de rigueur* during the Regency crisis. In 1788, the old king, George III, appeared to have lost his reason. A Regency Bill was hastily drawn, expecting the imminent rise to power of George, the Prince of Wales. The prince's political sympathies were on the side of the Whigs. The ladies of fashion who also had Whig inclinations hastened to decorate their hats with three ostrich feathers, much to the delight of the cartoonists, who had a field day. A more quiet way of anticipating the prince's ascendancy was to have one's box discreetly inlaid with the prince's symbol. Unfortunately for the Whigs, and in spite of the buffoonish doctors, the king recovered and the Regency was postponed for another twenty years, by which time the political affiliations of the prince were totally confused.

Crossbanding in kingwood, serpentine forms and generally more robust decoration featured strongly in Hepplewhite's designs. Another element that also crept in was folding arrangements and mechanical devices. Neoclassical design was adapted more to real needs. In fact, the preface to the *Cabinet-Maker's Guide* begins: "To unite elegance and utility and blend the useful with the agreeable, has ever been considered a difficult, but an honorable task." However, the preface is careful to assure the reader that there is no "violation of all established rule."

Leading cabinetmakers of the period studied the designs of architects and transposed them into their own work. Thomas Chippendale cooperated on many important projects with Robert Adam, such as Harewood House and Syon Park. It was inconceivable that serious cabinetmaking could be undertaken without a thorough study of such luminaries as James "Athenian" Stuart, Sir William Chambers, and of course the Adams. Bearing in mind the principle of a unified whole that pervaded the period, it is easy to understand how the rules of proportion and the aesthetics of ornament were applied to boxes, which are after all small pieces of furniture. This is an important point to remember when judging the authenticity of an item.

During the last two decades of the century, other important architect-designers were exploring the classical world. Henry Holland, who had been commissioned by the Prince of Wales to redesign Carlton House, sent Charles Heathcote Tatham to Rome to draw classical details so that he could use firsthand information for the royal residence. These drawings were published between 1796 and 1799 as *Etchings of Ancient Ornamental Architecture Drawn from the Originals in Rome and Other Parts of Italy*. Accuracy of "grammar" was again reinstated. However, Holland was far from being a one-style designer, and his diversity already began to sow the ideas of the Regency.

By the last years of the eighteenth century, neoclassicism became less rigid, foreshadowing the more flexible and varied style of the early nineteenth century.

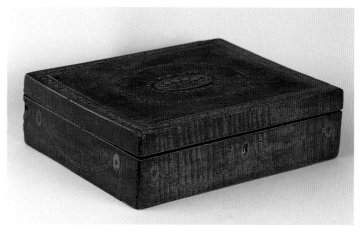

*Above and below:*

Figure 29. Veneered in very thick harewood veneer and banded in greenish sycamore, this is neoclassical work in perfect harmony with woodworking craft. The box is edged in boxwood, which is also used as stringing between the main panel and the border. There is also a very fine line of half herringbone stringing between the boxwood line and the main panel. Navicular and dot inlaid pieces form oval and straight patterns on the top. These are more complex than usual in that they are made of a central dark-wood part and an outer part in lighter wood, suggesting open seeds. The center is inlaid with a marquetry oval of a shell. All around the sides, dot-and-leaf garlands drape over ovals edged in half herringbone. The box retains much of its original varnish and has patinated to a warm glow. 10.9" wide. Ca. 1780. $4,500–6,000.

# CHAPTER 3 *Chinoiserie*

t is paradoxical that it was during a period when classicism was acknowledged as the epitome of culture and taste that the bewitching vision of the East captivated the hearts and minds of Europe. Perhaps the human imagination needed to break the confined boundaries of classicism and embrace this magic world, where rules seemed to swing on gossamer threads carried about by fabulous birds over fantastical landscapes.

Chinese life and art invaded the artistic consciousness of Europe and found expression in two ways: decoration and shape. Decoration that appears on boxes is now generally called chinoiserie, although during the seventeenth, eighteenth, and nineteenth centuries it was confusedly termed Chinawork, japanning, or India work. Anywhere east of Constantinople was so alien at the time that cultures and countries remained indistinguishable in the popular mind. The only available sources of information were enhanced travelers' tales, geographically inaccurate maps, and fantastical sketches.

The correct terms accepted today and which I will use are "chinoiserie" for the style of decoration, which was applied in many forms, and "japanning" and "lacquering" to mean the technical treatment of the surface of the box to make it look as if it was finished in oriental lacquer. Chinoiserie was not always applied to japanned articles, and japanned surfaces were not always decorated in chinoiserie (see figure 563).

The land beyond, somewhere in the East, was generally called Cathay and was perceived as nothing short of miraculous. Marco Polo (1254—1324) was the first to bring the world of Cathay to the attention of Europe. Although this work appeared centuries before chinoiserie was first attempted in the West, the descriptions of the splendors of such places as the winter palace of Kublai Khan, with its fabulous Green Mount garden, had a profound influence in the many attempts at re-creating the fairy tale world of the paradoxically arranged "natural" landscape of the East.

By 1700, most enlightened Europeans would have been familiar with Marco Polo's *Travels* and would have been eager to expand their knowledge by reading the more up-to-date travelers' tales. The Dutch were a nation of traders who, by the seventeenth century, had established strong links with the Far East. It is not surprising that it was a Dutchman by the name of Johan Nieuhoff who provided the next important text and, particularly, the first visual images of China. In his *An Embassy to China*, published in 1669, Europeans gazed for the first time at engravings of such extraordinary buildings as the Porcelain Pagoda of Nanking, and at Chinese street life, temples, palaces, bridges, and, most importantly,

Figure 30. The front of a table cabinet painted with oriental figures. The dignified posture and costume are in the manner of Du Halde, who published in 1736. The original varnish is still present, with some chipping revealing even-brighter colors. Mid-eighteenth century. 13" wide. $?

the artificial rock structures found on almost every eighteenth-century chinoiserie decorated box.

As well as the general representations, there were details of ornaments, columns, arches, fabulous beasts, strange trees, people, banners, and bells, all quite new, exciting, and intriguing. Other accounts followed, often peppered with yarns of fictitious wonders, beasts, and peculiar, even monstrous, practices. However, it is the idyllic gardens and the elegant, calm figures that, in the West, were transposed into chinoiserie.

The first Europeans to penetrate the inner routes of China in any number were the Jesuits. Louis XIV of France was presented by a Jesuit with several volumes of Chinese paintings as early as 1697. A little later, Father Matteo Ripa, an Italian, produced some fine engravings of the emperor's summer palace at Jehol. Thirty-six of these were circulated in London in 1724.

Figure 31. A small but significant japanned box with exquisite chinoiserie decoration. The surface of this piece is almost indistinguishable from oriental lacquer. It is decorated in raised and flat gold painting, both executed with virtuosity. The upward-winding road with trees and exotic buildings with small figures, just in the lower part of one corner, is in the Chinese tradition of decoration. Inside the box is sprinkled with gold powder, an oriental technique rarely employed in chinoiserie. Last quarter eighteenth century. 2.5" wide. *Courtesy of Joan Kiernan.* $1,200-1,500.

The engravings were pretty accurate and showed the beautiful landscape, including the huge artificial calm lakes. The third Earl of Burlington obtained a set of the engravings, and he must have gazed from his library in Chiswick at the "small pleasure houses ... which are reached by means of boats or bridges" and thought of the emperor, who "when fatigued by fishing . . . retires, accompanied by his ladies" (*The Memoirs of Father Matteo Ripa*, translated by Fortunato Prandi, 1844).

Another Jesuit, Jean-Denis Attiret, whose work was translated and circulated in England in the 1750s and 1760s, produced a record of another imperial garden, *Yuan—Ming—Yuan*, which translates as "Round Bright Garden." This fabulous garden was established by Emperor K'ang Hsi and was further enhanced by Ch'ien Lung (1735—1796). The description of its steep hills, broad lakes, temples, pavilions, grand halls, and other man-made and natural beauties provided rich food for the imagination of the chinoiserie artists.

To the Western mind, the fabulous gardens, with their artificial rocks, lakes, pagodas, temples, and fairy tale pavilions, seemed the perfect escape from the all-too-solid and rule-riddled life of Europe. The little figures, who looked as if they glided along dressed in long exotic robes without a care in the world, appeared to have mastered the essence of wisdom and serenity.

Indeed, the garden-strolling oriental figures were probably in a state of bliss. The activities that went on in the oriental gardens were designed to induce contentment. Gentle intellectual pastimes, such as music playing, chess playing, and studying, were carried on in the pavilions. More rarified, esoteric pursuits took place in cool chambers hidden inside what appeared to be artificial rocks. There sages sat, read, contemplated, and composed poetry. When they felt in a more social and playful mood, they retired into a chamber that had an artificial rivulet running through its floor. A glass of wine was floated on the water, and each wise man was obliged to compose a new line of poetry every time the glass passed in front of him. If he failed to do so, he had to drain the cup. How much drinking was done for every line of poetry written is not clear, nor do we know if the poetry improved with every cupful. To the European mind, what went on in the gardens of Cathay was the pinnacle of happiness. It combined beauty, intellectual stimulation, sensual pleasure, and companionship mixed with the right amount of whimsical humor. One could indeed imagine oneself in the land of the immortals.

Many European intellectuals eulogized on the ways of the Chinese, Voltaire being perhaps the most notable exponent of oriental virtue. To an age when "doing right" had to be incorporated within artistic expression, chinoiserie decoration seemed a more seductive alternative to classicism. Exercising a variety

*Center and left:*
Figure 32. Decorated in raised and flat painting, this example typifies both the wayward perspective and the delightfully amusing essence of chinoiserie. Although inspired by China, the arrangement of the landscape, figures, plants, birds, and insects is interpreted through European perceptions. It is both fantastical and fun. 11" wide. Ca. 1780. $2,000–3,000.

Figure 33. A beautifully composed chinoiserie scene of figures in pavilion gardens, some playing musical instruments. It is executed in raised japanned and flat painting. It evokes the European impression of a happy people pursuing artistic pleasure. The piece, which is a tea caddy, is cartouche shaped. French. Ca. 1800. *Courtesy of Charleen Plumly Pollard.* $2,000–3,000.

of art disciplines in an environment of bold shapes and unconstrained landscapes where fabulous birds flew among exotic plants was the perfect marriage of intellect and sensual pleasure: the Cathay recipe for sanity, wisdom, and happiness. It was not possible for many Europeans to go to China, but this did not stop them from re-creating a token piece of oriental terrestrial paradise at home. It was important to demonstrate that a person understood the East.

By the middle of the eighteenth century, the fashion for engravings and designs purporting to be "Chinese" proliferated. Many were derived from secondary sources with emphasis on what may be construed as commercially desirable. As a result, they were inaccurate and often naive. Others deliberately introduced European artistic elements to appeal to patrons who found unadulterated orientalism too strong to adopt. Even woodcuts and paintings by Chinese Court artists incorporated rococo cartouches and scrolls to suit the West.

Jean Baptiste Du Halde (1674—1743) was very influential in introducing European elements into chinoiserie. He published the accounts of twenty-nine missionaries with engravings of Chinese life. His work, *The General History of China*, which he claimed was "a Description of the Empire of China," was published in France in 1735. It was translated and published in England in more than one edition between 1737 and the early 1740s. The buildings on the engravings swirl and curve unrealistically, as if they were made by a confectioner. In contrast, the people are rigid and pose with the air of Romans, rather than orientals.

At about the same time as the increased availability of diverse "Chinese" designs, the rococo style was gaining ground over the earlier, heavier baroque and the austere classicism of the early eighteenth century. Rococo elements, with their whimsical curves and spikes, were very suited to the freer, lighter, fanciful Chinese designs with their towering flowers,

Figure 34. Canopied by a rococo cartouche, an oriental figure is playing a drum and another is standing by. The European cartouche and the chinoiserie scene are executed in raised and flat colors. The pennant and the plants outside the cartouche are in typical chinoiserie fashion, as are the bunches of flowers on the sides of the box. These are very similar to Stalker and Parker designs. The structure is English, which makes this a rare example of rococo chinoiserie. 11" wide. Mid-eighteenth century. $2,000–3,000.

pagoda roofs, trellised woodwork, delicate bells, and overall air of ethereal unreality.

France, where rococo blossomed, was also the source of the choicest Chinese rococo designs. Some of the most influential artists of the period gave expression to this genre, among them Antoine Watteau, who mixed European scrolls and zigzags with Chinese figures, pagodas, and landscapes. By the 1740s, François Boucher transposed his orientals into European gardens. In terms of decoration on boxes, this mid-eighteenth-century Sino-European flavor found expression mostly in mainland Europe.

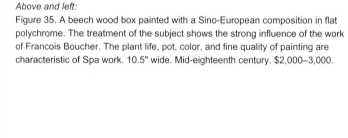

*Above and left:*
Figure 35. A beech wood box painted with a Sino-European composition in flat polychrome. The treatment of the subject shows the strong influence of the work of Francois Boucher. The plant life, pot, color, and fine quality of painting are characteristic of Spa work. 10.5" wide. Mid-eighteenth century. $2,000–3,000.

Lighter chinoiserie designs, featuring whimsical curvatures, were produced and published in the 1750s by artist Jean-Baptiste Pillement (1728—1808). Although French, Pillement worked throughout Europe and was very influential in establishing a style of delicate and elegant fantasy. He encapsulated the spirit of rococo with large trees, fine birds, light ornaments, supporting scrolls, and precariously spindly bridges and peaks. His wispy figures often wear fairy flower hats, and his occasional monkeys are sinewy and elegant, unlike the monkeys in "signeries," where they are deprecatingly used in place of oriental people.

In 1750, Messrs. Edwards and Darly published *A New Book of Chinese Designs Calculated to Improve the Present Taste*. Darly was a versatile designer and cartoonist. He engraved many of the Chinese-inspired designs in Chippendale's *Directory*, which demonstrated his understanding of oriental structure and architectural grammar. His cartoons showed shrewd social perception and lightness of touch. His chinoiserie designs, which were very influential, were a mixture of architectural soundness and capriccio, which make them credible yet exciting. His real and accurate-looking structures host fabulous birds, butterflies, and elegant figures, sometimes looking as if they are about to levitate from grassy roofs.

Although by the middle of the eighteenth century most fashionable people had accepted chinoiserie as one of the stylish decorative alternatives, some old establishment figures were reluctant to allow it the credibility of European-derived alternatives. The decisive accolade for the Chinese taste was given in 1757 by Sir William Chambers, who was already an acclaimed architect. After spending two years in China, Sir William came to London, where he published *Designs of Chinese Buildings, Furniture, Dresses, Machines, and Utensils*. Chambers's credibility as an exponent of the Chinese taste was further enhanced when, following the publication of his designs, the Dowager Princes Augusta commissioned him to redesign the royal garden at Kew. Chambers created a true fairyland, complete with a Turkish mosque, a five-arch alhambra, a Gothic cathedral, a ruined arch, and a temple. To crown it all, he erected a splendid pagoda that was designed to resemble the Porcelain Tower of Nanking, first glimpsed in the seventeenth-century engravings of Nieuhoff's *Embassy*. The oriental and Moorish buildings at Kew were enormously influential in disseminating the oriental taste.

In 1772, Chambers, secure in his reputation, published his *Dissertation of Oriental Gardening*. This was on the side of the rather absurdly fantastical, but it did have the effect of shocking people out of pompously serious landscape design, which had come to be regarded as good taste. Chambers tried to infuse a sense of fun and whimsy suited to the outdoors. In correspondence, he even suggested the introduction of Roc, the fabulous bird able to carry off an elephant, found fluttering about in the fables of Persia and the Arabian Nights!

In spite of the oddly raised eyebrow, garden designers followed Chambers's lead, both for public and private gardens. All classes who could afford to flocked to the public pleasure and tea gardens, and to the gardens on the grounds of the grand houses. Transport improved dramatically in the second half of the eighteenth century. By the beginning of the nineteenth century, visiting important estates had become a favorite pastime, especially for the rising and aspiring middle classes. Jane Austen's people are forever discussing grand houses, their "aspects," their grounds, and their vistas. Her heroines are visiting, planning, and walking through gardens in endless pursuit of pleasure and husbands.

The ladies and gentlemen who lived in the grand estates wished for the oriental flavor to also permeate the interiors of their homes. Chinoiserie furniture and objects were made both for country houses and for the town houses the rich occupied during "the season." For the middle classes, who did not have the land on which to indulge their desire for oriental pavilions and pagodas, objects were their only way of proving their style credibility. Enchanted by the gardens, the chinoiserie furniture, and the boxes of the rich, they hurried home and either commissioned or set about creating their own Cathay microcosm. In an age of no moving pictures, of no photography, when very few people traveled and when information was sparse and often prejudiced, the glimpse of a strange way of life and a new aesthetic concept must have been exhilarating to a degree difficult for us in our information-flooded world to understand. The fascination was total.

During the eighteenth century, boxes decorated in chinoiserie were entirely, or to a great extent, japanned. It is not surprising that the terms were confused, since japanning was the European attempt at re-creating the effect of oriental lacquer. Japanners became the aristocrats of the cabinetmaking trade, commanding higher salaries than craftsmen working in many other disciplines.

In France, where the concept of style had by the mid-seventeenth century already assumed gigantic proportions, japanning and chinoiserie featured heavily in the palaces and chateaux of the king and the aristocracy. The passion continued well into the eighteenth century, with Mme. de Pompadour, the diva of style, commissioning suites of chinoiserie furniture and objects.

It is not surprising that in England, after years of Cromwell's austerity, Charles II upon his return from the Continent introduced a taste of extravagance and frivolity and a thirst for the strange and the magical. According to diarist John Evelyn, the king's bride, Catherine of Braganza, brought with her in 1662 as part of her dowry, "such Indian cabinets as had never before been seen here." The time was right, the conditions ideal, and the desire for things exotic all embracing. This desire grew and grew until the perception of the world changed with the coming of the age of Victoria in the late 1830s.

Some of the cynical wits of the eighteenth century could not help but pour a little vitriol on the obsession with style and the taste for the exotic. In his *Epistle to a Lady*, a bitter Alexander Pope writes:

*She, while her lover pants upon her breast,*
*Can mark the figures on an Indian chest …*
*(Epistle II to a Lady, 1735)*

During the eighteenth century, an "India" chest was indeed a prized possession. Decorating in the oriental taste was practiced both professionally and at home. Home artists drew inspiration from published designs and travel accounts and composed their own, often-charmingly muddled vision of Cathay.

The practical side of japanning—that is, the preparation of the surface to be decorated, the method for applying the decoration, and the final varnishing—had to be learned. Schools for young ladies began to offer it in their curriculum, and instructions were available in books and periodicals. The aim was to

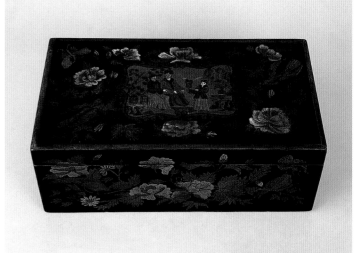

achieve as close a resemblance as possible to the oriental lacquer objects imported from China.

The first pieces of lacquer furniture, cabinets, and boxes decorated with oriental scenes that people in England saw were most probably plundered from Dutch and Spanish ships. The British had not been able to establish and sustain trade with the East. Frustrated in their efforts, the British merchants, with the blessing of Queen Elizabeth I and the support of arms, made free with the cargo of other nations. Such important figures as Sir Francis Drake owe their place in history to their license to plunder Catholic Spanish galleons and Portuguese carracks. The great queen saw nothing wrong with national piracy, which continued throughout the seventeenth and eighteenth centuries and even stretched into the nineteenth century, although by this time more indirect and effective methods of plunder had been established. All the dashing young officers in their splendid uniforms that crowd late-eighteenth- and early-nineteenth-century novels and paintings were out to make their fortunes by fair means or foul.

In 1599, the East India Company was founded, and in 1600 it was given the Royal Charter. Although the methods of the company were both jingoistic and self-promoting—the jingoism supporting the self-interest and vice versa—a veneer of honorable "trade" had to be established to obscure some of the worst excesses of the Crown and its servants. The establishment of the East India Company helped promote trade and widened knowledge about the Far East, its art, and its way of life.

Some of the earliest imports of the East India Company were oriental lacquer panels that were incorporated into furniture and objects made by English cabinetmakers. Complete pieces followed and continued to be imported well into the

*This whole page:*
Figure 37. The surface of the box is japanned, but the painting is executed with flat colors and colored varnishes over gold leaf. The cartouche-enclosed chinoiserie scene is characteristic. The treatment of the exotic flowers, birds, and butterflies shows an assured hand and a bold sense of design. Strong groups of exotic flowers were featured in Mathias Darly's drawings. The arrangement is unusual in that the framing flowers predominate over the central scene. The interior has a lift-out compartmented tray, each compartment covered by a lid that is japanned and treated with metal dust, aiming at reproducing aventurine lacquer. The inside of the lid is covered with a painting of exotic birds and butterflies among flowers. This is on a dark-pink background and is executed in clear, bright colors in the style developed by the Chinese for export painting. 11" wide. Third quarter eighteenth century. $3,000–5,000.

*This whole page:*
Figure 38. A thickly japanned table cabinet, the interior with similarly japanned drawers. The decoration is inspired by but not directly copied from Stalker and Parker. The artist was obviously influenced by other representations and oriental work showing an upward movement. The varnish has crackled and darkened, and some of the fine detail is now obscure. An elegant, well-balanced, and executed composition. 15" wide. Ca. 1760–80. $6,000–8,000.

nineteenth century. These pieces were fascinating both because the lacquer surface was something entirely new and because the scenes depicted in the decoration opened up the vision to an unknown world. The demand for items in this new medium and decoration soon outgrew the supply. English cabinetmakers saw the opportunity of fulfilling this demand by producing their own version of lacquer. Because true oriental lacquer comes from the sap of a tree grown only in the Far East, alternatives for creating the glossy surface and decoration had to be found. Much experimenting went on, with japanners vying with each other for best results.

Small items such as boxes gave plenty of scope for individual interpretation. The need for personal involvement in the decoration was harnessed by publications giving quite accurate and detailed instructions, both about the technicalities and the decoration. The building-up of the surface and the design were inextricably linked at this stage of the "new taste."

As early as the 1660s, Samuel Pepys mentioned chinoiserie designs in a "book with rare Cutts." However, it was not until

*This whole page:*
Figure 39. A significant tea chest, in that it provides a wonderful illustration of the influence of Stalker and Parker over a long period of time. The outside is japanned and decorated with raised and painted designs, which were either directly copied or modified from the examples in the *Treatise*. The interior of the box is decorated in the later penwork and paint technique, again copying the Stalker and Parker designs. Because of the different nature of the work and because it was more protected, the interior has not darkened. The designs remain clear and easy to identify. The naive and somewhat awkward lines create delightful vignettes, which are characteristic of early chinoiserie. This box is full of surprises, with every facet offering a new treat. It is most unusual to find both japanning and penwork on the same piece, and it is interesting to compare how the two techniques were used to interpret the same designs. It is also interesting to compare how the differently treated surfaces have aged. Rare. Ca. 1800–1810. *Courtesy of Charleen Plumly Pollard.* $9,000–12,000.

1688 that a really comprehensive and well-distributed publication appeared that was to influence chinoiserie for the next 150 years. This was a book by J. Stalker and G. Parker that explained how to prepare the surface, build up and paint the decoration, and prepare and apply varnishes. The book also provided designs for copying. The designs, with their precise shapes and well-defined lines, were easy to follow and are recognizable in many a box. There were complete scenes, as well as pages of specific items to copy from (for example, various birds), so that a person could choose and compose scenes according to individual preference.

The Stalker and Parker book epitomizes the confusion that prevailed in Europe regarding anywhere east of the Mediterranean Sea. The title reads *Treatise of Japanning and Varnishing*. The designs are *Patterns for Japan-Work in Imitation of the Indians*! The advice given in the book was most probably deduced from Chinese imported lacquer and from Dutch craftsmen who had observed Chinese and Japanese lacquer workers.

Confusion of terms apart, the contribution of this book to the spread of japanned chinoiserie cannot be overstated. Arcane information about the properties of gums and varnishes was freely given. Instructions on how to coat a wooden surface and how to varnish to a mirrorlike finish were explained in detail. Pigments to be used for the attainment of different colors were listed with their properties. The reader was also tutored in the use of metal dusts for creating special effects, a direct copy from Chinese and Japanese practices. The different instruments needed were also described, such as quills,

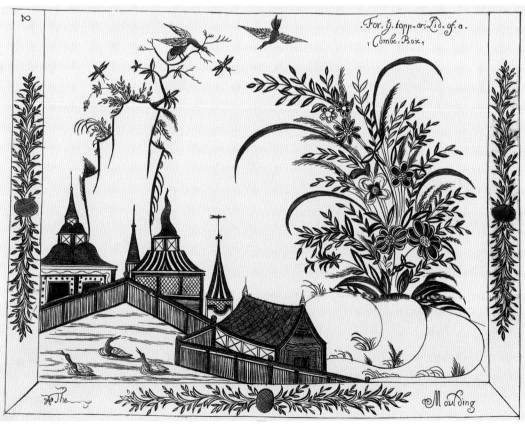

*This whole page:*
Figure 40. Two illustrations from the 1688 edition of Stalker and Parker's *Treatise of Japanning and Varnishing*.

*Above and right:*
Figure 41. Japanned, raised, and polychromed, the decoration on this sewing box is a truly golden vision of Cathay. Figures relax in a garden with a distant rock in the background and the ho-ho bird above. This is a relatively late example of such work, and it does not have an overall varnish. Note how the gold and the colors have remained brighter than in earlier examples. 8.5" wide. Ca. 1820. $4,000–5,500.

varnishing pencils, and Dutch rushes (a horse tail used for polishing).

The gist of the instructions—and of similar instructions given in other publications—was that the surface of the wood should be coated in whiting and parchment size in as many layers as was necessary. Each layer should be dried completely before the next coat was applied. If the decoration was to incorporate raised parts, these were to be built up with a paste made of gum arabic, water, and whiting. For extra hardness, fine sawdust could also be mixed into the paste. A rush pencil stick was to be used to build up and shape the raised surfaces, which were to form the artificial rocks, mountains, and other features in the landscape. People, birds, buildings, animals, and plants could be given a three-dimensional effect by first raising and then incising and painting their shapes.

Stalker and Parker's work was the inspiration for later imitations, the most influential of which was the 1760 publication of *The Ladies Amusement, or The Whole Art of Japanning Made Easy.* The practical advice was simpler than in the earlier book, but the designs were plentiful, and many were of high aesthetic merit. Among the fifteen hundred designs there were contributions by eminent artists, including Jean Pillement. The figures had more grace and movement; the flowers and birds were luscious yet elegant. The writers warned against absurdity of composition, although they allowed more liberty with "Indian and Chinese" designs.

The instructions were for the surface to be brushed with melted clear size and then to be painted with the ground color three or four times, drying between coats. The colors for the decoration were to be mixed with gum arabic, and the

"embossed parts" to be accumulated by building up layers of Paris white mixed with size "finely ground to the consistency of cream." The raised details could be scraped, painted, and gilded to give the required effect. The described method allowed for a thinner surface and paved the way for the later polychrome and penwork chinoiserie of the late eighteenth and early nineteenth centuries.

In 1758, Robert Dossie wrote that the art of japanning was "covering bodies by ground of opaque colors in varnish"; this vague and flexible description encapsulates the flexibility and variety of the methods used.

Because there was no exact way of preparing either the coating materials or the varnishes, and since many professional japanners guarded their secret recipes, there was no standard way of producing japanned boxes with chinoiserie decoration. The wood that was used to make the basic box, which was supplied decorated or "in the white" for home decoration, was deal (a board of softwood, usually fir or pine) or occasionally mahogany, beech, or maple. Other woods were not often used, although I have come across examples in oak, fruitwood, and ash. In large pieces of japanned work the joints were covered in muslin before the gesso mixture was applied. In boxes this was not necessary, and I have come across this practice only on table cabinets. Originally the objects were dried in the air, and this practice continued for home-decorated boxes. Linseed oil could be employed to quicken polymerization. Professional japanners used special ovens, which occasionally caused fires. There are references to "lacquer ovens" in workshop descriptions, including that of the workshop of Thomas Chippendale.

Figure 42. Tea chest painted predominantly with green on a cream background with chinoiserie scenes of oriental figures delighting themselves under exotic giant blooms. 12" wide. Ca. 1820. *Courtesy of the Bielstein Collection*. $8,000–10,000.

Figure 43. The surface of this box is japanned and painted to simulate tortoiseshell. This is a very unusual treatment. It is further decorated with oriental figures in a garden and a pavilioned island in the background. The decoration is raised and painted in gold. In front of the figures there is a frame made up of what appears to be bamboo and trellis in an angular, asymmetrical arrangement. This is interesting in that it is an adaptation of the rococo principle to the form of the oriental railing. The plants, figures, and building are firmly rooted in the chinoiserie tradition and are of the elegant, elongated variety favored by artists of the mid-eighteenth-century period. Probably made in the town of Spa. 12" wide. Mid-eighteenth century. $3,000–4,000.

The varied ways of drying, as well as the different gums used, explains the reason why the surface on japanned boxes shows varied signs of aging. Some boxes have darkened, some have fogged, and some have crackled. Some have done all three.

True to form, the East India Company used their exclusive trading rights to forbid private trading in gum lac, so that they could be the sole importers and control the price of supplies to protect their own imports of real Chinese work. Even by 1700, English "Patentees for lacquering after the manner of Japan" complained of the vast number of items imported, including 4,120 powder, comb, and dressing boxes. Faced with the wrath of the home lacquerers, in 1702 the English government imposed higher duties on lacquer imports, paving the way for new inventions for japanning at home.

"Spirits of wine" (ethyl alcohol) were mixed with resins such as copal, sandarac, *pix greca*, amber, isinglass, and *sanguis draconis* (dragon blood, a red-colored resin) in an effort to achieve parity with oriental work. Robert Dossie, in his published thoughts on japanning, even suggests honey as a mixing alternative. Most workshops of note were clustered around St. Paul's Churchyard, in the city of London, and this is where most professionally made items would have been constructed and decorated. However, the fashion traveled fast, and as early as 1749 there is mention of "Chinese gout" items being supplied in Tunbridge Wells, the home of the very English Tunbridge ware boxes.

Chinoiserie, which is a hybrid style of decoration resulting from oriental life and art diffused through European preconception, has a timeless quality. Therefore, it is not easy to date such boxes very accurately. Since the wood on the boxes that were japanned is completely covered, we have to look at shapes and fashionable uses as well as the interiors for some clues. The thickness of the surface coating can also be a pointer, since most boxes made after 1760 were more lightly coated, or simply painted and gilded. This is not a strict criterion, since complex mixtures and varnishes were used up to the third decade of the nineteenth century.

During the eighteenth century, most boxes had a black background. There are a few rare exceptions to this. Red, in the shade of early carved Chinese lacquer, was favored by Giles Grendey, a distinguished cabinetmaker who was commissioned both by English and Continental aristocracy and royalty. Furniture in this color commands much-higher prices than the black equivalent and very rarely comes on the market. Boxes in this color are virtually unknown (see figures 302 and 325).

Thomas Chippendale used white with green chinoiserie decoration for furniture he made for actor David Garrick. He used green with gold decoration for Nostell Priory. These two combinations of color are also rare in boxes, as indeed are most colors other than black. Presumably this is because it was more difficult to get an even surface color in lighter shades and because most makers tried to imitate Chinese work, which was mostly gold and had some color decoration on a black background.

Stalker and Parker did give instructions for various colors, including Chestnut, Olive Yellow, Counterfeit Tortoiseshell, and the very difficult and complex "Blew Japan." However, none fired the imagination to the extent of black, which provided a good background for most colors and a glamorous contrast to gold.

By the end of the eighteenth century, every fashionable lady must have had her chinoiserie box, yet the fascination with China grew. With increased trading, more information became available. This later influx of knowledge was more refined and varied than what had been previously available.

Trading concerns made it imperative for England to try to establish more-favorable trading terms with China. In 1787, an abortive attempt was made at sending an embassy to the Chinese Court. This ended in failure, as did the more concerted and carefully prepared delegation headed by Lord Macartney in 1792.

In terms of public and trading relations, the ambassadors achieved nothing more than annoying those on top of the Chinese hierarchy and amusing others with their strange looks and outlandish behavior. In spite of the chasm of culture, the true China—not merely the trading posts of Canton—was for the first time exposed to English eyes. The English embassy was received at Jehol, which early in the century was glimpsed at in the engravings of Matteo Ripa. Emperor Ch'ien Lung was not impressed with the English or their offerings. In contrast, the ambassadors of King George III marveled at the wonders they encountered as they traveled one hundred miles north of Peking, beyond the Great Wall, to the fabulous gardens and palace of Jehol.

Fortunately the embassy included a "Draughtsman," William Alexander, who took pains to record scenes of Chinese life, complete with figures and buildings. He also drew ships, fauna, and flora. Alexander prepared a set of impressive paintings that were later exhibited at the Royal Academy in London. This was a fresh look at China offered by an English artist from firsthand observation.

The interest was sustained by accounts of the journey published by others who had taken part in the expedition. Sir George Staunton's account (1797) with engravings after Alexander was widely distributed and must have contributed to further stimulating interest in China, which continued well into the first decades of the nineteenth century. Lord Macartney's private secretary, Sir John Barrow, left an invaluable record of the journey. In quoting Lord Macartney, he describes many scenes that could have inspired chinoiserie. For example: "A Chinese gardener is the painter of nature and though totally ignorant of perspective as a science, produces the happiest effects by the management, or rather penciling, of distances." He tells us that Jehol was called the Paradise of ten thousand (or innumerable) trees, and he marvels at the "extensive lake." He talks of the emperor appearing "on a high open palakeen," of how "almost every stroke of the oar brought a new and unexpected object to our view." He describes the islands as "one marked by a pagoda, or other building; one quite destitute of ornament; some smooth and level; some steep and uneven; and others frowning with wood, or smiling with culture" (Barrow 1804).

In Jane Austen's *Mansfield Park* (pub. 1814), Edmund asks his cousin Fanny, "You in the meantime will be taking a trip to China, I suppose. How does Lord Macartney go on?" Such imaginary trips to China were not taken only in fiction but must have been indulged in by many a real person who wished to be well informed about the culture of the East. Chinese scenes were once more the inspiration for drawing and painting, only now there was a desire for more refinement of line and more individual freedom of interpretation. Japanning and decorating using raised surfaces created technical restrictions, so new ways of painting on boxes had to be found. Drawings and paintings of China on paper were already proliferating, so it was a natural step to transfer direct painting onto wood. Chinoiserie, as a style of decoration, was no longer practiced as an integral part of japanning; instead, it was executed by using the new method of direct penwork and painting.

The influence of some of the best eighteenth-century artists, such as Pillement, did not make its mark in box decoration until the turn of the century, when methods of painting were more conducive to delicacy of line. The charm factor of the earlier chinoiserie decoration was replaced with more sophisticated and refined ornamentation.

Publications, design books, articles, paintings, and firsthand accounts and letters continued to circulate, bringing Chinese pagodas, temples, palaces, waterwheels, plants, animals, and people into libraries and drawing rooms throughout England.

Attempts at Chinese writing were the epitome of kudos. Such decoration is very rare, and even when it is found on European work, it does not usually make much sense. More interesting and prestigious are attempts at writing that do make sense but give the nationality of the artist away, since the strokes of the calligraphy are not painted in the right order. The exquisite precision necessary for Chinese calligraphy was then, as always, difficult to grasp for the untutored hand.

By the end of the eighteenth century, the royal arbiter of taste, George, the Prince of Wales, was also enchanted by the wayward fancies of chinoiserie design. In spite of the fact that the Chinese treated the English delegation with nothing more than polite contempt, the prince was not put out. He was able to separate his Whig-oriented political sympathies, which included aggressive trade expansion, from what he saw as an aesthetically important development. A modern psychologist may attribute his love of Cathay to the fact that for his first public appearance at age twelve, he was placed behind a screen of Chinese lattice work. The plain fact is that the fantastical suited his inquiring and restless personality.

The official residence of the prince was Carlton House, which was to his mind in need of improvement. He commissioned Henry Holland, an erudite and respected architect, to undertake the project. Holland designed different rooms in the various fashionable styles of the period, including a Chinese salon. This was the forerunner of the building that came to epitomize the exoticism of the early nineteenth century: the prince's summer palace, the sumptuously oriental Brighton Pavilion.

Figure 44. An example of a rare blue japanned box, decorated with a raised and painted picture of oriental figures fishing. Fishing, without seemingly a care in the world, was depicted by many artists, including Mathias Darly. Note the precarious way the pavilion is perched on the edge of the land, and the tall rocks that appear to be erected behind it. Note too how the trees are bending and peeping from the side of the rock or seem to grow from nowhere. These all are typical elements of chinoiserie. French. 12" wide. Ca. 1780. $2,000–3,000.

The Pavilion was a farmhouse the prince bought in 1787. After many plans and changes of heart, Henry Holland began the conversion of farmhouse to palace in 1801. The Pavilion became the focus of fashion for the first four decades of the nineteenth century, even during the period of its conversion. In fact, it did not emerge as the wondrous microcosm of eclectic orientalism until 1822, when John Nash, the prince's latest favorite architect, completed the remodeling he was commissioned to undertake in 1815.

Nash gave the exterior a Mughal-inspired look—demonstrating the Indian influence that was beginning to gain ground—while the interior continued to develop in the Chinese taste, with Chinese wallpapers, figures, dragons, lanterns, vases, faux bamboo, trellised banisters, screens, lacquer objects, bells, and drapes.

The prince imported furniture and objects from China through Crace and Sons and also commissioned pieces in the oriental taste from English cabinetmakers, including "Crace specialists in exotic designs for five generations." The prince's active patronage of the style made it imperative for the beau monde to follow. Not only was the Chinese taste given another tremendous boost, it also moved into more rarified and eclectic realms, despite the fact that the prince's efforts were at times tittering on the prodigious. (See the chapters "Papier-mâché" and "Card Boxes": 8/01, 8/12, 18/06—7.) Even when in 1816, Lord Amherst and his embassy suffered more-severe humiliation in China than previous British delegations had done, the Prince of Wales, who by now had become the Prince Regent, was undeterred in his avid zeal for amassing oriental and oriental-inspired treasures.

*Below and left:*
Figure 45. A box decorated in penwork like a sampler of its owner's preferred chinoiserie designs. There are copies from Stalker and Parker, *The Ladies Amusement*, Darly, and other sources. The hand is that of an enthusiastic amateur, and the whole composition has the curious charm of surprise. The different designs are arranged like scraps, without any thought for relevant size; a rabbit, for example, dwarfing a boat. The detail shows an interpretation of Stalker and Parker's design of *A Pagan Worshipp in ye Indies*. 10.3" wide. Ca. 1820. $2,500–3,000.

While the prince was amusing himself collecting and making plans both for his own residences and the whole of London, the country was embroiled in the Napoleonic Wars. The people were not happy. They began to disapprove of their extravagant prince, especially after his marriage had degenerated into a public shambles.

The prince tried to provide diversions such as royal visits, which, while providing spectacle and excitement, also disrupted the life of the city. The people neglected their work and crowded into the streets of London, creating a veritable pandemonium. Even the cows in Green Park, frightened by the noise of the gun salutes and the cheering, registered their protest by refusing to produce any milk. In summer 1814, in an effort to raise his popularity and the spirits of the people, the Prince Regent instigated the staging of a grand public party, "the Grand Jubilee." The celebrations were sumptuous and spectacular. There were grand fêtes in London's Hyde Park, St. James's Park, and Green Park. Nash was given the job of transforming St. James's Park into a mini-Cathay. Oriental bridges, temples, pavilions, and ornamental structures were erected among the familiar English trees. The Grand Pagoda was reported as particularly magnificent. The dream of Cathay had moved into the public heart of London and worked its magic. Even cynical critics such as *The Times* had to bow to the demonstrable delight of the public.

While George (1762–1830) was the young Prince of Wales and the Prince Regent (1810–1820), his energies were very much taken up with stylistic concerns. During the last decade of his life (1820–1830), when he became King George IV, he was still fierce of his aesthetic standards, but not quite so absorbed by them. It was still perceived that he approved of the oriental style, and the fashionable world continued to decorate in chinoiserie or buy imported Chinese works of art.

Figure 46. A penwork chinoiserie design of oriental figures and giant blooms. This is a professionally decorated piece of early Tunbridge ware. 6.5" wide. Ca. 1800. $600–800.

*This whole page:*
Figure 47. A table cabinet decorated in penwork with striking Chinese figures. The warriors with their flying pennants, the figure holding the bird, and the other representations must have been copied from drawings executed from life. Quasi-Chinese writing was added to render the composition more realistic. This is a very interesting departure from chinoiserie convention. Although still within the genre, the artist tried to portray Cathay according to the latest firsthand observations. Perhaps he himself had been to China? 13" wide. Ca. 1810. $4,500–6,000.

Figure 48. The most delightfully fanciful vision of Cathay in a tea chest. The interior of the lid is painted with three oriental child clowns, standing on a platform made up of what looks like tea chests. Their costumes are more in the Turkish-Moorish fashion, except for the hat of the central figure, which is in typical chinoiserie of the inverted flowers variety favored by Pillement. It was a fad among European aristocracy to dress their own children in "Turkish" costumes. Unusually, the building behind them is drawn in perspective, although the bridge in the distance is more in the tradition of chinoiserie. The enormous flower pot and the gigantic plant, which looks as if it is the continuation of a metamorphic spout, are influenced by French mid-eighteenth-century tradition. Pillement liked to dwarf his figures by shading them in enormous two-dimensional plant life, although these youngsters are too solid looking for Pillement. The composition is most unusual in that it combines quite earthly looking elements with total fantasy. The painting is of exceptional quality, the vivid colors of the clothes and plants contrasting with the delicately shaded faces. A rare whimsical vision perfectly composed, placed, and executed. 9" wide. Ca. 1810. $?

William IV succeeded his brother George in 1830, and for the seven years of his reign the Pavilion enjoyed more royal visits. Neither the king nor his queen were great style leaders, and there was not much development in oriental trends during the 1830s. Furthermore, the traders of the East India Company were importing real lacquer boxes from China, with scenes painted by the Chinese themselves. For a time, these boxes coexisted with chinoiserie-decorated boxes. After about 1830, chinoiserie work all but disappeared.

When Queen Victoria succeeded her uncle to the throne in 1837, she was not quite so taken by oriental fashions. The political climate had changed. Previous monarchs could keep their political agendas and fiscal interests separate from their cultural and artistic concerns. As the nineteenth century

progressed, trading became more aggressive. Brutal measures had to be taken to expand trading rights. Queen Victoria and her government saw their role as empire builders both by acquiring land and financial supremacy. Since the loss of America, England's position in the world appeared to be shrinking. The young queen, guided by her ambitious politicians and the huge financial interests of the middle classes, was determined to regain her position in the world.

For nearly two centuries the oriental way of life and oriental culture had been promoted as refined and wise. It was difficult to justify to the people going to war against the Chinese and their ancient culture. Faster communications meant that information was more widely disseminated throughout the population, and as a result, dissident voices were beginning

*This whole page:*
Figure 49. A box decorated all over in penwork, with scenes of idealized Indian life featuring figures in gardens with musicians.
Feet and handles in contemporaneous Regency style. The handles are of an exceptionally striking design of a star shape made
up of bunches of grapes alternating with vine leaves. 11.75" wide. Ca. 1815–25. $3,000–4000.

to condemn the imperial drive. The only way to sell the change of attitude toward Cathay was to demonize the orientals—both the Chinese and the Indians—and demote them to no more than savages who needed England's civilizing influence and, of course, religion.

Victoria sold the Pavilion to the town of Brighton in 1850 for a fraction of what it had cost to create. It was curtains for the Chinese taste. Victoria would go to Balmoral in Scotland when she needed a retreat. The cold, sober air suited her best.

The last real glimmer of Cathay was seen in 1842, in Hyde Park in London. It was an exhibition that previously had been seen in America and was brought over to England by the man who had first organized it in his native land, Nathan Dunn of Philadelphia. Nathan was a Quaker merchant who had amassed an eclectic collection of Chinese objects. He had the reputation of being well respected in China for his fair way of dealing and for not trading in opium. For this reason the Chinese sold him their finest pieces.

The exhibition, which featured oriental life and authentic-looking pavilions, attracted crowds of lookers, but not many buyers. The only thing to sell well was the catalogue; 100,000 catalogues were taken away by the visitors as souvenirs of the visit. The upper classes were no longer buying Chinese; they were certainly not used to buying in public, crowded places. The middle classes did not have the assurance of their own judgment. From thence it was the American traders who had the choice of the treasures of China.

It is ironic that 1842 was also the year that saw the signing of the Treaty of Nanking. This insult to China was brutally accentuated by British seamen, who vandalized the Porcelain Tower of Nanking, the inspiration of so much chinoiserie decoration and the ultimate symbol of Cathay.

## THE INFLUENCE OF INDIA

India was more swiftly and brutally taken control of by the British, and therefore its artistic influence was not felt to the extent that Chinese influence had been felt. Such as it was, it was often as part of an overall exotic scheme, or as an adaptation of Indian craft techniques.

Penwork boxes of the early nineteenth century that appear to be chinoiserie are often a mixture of Chinese and Indian scenes. Sometimes both Chinese and Indian elements coexist on the same scene in charming confusion.

Indian art was first introduced to Europe by the Dutch in the end of the sixteenth century. During the seventeenth and eighteenth centuries, the British were aware of Indian art, but it was not until the 1780s and 1790s that most people in England had any idea of what India looked like. The first view of India was provided by William Hodges, who published engravings of *Select Views of India*. Hodges was an artist under the patronage of Warren Hastings, who until 1784 held various high offices in India, including that of governor general. Hodges's painting of the Mosque at Gazipoor is a brilliant example of the onion-domed roof that was transposed to exotic European buildings, including the Brighton Pavilion.

At the turn of the century, two brothers, Thomas and William Daniell, published engravings of the aquatints they painted while traveling through India and China. The Daniells were influential in conveying the mystique of India and were no doubt responsible for inspiring designs featuring Indian architecture, costume, and animals, which were soon transferred from pattern book to penwork box.

During the second half of the eighteenth century and the best part of the nineteenth century, British officials in India commissioned paintings and collected Indian artistic objects. For a brief period, such work was held in high regard and inspired some wonderful work in the field of decorative objects, including boxes. As the hold of Britain on India strengthened, Indian-inspired decoration declined.

In addition to the pictorial contribution made by the influence of China, and to a lesser extent India, the buildings of the Orient helped extend the possibilities of shape and structured ornament. During the first three decades of the nineteenth century, some boxes had lids inspired by pagodas or Chinese ceramic pillows. Sometimes such boxes were of Chinese inspiration, and sometimes the pagoda element was incorporated within a hybrid design.

The inspiration of Cathay went further than mere decoration and form. It contributed to the liberation of design from the restricted interpretation of late-eighteenth-century neoclassicism.

# CHAPTER 4 *Regency*

Historically, the Regency lasted only for the second decade of the nineteenth century. Stylistically, it developed from the last ten years of the eighteenth century up to about 1835. The figure who infused this period with its particular quality was George (1762–1830), Prince of Wales, Prince Regent (1810–1820), and finally, until his death in 1830, King George IV. From his coming of age in the 1780s, George's main interest was the expansion of the stylistic horizons, not only for his own residences, but for the whole of the country.

Before the end of the first quarter of the nineteenth century, the Regency style reached the pinnacle of its very distinctive flavor. Taste expanded and reached that delicious largesse that absorbed and interpreted epochs and men without aesthetic inhibitions. True, sometimes it was precariously poised between excellence and vulgarity, but it always evaded banality by rising above the commonplace with vibrancy and vision. Regency boxes are not merely good taste; they are significant testimonies of the aesthetic turmoil of their time.

George was frustrated in his desire for a military career by his father, King George III. In later life, when he was himself the king, George appeared to have convinced himself that he had been at the Battle of Waterloo, so strong was his wish to distinguish himself with his own royal hussars! However, King George III decided that his younger son, the Duke of York, had the right gravitas for the army. Contrary to expectations, the duke did not distinguish himself in battle. His only contribution to the collective memory of the nation is this rhyme:

*The Grand old Duke of York*
*he had ten thousand men,*
*he marched them up to the top of the hill*
*and he marched them down again*

The Duke was a bon viveur who strayed into roguish deeds. To augment his income, he clandestinely sold army commissions with the help of his mistress. In a way he embodied the spirit of the Regency, which was style before propriety. Taking the lead from his brother, he too commissioned many beautiful objects.

With such ardent royal patrons, style became a very serious consideration. Having no other specific occupation, George, the Prince of Wales, applied all his energies into orchestrating grand architectural schemes. The repercussions of this new stylistic impetus were felt throughout the country and left a legacy of beautifully laid-out squares, parks, crescents, and roads, not just in London but in other cities, such as Tunbridge Wells, Brighton, and Bath.

George was not only an active patron of all the arts, but also an acknowledged connoisseur. At the annual banquets of the Royal Academy he was considered a serious speaker, and although the building of the National Gallery did not start until two years after his death, he was instrumental in its implementation. In 1823, when he was king, he presented the nation with his father's 70,000-volume library, which became the foundation of the British Library (I used the B.L. during my research for this book). He also took the first steps in planning a new building for the British Museum, although the project did not take off until after his death.

His most direct contribution to the vernacular style of the period was the transformation of his London home, Carlton House, and particularly his summer palace, the Brighton Pavilion. The Pavilion still stands in all its external glory and fixed decorations, but alas, with only some of its interior furnishings and objects. The characters who buzzed in it with such panache and vibrancy have long since departed. So has the particular royal presence of George and his period. The Pavilion was not just the zenith of Regency style; it was a microcosm of Regency high life.

Before he came of age, George was not allowed to go to Brighton. The company the town attracted was not considered respectable by his parents. The prince, on the other hand, was drawn to society on the edge, as long as it was witty, fashionable, stylish, and socially liberated. It was inevitable that he would establish his base of pleasure on forbidden ground.

Looking at the Pavilion, any idea that George was a connoisseur of the strictly academic type vanishes. The building is such a fantastical concoction that attempts at precise classification and description are futile. The Pavilion is a distillation of many influences drawn from many cultures, and is infused with such idiosyncratic whimsy that the sober observers thought it a manifestation of madness; the imaginative spectators, a bold statement of inspired magnificence.

George did not just immerse himself into art. He also immersed himself into life. At eighteen, he had his first serious affair with an actress. At twenty-three he married in secret Mrs. Fitzherbert, a Catholic widow a few years older than himself. This marriage was never officially acknowledged. It was totally ignored by his father, King George III, who in 1793 arranged for George to marry Princess Caroline of Brunswick. Unfortunately, Caroline was far from being a style guru. She was said to be gross, uncouth, and malodorous. George, who asked for brandy

*Left and below:*

Figure 50. An extraordinary mahogany box with shallow carving depicting a lyre in the center of an equal-sided boat. The lyre also suggests a sail. The sides of the boat, which curve up in an almost straight perpendicular manner and then curve outward, are reminiscent of pictorial Egyptian art. The lyre is rich in mythological connotations. The sides of the box are also carved with lyres. The box is constructed like a building supported by four pillars, which start from bases and conclude in capitals. The top is shallow, with a slight taper to a central raised part. The four corners are inlaid in coromandel wood, with branches that suggest palms. The central part is decorated with a symmetrical motif of a moth flanked by stylized foliage, executed in shallow carving, the details emphasized in inlaid coromandel wood. There is a drawer in the lower part with a central "blind" escutcheon. This is constructed so as to suggest a vaulted entrance. The surround is in stepped carving that leads into the inner part, which is in mother of pearl. There is shallow, fluted carving and shallow, sharp molding defining areas of the box. The piece is rich in cultural associations characteristic of the early part of the nineteenth century, although the manner in which these are translated into aesthetic symbols is rare. The patination is exceptional, with raised and flatter parts having faded in differing degrees. There is nothing inside. It could have been made for a special purpose, although the depth and the proportions suggest a tea chest with a drawer for tea spoons. 16" wide. Ca. 1810. $?

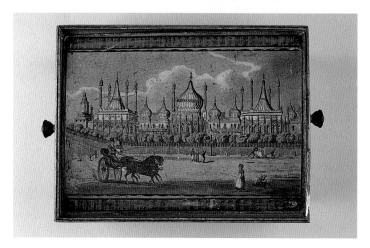

Figure 51. The top of a basket-shaped box with a contemporaneously colored print of the Brighton Pavilion. In front of the building there are people traveling in fashionable conveyances, and, in true Regency whimsy, a child pulling a carriage with two fashionable dolls sitting in it. 7.5" wide. Ca. 1822. $1,000–1,500.

*Above and right:*

Figure 52. This is a truly regal Regency piece. It is constructed with no concern for cost. The flat panels of rosewood are strung and inlaid with brass in robust lines and distinct defined ornament. The box is framed in deep carving. The pattern is arranged in mirror image. The top is constructed with alternating bands of carving, which are not just decorative but are integral to the form. The uppermost part is slightly rounded. The straight lines juxtaposed with the rounded elements are orchestrated with true virtuosity to give this box a severe yet vibrant strength. 14.5" wide. Ca. 1820. $?

when he first saw her, prepared himself for the wedding ceremony by getting seriously drunk. Neither the bride nor the idea of bigamy could have been very appealing. The marriage was disastrous and ended in vexatious divorce, causing George a period of intense unpopularity and much embarrassment. The only child of the union, Princess Caroline, died very young, giving birth to her first child just when her relationship with her father was beginning to take a meaningful direction.

In a way, the Prince of Wales was left with no other occupation or concern except style. He surrounded himself with men and women in the hubbub of cultural and social life and dallied with intelligent socialite mistresses throughout his life. Neither as the Prince of Wales nor as the Regent did George see eye to eye with his father. Politically, they had different affiliations. In terms of character, they were eons apart. George III was a sober man of frugal taste who felt humbled by the loss of the American colonies and was worried about the finances of the nation. On the other hand, the prince saw his royal role as establishing a magnificent style, harking back to the period of the Bourbon kings of France.

To celebrate his ascendancy to the Regency, in summer 1811 the prince gave a grand fête at Carlton House. The pretence was that it was in honor of the exiled Bourbons of France. He appeared to his guests under blue drapes decorated with gold fleur-de-lis, the emblem of the Bourbon French monarchy. Some of the Carlton House carpets also featured this design. On April 23, 1814, he entertained Louis XVIII to dinner at Carlton House before the latter set off for Dover. He arranged other royal visits, gathering the Tsar of Russia, the King of Prussia, Prince Metternich as a representative of the Emperor of Austria, and other royal persons to London, staging pageants and

sumptuous feasts in an almost hysterical pursuit of grand splendor.

The Prince Regent certainly saw himself as part of an ancient royal tradition. The extravagant spending on his houses may have brought the country to its knees, but it also stimulated design and commerce. He established style as the ultimate social accomplishment, so important in fact that it became an end in itself. It was not just the mid-eighteenth-century idea of classical form and moral rectitude being inextricably linked; it was taste as an indicator of social superiority and, as such, pursued to perfection.

Figure 53. Paper and mirror box with a central watercolor. This is a piece of characteristic Regency fantasy. The fragile materials are treated with utmost respect, the work being as fine as if it was executed with precious metals. The watercolor picture is of two figures in theatrical, idealized costumes discussing a baby sleeping under a tree. Perhaps a christening present, it is imbued with the romanticism of the period. 4.5" wide. Ca. 1810. $800–1,000.

*This whole page:*
Figure 54. A leather-covered box that combines many Regency features: shape, applied gilt ornament, lion handles, ball-and-claw feet, and impeccable workmanship. It bears the label of T. Lund, 56 Cornhill. The corners of the top are decorated with pressed metal gilt pineapples; the cartouche around the central handle, with a laurel wreath and flowers. The printed silk depicts Demeter, the goddess of agriculture, with figures holding emblems of her attributes. The piece combines classical decoration with freer and more organic form. 12.5" wide. Ca. 1820. $3,000–4,000.

The interesting result of this cultivated style consciousness was that a person of acknowledged taste could feel himself on par with people of superior social standing and, to this end, the increasingly prosperous middle classes spared no effort. Ironically, the prince's philosophy robbed him of some of the reverence owed to him as a royal person. In 1813, when George was already Prince Regent and rather corpulent, he attended a "dandy ball" in London. The prince was talking to Lord Alvanley, ignoring another guest—George "Beau" Brummell, a former friend with whom he had fallen out three years previously. Beau Brummell returned the snub. He turned to Alvanley and asked loudly and clearly, "Alvanley, who's your fat friend?"

Beau Brummell was the undisputed king of dress style. Lord Byron had once declared with caustic affectation that "there are but three great men in the nineteenth century, Brummell, Napoleon, and myself." In 1826, *The English Spy* wrote of Brummell, "When he first appeared in this stiffened cravat, its sensation was prodigious; dandies were struck dumb with envy and washer women miscarried." The prince himself had admired the way Brummell, the grandson of a gentleman's gentleman, had stiffened his cravat and mixed his snuff. Style had elevated Brummell to the stratosphere of emperors.

George's greatest triumphant lifestyle statement, his Brighton Pavilion, was said to have been partly inspired and derived from Sezincote, a very significant exotic grand house built for a retired trader of the East India Company. The luster of royalty was tarnished sufficiently to allow renewed aesthetic input from trade.

To be fair, the new air of egalitarianism ushered into the hitherto stuffy salons not just people who had new money and experiences to offer, but also more intellectuals, wits, and interesting characters, all contributing to the cultural vibrancy of the period. Another new phenomenon was the appearance of the first lady decorators. Lady Anne Barnard and her sister shocked society by subsidizing their genteel living through "doing up" and letting houses.

As more people pursued style, more cabinetmakers tried to fulfill the demand for new designs. There was a flourishing of ideas, incorporating elements of such diversity as never seen before. The neoclassical and Chinese fashions were already well ensconced in the pattern books. With the exception of a limited rococo element in certain chinoiserie designs, box styles had remained separated up to the 1780s. As the eighteenth century was drawing to a close, there was a new drive for more individuality and freedom of expression that surpassed the rigidity of prescribed rules and strove for a new rule of Style with a capital S, which, while respecting form and proportion, allowed for ingenuity, imagination, and innovation.

Historical events opened up more cultural doors and introduced fresh ideas to the design palette. By far the most important of these was the Egyptian influence, which at its most restrained took neoclassicism into a more robust direction and at its most extreme developed into a much more sumptuous and sensual genre. Both England and France incorporated Egyptian elements into the Regency and Empire styles, respectively. Many English aspiring and true connoisseurs had

Figure 55. Veneered in well-figured mahogany, this box is inlaid in boxwood with a restrained classical pattern. However, the tapering form, which gives the illusion of towering height, and the domed top are more typical of the nineteenth-century phase of neoclassicism. 12" wide. Ca. 1810. $1,400–2,000.

Figure 56. A box in a very unusual shape attesting to the sophisticated understanding of ancient form. It is very deliberately structured to imply three dimensions. The central panels are sunk and edged in gadrooning. The inlay is in pewter and mother of pearl. Note the ornament that suggests spearheads, and the foliated scroll feet. The flat top is suggestive of a classical support. The whole piece in fact could be a trapezophoron. This is a true distillation of the principles of one discipline transferred into another. 12.5" wide. Ca. 1820. $3,500–4,500.

Figure 57. Truly monumental, this tea chest is veneered in richly figured mahogany. The structure uses paneling and gadrooning to create a sense of depth and weightiness. The exceptionally large size is suited to the complicated architectural design. 17" wide. Ca. 1825–30. *Courtesy of Berry and Marcia Morton.* $3,500–4,500.

*Above and right:*
Figure 58. A tea chest in subtle sarcophagus form, the top made of a gently stepped concave border around four low pyramid-shaped sides culminating in a flat center. Note the very strong ball-and-claw feet. Note also the handles with the feature of the extra gilt brass ornament so that the loop does not mark the wood. Interestingly, the head is not of a lion, but more of a leopard, suggesting more Egyptian rather than Greco-Roman influence. Ca. 1820–30. *Courtesy of a private collection.* $4,500–5,000.

encountered Egyptian design since the 1760s, during their stay in Italy. There was printed information about Egypt in the Vatican, which some of the most astute travelers had the opportunity to study. For the others, there were the etchings of Piranesi, and also the painted walls of the English coffee house in Rome, which were painted by Piranesi in the Egyptian manner. In Patch's *The Golden Asses*, already mentioned in the chapter "Neoclassicism," Egyptian objects adorn the walls of the room where the aficionados are gathered.

In 1798, when Napoleon set off on his expedition to Syria and Egypt, he took with him archaeologists and artists so that they could record the culture of the people he intended to conquer. The later concept of obliterating the heritage of colonized nations was quite alien, both to Napoleon and to George, then the Prince of Wales. Both of them were eager to allow their opponents the integrity of their own heritage. Furthermore, they were willing to enrich their own aesthetic knowledge both by studying newly explored worlds and assimilating into their own consciousness the culture of their enemies. It was a unique form of imperialism, rejecting both the ancient Greek label of barbarian for the defeated and the future European label of demonic savage. It is said that when Napoleon's men first set eyes on the temple of Thebes, they burst into applause. Unprepared for such monumental structures, the sight must have been truly awesome.

Napoleon's expedition increased the knowledge, and thus the influence, of the Egyptian world both in France and England. In 1802, on his return to France after the expedition, Vivant Denon published his work *Voyages dans la Basse et Haut Egypte*. The book was avidly devoured by English culture seekers and encouraged a style that was already beginning to take hold. In 1812, a collector by the name of William Bullock created the Egyptian Hall in the heart of London—the south side of Piccadilly. William was the brother of George, one of the most innovative of the Regency cabinetmakers. The frontage of the building was modeled as an Egyptian temple, with a tapering facade complete with large supporting figures and heavy

Figure 59. The pure neoclassical form, taken a step toward the Egyptian-inspired sarcophagus shape. The gilded applied escutcheons and handle are influenced by French work. Veneered in kingwood, perfectly proportioned, and subtly strung and edged. 12" wide. Ca. 1810. $1,500–2,000.

Figure 60. A tea chest of strong form. The lower part of inverse sarcophagus and the top elaborately structured to give the illusion of a roofed building. Veneered in figured rosewood, it is inlaid in mother of pearl and pewter lines, which serve to emphasize the dramatic shape. 13" wide. Ca. 1830. $1,800–2,500.

reeded columns. The hall, which functioned as a museum, survived until 1905.

In the last two decades of the eighteenth century, encouraged by the proclivities of the Prince of Wales, French influence was felt much more strongly in England than it had been since the seventeenth century. This influence encouraged stronger use of metal ornament and more curvilinear shapes and was in tune with the expression of the new Egyptian-inspired designs. After the signing of the Anglo French Treaty of Commerce in 1786, there was increased traffic both in goods and craftsmen from France. Certain cooperative arrangements were struck up, the most notable of which was arguably that between Henry Holland and the French cabinetmaker and dealer Daguerre. Henry Holland was the architect commissioned to redesign Carlton House, the London residence of the Prince of Wales.

Daguerre, who also imported other French makers' work, set himself up in London with a showroom in Piccadilly. He supplied furniture for Carlton House, which was of course a wonderful start to his London venture. After the French Revolution, Daguerre, who also operated from a Paris showroom with a partner, smuggled into England several choice pieces that had previously belonged to French aristocrats. It was rumored that his partner was trusted by Marie Antoinette with many of her treasures for safekeeping.

Later, Daguerre also supplied furniture for the Brighton Pavilion. In 1791, some of the smuggled French furniture was sold by the auction house Christie's. Daguerre never returned to France, dying in London in 1796, by which time the French and English styles had been drawn closer, although the English still preferred a greater degree of robustness, strength of line, and decorative restraint.

The prince's architect, Henry Holland, not only bought French furniture for his clients; he also employed French craftsmen on several of his projects, such as Woburn and the redecoration of Althorp for Lord Spencer. Thus, up to his death in 1806, he did much to soften the strict classicism of the earlier period with the input of opulent French-inspired decoration. It is interesting that one of the architects to introduce the newer style was Holland, who had impeccable neoclassical credentials. Holland was one of the pioneers who had the good fortune to also have pioneering patrons.

Holland enhanced mahogany using brass, ormolu, and ebony bandings. The decorative motifs were in the classical tradition of acanthus leaves, honeysuckle, and stylized flora. The more varied structural shapes were complemented with the use of lion feet and monopodia. The use of these features was a great inspiration for box makers, who stood the new shaped boxes on feet and further enhanced them with lion mask, cornucopia, stylized basket, or floral handles and escutcheons.

Another pioneer of the new freer style was Thomas Hope. Hope came to England after spending eight years traveling, studying, and drawing the ruins of Greece, Asia Minor, Turkey, Syria, and Egypt. Five volumes of his drawings still exist. He collected artifacts of all kinds, which he displayed in his house on Duchess Street, London. He set up different rooms that reflected styles derived from different countries. Hope was first and foremost a connoisseur collector and secondly an amateur architect-designer. He was an amateur in the old sense of being equal with the professionals, but more of a gentleman than a trader.

Hope was highly respected, and his 1807 publication *Household Furniture and Interior Decoration Executed from Designs by*

Figure 61. A carved-mahogany tea chest bearing the stamp of Robert Wright of Hull. Records indicate that Wright was working as a cabinetmaker in Bond Street, Hull, from 1814 to 1839. It is most unusual for boxes to be stamped, since this treatment was reserved mostly for furniture. This is an extraordinary caddy and must have been made in the early years of this maker's career. The caddy conforms to the form of boxes popular during the Regency period; that is, of the late neoclassical phase, which was heavily influenced by the discovery of the ancient Egyptian world. The treatment of the form, however, harkens back to the eighteenth-century interpretation of the classically inspired cellaret. This was a rendition in wood of ancient Greco-Roman shapes, which were originally carved in marble or cast in bronze. Ca. 1815. $6,000–8,000.

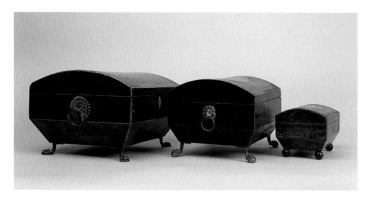

Figure 62. Side view of three boxes in the same design in three different sizes and woods. The rounded tops and the tapering lower parts standing on lion paw or ball feet give the structures a more organic appearance than that of the earlier neoclassical rectilinear forms. The large box is veneered in burr yew and has a border of fine geometric inlay. The middle box is veneered in coromandel; the smaller box, in kingwood. These have oval cartouches decorated with colored prints of the period. The smallest has a label inside attributing its print of the Brighton Pavilion to the Tunbridge ware maker Wise. 10.75", 9", 6" wide. Ca. 1822. $1,000–3,000.

*Thomas Hope* was consulted by cabinetmakers and clients alike. He was a friend of the French architect Percier, who was influential in promoting the new Egyptian style. In 1801, Percier had cooperated with Fontaine in the formulation of a complete set of designs reflecting the new thinking. A major element in their designs, adopted by Hope, was strong animal symbolism, encouraging further use of metal animal feet and handles as well as animal decoration.

Hope advocated plain surfaces that would be enhanced by inlaid motifs of brass and ebony, providing striking but restrained contrasts. Metal inlay on dark wood would provide "that distinctness and contrast of outline, that opposition of plain and enriched parts." There was a severity in Hope's designs consistent with the more weighty classicism of the first years of the nineteenth century. The decoration had symbolic cultural meaning and was applied with precision, within a classical framework.

In 1808, a more accessible version of Hope's designs was published by George Smith, and this promoted a wider following of the style. Egyptian monopodia, palmette and lotus motifs, Egyptian lion or leopard heads with smooth hair, columns, and reeded carved ornament joined the repertoire of already existing decorative elements sharing a common classical tradition.

The shapes of the new classicism were liberated from the strict lines of the earlier Adam style. The sarcophagus shape is of course what immediately springs to mind, but the influence was much more subtle and varied. Champolion (1790—1832), the translator of the Rosetta stone hieroglyphics (according to the West) and the founder of modern Egyptology, said of the Egyptians that they thought as if they were 100 feet tall. This essence of monumental strength found expression both in furniture and boxes. Although small, the box shape was transformed in many ways by using structural grammar derived from architecture. Sometimes a true master of his craft used an almost imperceptible change of angle within a deceptively simple design and transformed a simple box shape into a magnificent and dignified structure. Boxes were often built with bases, supports, pedestals, and structured stepped tops.

More complex designs drew the eye into an inner surface by using fielding (the enclosure of a panel within a framed structure. See figures 379, 442) and, from the 1820s, fielding in conjunction with gadrooning. Gadrooning, or deep continuous carving as a means of accentuating strength and depth, was already used in the later part of the eighteenth century by important cabinetmakers, such as the royal maker, William Vile. This technique, which was costly both in materials and time, was adopted for boxes slightly later and produced strong and impressive pieces.

The other shape derived from Egypt was the pyramid. This was used in two ways. In the earlier boxes of the very late eighteenth and early nineteenth centuries, pyramid tops would crown boxes with straight sides, giving just a hint of departure from neoclassicism. In the 1820s and 1830s, the pyramid top

Figure 63. This is a piece of compact furniture in box form. It is made with incredible precision by a master craftsman capable of impeccable work of the highest quality. Simply, the box would not work if there was the slightest miscalculation or imperfection. The timbers and the construction had to be absolutely stable and able to withstand the sometimes less-than-comfortable travel arrangements of the time. When closed, the box presents a compact Regency form in rosewood veneer strengthened with brass edging and enhanced with an ornament of brass line concluding in fleur-de-lis, the Prince Regent's favorite motif. The surprise comes when the box unfolds into an astonishing all-needs-served compendium. The top part lifts and the double-hinged slope (the double hinges enable the slope to fold upward into the box) folds down to provide a baize-covered writing surface. Facing the writing tablet there are small drawers in the manner of a Carlton House desk. The drawers are impeccably made in mahogany veneered in rosewood, like the exterior of the box. The joints are dovetailed. The surface is edged with boxwood. The framing is finished neatly with beading. Such drawers could hold writing necessities, trinkets, or collector's treasures. Collecting of all sorts of things was very fashionable at the time. The relatively new fad for traveling made acquiring objects of natural history, antiquity, or simply beauty an assertion of a person's worldly erudition. The top drawers are secured in place with a brass rod when the box is closed. The large bottom drawer is fitted with a lift-out tray suitable for keeping jewelry. There are two side drawers, which open externally: one holds writing implements, and the other is fitted with exquisitely turned sewing spools and other sewing tools. This box can stand favorable comparison with any portable, durable piece of furniture that stands elegantly and gracefully and approved of by Mr. Sheraton or Mr. Hepplewhite. The construction gives it strength in spite its delicate appearance. 14.2" wide. Ca. 1810. $10,000–12,000.

was occasionally used as the topmost part on boxes of sarcophagus form, especially in conjunction with reeded carving as in Anglo-Indian boxes.

Reeded radiating carving was seen in wooden furniture as early as the late eighteenth century, especially in cellarets. A cellaret in Harwood House made by Thomas Chippendale and a design in Thomas Hope's *Household Furniture and Interior Decoration* present two examples of this type of carving on a shape reminiscent of an ancient krater, rather than a sarcophagus. This particular structure, of elongated shape with segmented carving, was rarely adopted by English box makers, although it became very popular in Vizagapatam in India by the second decade of the nineteenth century. (See Fig. 268)

Although not the first exponent of the newer manifestation of the neoclassical style, Thomas Sheraton is perhaps the name most frequently applied to boxes that manifest a mixture of Egyptian, Greek, and Roman influences somewhat distilled through the spectrum of France. Sheraton was an interesting character, vacillating between a career in the church and a career as a designer. He may have been an itinerant cabinetmaker, but it is not clear if he himself had ever made any of the pieces he tried to teach others how to make. Although the designs in his *Cabinet-Maker and Upholsterer's Drawing-Book*—published first between 1791 and 1794—do not greatly vary from those of Hepplewhite, by the time he published his *Cabinet Dictionary* in 1803, he had moved more decisively toward the new Egyptian-inspired direction.

Sheraton made a strong point of promoting himself as the exponent of the new fashion, disregarding completely Thomas Chippendale, whose designs he claimed were "wholly antiquated" and curiously claiming that Hepplewhite had already "caught the decline." Sheraton made a great play of his understanding of geometry, giving detailed instructions as to perspective, both in drawings and text. His front piece was a labored allegorical composition of figures representing geometry and science and architecture, with temple and columns, and drapes and cabinetwork, and a putto for good measure. The departure from strict classicism was not allowed to imply a slackness of composition.

Sheraton explored bowfront and serpentine shapes, as well as tambour and domed tops. These forms were very successfully translated into boxes, giving an organic look that could not have been achieved with straight lines. Sheraton's decoration was within the genre of the time. He employed crossbanding, inlays, and marquetry, but he also expanded the repertoire of ornament to allow for more-naturalistic flowers, fruit, and figures. For example, his painted figures were not always drawn from antiquity. Even if the composition had classical elements, such as an urn, temple, or column, the figure could be contemporary. He even went further and designed

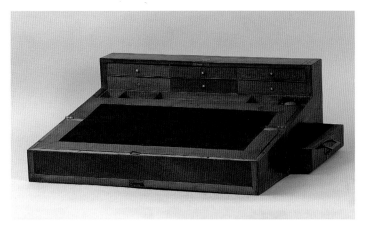

*Above and right:*

Figure 64. A mahogany-veneered writing box crossbanded in kingwood. This box is truly a portable desk in that it is very close in design to a desk. It has two side drawers, in the characteristic manner of a writing box, but the way it opens to reveal a number of drawers at the raised back section is reminiscent of furniture pieces designed by Hepplewhite and Sheraton. The whole look and structure of the box are similar to Sheraton's Lady's "secretaries," where he recommends the use of crossbanding and has small drawers facing the user. The two side drawers are an unusual feature. Taken with the good color of the wood and the crossbanding, this may be the work of Sangwine and Sons, who worked in Strand in London. Characteristic of the compact furniture that was gaining in popularity at the beginning of the nineteenth century. 21" wide. Ca. 1800. $8,000–12,000.

idealized rustic figures and rather silly-looking putti. Design began to move toward nature.

In his later publication of 1803 (*Dictionary*), Sheraton advocated the new fashion of brass inlay, which he went on to explain was a "very expensive mode" of decorating. In his last work, his *Encyclopaedia*, which was left unfinished upon his death, he explored the Egyptian element to the limit, introducing crocodiles and sphinx heads. In tribute to Lord Nelson, he also emphasized dolphins and other marine emblems.

Another new development Sheraton must be given credit for promoting, which influenced the design of boxes for the rest of the century, is his designs for compact pieces of furniture. These designs translated very well into the multipurpose boxes of the Regency and Victorian eras.

Although not a designer, Rudolph Ackermann (1764—1834) deserves mention, since without him we would not have such a complete record of the design of the period. Ackermann was a bookseller and publisher who (between 1809 and 1828) published *The Repository of Arts, Literature, Commerce, Manufacture, Fashions and Politics*. This publication was extremely influential and must have been instrumental in the rapid way that new ideas and designs were absorbed and developed during the years of its publication, making the Regency such an exciting and innovative period. He also sold prints and artifacts, including boxes, from his retail repository.

As well as influencing the designs produced by cabinetmakers, the French also had a significant input into the practical techniques of achieving these designs. Brass inlay had already been recommended by Hope, Sheraton, and others by the first decade of the nineteenth century. The Prince Regent encouraged this French-inspired fashion. The method of using brass in elaborate marquetry was first practiced during the

reign of Louis XIV by his *ébéniste*, Andre-Charles Boulle (1642—1732), with whose name it became synonymous. Boulle's inlays incorporated tortoiseshell and other materials, such as mother of pearl or silver. The fashion of the Regency brass inlay was principally, but not exclusively, for brass on dark wood; however, the technical principle was the same, even though the effect of the English work was different from the earlier Boulle work. Briefly the work carried on in England veered toward the classical tradition, rather than the more opulent and heavy baroque of the French.

The earlier pieces featuring brass inlaid ornament have an unrivalled purity of design. The brass motif is well separated and is of stylized and restrained form. The decoration is classical rather than naturalistic, employing such ornaments as the anthemion, fleur-de-lis, or a border in a single leaf shape. These pieces were executed with immaculate precision, respecting and enhancing the natural beauty of the wood. Thomas Hope designed furniture with brass and ebony inlay in controlled, stylized patterns.

Brass inlay was adopted very successfully as box decoration. In the early 1800s, boxes decorated with this work featured the more sparing type of separate ornament. Some were made in kingwood, which, although similar in appearance to rosewood, is not as open grained and does not require grain filling and French polishing to acquire a smooth surface.

The next stylistic development in brass inlay work was mainly the contribution of George Bullock. George was the brother of museum promoter William, and he was credited with producing the first Boulle-style inlays in England. George Bullock was a very talented artist who began his career as a sculptor in his native Liverpool. This early work must have given him a tremendous understanding of perspective and composition. Furthermore, the strength of his work in wood with metal mounts and inlays must have derived from the robust discipline of sculpture. Bullock used marble in conjunction with exotic hardwoods in his earlier furniture. Later his work became more patriotic. He designed in the Gothic style, using native oak. During the early nineteenth century, he worked within the Regency tradition of structured and weighty composition.

The first known work by Bullock was in 1805, for Cholmondeley Castle. In 1810, he moved to London, where he established his "Grecian Rooms" in his brother's Egyptian Hall in Piccadilly. By 1815, he had moved his business to Oxford Street, where he remained for the last few years until his death in 1818.

Bullock's career was cut short by his early death. Although very distinguished—he could claim the Regent among his clients—he did not attain financial success, probably because of his scheming business partner, an ex—East India Company man.

Bullock's designs influenced other cabinetmakers and commissioning clients well into the 1840s. His brass inlay designs were stylized, forcefully assertive, and totally controlled. In this, they adhered to the spirit of neoclassicism. But Bullock abandoned the motifs of the ancients in favor of floral and foliage patterns reminiscent of British plants. His inlays were in the form of continuous, repetitive patterns and scrolls, rather than more-severe separate ornaments. He injected an element of romanticism within the "antique" tradition, and the result was a style close to the French work, but still remaining distinctive.

By the end of the second decade of the nineteenth century, brass design on boxes became more naturalistic and was applied in the form of foliose and floral scrolls as borders, or as stylized compositions on the whole surface. As the fashion became more popular, some of the work lost its earlier vigor and precision. The patterns became larger and less well controlled. One clever innovation was a running pattern reminiscent of a Vitruvian scroll, which, although not as difficult to execute as the more complex floral motifs, was very effective, especially against rosewood and rich mahogany on large writing boxes.

There were other notable exponents of the brass inlaid decoration, one being Louis Le Gaigneur, who also used pewter, brass, copper, and shell, much in the French tradition. Thomas Parker of Air Street advertised his "Bulh" furniture, in the anglicized form of the term. Such work was done mostly in London, presumably because the makers had the means to invest in the process and because their fashion-conscious patrons demanded it. In the early decades of the nineteenth century, designs for metal inlays were available. A set of drawings dating from 1816 reside in the Victoria and Albert Museum in London.

The wider introduction of exotic woods, such as rosewood—which was very sparingly used before 1800—also gave an impetus to the new style of decoration. Rosewood, being a dark wood, looks good combined with metal inlay or applied ornament. Moreover, rosewood is an open-grained wood that responds well to French polish. French polish was introduced to England in the early 1800s and was in general use by 1815. The polish, which is a mixture of shellac and alcohol, gives a glossy and even finish. It was painstakingly and carefully applied to grain-filled wood.

The word "shellac" comes from the Sanskrit word "lakh," meaning 100,000, and refers to the secretions deposited on tree branches by shell lice. This deposit is scraped and sold as stick lac, which is raw or seed lac that is purified. After the Peace of

Figure 65. A tea caddy in rosewood with very well-defined separate ornament. The striking yet unfussy appearance of such pieces is typical of the earlier phase of the metal inlaid decoration. Ca. 1815. *Courtesy of the Bielstein Collection.* $3,500–4,500.

Figure 66. Rosewood and inlaid-brass box. The ornament of stylized leaves is arranged in two symmetrical halves, very much within the neoclassical tradition. The form of the box too is in severe neoclassical lines. The use of rosewood and brass, however, is more characteristic of early-nineteenth-century work. 9" wide. Ca. 1810. $1,000–1,400.

*Above and left:*
Figure 67. Rosewood and inlaid-brass box. The foliated borders are exceptionally well designed and executed with looping stems arranged in a mirror-image fashion. The two sides of the pattern are separated by a palmette motif. The palmette is repeated as the central motif on the sides of the front of the box. The corners are inlaid with squared leaf designs. The severity of the lines, the arrangement of the design, and the palmettes are rooted in the neoclassical tradition. The design, however, is more naturalistic than the design on the two previous boxes, attesting to the influence of the later years of the Regency. The box is of exceptional quality, with a very particular hinge patented by E. Wells. The hinge is sunk into the wood, and the whole back of the box opens very smoothly in a cylindrical motion reminiscent of the Scottish hinge. There is a centrally positioned silver gilt plaque on the top of the box, with the name of one of the early owners. The silver mark is of London 1824–5. The name reads "The Countess of Kinnoull." This was probably a gift to Louisa Rowley, who married the 11th Earl of Kinnoull in 1824. 15.5" wide. Ca. 1820. $12,000–15,000.

Figure 68. Rosewood veneered and inlaid in brass, this box typifies the combination of dark wood and metal inlay. Such boxes are invariably of high quality. 11.5" wide. Ca. 1825. $2,000–3,000.

1814, French cabinet workers popularized "French polish" throughout England. The new method enabled cabinetmakers to give quite a different gloss from that achieved through the application of earlier varnishes or wax finishes and was very well suited to new decorative techniques.

At this stage some earlier pieces were refinished. The results were more uniform than in earlier work, since makers followed more or less the same method and used the same ingredients.

The new woods did not take over completely from old favorites such as mahogany, harewood, maple, partridgewood, yew, and fruitwoods, but they were on the whole preferred for the new designs. During the Napoleonic Wars, direct trade with Spanish America and the Portuguese colonies of South America opened up as new trade alliances were forming. From Brazil came striking zebra wood and Brazilian rosewood, which has a much-stronger figure than Indian species.

The cutting of veneers was also getting marginally easier. Previously, a pair of expert cutters could get six to eight veneers per inch after long and hard work that required concentration and skill. In 1806, the *Annual Register* records the first appearance of steam-driven saws. Although these saws were not immediately employed by all cabinetmakers or mills, and hand cutting continued for many years, some of the pioneers must have taken advantage of this new technique, enabling them to produce predictably even veneers.

By the end of the 1820s, there was a revival of interest in lighter woods such as maple, amboyna, and satinwood. The brass inlays were still fashionable, but wood inlays and mother of pearl were beginning to gain in popularity. There was not a decisive swing in fashions, but rather additions to the repertoire. Mahogany was also used throughout the 1800s, as were most of the other woods mentioned, with the occasional use of oak (straight or pollarded), birch, elm, coromandel, and other native and exotic woods.

The third decade of the century, when George was finally crowned King George IV, saw the Regency style already fully developed. When George IV died in 1830, his style-conscious brother, the Duke of York, was already dead, and the Crown rested on the middle-aged head of the Duke of Clarence, who became William IV. Although William and his queen liked the Pavilion and paid several visits to Brighton, they did not have the stylistic vision of George IV. Furthermore, the rising middle classes were getting a stranglehold on the spending power of the nation and demanded to be catered to. A few years later, in 1837, Victoria succeeded to the throne. By this time the whole ethos of the client and supplier relationship had changed.

The Regency was a time of exquisite and magnificent excess. The scholarly deliberation of the eighteenth century was infused with strange, exotic ideas, with a zest for life championed by the Prince Regent, and by a fresh breath of individual liberty. At its worst it became obsessively selfish, as when the collecting of artifacts became so avid that it culminated in Lord Elgin's acquisition of the "Elgin marbles." At its best it gave rise to insightful writers, deliciously wicked cartoonists, and of course the great romantic poets. Lord Byron went off to fight for Greece and died in Messolongi. The Regent espoused both the classical and the oriental world, and through his human alchemy he caused them to reemerge with energy and humor.

The Regency was a period sandwiched between the age of reason and the age of outward respectability and inward hypocrisy. It produced art that could not have been produced at any other period. The cabinetmakers seemed to have a genius for fusion of ideas and styles, not just within a project but within a single item. They still had respect for the old orders of perspective and symmetry and could master the incoming influences. They employed their informed talents to inspire and create things of beauty and originality. At no other time was finesse and vibrancy so consummately united. It was a unique time in history, when social and economic transition was at a perfect pace for innovation without confusion.

Figure 69. Concave box, the whole front and top of which are made up of rosewood and brass marquetry. The striking form is shown to advantage by standing on ball feet. This box is characteristic of the later phase of brass inlay work. Both the fluid shape and the robust pattern attest to the bolder use of shape and decoration. 11" wide. Ca. 1825. $2,500–3,000.

Figure 70. A fitted sewing box. Veneered in rosewood and inlaid in mother of pearl, a material used in the later part of the Regency period. To be more precise, we are moving into the era of George IV and William IV. The form is in the established Egyptian-inspired tradition. What is particularly interesting about the decoration is that it is directly influenced by Egyptian visual tradition. The fine ornament is formed by two symmetrical and identical parts that are given a sharply upward and a precisely angled outward direction. 12.5" wide. Ca. 1830. *Courtesy of Susan Hannon.* $1,800–2,400.

*Above:*

Figure 71. In rosewood and amboyna, the marquetry on this box draws its inspiration from native plants. However, the treatment is still very formal. Note the strong treatment of the fern pattern. The central mother of pearl motif is not symmetrically arranged, but it is still contained within a very precise boundary. The work is very fine. 12.5" wide. Ca. 1830. *Courtesy of Amy Stevens.* $2,500–3,000.

Figure 72. Rosewood veneered with an arabesque floral inlay, this box indulges in Regency whimsy. The escutcheon is in the form of an urn-shaped flower pot with three blooms growing out of it. The center of the slightly domed top is inlaid with a Chinese person in typical chinoiserie inverted flower hat, wheeling a wheelbarrow. 11" wide. Ca. 1825. $1,000–1,500.

Figure 73. A mahogany tea chest with the details accented in boxwood. The inspiration of this piece is directly derived from classical architecture. The columns at the front are constructed so that they are three-dimensional, giving the impression of perspective and structural depth. The top part is wider so that it meets the top of the column like a pediment. The lyre in the center is a classical motif. The strings are in brass. 13" wide. Ca. 1810–15. $6,000–8,000.

# CHAPTER 5

# *Trade and Taste*

n 1836, Sir John Barrow wrote in the *Quarterly Magazine*:

*… it is a curious circumstance that we grow poppy in our Indian territories to poison the people of China in return for a wholesome beverage which they prepare almost exclusively for us.*

This, in a nutshell, was the core of the trading practice of the East India Company from the middle of the eighteenth to the middle of the nineteenth century. This is not to say that the Company traded only in these two commodities. It is just that this particular trade influenced the aesthetic of the arts to such an extent that an understanding of the stylistic development in England cannot be complete without reference to the historical background that gave it birth. I have referred to relevant events and personalities in other chapters. Here, I am attempting to place their role in context with the political scheme of the period. This chapter is only a sketchy account of the historical aspect, which was inextricably fused with trade and, at first, promoted and finally rejected the oriental taste.

The trade grew out of a whole labyrinthine pattern of business. It generated expansion and profits, both for the Company and its country of origin, England. The Company traded in spices, silks, lacquer, lac, ivory, wallpapers, china, paintings, and other commodities, the most lucrative being tea and opium.

The cozy image of the eccentric English person making such a performance of drinking tea in a genteel way is somewhat shattered by the knowledge of the Company's practices. Contemporaneous eyewitness accounts and letters from Company servants to their relatives are pretty damning. Writer and lecturer James Silk Buckingham (1786—1855) thought it preposterous that a country of a hundred million souls (India) should be run as a commercial enterprise by a company whose only aim was to produce dividends. But this is how it was; a huge enterprise set up to support the mother country.

Behind the facade of respectability, the history of tea trading is a sinister chapter of government manipulation. It can be argued that it was the foundation on which the British Empire was built. The East India Company was certainly the agent of state that brought about the expansion of the empire. Historically, its influence on Eastern nations was deleterious. In terms of cultural expansion within England, and even Europe and America, its contribution was positive and vast. It made accessible worlds of knowledge and aesthetic appreciation that scholarship would have taken infinitely longer to reach.

The Company was the first major marketing concern, even though the word had not yet been invented. Profit oiled the wheels of the engines of exploration that sought out and presented new ideas. In this respect, the Company was instrumental in pioneering style and also in supplying many of the raw materials, as well as the finished items, to satisfy the newest fads. The Regency would certainly have been less dazzling if it was not for the Company, and, ironically, the Victorian period may have been less xenophobic if it were not for commercial drive getting out of hand in the 1830s and 1840s.

The East India Company was set up as a joint stock company in 1600 by Royal Charter given by Queen Elizabeth I. The queen's astrologer and secretary, Doctor John Dee, saw it as an opportunity to place England on the top of a European hierarchy that would herald the dawn of a new golden age. There was uneasiness about the Catholic Portuguese, Spaniards, and Dutch, who had supremacy over the English in foreign trade. A strong company driven by promise of mythical profits was seen as the best way forward. The Company was set up with 218 merchants and traders in the city of London and was given the monopoly of trade east of the Cape of Good Hope. By the end of the seventeenth century, it even minted its own coin, which as business grew became widely accepted.

Early in the seventeenth century, the Company was granted trading rights in India by the Mogul emperor. In 1637, the first Company ships sailed to China with a view to exploring trading possibilities with the Far East. In this, they were joining traders from other nations who had already established links with the Chinese. As foreign activity increased, the emperor of China began to be concerned about the corrupting influence all the foreigners could have on the Chinese people. In 1729, foreign trade was strictly restricted to Canton, and only during a trading season lasting for about six months, avoiding the monsoon.

The foreign companies established "factories"—that is, living quarters and warehouses—in the allocated area along the Pearl River, outside the walls of the city of Canton. All the buying and selling had to be negotiated through specially licensed Chinese merchants, the Co Hong. The nearest that foreign ships were allowed to approach was thirteen miles downriver from Canton, at Whampoa island. The Chinese emperor's imperial agent was responsible for overseeing the correct procedure. If the English merchants remained in China during the time when they were forbidden to trade, they stayed in Macao, which had already been leased to the Portuguese.

As the eighteenth century progressed, the Company became increasingly aggressive. This was actively encouraged by the government back in England. Trade was seen as the way to gain influence, to increase income so that wars could be fought successfully and people at home would be kept prosperous and happy. Daniel Defoe, whose own creation, Robinson

Figure 74. A Napoleonic prisoner-of-war straw workbox. The lid is decorated with a straw marquetry picture of the East India House in Leadenhall Street in London after its late-eighteenth-century transformation from an Elizabethan building into a neoclassical edifice. Although the Company's vast wealth came from the East, the Company headquarters were designed in the European neoclassical style. The interior of the box is very much within neoclassical tradition. The exceptionally fine quality of the work and the identifiable and precise illustration points to a specifically commissioned piece. The angle and the treatment of the building on this box are similar to a straw work picture of Peterborough Cathedral, now in the Peterborough Museum collection; this is attributed to M. J. De la Porte, an acknowledged master of straw work. 13" wide. Ca. 1800. $?

Crusoe, was the archetypal trader of the early 1700s, put it in a nutshell: "The Commerce of England is an immense and almost incredible Thing." This was a good fifty years before it had become not just incredible, but also monstrous.

By the end of the eighteenth century, the use of tea in England was inextricably and irrevocably interwoven with opium, rendering it one of the two crops whose interdependence yielded vast financial and, consequently, political influence. Many an English bank was set up on money earned from opium and tea dealing. The coffee and tea houses became embryonic financial institutions. "Jonathan's" in Change Alley did a good trade in stocks and shares, eventually giving its name to the stock exchange. Originally, messengers were called waiters.

The late eighteenth century was a time of social unrest. Vast areas of countryside were already "enclosed" and owned by rich landowners. The peasants had nowhere to eek out a living. Farm workers were badly paid; cottage industries, although still robust, were damaged by new mechanical inventions. People were flooding into the towns in search of work. For the unskilled, this was invariably hard and poorly paid. Scattered around the country, the poor were not much of a threat; crowded in city slums, with the possibility of hearing subversive views already circulated in magazines and pamphlets, they were potentially explosive.

It was all very well for poets such as William Wordsworth to write in the first decade of the nineteenth century about the French Revolution:

*Bliss was it in that dawn to be alive,*
*But to be young was very heaven!*

—William Wordsworth, The Prelude xi, 1805

But it was hell if you were a royal, an aristocrat, or a member of the establishment. The French Revolution was masterminded by the middle classes, who harnessed the anger of the poor. The poor were getting angry in England too. The rich were getting nervous. Drastic social change has never been in the nature of the British, but Cromwell and the odd rolling kingly head were less than two centuries back. Change there had to be, but not of a kind that would damage the body politic, or the real power class. The method of change most preferred by the government and the Crown would allow the middle class to

*This whole page:*

Figure 75. A note in this caddy tells us that it was painted by Miss Anne Isaac. Miss Isaac must have been an extraordinarily talented and erudite woman. At the time when this work was done, women had very few opportunities to express their intellectual and artistic talents. Paint or penwork on domestic objects was one of the ways they could do so, without offending the egos of the men in their lives. This is a truly original, stunning artwork. The usual composition for penwork is for the main picture, often depicting figures, to be framed by flora. The convention is reversed on this piece. The front features an explosive arrangement of classical stylized flowers and motifs, which break through the austerity of neoclassicism with their bountiful exuberance of movement. The work around the keyhole is a little gem of composition, the central shell introducing a rococo hint in its asymmetry. This tea chest is a veritable time capsule. It is a symbol of all that was important when it was made. The stroke of genius that enables this object to deliver such original artwork is the inversion of scale. The top narrow edge of the lid depicts figures in action. This narrow strip, which goes all around the chest, is painted with people on the move. Placed above the large plant life of the front, the juxtaposed narrow space of the top suggests an extending road stretching over vast and varied landscapes. The figures are exotic. There are variations in their head covers and garments, but they all look Eastern. There are rounded and pointed hats and umbrellas. There are strange and wondrous plants. On one vignette, a figure is trying to climb a miraculous-looking tree and harvest an exotic fruit. The travelers are accompanied on their journey by camels, elephants, and horses. Among the tropical palms and strange trees and plants, they come across bridges and pagodas. Sometimes they point to the way forward; sometimes they meet up with fellow travelers. This is a vision of the Silk Road. Reports and sketches were avidly pursued by persons curious about the exotic East, which was beginning to interact with the West. The plant life may be unrealistic; the perspective, strange; the animals, not anatomically correct. Although Anne Isaac, who drew these creatures, had not studied them in real life, she had understood the essence of the idea of the Silk Road. What is more, the top strip on this chest captures these magical lands that promise so much—especially bringing to Europe the magical beverage TEA. The top features exotic figures relaxing under trees. Have the travelers arrived? The back is decorated with floral designs reminiscent of sixteenth-century "black-work embroidery." This adds a touch of home, the opulence of which had to be supported from the bounty of the Silk Road. The truly inspiring design is executed with a finesse of touch, which to my mind elevates this piece to a true work of art. It is a pity that the artist remains elusive and unsung. 12.1" wide. Ca. 1820. $?

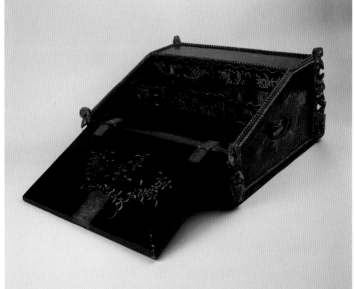

Figure 76. A portable lacquered writing desk. The gold decoration is in the oriental tradition of landscape painting. The form conforms to European style. In 2004, the *Encounters* exhibition at the Victoria and Albert Museum featured a portable altar that was made in China for a Jesuit priest in 1700. The exhibition piece has similar decoration and the same interior red lacquer color as in the drawers of this writing desk. It is very likely that this piece was also made for a European, since the structure follows a European design and the lacquer and decoration are Chinese. Such pieces are extremely rare, in that very few Europeans had ventured to the East before the end of the eighteenth century. Ca. 1700. 18" wide. $?

aspire to social and financial promotion by cooperating with, instead of antagonizing, the aristocracy.

The East India Company did exactly that. It became instrumental in creating new money that chased after the old money and social position. The old money went after the new money, created partnerships, intermarried, and pulled strings to get commissions and jobs in the civil service or, in the Company, for poorer friends and relations. The poor aspired to get a small share of the new wealth created by trade and manufacture. It was easier not to rock the boat that may be one's means to betterment. Thus, large numbers of the population could aspire to a more prosperous life. So it was imperative for the government to support the Company, and support it, it did.

When trading in opium was seen as the way forward, the Company and the Crown proceeded in total accord. The opium was derived from the opium poppy, *Papaver somniferum*, grown in British-controlled India for the purpose of selling the processed product, opium, to China.

The whole operation of growing the poppy was ruthlessly organized by the British East India Company. Even a British plantation superintendent, C. A. Bruce, found it difficult to accept how his countrymen were responsible for the degeneration of the Assamese from a fine to an abject and demoralized race. By 1820, producing opium on Company-owned or -controlled land and packing it at the Company's depot had been well established.

During the eighteenth and early part of the nineteenth centuries, selling opium to the Chinese was pretty straightforward. After 1813, when the Company lost its monopoly of trade in India

except for the growing of the poppy, the selling of opium to the Chinese grew at an accelerating rate. The problems of addiction in China became so acute that it was no longer possible for the Chinese authorities to turn a half-blind eye.

The events that culminated in the Opium Wars of 1839—1842 are complex and confused. Different interests of involved parties often resulted in bungled outcomes. Here I am only trying to give the essence of the tea/opium trade and its decisive part in shaping the fortunes and taste of the English.

Tea was on sale in England by the middle of the seventeenth century. It is not clear when opium was first sold to China by the Company. English traders first bought it in India in the seventeenth century, but neither the Company nor the English government admitted to the sale of it until there was irrefutable evidence.

The English government of the day saw its chance to augment revenue by imposing heavy import duties on tea, which was hyped as a rare and precious beverage. In 1701, less than seventy pounds (lbs.) of tea was imported, rising to about 1,000,000 pounds (lbs.) by 1730 and nearing 20,000,000 by the last decade of the century. As the eighteenth century progressed and demand rose, the inevitable result was greed for more profits by more people, and especially by the Exchequer.

In an age of social climbing par excellence, opportunists saw tea as a way of profiteering from a commodity, the consumption of which was encouraged with the blessing of the government. It is not easy to be certain about the cost of tea. There were claims of £10 a pound (lb.) early on, but by the end of the eighteenth century it settled to about 16—30 shillings per

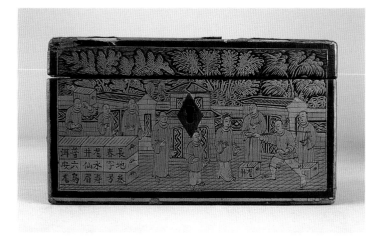

*This whole page:*
Figure 77. Various depictions of the trading of tea on two Chinese lacquered boxes of the early nineteenth century. Note the names of the different varieties of tea written on the boxes. These include both green and black teas. There are such poetic names as "water fairy" and "harmonious gem" as well as more-familiar tea names such as oolong. On one side of the tea boxes there is a drawing suggesting five bats, a symbol of good fortune. 9" wide and 6" wide. $4,000–6,000 and $2,000–4,000.

pound. The poor bought secondhand tea leaves from inns. Smuggling and adulteration became rife. Even so, legitimate imports continued to rise.

To people who did not know all the machinations of the government, it looked as if the scales of trading had tilted in favor both of China and Holland, whence a lot of the smuggled tea came to England. The general perception was that too much coin was leaving England to pay for the tea, and even though the Exchequer was doing very well out of import duties, there were rumbles of discontent, and a concern that the country's economy was doing less well out of it than it potentially could. Thinkers were beginning to air their views on what they saw as a beverage of little value—except perhaps for weaning people off the gin.

There are numerous references to tea in literature and diaries of the period. Especially significant is the mention of tea in satire and caustic verse. The English had a genius for print caricatures, in which social and political evils were exposed with savage humor. Perhaps this was another safety valve that prevented public anger from boiling up to the revolution point. The intellectuals suspected the social manipulation going on in the teacup, and their rumbles were beginning to be audible.

The government did not want such a good revenue spinner to disappear from the English table. Far from it. Tea image and drinking were actively encouraged by sustaining the social status of the new beverage. On the other hand, it did not seem expedient to let the public know that the state was encouraging the opium trade to pay for the tea. This would have created more discontent.

Mindful of the criticism—both actual and potential—that threatened such a good earner, the English government in the late eighteenth century set out to create an alternative way of paying for the tea. Attempts to sell large amounts of tea to America failed dismally. By the end of the eighteenth century, one way forward was seen to be the creation of new markets for new British products. And where better to start but the very place that grew the precious leaf?

In 1793, an attempt was made to interest the Chinese in British-manufactured goods. A delegation headed by Lord Macartney made the arduous journey to China, bearing gifts for the emperor and samples of British wares. The Chinese were not impressed. The ambassadors were firmly dismissed, albeit with impeccable courtesy. However, in terms of gathering cultural information, the embassy was quite successful. Macartney's delegation was a complex affair. There was an entourage of ninety-five, including five German musicians, presumably in the ill-informed belief that the Chinese would have liked Western music.

More successful was the inclusion in the party of William Alexander, who—as already mentioned in the "Chinoiserie" chapter—did much to further the appreciation of Chinese art and life with his firsthand artistic rendition of his experience. Frederick Crace and his team of thirty-four artist assistants re-created this exotic vision in the music room of the Brighton Pavilion. The designs for this work were based on Alexander's aquatints, published in 1805.

By the time Lord Macartney had set foot on Chinese soil, China had developed a complex and sophisticated culture spanning over many centuries. The Chinese were the inventors of paper and printing and arguably had more printed books and texts than the rest of the world put together. The Chinese emperor, secure in the belief of the superiority of his people, saw himself as the ruler of the world. All other nations were classed as vassals. The delegates were looked down upon with indulgent curiosity.

The Chinese considered the English, in their elaborate but inelegant dress, as little more than "monkeys in an opera" or "prancing ponies," and their goodies as quite irrelevant to the spiritually superior oriental way of life. Their manner was thought to be crude and overbearing. The English just did not have the skill to engage with the Chinese and arouse their interest in British goods. The complex cultural significance with which the people of China endowed even the slightest of commodities was quite alien to the British way of trading.

For their part, the official English line was that the Chinese were backward. The British sense of superiority was nurtured by the fact that England was stronger in terms of military might and manufacture. It was inconceivable to the king's representatives that their industrial products would be scorned. It is poignantly ironic that the Chinese invented gunpowder but did not exploit its use in the manufacture of armaments to the extent the British had done. To the Chinese, war, like everything else, had a large element of art integrated with it. The result was that their own invention, which they themselves applied to the making of splendid fireworks, was utilized in the devastation of their country.

The chasm between the two cultures was enormous. In diplomatic terms, there was absolute mutual incomprehension. Subsequent attempts by England and, to a lesser degree, by Holland and other European countries failed. The Chinese did not need anything from Europe. In fact, by the time of the next delegation in the second decade of the nineteenth century, the monster originally created by the British government—the Company opium merchants—sabotaged the proceedings by giving the ambassadors wrong advice as to protocol. They did not wish the importance of the opium trade to be diminished by alternative products.

The attempts at diplomacy were certainly disastrous. There were endless discussions about minutiae of form, such as number and depth of kao tao, with both sides being equally, absurdly stubborn. However, underneath the rigid mantle of governmental statement and posture, the human element on both sides, spurred by the curiosity of the new and unexpected, was busy sculpting new insights. It is very probable that both the Chinese mandarins and the British officials who were part of this elaborate engagement enjoyed the joke behind their superiors' backs. The Chinese were masters at exquisitely artful social games; the British had a genius for irony and satire. There are reports of clandestine get-togethers, including a dinner on a boat arranged for some of the British by Chinese mandarins. The evening was greatly enjoyed, both for the delicious food and the music-playing girls! Understanding of the finer aspects of China was certainly being fostered.

In the meantime, the East India Company was colonizing large parts of India on behalf of the English Crown. As early as 1639, the British had a permanent foothold in Madras. When Charles II married Portuguese Catherine of Braganza in 1662, he was given Bombay (now called Mumbai) as part of her dowry. Bombay was leased by Charles II to the Company for ten pounds a year. A hundred years later, the Company was establishing a really strong power base in India.

For England, India was a gold mine in all respects. It had vast areas of fertile land, and it had precious gems and silver. It gave access to a huge labor and military force. India was a good in-between point bridging the East and the West. It was fragmented by religion and system of government. Different rulers administered different areas. A sophisticated and

*This whole page:*

Figure 79. A Chinese-export lacquer tea chest decorated with scenes that are significant both in trading terms and in Sino-European relations. All the figures appear to be men. They are "toing and froing" from the focal point, which appears to be a table at which some important figures are gathered. The impression given is of negotiation rather than festivity. The most unusual feature of the decoration is the border, which features Chinese coins interwoven with bamboo and bamboo and flowers on the top. The coins bear the reign titles of Ming and Qing emperors. The latest-minted coin is the one centrally placed above the escutcheon. This was minted in the period of the Taiping rebellion (1850–1864), during which Hong Xiuquan declared himself king of Taiping, the Heavenly Kingdom of Great Peace. He self-styled himself as the brother of Jesus, rejecting traditional Chinese beliefs. The embracing of Western religion, fanned by the discontent of the workers in southern China, nearly toppled the Qing dynasty. Because Canton was not under the control of the Taiping, the inclusion of this coin strikes a very rare, bold seditious note. It must have been inserted in honor of the commissioning client. Curiously, I have discovered that one of the coins is that of Puyi, the last emperor of the Qing dynasty from 1908 to 1912, and that during his brief restoration in 1917, Puyi's era name was Xuantong, so he was known as the Xuantong Emperor. Coins in this context must be symbolic of the wealth generated through trade. The "bamboo," a richly significant oriental motif, is meaningful here in its quality as a homophone with the Chinese word "to wish." The straight form of the chest accentuates the significant nature of the border. Although a rather late example, this is a rare and important piece. 11" wide. Ca. 1910. $?

Figure 80. A superb rendition of company-style painting on an English writing slope. The lid depicts a very important nobleman/merchant, the superiority of his person denoted by his long beard and magnificent costume. A rich beard is a stylistic convention used in Chinese art to signify rank. He is attended by figures of some, although lesser, status. The standing figure is offering a box with Chinese characters, which were copied by a European who had not mastered the language or the order of painting the strokes. One of the characters looks like an attempt to write "jade," a precious and important commodity worthy of the attention of such a person. Note the formal poise of the scene in spite the fact that there is activity. The oriental art of negotiation is perfectly captured in all its subtle nuances. The inside of the lid is decorated with a scene in the lighter, more playful chinoiserie style. All the painting is done using clear, bright colors and defining the lines precisely. The mood of the composition is captured in the interaction of the posture of the protagonists. 14" wide. Ca. 1790–1800. $15,000–20,000.

ruthless power such as England could easily manipulate and control them by playing the interests of one against the other. Systematic colonization and wealth extraction became policy.

The East India Company was the body responsible for most trading between England and the East. Although it was supposed to exist as an independent entity, the Company operated and administered the will of the British government. It resembled present-day government agencies and quangos (a quasi-state agency). It provided an underhanded way of flaunting international laws and agreements. Contracts were set up in circuitously devious ways so that the government could wash its hands of blame. The Company could not have been sustained without the support of the government. On the other hand, the government could not have earned so much revenue without the covert criminality of the Company. When, in 1773, the Company ran into financial trouble in India, before the opium operation had reached significant production levels, the British government bailed it out and staved off its bankruptcy. In 1784, Prime Minister William Pitt divided control of the Company between the Court of Directors and a government board.

The partnership was complete, as was the hierarchical opacity that fostered irresponsibility.

The East India Company set out to establish control of India by subterfuge and force. In 1757, Robert Clive won a decisive victory at the Battle of Plassey. Although this was not the result of pure military excellence, it had the required effect: it turned the tide in England's favor and terminated French colonial aspirations.

The relationship between England and India changed from that of trading cooperation to that of imperialism. The British ruled and the violence continued for several decades. In 1773, Warren Hastings, who was the governor general, excused the use of force by the British as being compatible with "the customs of the country!" Ironically, Clive himself died in England in 1774, possibly from an overdose of laudanum.

The Company financed its own armed forces, mostly via revenue derived from growing the opium poppy. The Company was given the monopoly for opium growing by the British government, and it set out to grow the crop with fanatical zeal. Indian farmers were often forced to destroy other crops to grow

*This whole page:*
Figure 81. A most unusual Chinese-export lacquer box. It combines gold-painted borders with figures in paper decoupage. The faces are ivory or painted. The figures are reminiscent of European chinoiserie techniques, while the gold borders are in the finest oriental tradition. The figures are striving for a realistic representation of people, clothing, and objects. They reflect the tranquility and poise of the oriental life, as they are serenely poised on either side of their well-ordered table. 11" wide. Ca. 1820. $5,000–7,000.

opium for the Company at below subsistence income. The Indian cotton industry was devastated by the importation into India of duty-free cotton from England, while the export of machinery to India for processing cotton was banned. Even English observers at the time commented on how prosperous areas in India were destroyed for the sake of growing opium destined for China.

Opium had been used both in India and China for many centuries in small quantities for medicinal reasons. It was probably first imported by Arab merchants, who had been trading with China for centuries before the Europeans arrived. The British selling drive was something quite different. It was a systematic and deliberate attempt to foster addiction among healthy people. Up to the seventeenth century, opium was smoked only mixed with tobacco. In the eighteenth century a new way was found, enabling pure opium sap to be smoked in a pipe.

The opium, already processed and ready for smoking, was carried to China in the Company's clipper ships, which then brought tea and other goods back to India and England. When the going got tough, with the Chinese complaining and refusing to sell tea, the trading simply changed cover and business was carried out by "independent" merchants, or servants of the Company acting privately.

At first, Chinese authorities did not actively object to the importation. The Imperial Court in Peking tried to impose an edict in 1729, forbidding the use of opium for anything except medicinal reasons, but nothing much was done about enforcing it. Cocooned by layers of officials and courtiers, the consequences of the activities of their own Hong merchants, who negotiated the buying of the drug, took some time to penetrate the ears of the Son of Heaven.

The addiction in China was well advanced before the scale of importation was realized and effective measures were taken. In 1815, an imperial edict from Peking forbade the traffic and use of opium. In 1819, a new emperor, Tao Kuang, ascended the imperial throne, and hostilities between Company merchants and authorities began to escalate. In the early 1830s, the emperor's own son died of opium addiction. The Chinese determined to deal with the opium problem resolutely.

An unsuccessful attempt was made to ban the export of tea and rhubarb. The Chinese hoped that by stopping the supply of rhubarb they could inflict terrible constipation on the whole British nation! Vast amounts of Company opium were confiscated and destroyed. Complaints were dispatched to the government in England.

The British government made disingenuous agreements with China not to allow the East India Company to export opium. However, the Company was allowed by the British government to keep the monopoly of growing opium in India, only by strictly adhering to the rule that the opium would be sold only to merchants who would export it to China! Opium was for a time transported in what were called "country ships," supposedly controlled by independent merchants. True to modern state methods, the public political stance was at complete variance with the real policy, which was to serve the treasury at any cost.

For their part, the merchants of the Company were finding other ways of disposing of their merchandise. They sailed their ships to the small island of Lintin, in the Canton estuary, and with the help of corrupt and bribable officials continued their business with the Hong merchants. The profits were vast. It is difficult to have precise figures for such an illicit trade, but records suggest that up to a 2,000 percent profit could be made on the original investment. At the beginning of the nineteenth century, only one to three thousand chests of opium were sold, but by the 1850s, some twenty thousand were sold, which brought around £3,000,000. In the following decades, possibly three or four times as much was sold. In 1860, China was forced to legalize the trade. Thirty million users, of whom fifteen million were addicts, swelled the coffers of the British Exchequer.

Before the final surrender, the Chinese tried again and again to stop the trade. Commissioner Lin, who was in charge of the decisive drive during the 1830s, even wrote to Queen Victoria, pleading with her to stop her subjects from what was so blatantly "against the will of Heaven." He never received a reply. It is doubtful if Queen Victoria had much idea of what was really going on. She was barely twenty at the time, and in her early years she was not likely to have been informed by her advisors that the opium sent to China was any different from laudanum! She herself used the opium-based drug quite freely, as did many an English person. Her uncle, George IV, had retired to bed for a fortnight on laudanum, when in 1811 he injured his ankle showing Princess Charlotte the Highland fling.

Basically without tea and opium, English fiscal policy was unsustainable. Already by the end of the eighteenth century, England really needed the revenue from tea to finance the Napoleonic Wars. Figures suggest that in 1800, one-tenth of the import tax revenue was derived from tea. This is without the indirect income from opium, which was vast. By 1833, when the tea trade was at its peak, it brought in up to £4,000,000 a year, two-thirds of what was needed to keep the civil establishment, including the Crown.

In the meantime, fortunes were made by exploiting opportunities offered both by the war and trading. The Company was given privileges over other merchants in trading in all kinds of products. For example, Company-imported wallpapers had no duty, in contrast to other wallpapers, which had excessive import duties. The Company had the monopoly in the importation of lac, so they could control the price of home japanning. A vast trading empire was created. The class system became more accommodating to new money. Entrepreneurs mingled with the landed gentry in unholy alliances. Great financial power was created that cemented the country's position as an imperial power. The contribution to England's success of the two beautiful plants—the tea and the poppy—cannot be overstated.

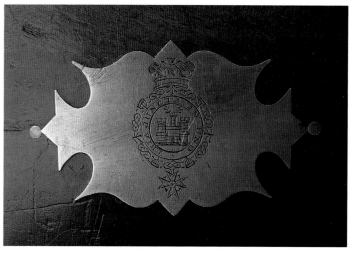

Notwithstanding the harm inflicted, the trade between England, India, and China did have some positive aspects. For example, Chinese skilled craftsmen were brought to India and imparted their knowledge to local cabinetmakers. Chinese tea workers were also brought to India to help with the development of the Indian tea plantation. The very English Earl Gray tea was, in fact, the result of the exchange of observations between two botanists, Sir George Staunton and Sir Joseph Banks. Banks, who was an advisor to the Company, was the first to prepare plans for growing tea in India. He showed Staunton a drawing of the Bergamont orange, which prompted Staunton, who had been to China, to report how the Chinese grew tea among the bitter orange trees. The result was the inspiration for "Earl Gray," the bergamont-scented tea named in honor of the then prime minister.

The skills and artistic perceptions of the English, too, grew as a result of their interaction with such distinctly different cultures. It is true that Chinese artifacts had found their way into Europe nearly 200 years before. Marie de Medicis went as far as to install a seller of Chinese wares in the gallery in the Louvre, but secondhand observation was nothing compared to the real live experience.

While Company traders lived in their allotted quarters in Canton, a whole microcosm of activity grew around them. The European "factories" were impressive buildings, built in classical Western tradition. Although a deliberate effort was made to keep the national character by attending Christian mass every day and hoisting the flag on Sundays, it was impossible to ignore the pulsating world outside the walls. There was Hog Lane, where the foreigners could experience the less savory side of Chinese life. They could mingle with thieves and prostitutes or get drunk on Chinese spirits. After arduous and perilously long journeys, sailors found solace in native alcohol mixed

with tobacco juice, sugar, and arsenic! The locals assured them it was an aphrodisiac as well as an intoxicant!

There were also the respectable streets, catering mainly for the more refined needs of the incomers. Old and New China Street, complete with shops and studios, provided all the beautiful things the country produced: silks, china, silver, paintings, and lacquer boxes of exquisite quality. Furthermore, craftsmen could be seen at work, creating exotic and exciting objects.

Chinese artists painted portraits of the Europeans to take home with them, or created oil paintings from prints and sketches provided by their clients. Chinese landscapes, scenes of Chinese life, and of course the Canton estuary with the ships and Company buildings were painted from every conceivable angle both by Chinese and European artists. Some pictures looked like stage sets of a way of life. Although this element was reminiscent of European art, the result was recognizably Chinese. A hybrid artistic style developed, with precise, assured lines, and with the human subjects looking ahead in calm contentment.

Some painted boxes acquired the distinctive Company-style painting. Like in portraits and landscape and floral paintings done by Chinese artists for Europeans, the colors are clear and precise, and the figures are imbued with a stillness and serenity with which they measure the world as they stare at a point in the distance.

The richest of the Hong merchants who negotiated the trading commodities with Europeans were men of substance and means. They lived in beautiful houses, built in splendid gardens. The Company merchants accepted personal invitations and ventured to these paradisiacal settings to partake of the magic of Cathay. Their reports and impressions must have stimulated the more fluid and refined last phase of chinoiserie. During the early part of the nineteenth century, foreigners were

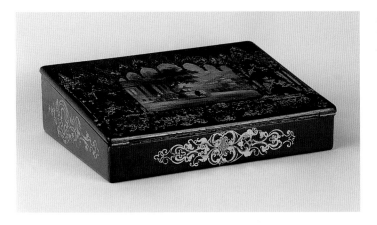

*Above:*
Figure 84. A papier-mâché writing slope painted with a scene of Europeans in front of a Chinese tea house with an oriental figure sitting in the background. It is inscribed *Tea House at Kow Loon*. Kow Loon, which is located on a peninsula across the water from Hong Kong, had—by the middle of the nineteenth century— acquired the reputation of a place for the negotiation of stolen goods. The English merchants soon spread their control over this illicit corner of China. The decoration is very interesting and most unusual, in that it combines neo-Gothic elements with an oriental scene populated by Europeans. The piece encapsulates the moment in time when English traders felt at home in parts of China. 11.5" wide. Mid-nineteenth century. *Courtesy of Anne Brooks.* $4,000–6,000.

also allowed to visit the public gardens on Honan Island three times a month. When hostilities turned nasty, this privilege was withdrawn. The growing appreciation of the Chinese garden and flora prompted the importation of many new plants, including the group of roses named "tea roses," which rooted so successfully in British soil.

Chinese artistic and leisure activities, as well as work practices, were quite different from European ways, and as such the traders wanted to preserve and communicate their experience of this exotic lifestyle. This prompted a new direction for the development of Chinese lacquer decoration and infused English chinoiserie with greater reality, especially in figures and animals.

Another artistic import from China was reverse painting on glass, often backed with metal foils. This work is called *verre églomisé* (derived from the name of the French craftsman Jean Baptiste Glomy) and was practiced in the Levant from very early times. It is likely that it was introduced to China by Arab traders, and by the time the English arrived, the Chinese had perfected the technique. Reverse painting on glass was readily adopted by English box makers, especially for landscape and building painting. Its most widespread use was on papier-mâché and small tortoiseshell boxes in the mid-nineteenth century, ironically at a time when the Chinese stylistic influence was in decline.

For a time in the early nineteenth century, it looked as if the opium/tea trade and the life that had expanded with it were going fine. As more land in India was given over to opium growing and more tea was imported and consumed in England, more people wanted a share of the lucrative trade. Overexpansion brought about its own problems.

Bribery and discretion were keeping the trade going in China through the Hong merchants, until eventually the addiction and its repercussions became too severe to be tolerated. After the first unsuccessful attempts, the Chinese tried to use force in their effort to destroy the opium trade. Unfortunately, their beautiful swords and spears, however artfully employed, were no match for British military might.

The warring agenda was firmly set by Lord Napier. In 1833, Napier was dispatched to China as the "Superintendent of Trade." His job was to safeguard British interests, but he was a bad choice for such a delicate mission. The Chinese considered his manner provocative and bellicose. They accorded him the epithet "laboriously vile." The Chinese were already aware of English intransigence. By that time the English were no longer seen as merely ridiculous; the "monkeys" were now firmly labeled the "foreign devils." They had not kept to the agreements and they were getting violent.

Serious hostilities started in 1839. Capt. Elliot—a man with colonial and naval experience—replaced Napier. His agenda was to pursue a policy formulated since 1780 and lobbied for by Company merchants, especially Jardine and Matheson. The demands were for more trading rights to be conceded by China to English merchants. Having abused their trading rights to the detriment of the host country, this demand was nothing short of blackmail; the only possible answer was a refusal.

*Above and right:*

Figure 85. A box veneered in tortoiseshell, the top decorated with a reverse painting of St. Paul's Cathedral backed with silver foil. This famous landmark is in the city of London, in the area where the East India House was located. The box and therefore the painting are larger than usual and executed with great skill. It could have been done in China and brought over to be inserted in the box, or it could have been painted in England, inspired by oriental work. 10.75" wide. Ca. 1840. $6,000–8,000.

In 1840, men-of-war ships and armed steamers were prepared in India and dispatched to China. By that time India had become a firm power base for England. Company mills ground gunpowder in India, ships were prepared and docked in Indian waters, and soldiers were gathered and trained on Indian soil. The "Opium Wars" started in earnest, without most people in England having any idea of what was happening. The military superiority of the English was overwhelming and the hostilities were short lived. In 1841, China was forced to cede Hong Kong as a trading base for English merchants.

Young Queen Victoria, who had been cast by her officials in the role of the first drug baron, was not pleased. She thought that her negotiators—namely, Capt. Elliot—should have extracted more! Her foreign secretary, Lord Palmerston, was also vexed. His philosophy was that the business of government was "to open and secure the roads for the merchants." Hong Kong was considered too narrow a road. So the war went on for another year, until the Treaty of Nanking was signed in August 1842. The Company was compensated for opium burned by Chinese authorities, and five more ports were opened to English merchants. There was nothing more the Chinese could do to stop opium reaching their shores in vast amounts.

By the time England had taken hold of Hong Kong, the opium and tea trade had become more complex. Other countries were beginning to control opium production in parts of India not under British control. More mobility on the high seas weakened the English monopoly. The floodgates were opened.

Some eminent politicians, such as Gladstone, had spoken out both against the war and the opium trade. Writers and the press were beginning to inform the public. Consciences were stirred. Opium for tea was no longer an easy option.

The Company's monopolies were first eroded and later formally terminated by Parliament. In 1833, the Company's monopoly in China was ended. What happened to the Company between 1740 and 1840 is a most interesting metamorphosis. The Company was set up to further the interests of the Crown by harnessing the self-interest of its shareholders and merchants. It grew into quite an organism, with hierarchical structures parallel to that of a state. Like any large group of people, individual characteristics and common human needs had to be interwoven into the fabric of the organization.

The first servants of the Company, who were stationed in India, appreciated Indian culture and, being so far from home, saw nothing wrong with being integrated into local life. In fact, it must have been quite exciting to escape the British social straightjacket. Most of the men—about 90 percent—married local women, many of them following local custom and marrying several! These ladies were called *bibis*, which is the Hindi word for "lady," or the title for a married woman. As dutiful wives, they produced several children of Anglo-Indian parentage. These children had the best of both cultures: they could understand the Indian mentality, and they could also deal with English merchants and authorities. A new race was growing up, threatening the jobs of the English-born hopefuls who sought their fortunes by joining the Company.

Already by 1791, the problem was acute enough for a parliamentary edict to be put in place excluding Anglo-Indians from the Company's military and civil service. The British government was afraid that the monster it had created—the Company—would grow independent of its supporting country and keep the benefits of its trading for itself, with its financial base in India. Although excluded from the first-line

*This whole page:*
Figure 86. A tea chest decorated in penwork. The scenes are of Indian inspiration, with figures and elephant among gigantic leaves and blooms. However, the exoticism of the composition is tempered and given an extra dimension of charm by introducing domestic themes. For example, there is a child with its skipping rope with a lady, in an Indian landscape framed by huge stylized flowers. Is this a *bibi* and her child? The back shows another child in Indian costume opening its arms to a bird, while another young-looking figure in exotic costume and European-looking hat reads a book while leaning on a tree. There is English writing on his book. It is not very clear, but I think I can make out the words *Honor, God and King*. This piece is unusual in that it introduces an everyday Anglo-Indian element in the decoration and, furthermore, English writing in an exotic scene. Writing in exotic penwork decoration is usually quasi-Chinese, and even this is rare. 13" wide. Ca. 1815. $15,000–20,000.

jobs, there were so many circles within circles in the activities of the Company that Anglo-Indian families continued for another four decades or so. In 1835, intermarriage was forbidden and scores of hapless English girls were shipped over to India to become the Mensahibs. Some men continued to have both English and clandestine Indian families for many more decades.

By the third decade of the nineteenth century, the balance between government and Company control had already changed. It was no longer a partnership, but a tug of war for control. Without the power to hold on to the monopolies, the Company could not win. It had taken control of India for the Crown, and the Crown now demanded the whole cake. The government exercised its power to hijack the entire structure. In 1858, the Company gave control of India to the British Viceroy. In 1874, the Company's charter expired. By that time there was not much breath left in it.

Fortunes had of course been made. In 1758, Horace Walpole described Gen. Clive as "all over estates and diamonds." There were other considerable accumulations of wealth, some of which filtered down to the middle classes. By creating this pool of funds, the Company also created a market at home for objects that previously had been the prerogative of the aristocracy. It also stimulated industrial expansion and trade, so that when the Crown took control of India there was already a thriving middle class in England, as well as a large expatriate community in India, ready to serve queen and country. The main players in the Company had made their own fortunes and built their own grand estates. Their families continued, and many still continue, to be influential in subsequent financial and governmental structures.

Paradoxically, the Company, which was instrumental in the introduction of the exotic artistic influences of the eighteenth and nineteenth centuries, was also pivotal in the creation of the Victorian middle class, which rejected the "foreign" and turned to home inspiration and methodologies. The next big step was the Great Exhibition of 1851: the apotheosis of England, the empire, and Victorian philosophy.

Figure 87. Detail from a mahogany box showing a marquetry oval. It depicts Britannia in a diaphanous top, brandishing a triumphant palm branch and resting on her shield, her pet lion by her side. Ca. 1780–90.

*Above:*
Figure 88. Writing slope covered in embossed leather made as a memento of Queen Victoria's coronation in Westminster Abbey on the 28th of June 1838. The center features the young head of Victoria with the words VICTORIA CROWNED REGINA JUNE 28 1838. The surround is embossed with fruiting looping vines. 10.5" wide. $?

By 1837, when Queen Victoria came to the throne, stylistic innovation had already slackened. It was a case of experimenting within known forms and taking advantage of the newest mechanical developments to refine technical processes, both in structure and ornament.

The time of the architect designer was drawing to a close, but not without a core of eclectics refusing to adapt to the new demands of the market. Architect/designer J. B. Papworth (1775—1847) still advocated that objects should be part of the overall design; if they were not designed by architects, they were of inferior caliber. Papworth worked closely with leading cabinetmakers of the period, cooperating in the production of top-quality pieces for discriminating patrons. Until the middle of the century, boxes displaying style consciousness continued to be made in some numbers.

The nature of patronage was changing. Increasingly the middle classes demanded more furniture and accessories and had the means to pay for them. J. C. Loudon tapped into this market and published a vast catalogue of designs, plagiarizing some of Papworth's ideas and also offering other extensive style possibilities. His *Encyclopaedia of Cottage, Farm and Villa Architecture and Furniture*, which appeared in 1833, allows for the Grecian, Gothic, Elizabethan, Louis IV, and Italian styles, with the Italian described as curvilinear and florid.

What was beginning to emerge was a separation, rather than a fusion, of styles that had prevailed during the Regency. This new development made it easier to copy designs. A deep understanding of cultural reference and rules of perspective was not necessary if a person was simply copying within a consistent style. The danger was that in the hands of the untalented, this could lead to rather repetitive and pastiche objects. In terms of commercial success, copying was not necessarily a bad thing, since work could be delegated without the necessity of the strict supervision demanded in the making of more unique pieces.

The social landscape was changing at an ever greater rate. Cities were bursting at the seams. London grew from less than one million to over two and a half million inhabitants in the first fifty years of the nineteenth century. Traveling became easier, as did communications in general. A new urban culture was overtaking the previous Grand House—based society. The opulent country estates created by the enclosures of the eighteenth and early nineteenth centuries were still centers of style, but the rich had their town houses too, and this gave an ever-greater incentive for the middle-class town dwellers to emulate their social superiors and spend money on furnishings and objects.

The health of the English nation was already more robust than it had been during the previous centuries. Local boards of health were established in 1831. The middle classes could afford the services of doctors, who had achieved professional status and charged appropriate fees. Other professions too came to be seen as "respectable" rather than "trade." Lawyers, bankers, schoolmasters, and other occupations that were supposed to exercise the intellect went up in the "sociometer." The consolidation of the middle class was a new phenomenon worthy of the attention of the purveyors of luxury goods.

The early Victorian era was a period of security for the upwardly mobile. Most of the members of this newly "arrived" class conformed to the rules of respectability, in case they were blown off their newly arrived at perch. Wars were kept away from home and resulted in even greater moneymaking colonial expansion. The imperialistic stance was sold to the people by painting the foreigners as uncivilized heathens in need of religious and cultural instruction. This precluded any hint that the British could learn anything from far-off lands, and encouraged an attitude of looking for inspiration in past periods of English history. Objects that had no offensive foreign connotations became desirable.

The beginning of the nineteenth century saw many new patents in all types of mechanical methods. Messrs. Watson's works at Battersea was reported as having installed Brunel's steam driven veneer-cutting machine, which was patented as early as 1805. A description of such machines was published in 1829, by which time they were widely used in many sawmills. By 1840, the steam-driven bandsaw was also invented. Communications made it easier for specialized work to be done in separate workshops. Hardware too was easier to make with the help of new machinery. Machine made screws with pointed ends were exhibited as a novelty at the Great Exhibition of 1851.

In 1840, at the young age of twenty-one, Queen Victoria married Prince Albert of Saxe-Coburg. Victoria did not have the exuberant personality and visionary gifts of her uncle, George IV. Marrying Albert, who was by all accounts a solid and sensible young man, influenced her character towards sense and sobriety, rather than grandiose extravagance. It appears that Albert imbued the age with a certain earnestness and commercial ambition, precluding both artistic and moral frivolity. The landmark that epitomizes the Victorian era was Albert's brain child: the Great Exhibition of 1851, held in the Crystal Palace.

The Great Exhibition of 1851, although presented as an "Exhibition of All Nations," was very much an exhibition where Britain was like the mother hen of all nations. Queen Victoria

Figure 89. The form of this box is characteristic of the Regency, but the coromandel wood veneer and the rather uniform inlay of mother of pearl date it to the late William IV or early Victorian periods. 12" wide. Ca. 1835–40. $2,000–3,000.

Figure 90. Veneered in parquetry designs reminiscent of early nineteenth century Tunbridge ware. The limited variety of timbers, the thinner veneer, and the arrangement of the patterns date this box in the mid-Victorian period. 12" wide. Third quarter nineteenth century. $1,000–1,500.

Figure 91. A combined envelope box, inkstand, and stationery drawer. Veneered in burr walnut and embellished in applied brass in the neo-Gothic taste, this is a characteristically glamorous desk piece. Last quarter nineteenth century. $2,000–3,000.

Figure 92. Veneered in a parquetry of kingwood, this box features an extraordinary design executed in metal, ivory, and shell inlay. It represents a person emerging out of a bird persona, playing the violin. Metamorphic bird/human creatures were a traditional oriental motif, and this may have been a cultural import from the East. It may refer to the birdskin Little Prince God, who, in Japanese legend, assisted in consolidating the land. French. 8" wide. Mid-nineteenth century. $1,200–1,500.

described the opening day in her journal as "one of the greatest and most glorious days of our lives." Some 25,000 people were present to hear the "Hallelujah Chorus" reverberate among the merchandise. Albion wished to show off all the latest achievements of her children, and this she did with great success. Some cynics criticized this monument to consumerism, but their voices were drowned in the hubbub of the crowds that literally rushed to view the newest fashions in the living arts.

The home section of the exhibition reasserted "Britishness." It included a medieval court designed by Pugin. The Gothic revival was well on its way, and this spectacular exhibit cemented its appeal. The attitude of self-sufficiency was encouraged further by showing the best of what was available at home. And what was available at home was the industrial process. People saw the new machinery and railway equipment, and they also marveled at the photographic apparatus on display. Although photography was still in its infancy, it was a further pointer to the march of style toward greater uniformity and egalitarianism. Victoria loved photographs; so did the people. The greatest proof of British industrial superiority was the Crystal Palace itself.

In terms of manufacturers' exhibitions, London was already trailing behind other European nations—notably France, where such activities had started in the eighteenth century; Belgium, where many successful exhibitions had already been staged; and Berlin, where a significant show had taken place in 1844. No sooner did Albert feel his feet safe under the royal table than he set about organizing this great event. The exhibition was to be in Hyde Park, and after much prevarication, the design chosen was a huge glass structure resembling a greenhouse. Appropriately enough, this was the brainchild of a designer/gardener, Joseph Paxton.

The satirical magazine *Punch* called it the Crystal Palace and the name stuck. The Crystal Palace epitomized Victorian thinking. The frame of the building was made of cast-iron components that were then dressed in glass. The columns, girders, and glass panels were brought from their different locations of manufacture and assembled on-site. At the time, this method of building was seen as a great advancement on the more traditional bricks and mortar.

The Crystal Palace hosted 14,000 exhibitors from all over the world, displaying a huge range of products. It also hosted a great many sparrows who nested in the elm trees left inside the building and who went about their business, unconcerned about the nuisance they caused to humans. The exhibition was indeed a *tour de force* of manufacture. Fortunately the nineteenth century never hardened to a rigid monolithic industrial and commercial era. It refreshingly allowed room for a few individuals who were determined not to be drowned in the new waves of industry. Among them was Kate G. Fonnereau of Ipswich, a lady of Huguenot origin who was described as an amateur and who displayed an "Octagon box, in imitation of inlaid wood."

Figure 93. Rosewood veneered and inlaid in an exceptionally finely executed design in brass and mother of pearl; the arrangement of the pattern, the thinness of the brass, and the attempt at naturalistic leaves date after the early part of the nineteenth century. French. 10.75" wide. Ca. 1840. $1,000–1,500.

Half the hall was given over to the British and Colonial section, where a great variety of items were displayed, including many boxes, particularly in papier-mâché, a process that made great strides in the second quarter of the nineteenth century.

The exhibition was seen by more than six million visitors, a credit both to its appeal and to the new ways of traveling, notably the railways. The Crystal Palace was indeed the greenhouse for new ideas on manufacture that nurtured and matured in a climate of middle-class affluence and promised a secure future of plenty for the whole country.

Manufacturing in the 1850s did not have the connotation of mass production at the expense of high quality. On the contrary, machinery was seen as a means of improving quality. Thus, a cabinetmaker could use a machine to make his dovetailed joints, but this could give him more time for embellishment or French polishing. Joiners came to call themselves cabinetmakers in the eighteenth century. Many now

Figure 94. This is really the epitome of Victorian craftsmanship. It is a box made with utter precision by using machine-cut components to achieve smooth and complex openings. It is veneered in thick coromandel and was French polished to a high level. The brass edgings provide both enhancement and strength. The different parts open by releasing catches and springs. Note the gilded brass gallery around the part where the silver-topped bottles are fitted. This strengthens this section and also provides an extra level of glamour. The box is marked Betjemann's patent. The lock is marked Asprey's. This patent was taken by the firm of Betjemann in the 1870s. Although the sewing tools match the date of the patent, the silver tops are of an earlier date, 1843 and 1859. It is very likely that this was a box made to order for a customer of Asprey's who wished for a more glamorous box for their dressing bottles, which in the pre-trick-opening days would have been housed in a simpler dressing box. This was not unusual. Many retailers and makers advertised refitting services. The allure of the super-glamorous dressing box is easy to understand. 13.75" wide. Last quarter nineteenth century. $12,000–15,000.

*Above and right:*
Figure 95. Veneered in amboyna and edged in engraved brass, this is another example of complex unfolding and opening. Impeccably made, it works with precision to provide a glamorous traveling companion. 12" wide. Last quarter nineteenth century. $2,500–3,000.

called themselves manufacturers, and they were proud of it. According to the late poet laureate, Sir John Betjeman, his father (Ernest Betjemann), who was the third generation to run the family firm, called his workers "artist craftsmen." Betjemann's was a typical mid-Victorian company. It embraced the mechanical processes with great enthusiasm and secured many patents without compromising the quality of the work.

One of the design avenues that was avidly explored by Victorian makers of high-quality boxes was different ways of opening boxes by using elaborate springs and catches. These boxes have a very professional feel to them as they glide or spring open, revealing exquisitely dovetailed joints and immaculately polished surfaces. Their interiors are also lined very carefully with leather or velvet, or both. Such boxes utilize manufacturing processes to achieve perfect balance of form and hand-finishing methods to give the box an opulent quality.

Because the more efficient manufacturing methods encouraged the production of several similar items at the same time, boxes were made in more-uniform designs. The first element to go was the variety of form. Boxes were again made in straight lines, allowing for easier production of the basic box, more-straightforward veneering, and simpler application of hardware. Furthermore, the flat surfaces could be more easily French polished, giving a flat, glossy surface. The simpler shapes conformed to the new ideas of the age: their designs were not derived from temples, pagodas, or sarcophagi. They were sensible and useful. Their chief purpose was to complete the picture of comfort promulgated by the royal family, who

had abandoned the excesses of Victoria's uncle George for a domestic life of parochial coziness.

With the exception of special types of boxes, such as Tunbridge ware, the varieties of woods used from the middle to the end of the nineteenth century were more limited. As veneers were cut in greater quantities in specialized mills, it was inevitable that certain species would be preferred due to availability and size of logs. Thus, wood from small fruit trees all but disappeared, as did other species that could be rendered only into narrow veneers, such as kingwood and yew.

Walnut was now the favorite wood, both in straight figure and in the more expensive burr. Walnut could be sliced very thinly and therefore provide many veneers from one piece of wood. This enabled makers to utilize the prettiest pieces to cover many boxes. Coromandel wood was also used, often cut in thicker veneers that were applied to more-special boxes. It provided a wonderful background for brass decoration, contrasting the shiny metal with the darkly striated polished surface of the wood.

Both rosewood and mahogany continued to be used, but very rarely was mahogany cut or chosen to provide rich figure, and rosewood was mostly of the lesser-figured Indian variety. Boxes of superior quality were occasionally veneered in bird's-eye maple, satinwood, amboyna, ebony, and other costly woods. By the end of the century, oak was also used, predominantly in the solid form.

The decoration on Victorian boxes—excepting special categories such as papier-mâché and Tunbridge ware—falls into three categories:

**1.** Very restrained brass bindings, straps, and inlaid lines. By now, box makers were able to glue brass securely enough, obliterating the need for large screws. The brass was also thinner than brass used in earlier periods, and it was nailed onto the wood with small brass pins that when polished were invisible.

**2.** Brass surface-applied decoration, often in the Gothic style, especially in domed or pointed-top boxes. The cutout brass designs were often engraved, and on some costly boxes gilded. Matching gilded, engraved hinges and locks was a feature adopted by some makers. Wedgwood or other plaques were sometimes added as central focal points.

**3.** Inlay was in fluid, naturalistic motifs, in any combinations of wood, metal, mother of pearl, and very occasionally ivory or bone.

The possibility of using thinly cut veneers, thinner brass, and acid-cut mother of pearl made it easier to compose designs in a freer hand. These designs were more in keeping with the Victorian age that had rejected the more culturally derived motifs of the Georgian periods in preference of the recognizable and the familiar.

The quality of the structure, as well as the decoration, varies enormously. It is almost as if the top-quality boxes had to be made to a much-higher specification, in case they were mistaken for more-modest boxes, which may superficially have had some similar characteristics.

Design, as it was understood in the previous hundred years—that is, as part of an integrated whole—did not have very much relevance in the Victorian home. Families grew in numbers as medical care, hygiene, and nutrition improved with prosperity. Drawing rooms where the family gathered were turning from showpieces into living spaces. This is not to say that care was not taken in the furnishing, but the care allowed for an element of comfort and practicality. The different members of the family would have their writing, sewing, or other boxes that they would use for their own private work or pleasure, bringing them in and out of rooms and placing them wherever was appropriate—sometimes on their knees, or even on the floor. Flat-based boxes were preferable, since they were easier to handle and also maximized the space available for holding useful items.

Drawing rooms were often cluttered with many objects that were seen as a must for the new well-to-do. There were also souvenirs brought from different parts of the country, and even the Continent, where the family could now travel with relative ease. The Victorians cultivated the cult of memories, which is very understandable. They were the first generation to have the chance, *en masse*, to accumulate different impressions, and as such they treasured them. Nesting in the rich patina of life that the family had built developed a comforting feeling that caressed human sensibilities and created an aura of well-being.

Figure 96. A box that typifies the best of nineteenth-century work. It is veneered in thick ebony and is inlaid in floral designs. Although symmetrically arranged and superficially similar, when examined the plants differ in each corner, the most striking being the rose and honeysuckle. The inlay is unusual in that it is in silver. It is finely chased and precisely formed, as if it is a piece of jewelry. The interpretation of the flora is aiming at realism, albeit romantically stylized. There are five different dates subtly engraved in different parts of the design, ranging from 1845 to 1859. The central scrolling pattern forms initials. The dates are perhaps significant to the family who owned it. Birthdays? The lock and hinge are long and of exceptional quality. French. 10" wide. Mid-nineteenth century. $3,000–4,000.

Figure 97. A typical envelope box veneered in pretty burr walnut with applied brass escutcheon. Last quarter nineteenth century. $800–1,000.

Figure 98. Veneered in thick rosewood and inlaid in brass and shell, this box is a good example of the way that brass was used in the mid-Victorian period. The pieces are cut in swirling delicate shapes and engraved to give further definition to the design. The metal is used not to convey strength or to suggest ancient ornament, but as a material to form pretty and aesthetically accessible ornaments. This type of work was influenced by French usage of brass and shell. Ca. 1870. $1,200–1,500.

Figure 99. Very fine inlay in mother of pearl and silver on a Rosewood veneered box. French. 6.6" wide. Ca. 1840–50. $800–1,000.

It did not matter if not all of the things matched. The whole ensemble was a treasure trove that bestowed status, security, and respectability.

An interesting characteristic of Victorian boxes is that they were invariably made for a purpose, such as writing, sewing, dressing, tea holding, etc. In previous times some boxes were made for specific purposes, but they were also made as objects in their own right, something that almost disappeared by the 1850s, except in regional or special categories.

The Great Exhibition opened the doors to real marketing and marked the turning point of the splitting of the two disciplines: the maker and the retailer. This is not to say that 1851 was a decisive and definite date. Cabinetmakers retailed other peoples' goods way back into the eighteenth century, and makers sold their personally made objects well into the nineteenth century. Some do so even to the present day.

However, once the scales were tilted in favor of manufacturing rather than handcrafted processes, the swift rise of the retailer as the pivotal figure in the distribution of goods became inevitable. In the last few decades of the century, boxes were catalogued in great numbers in retailers' brochures, giving choices of woods and interior linings to prospective buyers. The boxes in these catalogues were very carefully defined; for example, "Desk (Ladies), Desk (Gentleman's), or Papeterie," or "Dressing Case (Ladies), Dressing Case (Gentleman's)." "Workboxes" did not define the sex, nor did combinations of "Workbox and Desk," which were called Victoria or Princess. Presumably, the idea that men, who ran the empire, could thread a needle was inconceivable.

In the last few decades of the century, a prevalent style of box was made that was walnut, or occasionally other wood veneer, on pine. These boxes were decorated with strips of geometric marquetry and escutcheons in wood or mother of pearl. The quality of the decoration on these boxes varies enormously, from quite simple stripes of stained woods to complex and competently executed designs. In retailers' catalogues this decoration is sometimes given the laconic description of "fancy straps" or "fancy panel." Often wrongly labeled as Tunbridge ware, these boxes were in fact blamed by Tunbridge ware makers for the demise of true Tunbridge ware.

Papier-mâché and Tunbridge ware boxes have already been mentioned in this chapter. They are two of the specialized branches of box making that flourished during the second and third quarters of the nineteenth century, quite independently and distinctly from the general flow. Other categories are Scottish and Irish boxes, again in a style of their own. This is another feature of the Victorian age. While earlier papier-mâché and Tunbridge ware boxes were within the prevalent cultural and aesthetic traditions, the later boxes developed a personality exclusive to their own genre. Perhaps the lack of direction

Figure 100. An excellent example of a Victorian box veneered in burr walnut and banded with geometric inlay. $1,000–1,200.

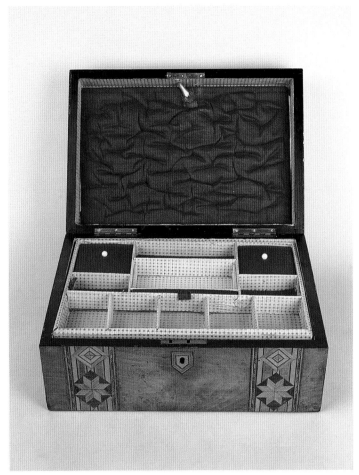

*Above and right:*

Figure 101. Boxes and tea caddies with geometric-band marquetry decoration were made in many sizes. Most of the boxes were sewing boxes with lift-out unfitted trays. The covering veneers were walnut, the more special ones in burr figure. A few were veneered in mahogany or rosewood. $300–1,200.

within the general development of box style allowed these branches to develop their own characteristics and find their own specific patrons.

An appropriate conclusion to the Victorian chapter is perhaps a mention of Prince Albert's memorial. Much to the chagrin of Queen Victoria, her husband died prematurely in 1861. The memorial she erected to his memory, appropriately in the vicinity of the site of the Great Exhibition, is a distillation of the Victorian era. Reference is made to the four continents, with allegorical representations on the four corners. Oriental figures and animals feature prominently, alluding to Eastern trading connections. However, the overall structure is pure domestic Gothic. In contrast, Sir David Ochterlony's memorial in Calcutta (now called Kolcata) is shamelessly foreign, mixing Greek, Egyptian, and Islamic themes in one structure. But he died forty years earlier, after a life with thirteen wives openly kept in Delhi. By the second half of the nineteenth century, the people of England had indeed been tamed.

Figure 102. Details of geometric-band inlays from mid- to late-nineteenth-century boxes. The variations are endless. These are among the most popular and widely distributed boxes ever made.

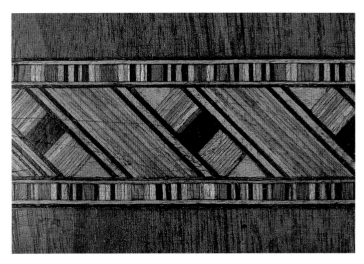

# CHAPTER 7 *Painted, Penwork*

The wealth of aesthetic and cultural influences that burst onto European applied arts from the second half of the eighteenth to the middle of the nineteenth century was dazzling. The Far East, the classical world of Europe and the Middle East, the beauties of the flora and fauna of the world, and the strange persons who inhabited lands hitherto unknown invaded the consciousness and the intellect of a society eager to inquire, learn, and experiment. Such a cornucopia of new ideas opened up infinite possibilities of diversification in the arts. It was the time of the romantic poets, of great creative novelists, and of travelers, merchants, botanists, and adventurers.

Added to this, a new awareness of the beauties of nature nearer home was awakened. There was renewed interest in the Physic Garden in Chelsea, in London, which had been gathering plants and momentum since the seventeenth century. During the eighteenth century, under royal patronage, the gardeners at the royal Botanic Garden at Kew were accumulating and cataloguing specimens, both for the erudition and the pleasure of an inquiring public. The cult of visiting gardens and spa towns and taking walks in the surrounding countryside was encouraged by easier traveling conditions and an increase in suitable accommodation.

King George III was a keen botanist. This royal inclination promoted the observation and rendition of flora in art form as a serious and fashionable pastime. Intrepid travelers, such as Lady Anne Monson (1714—1776), wandered around strange countries painting plants. Botanists accompanied Capt. Cook to Botany Bay and brought back a plethora of new plants and seeds. On their return to England, they actively encouraged and advised aristocratic patrons on expanding their horticultural interests. The Duchess of Portland was such a patron. She not only took a very keen and active interest in the development of her gardens, she also commissioned professionals to supply her with botanical drawings and paintings.

It was not just the exceedingly rich who had access to the new flora. Botanical drawings, prints, and books were becoming widely popular, as was the knowledge and appreciation of plants and flowers. This newfound enthusiasm was soon transferred to the very personal home accessory—the box. Decoration on boxes was either commissioned from professionals or done by ladies at home. Many of these "amateurs" were just as talented, skilled, and trained as the professionals. It was just not socially acceptable to work if one was a lady of certain social standing. Furthermore, with the mental and physical space that such ladies had at their disposal, they could concentrate on such "work" with real dedication.

The flowers they drew were sometimes directly observed from nature and sometimes copied from books or pattern books. The symbolism of plants was hinted at in floral compositions. The tree of life, a symbol imported from the East, appeared in many guises. The poppy, which was thought to aid restful sleep, was recommended as a motif both by Ackermann and Thomas Hope. The pansy, from the French derivation for "thought," and, of course, the English rose featured frequently on painted boxes, painted naturalistically or drawn stylistically.

Mrs. Delany—a lady who had the good fortune to be taken seriously by such intellectual giants as Jonathan Swift and Dr. Johnson and who was befriended both by George III and his queen—took up the gathering, sketching, and making of flower collages with passion. Her work was admired by all, including the royal couple. There must have been many such ladies, although most have remained anonymous. There is evidence of their work that betrays a wealth of personal idiosyncrasies and sensitivities.

Insects too were recognized as worthy of observation and visual interpretation. They could not really be missed, hovering over the plants and flowers in gardens and meadows. Perhaps the stimulation offered by the insects depicted on oriental lacquer goaded people in England to look at their own bees, butterflies, and dragonflies and accord them a place in drawings and paintings, both on paper and on wood.

Figure 103. Penwork reflecting the manifold cultural influences of the early 1800s.

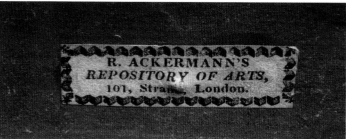

*This whole page:*

Figure 104. This is a *tour de force* of penwork. The drawing is of such incredibly high standard that it must have been a special commission executed by a very talented individual. The complex and culturally rich references of the work suggest that there was cooperation between the client and the artist. The cabinet was supplied by the prestigious repository of Ackermann (mentioned in the "Regency" chapter). This is the only box I have ever come across where the Ackermann label still survives. The illustrations on the top and back depict classical deities. However, these are not the formal Olympians intimidating in their austerity. The composition is infused with the romanticism of the early nineteenth century, and the gods are imagined as their playful infant selves. The work transcends convention and delivers images of energy, exuberance, and fun. The two front doors are framed by vigorous flora, which looks almost out of control. Acanthus leaves swirl with grasses and blooms to form not-quite-symmetrical patterns on each side. The subtle variations allow for the central design. On one side there is the infant Dionysus or Bacchus traveling on a goat, a symbol of lasciviousness that hints at his future. An adult Bacchante assists. On the other side there is a woman with two infants. She is probably meant to be Leto with her two twins sired by Zeus, the gods Apollo and Artemis. Leto is depicted in Greek iconography, albeit more formally, with her two children. There is more than a hint of movement in the landscape in both these scenes. The clothes float in the air, and the earth is fecund with crops, flowers, and greenery. The top picture depicts other gods in infancy, each carrying his/her personal symbol. There is Apollo playing his lyre, Pan, Athena (or perhaps Poseidon or Ares), Dionysus, and Eros (or perhaps Diana). The sides are further decorated with riotous depictions of classical flora. The eccentric use of leaves to form blooms relieves the symmetrical arrangement from predictable formality. The back depicts a romantic landscape, hinting at faraway travel and the contemporaneous cult of nature, framed by robust ancient motifs. The inside of doors continues the theme of ancient design, framing contemporaneous romantic scenery. The drawers are decorated with vigorously swirling acanthus leaves, the lower ones springing from classical masks. As well as an aesthetic delight, this piece is a microcosm of the cultural and social mores of the time: classical erudition, appreciation of nature and historical structures, travel, and, most of all, an inquiring mind, full of curiosity and zest for life. The proud owner would have been a truly erudite connoisseur, but also a bon vivant. 13" wide. Ca. 1810. $9,000–12,000.

*Above and right:*

Figure 105. A writing slope with a polychrome painting of naturalistically depicted fruit and bindweed in the center of the sloping front. The sides are decorated in penwork, with stylized representations of flowers and leaves. The penwork is within the tradition of fabric design that was popular during the eighteenth century. Such designs drew their inspiration both from Eastern work and from European sixteenth- and seventeenth-century embroidery designs. 12" wide. Ca. 1820. $4,500–5,500.

Birds, naturally, were great favorites. Both the exotic and the home flying species were painted. Interest in birds had been growing for centuries. Charles II had his extended menagerie of rare and exotic birds and animals in Birdcage Walk in St. James's Park. Presents of exotica were brought to him by the ambassador of the Sultan of Bantam, and he so much appreciated these exquisite feathered companions that they were even allowed access to the dining room. This royal passion continued through successive monarchs, and in the eighteenth century, one of William Chambers's garden buildings at Kew was the "Menagerie Pavilion," where everybody could go to watch and enjoy the birds.

The landed gentry could establish their own bird pavilions in their gardens if they so wished. Others had to content themselves with a few birds at home. During the eighteenth century, birds in cages were a feature of many a town house. Like with flowers and plants, birds were also observed and drawn, both in domestic and natural situations.

Animals were a different story. Very few familiar animals were ever painted on boxes. Although oil paintings of domestic, farm, and sporting animals abound, the animals that really captured the imagination of the box painters were mainly of exotic type. The East India Company imported animals mainly for royalty and rich patrons. There is a painting by George Stubbs showing two Indians with a cheetah, which was presented to George III. A deer looks on from the background, his supremacy challenged. Private zoos were set up on the grounds of grand estates, and as the fashion for visiting such estates developed during the second part of the eighteenth century, more people were able to see live exotic animals. Previously they had glimpsed them only in drawings and prints.

By the second decade of the nineteenth century, everybody willing to take the trouble could observe strange beasts at close range. This they could do in the heart of London, in the Strand, where Edward Cross set up his Exeter Change. The animals were displayed in cages, with no understanding or consideration for their needs. Sometimes they showed their disapproval by roaring so ferociously that the horses in the street took fright, but this did not put off visitors. Lord Byron was reputed to enjoy seeing "the tigers sup" and to have taken a fancy to Chunee, a five-ton elephant.

The Egyptian Hall, in Piccadilly, also exhibited animals in somewhat more appropriate settings. This was opened in 1809 by William Bulloc, who had previously displayed his collection in Liverpool. It was considered by many as "the most fashionable place of amusement in London." A herd of reindeer and a family of Laplanders (!) displayed against an arctic set proved to be one of its greatest attractions. Jane Austen was one of the visitors, her curiosity for the hall's many strange attractions much in keeping with the times.

Figure 107. A bird's-eye maple box painted with a naturalistic bouquet of flowers. The painting is of very high quality, and the colors have not lost any of their clarity. Boxes of many sizes, but usually smaller than this, were made in the town of Spa, in present-day Belgium, where they were bought by the travelers who went to take advantage of the soothing waters. By the nineteenth century, however, they were commercially imported into England and sold through English retailers. Most of these boxes were professionally painted with flowers. This particular box is quite special in that it has a complex shape and is veneered with a well-marked veneer. 9" wide. Mid-nineteenth century. $800–1,100.

Figure 106. A card box covered in cream paper and painted with flowers. The flowers are painted from nature, the artist striving to achieve an accurate representation both of color and form. The standard of the painting is extremely high, and the composition is arranged with artistic sensitivity. Gold paper is used as an edge, giving a hint of glamour. The box has gilded handles and stands on gilded feet, which enhance its tapered form. Both the handles and the feet continue the floral theme. A very fine example of painted work. 11" wide. Ca. 1815–20. $5,500–6,500.

Exotic animals found expression on painted or penwork boxes, mostly in chinoiserie or scenes inspired by India. Although not always anatomically accurately drawn, the expression and gait on the best of such work bears witness to the fact that the animal was observed firsthand. Even though the scenes were probably copied, or inspired from pattern books, there is sensitivity in the interpretation of the wise and dreamy stoicism in the faces of the beasts.

Marine life was not a strong favorite for box decoration, but Mrs. Delany displayed an interest in shells as well as flowers, and this must have been shared by other ladies who lived during the eighteenth and early nineteenth centuries. Although the shell motif was very much in keeping with the period, shells were rarely painted on boxes.

The period spanning from the last decades of the eighteenth century to the end of the Regency was a very strange time, during which information was disseminated through publications and reinforced through partial firsthand observation. The group of boxes that can be described as painted or penwork reflects more than any other group this curious intellectual and artistic mélange that captivated the imagination of society during the reigns of George III and George IV.

As already discussed in the "Chinoiserie" chapter, exoticism was on the ascendance. The published accounts of the first tentative diplomatic steps to the Far East, as well as firsthand narratives, conjured up pictures of men, beasts, and plants never previously exposed to such an extent to the nonspecialist public. The Regent himself gazed at Alexander's version of Cathay on display at the Brighton Pavilion.

The classical world also had its followers. Even if a person had not traveled in person, there were fragments to copy from in private libraries and a plethora of published material.

Both the professional artists who specialized in chinoiserie and classical decoration and the private ladies who decorated their own boxes were eager to prove to the world that they were

*Above:*

Figure 108. A small Spa box with importer's label on the underside, beautifully painted mainly with pansies. Mid-nineteenth century. $400–600.

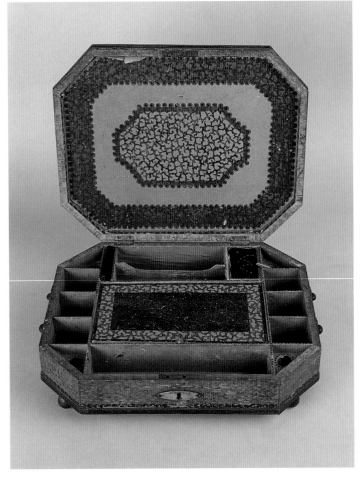

up to date with their cultural reading. Designs showing an understanding of classical symmetry and pictures experimenting with peculiar Eastern perspectives of "pagodas and the fantastic fripperies," as Hogarth called chinoiserie, all were painted or drawn on boxes dating from the end of the eighteenth to the third decade of the nineteenth century.

Exoticism was also found nearer home, in the romantic cult of the neo-Gothic. Going back to Bullock and his Egyptian Hall, another exhibit was his medieval gallery, complete with armory. Previous eras of English history, imbued with legend and romance, inspired the drawing of ruined castles, churches, and Gothic spires.

Another cultural revival was the illustrations of *Aesop's Fables*, which appeared in ecclesiastical art as early as the Middle Ages. Francis Barlow's illustrations in the 1687 edition continued to be used as inspiration throughout the eighteenth century in designs for architectural carvings and other decoration. During the middle years of the eighteenth century, with the renewed emphasis on the interdependence of morality and culture, it was natural for decoration based on fables to gain new impetus. It was the perfect blend of rustic charm and cerebral intent. Such themes are rare, but not unknown in box decoration.

Although the main categories of painted or penwork boxes can be classified as chinoiserie, neoclassical, nature inspired, or Gothic, many boxes in this group cannot fit neatly under a precise label. There are boxes incorporating various elements, and there is blurring of definition within the stylistic conventions that were followed. The aesthetics of the time were too fluid for consistent, rigid interpretation.

Like most observations that are perceived secondhand—as was the case with exotic designs—the result of the decoration was a distillation of the original, transformed by the perceptions and experiences of the receiver into his/her interpretation. In spite of the fact that the perspective may not be accurate and the representation may be fantastical, the pictorial boxes of this period have a unique and delightful quality resulting from the excitement of discovery and the eagerness to express it. Each one is a gem of social history, unique in its own way.

## FORM AND TECHNIQUE

Decorated boxes dating from the last two decades of the eighteenth century are usually of rectangular form, with perpendicular lines and flat tops. The decoration is primarily of home-inspired scenes. Boxes dating from the beginning of the nineteenth century are structured following the architectural forms typical of the Regency. They often stand on turned or metal feet and have side handles. They are mostly, although by no means exclusively, decorated with exotic designs.

Originally all the boxes in this category were varnished. Most of the varnish has become brittle with dryness and tends to fall off naturally. Caution! Do not try to take off old varnish, since it is likely to take off the decoration with it. Just leave it alone.

*Above and right:*
Figure 110. A card box with a finely executed painting of butterflies among ripe fruit. 11" wide. Ca. 1810. $2,000–2,500.

*Left and below:*
Figure 111. A penwork-decorated box showing drawing on a light background and also the reverse; that is, the background is inked, leaving the design in the white. The design around the box is exquisitely drawn in very fine lines. The flowers are stylized and executed as if they were Elizabethan embroidery, shaded parts filled with "stitches." (This was inspired by "black work" embroidery introduced by Catherine of Aragon, the first wife of Henry VIII.) Unusually so are the two birds, which are drawn on the two sides. The central picture of an oriental figure and an exotic bird is in the style of the second half of the eighteenth century. It shows a refinement of perception and a lightness of interpretation absent from earlier chinoiserie design. The back of the lid inside the box is painted with a scene of a Gothic ruin. 10" wide. Ca. 1800. $2,000–2,500.

Figure 112. Tea caddy decorated with a repetitive design of stylized foliage enclosing anthemia, the sides with acanthus leaves and seed heads. The center of the top depicts an ever-young Bacchus and a Bacchante, riding on a chariot. This particular composition refers to the expedition of Bacchus to the East, when he headed an army of men and women inspired with divine fury. They were armed with thyrsi and musical instruments. Note the thyrsus resting on the chariot and the tambourine held by the Bacchante. On this expedition, the Bacchic chariot was drawn by a lion and a tiger, as on the picture. Accompanied by Pan, Silenus, and Satyrs, Bacchus conquered without bloodshed, as the people joyfully embraced his cult of the pleasures of life and accepted him as a god. Worship of Bacchus spread from Egypt to Greece and Rome. His main attribute, that of a wine godhead, is symbolized on this box by the vine bush sprouting from the ground, the basket of grapes, and the wine amphora. The caddy, which demonstrates an accurate understanding of the ancient myth, dates characteristically from the time of the English bon viveur, the Regency. 11.5" wide. Ca. 1810–20. $8,000–11,000.

*Left and below:*

Figure 113. A wonderfully exotic procession complete with Indian figures, palm trees, horses, a charming elephant, and a stoical camel. All these on a tea chest complete with canisters decorated with stylized flora. An excellent example of a rich penwork piece. Ca. 1820. 9.5" wide. *Courtesy of a private collection.* $10,000–12,000.

# Penwork

Most penwork is reminiscent of linear lacquer decoration. The Anglo-Indian-engraved ivory work may have contributed to the spread of the technique, although this is another chicken-and-egg conundrum. Repair work on ivory items was certainly carried on in penwork. The feet of an ivory-veneered dressing table in the Clive of India collection were restored in what was described as "pencil work." However, we must not forget that the incised-ivory technique was not practiced by English cabinetmakers and that the same botanical designs were available both to artists at home and commissioning patrons in India. Furthermore, painted work and penwork were a natural progression from japanning. In fact, there are rare examples of both techniques applied to the same piece (see figure 39).

The technical quality of the drawing varies greatly, in that some were drawn by talented and inspired amateurs, some by less talented amateurs, and some by professionals. However, some pieces make up in charm quota what they lack in precision of line. The juxtaposition of different designs is sometimes predictable and sometimes startling. There was certainly scope for originality of ideas, as well as for accurate copying.

Techniques used for this form of decoration were not always consistent. The boxes were made in sycamore or other light-colored woods. Tunbridge ware makers simply referred to the timbers as white wood. When constructed, the boxes were either varnished or gessoed and then decorated. The gesso base technique, which was similar to the preparation for japanning, was not very widely spread. I have also found evidence of another interesting technique: A shallow, embossed imprint of the design was made on the wood. Then the design was painted in and the whole box was varnished, resulting in a flat surface.

Penwork decoration was done in black fine lines on a light background, or in reverse. That is, the background was painted black, leaving the pattern of the design unpainted and light colored. In such cases, the details within the light parts were drawn in black. Occasionally, other colored inks, paints, or gold leaf were used in addition to the black ink.

Often, hand-colored prints were pasted in the center of boxes decorated with penwork borders. The prints were edged with gold leaf decorated in lines of ink. The whole thing was then varnished.

This form of multidisciplinary decoration was done mostly in professional workshops, mainly in the area of Tunbridge Wells.

*Above:*

Figure 114. A domed box decorated in penwork. The theme on the box is the eighteenth-century *memento mori*, which is found on mourning jewelry of the period. This is the only example I know of on a box. Two classical figures guard a tomb. One is holding a crown, symbolizing earthly glory. The standing figure is holding a laurel wreath, which symbolizes spiritual achievement. A laurel bush is drawn on one side. The composition is framed in fruiting vines redolent of the ancient symbolism of immortality and fidelity. The vine, sacred to Dionysus, also acquired Christian symbolism. There is also what looks like the cross-shaped top of a sword stuck into the earth by the foot of the seated figure. On the sides there are lion mask handles. An extraordinary box in that it combines neoclassicism with the very private remembrance of the dead, which was used primarily on small personal items. 10" wide. Ca. 1810–20. $?

*This whole page:*

Figure 115. This tea chest is an iconic example of a piece that encapsulates women's desire to express both their talents as artists and also their erudition. Inside one of the canisters there are two very personal items, dated 1858. One is a short letter; the other, a funeral card for the late Mrs. Wickes. On the back of the card there is a very moving handwritten note by a Mrs. Smith, telling us that she received three items left to her by her friend: her bible, an obelisk, and a "Tea Chest the work of her own hands." Susan Wickes nee Watts was quite an important member of the Aylsham community in Norfolk, England, where she lived. She had extensive property, including a mill, in her own right. In addition to her commercial and administrative duties, she obviously had the time and the desire to inform herself and to exercise her talents. The chest allows us a glimpse of her inner life; it enables us to put some color and substance to a mere name from the past. The chest is decorated with classical figures. On the front, a winged Nike and another woman, perhaps a nymph or goddess, approach a seated warrior. On the top, a warrior rests while other people walk on. There is animation in the scene, a youth talking to a young girl, who is half turning round. There is real expression in both their faces, as well as on all the faces. They may be figures from the classics, but Susan depicted them as people from real stories. She was putting her knowledge of ancient legends on display. Inside there are two female ancients on the lids, facing each other—having a chat? The back is decorated with a contemporaneous family crest. The back is most intriguing. Susan left her bible to her friend, which makes me think that she valued the word of God and wanted to leave a token of this aspect of herself on her tea chest. There is the figure of Christ seated with a shepherd's stick on what hints at the surface of the earth, or is it heaven? There are no sheep for this shepherd; only the head of a stone lion and a whimsical eagle. Is the eagle a family emblem sitting next to Christ? And what exotic presence is in the sack? This is such personal iconography that it leaves us guessing. This scene is drawn sparingly with a very defined outline between darkness and light. A supreme example of a woman's grasp of the aesthetic, cultural, and social mores of her time. Thank you, Susan. 13" wide. Ca. 1820. $?

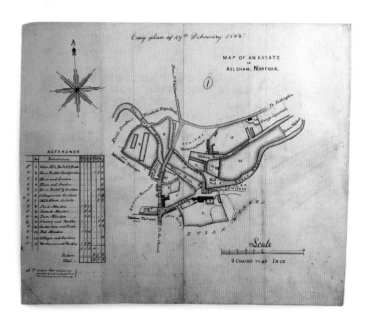

## Painted

It is not always possible to distinguish where the penwork ends and the painted work begins, since there was a whole range of painting and drawing instruments used in the decoration of boxes. Some work was done using paints rather than ink, with bolder brushstrokes, and with color used not as an infill but in graduated shades, as in water or oil color painting.

The themes mostly executed in this medium were inspired by nature and were either painted in a very realistic manner or in the naive tradition. Chinoiserie and classical scenes were rarely attempted, and the few that were are now exceedingly rare.

Because painted boxes needed a high degree of skill, very few were decorated in this way. Each one of these boxes has its own individual merit and beauty. They are some of the most stunning and idiosyncratic boxes ever made.

*Above and left:*
Figure 116. A box of complex form standing on talon feet, which enhance its curvatures. It is decorated all over in penwork, drawing its inspiration from the English countryside. The sides feature oak leaves and acorns; the top, a rustic cottage in front of Gothic ruins in an overgrown landscape. 9.5" wide. Ca. 1815–25. $1,500–2,000.

*Above and left:*
Figure 117. A tea caddy painted all over with ecclesiastical buildings, many of them in ruin. Very likely the artist drew them from life. Some are architecturally impressive and some have the charm of Gothic ruins. All the pictures are framed in trailing grapevines. The symbolism of this plant on this particular box must be meant to be strongly Christian. The grapevine traversed many cultures, from the ancient world to Judaism to Christianity. It was found in catacombs and early sarcophagi; it was popular in Renaissance Italy, which influenced eighteenth-century England, and is still a significant design in religious interiors. The strong vine is symbolic of Christ; the branches, of his disciples; and the juice of the fruit, of the Eucharistic wine. I have never seen another tea caddy carrying such strong religious symbolism and exclusively decorated with Christian buildings. It must have been a very personal piece. 10" wide. Ca. 1790–1810. $7,000–9,000.

*This whole page:*

Figure 118. This is a complete penwork collection on a single box. It has representations of almost all the major aesthetic and cultural trends of its period. The back and front are painted with glamorous Indian figures among stylized plants and exotic birds. The inside of the lid and the sides are decorated with scenes from fables. The fox and the stork were a particular favorite. Note how the chinoiserie convention of oversized flowers has crept into the fox scene and the "wolf in sheep's clothing" scene. The frieze of the box is decorated with a central basket of flowers and fruit with trailing foliage and birds, all arranged in the symmetrical neoclassical manner. The lids have penwork decoration in the manner of seventeenth- and eighteenth-century English embroidery. The top goes back to ancient Greece, with Eros on his chariot, which is driven by the doves of Aphrodite. Even then there is the most charming detail: Eros seems to have a very down-to-earth-looking doggie guide! A piece bursting with the confused charm of its period. 9" wide. Ca. 1815. $12,000–15,000.

## DECOUPAGE

Before abandoning boxes decorated at home, some mention must be made of the few, but very interesting, boxes that were enhanced with cutouts of paper or cloth. Flowers cut from colored papers were inserted into the borders of old Turkish manuscripts, although whether the eighteenth-century ladies who busied themselves cutting and pasting knew of this is not clear. It is more likely the fashion originated from the Venetian *lacca contrafatta*. From around 1730, when the fashion for chinoiserie decoration was sweeping through Europe, sheets of printed designs were sold in Venice. These were cut out and pasted on furniture and boxes, which were then varnished. The final impression, if well varnished and not too closely scrutinized, was of painted designs. This fashion was not widespread in England until the nineteenth century, when Victorian scraps were produced in profusion.

The idea of pasting and varnishing did inspire some interesting work. What is unique about boxes decorated in England in this way is that the person who decorated the box decided on what to cut out and paste. This resulted in each box being like no other and reflecting the artistic inclination of its owner. Two exceptional examples featuring decoupage are illustrated in the chapter "Card Boxes" (see Figs. 427, 428).

Figure 119. A box decorated with penwork and monochrome paint. The sides feature stylized oak leaves; the center, a charming representation of a millhouse at the side of a stream. Although the theme is rural and homespun, the arrangement of the decoration is very much in the neoclassical tradition. 9" wide. Ca. 1790–1800. $2,000–2,600.

*Above and left:*
Figure 120. A box made in beech and gessoed and decorated with penwork. This particular box is very reminiscent of Anglo-Indian work, both in the contrast of black on white, which resembles ivory, and in the style of decoration. The patterns of plants and flowers are executed in the manner of fabric and embroidery design, which was fashionable in penwork of the period. However, the top design goes further than most such work, in that the peacock is central to an asymmetrical tree-of-life motif, which is characteristic of eighteenth-century Indian inlaid work. Exceptionally well designed and executed. 11.75". Last decades eighteenth century. $5,000–7,000.

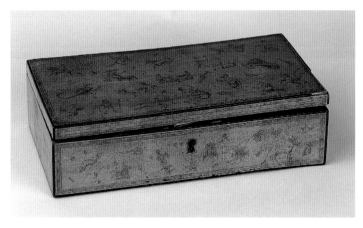

*Left and below:*
Figure 121. A box decorated either in penwork or pencil with symbols of the zodiac and of other arcane and intriguing arts. The idiosyncratic work of an eighteenth-century occultist? Saturn has Capricorn, the goat fish, on a lead, and Leo the lion makes an attempt at the fish tail. Exquisitely drawn in minute detail. Last decades eighteenth century. 8.5" wide. $?

Figure 122. A box decorated with a central topographical print and penwork. The arrangement, theme, and treatment of the floral border is characteristic of such work. 8.5" wide. Ca. 1815–25. $1,200–1,800.

*Above and right:*

Figure 123. A polychrome tea chest painted in a fluid hand with an exotic scene. The elongated figures, the inverted flower hats, and the lightness of execution suggest a knowledge of later, more refined chinoiserie design. The top is similarly decorated, gently built up into three dimensions using white size and fine plaster. The faces in particular display the sensitivity of the artist; the effect is of ivory. The tall female figures with their long feet and large, round eyes look European rather than oriental. A piece that echoes the Sino-European relationships of the early nineteenth century. The feet and handles are of strong Regency form. 12.5" wide. Ca. 1820. $7,500–9,000.

*Above and right:*

Figure 124. A box in beech, gessoed and painted. The sides are painted within ovals with landscapes with a small lone figure, buildings, and sheep. The top is ambitiously painted with people and their animals entering a courtyard. Well designed and executed, it points to the work of a professional artist. 12" wide. Made in Spa sometime in the middle of the eighteenth century. $7,500–12,000.

Figure 125. A box painted in the naive style, with girl and dog in country, the sides with roses. This is a manifestation of the fashion among the aristocracy to play at being country lads and lasses. A very charm-charged example. 10" wide. Fourth quarter eighteenth century. $3,000–4,000.

*Above and right:*
Figure 126. This is a good example of lacquer povera / *lacca contrafatta* with delightful vignettes of chinoiserie. These were typical of Venetian designs that were sold in sheets ready to be cut and used to taste. 12.5" wide. Ca. 1730. *Courtesy of Susan Webster* $6,000–8,000.

Figure 127. Detail: a box covered in colored scraps and varnished, the main figures harking back to medieval legend. Box is 10" wide. Mid-nineteenth century. $700–800.

# C H A P T E R 8 *Papier-mâché*

apier-mâché was the result of attempts by European craftsmen to produce a material with distinctive qualities: it could be carved and worked like wood, be durable and malleable, and take a finish to at least rival oriental lacquer.

It is difficult to say when papier-mâché was first made. Is the mixture of straw and mud used in construction since ancient times, or the plaster mixed with vegetable matter employed in the manufacture of architectural ornaments during the seventeenth century a form of papier-mâché? The step to mixing rags and paper into the pulp was only but a short one. In the second half of the eighteenth century, Robert Adam recognized the potential of a kind of papier-mâché mixture as a suitable medium for casting neoclassical ornaments. The

principle remains the same, whatever the ingredients, and it has manifested itself in many forms and many cultures since time immemorial.

In Europe, the most recognizable form of papier-mâché, as we know it today, was given a boost during the seventeenth century through examples of the work brought from Persia by early travelers. The French and Germans experimented with their own version of the material with varying degrees of success. During the eighteenth century, oriental lacquer posed a threat to the livelihood of European craftsmen. This led to serious attempts at reproducing finer forms of japanning that would incorporate both material and finish. The result was the successful development of papier-mâché as a medium for applied art.

*Above and right:*
Figure 128. A card box painted with scenes of Indian inspiration. The painting is of the finest quality, and it is reminiscent of the art of miniature painting. Against a black background, the artist has depicted scenes in exotic landscapes. The painted parts appear to be on a background of gold, so there is a glow under every color. Although the scene is arranged with an element of fantasy, it is painted by building up delicate and subtle shades of color in the manner of eighteenth-century landscape painting. Against this, exotic plants rise up in fine lines of pure gold accented with bright colors. The figures have well-painted expressive faces. Their clothes are painted in well-defined patterns, in the style of company painting. They resemble figures in traditional Indian illustrations. Two of the ladies appear to be European. The painting must have been executed by a sensitive artist who had understood different traditions and distilled their best qualities in this extraordinary composition. It is as if figures from Persian or Indian manuscripts leapt into an exotic landscape transformed by the alchemy of European perception. The piece transcends both chinoiserie and company painting. It is the work of a true master. 13.75" wide. Ca. 1800. $?

Figure 129. A pen box (a Qalamdan) decorated with a fine floral pattern of blue and gold. A traditional design for such boxes brought from India and Persia from the seventeenth to the nineteenth centuries. 11" long. $1,500–2,000.

"Vernis Martin," as this finish came to be known, was very successful, winning the accolade both of royalty and aristocracy. Some of its secret ingredients were reputed to be of a culinary nature, such as garlic and absinthe, but the exact mixture of spirit, lac, oil, resin, and other substances, in whatever combination, died with the brothers.

Germany, the Low Countries, Russia, and other countries produced their own versions of japanning and papier-mâché. However, it was in England that this material was developed as a very important medium for the production of larger boxes. It was eminently suited to the aesthetic climate of Victorian England. Furthermore, the mechanized processes of the age assisted in its meteoric mid-nineteenth-century popularity.

The first steps in modern papier-mâché manufacture were probably taken as early as the last decades of the seventeenth century, when a type of pulp was prepared from mashed paper, glue, chalk, and sand. It was used for moldings after it had been pressed, baked, and varnished. As late as 1763, it was still used as a medium for architectural ornaments by Peter Babel, who advertised himself as a designer and modeler.

Types of japanning in an effort to reproduce lacquer had already been produced in many parts of Europe. Early forms of japanning on wood necessitated coating the wood before decoration. It was an inevitable step to extend the function of the coating to incorporate the basic material. This could reduce the necessary processes from three to two and give a new substance that could be marketed as of superior quality and as quite distinct from oriental work.

The renowned Martin brothers in France were working during the earlier part of the eighteenth century toward perfecting a hard varnish with lacquer qualities. Guillaume Martin glued sheets of paper together, pressed them into molds while wet, and dried them in ovens. The japanning ovens were already in place, so the scene was preset for experimentation. After drying, the objects were coated with layers of hard varnish.

As the eighteenth century progressed, it was realized that to render the material suitable for the making of superior objects, it had to be refined. Henry Clay is credited with the next big step of the process, but it is more accurate to go one generation back to his one-time employer, John Baskerville, who was a manufacturer of tin japanned ware in Birmingham. He was also a printer with a passion for calligraphy. Henry Clay was apprenticed to him from 1740 to 1749. Baskerville was an inquiring and talented man who made his own paper and ink,

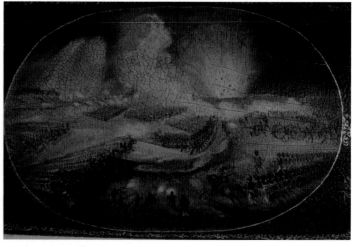

*Above and right:*

Figure 130. This box is the result of an extraordinary merger of two cultures: the decorative themes are all European, but the craftsmanship is Persian. The manner of painting is a manifestation of the long tradition of Persian miniature painting. The scenes are executed exquisitely, using a fine brush, which allows for a lot of action and detail to be depicted on a small surface. The scenes are titled in fine calligraphy in Arabic script. The front description translates, "the war between British and non British in Portsmouth which is a village in England [something something] from sea . . ." The boats with their sails are so finely painted that one needs magnification to appreciate the artist's virtuosity. The painting evokes the energy of the field of battle at Waterloo, "the war between British [army] in Hengan [?] never heard—port and China army waiting towards the sea." One end of the box is painted with an as-yet-unidentified palatial gallery, the other with a picture depicting the Bridge of Sighs in Venice, the "*Ponte dei Sospiri.*" The bridge was built in the seventeenth century by Antonio Contino to connect the old prisons to the interrogation rooms in the Doge's Palace (Lord Byron is credited with giving this name in the nineteenth century). During the nineteenth century, Persian artists produced a few boxes with European-inspired scenes, but I have never come across another example of such complexity. 12.25" long. Ca. 1850. $?

Figure 131. A papier-mâché box made by the first method of making boxes; that is, by using sheets of papier-mâché as wood, and working them as for cabinetmaking. The decoration is of a subtly painted chinoiserie scene with figures. Inside it is fitted with smaller card boxes and a counter box, decorated in foliage in a blue-gray color. 8.75" wide. Last quarter eighteenth century. $3,500–4,000.

*Left and below:*
Figure 132. A large box made out of flat sheets of papier-mâché cut and constructed as if made of wood. The painting of flowers and butterflies in pale colors and gold leaf is of exceptionally fine quality. 16" wide. Late eighteenth to early nineteenth century. $6,000–8,000.

and he already understood the principle of japanning. His printing work was reputed to be of exquisite taste. Everything was in place for the next logical step; that is, combining paper with japanning.

Baskerville and two other craftsmen had already experimented with making panels out of sheets of paper pasted together. In 1763, one of the other two men, Stephen Bedford, won the recognition of the Society of Arts for his superior varnish. It is likely that during the time when Clay was a young apprentice, experiments aiming at producing a superior form of papier-mâché took place in Baskerville's workshop.

As early as 1760, Samuel Derrick mentioned small items of papier-mâché produced by Baskerville. Unfortunately, to my knowledge, none has as yet been positively identified. For a time, after leaving Baskerville's employment, Clay became a printer while continuing to experiment with papier-mâché as a material. In 1772, his work finally paid off and he patented his newly perfected substance for "new Improved Paper-ware," which was heat resistant. Clay's method was followed by others, especially when his patent lapsed in 1802. The substance was now called "paper ware." This term remained in use for a few more decades.

Different makers introduced different techniques and variations, but the principle remained as Clay described it. Sheets of paper soaked in paste were pressed together on a flat plate or board. Equal numbers were pasted on each side. The paper sheets were then separated from the plate by planing or cutting the edges. They were then dried in a stove "sufficiently hot to deprive them of their flexibility and at the same time are rubbed over, or dipped in oil or varnish." The resulting material was used like wood, joining the parts by dovetailing or mitering. The final object was "coated with color and oils … and then japanned and highly varnished and can be brought to the highest polish by friction with the human hand."

The papier-mâché sheets were employed in the making of anything from coach roofs to boxes! The paper Clay used was made of cotton rags and had a greenish-gray color. Clay was given a patent by George III, allowing him to use dovetailing in the construction of objects by using his "paper ware." Clay first set up business with a man called Gibbons, but by the time he became established, his partner was out of the scene.

Although another important firm, Watson and Co., was listed as papier-mâché manufacturers in Birmingham as early

*This whole page:*
Figure 133. A caddy with typical characteristics of Clay work, such as the ceramic cameos of classical figures and the gilded internal facing, which is integrated with the hinge. This hinge construction overcomes the problem of the papier-mâché cracking with repeated openings of the box. The gold floral decoration is very fine and rather unusual, in that it is more naturalistic than the repetitive anthemia and palmettes that were painted as borders on caddies of neoclassical design. The rectangular shape of the caddy is also different from most eighteenth-century papier-mâché caddies, which are oval. An early Clay piece. 5.9" wide. $?

as 1770, it was Henry Clay who stole the limelight and became very successful. At about 1785, he acquired retail premises in London's Covent Garden. His manufacturing continued in Birmingham until about 1801, or even later. George III was one of his patrons, and by 1792, Clay was claiming the title "Japanner to His Majesty." In 1793, he presented his "new material for painting upon" to the Queen's Palace, as Buckingham Palace was then called. He presented the queen with a sedan chair painted after Guido Reni, and from this date onward he began to commission talented painters to paint ambitious scenes on his wares.

By 1803, Clay's billhead read "Japanner in ordinary to His Majesty and to His Royal Highness the Prince of Wales." Clay died in 1812, but the business continued until 1822 under W. Clay and Sons, from two different addresses in London. Items with his name attached to them were exhibited in the 1851 Great Exhibition by craftsmen claiming to be his descendants. His reputation certainly lived on.

Some of Clay's early objects are marked "CLAY PATENT" under a crown, but since much of the eighteenth-century work was personally commissioned, not every piece was marked. It is the style of work that identifies a Clay box. Caddies and dressing cases were two types of boxes made by Clay, and these were decorated in the fashionable styles of the day.

As early as 1775, when during a visit to England, Georg Christoph Lichtenberg—a German physicist—looked at the boxes and tea caddies produced by Clay at his Birmingham works, he commented on the orange color decoration reminiscent of Etrurian vases. This was in keeping with the neoclassical tradition of the second half of the eighteenth century. Another form of neoclassical decoration used by Clay was cameos of classical figures produced by Josiah Wedgwood. This type of ornament was particularly suited to small items such as tea caddies.

Clay was eager to use his newly "infinitely superior" developed substance as a background for fine painting. His work was skillfully painted with chinoiserie and also with European scenes. He strived to keep the standard of the painting high, and to this purpose he ordered copies of works by renowned artists, as well as prints and designs of antiquity. He also commissioned artists such as Paul Sandby, a prominent water colorist who was responsible for designing the table that Clay

Figure 134. An oval caddy painted in pale yellow with a large floral pattern reminiscent of chinoiserie. The decoration is unusual. 6.25" wide. Late eighteenth century. $6,000–10,000.

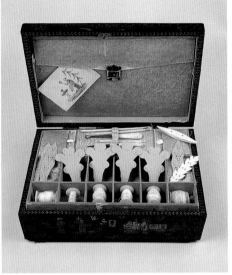

*This whole page:*

Figure 135. A sewing box that fits exactly the descriptions of the work of Joseph Booth. The surface is smooth and glossy like oriental lacquer. The work is executed with finesse and precision. The style of the decoration is in the later phase of chinoiserie, which was influenced by the work of Darly, Pillement, and Continental eighteenth-century artists. It has a lightness of touch and movement and is framed in rococo-style cartouches "filleted" in gold. The interior of the box is lined in water silk and fitted with ivory reels. Under the tray there is another compartment, which is enclosed by two leather-covered lids. These are painted and gilded. A most unusual feature. The whole piece is of exceptional quality. 11" wide. Early 1820s. $?

*Above and right:*
Figure 136. Rare, complex Toleware tea chest of rectangular form. The outside is decorated with painted decoration depicting rural scenes on a japanned ochre ground. This form of idealized country life found favor in the arts during the eighteenth century. The well-to-do often dressed up as country folk and pretended to work the land or to look after animals. Shepherdesses were de rigeur. The irony was that the wealthy attempted to mitigate the artifice of the period with the pretense of a simple life: a total sham. The painter has evoked the rural idyll in a simple but effective style. The artwork brims with naive charm. Inside the chest there are three canisters. The two with round caps would have been for tea; the central canister with hinged lid would have been for sugar. The chest stands on gilded brass feet. 8.2" wide. Ca. 1765. $5,000–6,000.

made for Horace Walpole. A visitor to Clay's workshop commented on a design that had been especially brought from Rome. When necessary, Clay employed professional painters from Wolverhampton, including the very talented Edward Bird, who was noted for his flower painting.

Clay also seems to have used mother of pearl decoration as early as the eighteenth century. When in Covent Garden, a chiffonier in his showroom was described as being decorated with groups of fruits and flowers in mother of pearl, gold, and colors. Clay's method for this type of decoration was to "inlay," implying that pieces of a certain thickness were inserted into pregauged patterns on the surface of the object.

A tea caddy he made for Horace Walpole in the late 1770s was described as painted "with loose feathers." It is interesting to note that a Clay caddy cost three guineas, which at the time was a great deal of money, and the equivalent of about three weeks' wages for a skilled craftsman. Patents at that time were costly affairs, and this may explain the reason why only luxury objects were worth the trouble of striving for such an accolade.

Clay's work after moving to London is sometimes marked "CLAY, KING STREET, COVENT GARDEN" and, after his death, "CLAY LONDON."

Although Clay's output was considerable by the standards of the time, there were other makers of papier-mâché and early pieces that must not be automatically attributed to Clay. A certain Godfrey in Hertfordshire claimed that his method was superior to Clay's. Unfortunately, in 1806 his stoves

overheated and his stock was lost. Overheating stoves were a regular occurrence in eighteenth- and early-nineteenth-century workshops.

After the death of Henry Clay, his Birmingham works were taken over by Small and Son, Guest, Chopping, and Bill. This firm continued the tradition of high-quality work and decoration. They also produced blanks for other firms to decorate. There is a theory that such firms, and even Clay, commissioned artists from Pontypool to decorate their "blanks." Pontypool, the center of excellence for tinned japanned ware, already had a core of talented artists working in the area. It had a long tradition for such decoration stretching back to 1730, when the "Japan Works" were established by the Quaker family named Allgood.

In 1816, Jennens and Bettridge—arguably the most successful of all papier-mâché manufacturers—moved into what had been Clay's Birmingham factory. During the first decade of their existence as a firm, Jennens and Bettridge established an ethos of excellence in the decoration of their work.

Mindful of the Regency fashion for chinoiserie, in 1821, they employed Joseph Booth, whose work in this field was second to none. It was reported that his chinoiserie work was indistinguishable from oriental work. He worked on a very smooth black background, building up part of his designs in a paste made up of whitening, size, and gold powder. Other parts were gilded in a mixture of lime and "filleting." Color was used sparingly and subtly.

One way of distinguishing between Booth's work and oriental lacquer is by smell. Papier-mâché has a faint linseed oil smell. Lacquer of that particular period has a weak cedar/pine smell. The reason for the papier-mâché smell is that papier-mâché objects, or sheets, were soaked in linseed oil—or linseed oil and spirits of tar—in between firings and before varnishing. This waterproofed and further hardened the material.

Linseed oil was also one of the drying oils used in the making of the finishing varnishes.

The employment of Booth was probably what attracted the attention of George IV to the work of this firm. In 1824, Booth painted a tray in chinoiserie for the king, and the following year, Jennens and Bettridge claimed to be "Japanners in ordinary to His Majesty." They continued to enjoy royal favor through the reigns of William IV and Queen Victoria. Booth left the firm in 1825.

In 1837, Jennens and Bettridge opened up showrooms in London's Belgrave Square. For a short period in the middle of the century, they even had a branch in New York for dealing with their exports.

Jennens and Bettridge were very business minded. They soon tried to establish brand recognition by marking pieces made in their workshops, although not all of their early work was marked. They reintroduced the term "papier-mâché" and strived to perfect and develop other methods of production and decoration. Most of the artists who worked for the firm—around sixty-four by the 1860s—had been trained at the London or Birmingham schools of design. They also employed instructors to train artists within their "works." The painting on their

boxes was well executed, mostly reflecting the taste of early and mid-Victorian England.

Ornaments, floral representations, and pictures of birds were more often copied from design books rather than directly from nature. By this time, the design books did not follow strict classical rules but offered decorative suggestions in a mixture of naturalistic, Gothic, and rococo styles. The work of the best artists must have also included some personal observation.

In 1834, a book titled *Fancy Ornaments* by Frederick Knight was published that proved invaluable to painters of papier-mâché. Knight was responsible for introducing rococo swirls and exotic birds on many objects of the period, hinting at the earlier exoticism of japanned and lacquer work. Many Jennens and Bettridge boxes feature rococo and other stylized ornament executed in gold. The gold was primarily gold leaf, unless it was used for raised decoration, in which case it was usually gold powder mixed in with the decorating medium. Such ornaments were drawn with care, sustaining a fine quality of line together with a fluidity of movement. John Breakspear, famous for his tulips, and Philip M'Cullum, known for his flower groups, were two notable artists whose work included pieces painted for Jennens and Bettridge.

In addition to paying special attention to the quality of the painted designs on their ware, Jennens and Bettridge sought to improve other methods of decoration. One of their employees, George Souter, found a superior way of shaping mother of pearl by using strong acid instead of scissors or cutting tools. This enabled the outline of the shell to be cut with greater precision and made it possible to cut several identical shapes at the same time. Birmingham had a thriving industry in mother of pearl

*Above and left:*
Figure 137. A tea caddy painted with the portrait of the young Queen Victoria and stamped JENNENS & BETTRIDGE LONDON. The shape of the box is already moving into curvilinear form. This is most effective, since it gives a good view of the main picture even when the caddy is viewed from the front. 8.5" wide. Ca. 1840. $4,500–6,000.

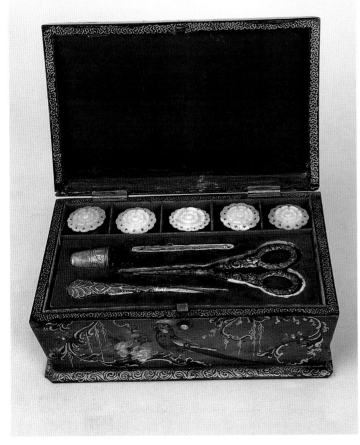

buttons, so there was a plethora of nautilus shell imported into the area. In 1825, the firm of Jennens and Bettridge took out a patent for "application of materials of the jewelry trade" for the purpose of "ornamenting papier-mâché with pearl shell."

Shell had been used in papier-mâché decoration as early as the end of the eighteenth century, and it had been used in lacquer for many centuries. In the seventeenth century, very fine shell decoration was applied to japanned work in Naples. So although Jennens and Bettridge had the patent for the method, this did not stop other makers from using mother of pearl decoration; it simply meant that they had to use more-laborious ways of cutting, often resulting in thicker shell. Thicker shell was not necessarily a worse medium. In high-quality work it could give more iridescence and depth of color. In poorer examples it resulted in crude, awkward lines.

When skillfully applied, shell, with its elusive quality of color and light, added another dimension to a painted piece. The way that Jennens and Bettridge used mother of pearl was this: Pieces that had already been thinned and shaped were affixed to the object to be decorated. More layers of tar varnish were then applied, until the shell was covered. The object was then rubbed down with pumice until the shell was revealed, this time level with the yet-unpainted surface. The parts depicted in mother of pearl were varnished with tinted varnishes, so they acquired a soft color without losing their translucent quality. The rest of the design was then painted and parts of it were gilded.

The iridescent effect of much of nineteenth-century pearl decoration has been destroyed by later inappropriate painting. It is not a good idea to paint over mother of pearl pieces, even

Figure 139. A writing slope painted with figures in an Egyptian temple. The light values of the work are enhanced with the use of mother of pearl inlay. It is stamped JENNENS & BETTRIDGE. An unusual theme for such work, it is influenced by the last phase of neoclassicism and the interest in Egyptian antiquities. Both the straight form and the theme point to a relatively early piece. 12" wide. Ca. 1825–30. $4,000–6,000.

*Above:*
Figure 138. A box with a lift-out tray fitted with sewing tools and five mother of pearl spools. It is stamped Jennens and Bettridge, under a crown. The top is painted with a peacock among flowers and grapes. Parrots and butterflies are painted all around. The main scenes are enclosed within fine rococo cartouches. Note the very fine quality of the painting and gilding, which attests to the work of one of the master painters. 6.75" wide. Mid-nineteenth century. $3,000–4,000.

Figure 140. Papier-mâché writing box, with the top painted with a still life of fruit and game, framed by gilded decoration. Inlays of mother of pearl are used to give translucence to the painting. The quality is of such high standard that it points to the work of a trained artist. The box is embossed to the base "JENNENS & BETTRIDGE." This firm trained and employed talented artists. 12.2" wide. Ca. 1830. $4,000–6,000.

Figure 141. A tea caddy with glass reverse painting of two small figures gazing at Westminster Abbey. The picture, which is very skillfully painted, is given extra radiance by having a backing of metal foil. The framing of the main picture and the side decoration are in bright colors and gold in the opulent style, which was inspired by Middle Eastern and Renaissance designs. All impeccably executed. 7" wide. Mid-nineteenth century. *Courtesy of Charleen Plumly Pollard.* $2,400–3,000.

if most of the colored varnish is gone. This has a deadening effect on the whole composition and destroys forever the knowledge of the artistic intention of the original painter.

The basic paper used for Jennens and Bettridge's papier-mâché was made of linen rag, which gave it a gray hue. However, the final product had a superior black color thanks to George Neville, another craftsman employed by this firm. Neville evolved a jet-black japan varnish that resisted fading. This provided a striking background for mother of pearl application, gilding, and, of course, painting. The varnish was made out of lampblack and tar varnish, the final coats consisting of just tar varnish.

Another decorative device patented in 1847 by Theodore Hyla Jennens was "gem laying," which was a jeweled panel of glass inserted in the center of a box. This was invented by Benjamin Giles, another of the firm's workers. It was reminiscent of Eastern art, with iridescent gems backed with bright colors and metal foils. It was a development of the reverse painting on glass already introduced from China and used for decorating both papier-mâché and tortoiseshell boxes. It was also only a tiny step further from Lane's patent for "Inlaid Pearl Glass." The Lane idea seems to have had two inventors: a Miss E. Tonge and Thomas Gibson. Gibson described it in 1846 as pearl on the back of painted and gilded glass, affixed either with tinted or transparent varnish.

Jennens and Bettridge marked most of their wares with an embossed or etched mark. A diamond mark denoted that the

Figure 142. A topographical picture of the Chapel, King's College, Cambridge, stamped "JENNENS & BETTRIDGE Makers to the Queen." Mid-nineteenth century. *Courtesy of a private collection*. $1,800–2,200.

object was also patented. If there was a patent pending, this fact was also recorded.

Jennens and Bettridge explored their own ideas, but they were also quick to copy the specializations of other makers. Sometimes it is difficult to ascertain who thought of what first, since employees and artists worked for different companies, and exhibitions helped cross-pollinate ideas faster than in previous centuries. For example, the firm of T. Lane was supposed to favor reverse glass painting, yet the same technique and even the same pictures turned up stamped with the Jennens and Bettridge stamp. Spiers and Son of Oxford specialized in topographical scenes of their area. Jennens and Bettridge also produced views both of Oxford and Cambridge. They also copied the "bronze interiors" for which the Old Hall in Wolverhampton was renowned, Foley (his real name was George Goodman) being their principal painter of such work.

The quality between marked and unmarked work is not distinguishable, and it is not possible to identify makers and artists with absolute certainty. Boxes must be judged on the merit of their aesthetic integrity and interest, and these pages serve to give an overall picture rather than an identification guide.

By the middle of the nineteenth century, Birmingham had developed a thriving papier-mâché industry. Many makers exhibited their wares at the 1849 Birmingham exhibition, and two years later, in 1851, they brought their best work to London for the Great Exhibition. Jennens and

Bettridge, T. Lane, G. C. Davies, Halbeard and Wellings, M'Cullum and Hodson, and I. Sutcliffe all came ready to dazzle the world. And the world was dazzled.

In the catalogue, Messrs. M'Cullum and Hodson are described as "deservedly stand in high repute." Among their offerings was a cabinet with painted pictures of Victoria and Albert, a bombe box, a writing slope, and other cabinets and compendiums painted either with flowers or scenes. The characteristic feature of the work of this firm was very exaggerated rounded shapes, with the boxes starting from a curvilinear base and getting narrower as they curved upward. The look had the opulence of the baroque mingled with more-familiar ornamentation.

G. C. Davies exhibited a workbox decorated with glass tablets depicting "English Monarchs from the Time of the Conquest": an ambitious work that must have played sympathetically on the newly found sense of inward-looking patriotism of the Victorians.

Jennens and Bettridge took the place by storm with, among other things, a pianoforte case. Among the smalls was a writing desk "inlaid with imitative gems by the patented process, employed exclusively by this establishment with the happiest effect." The firm had a very flattering entry in the catalogue for their "unceasing endeavors to improve the character of such productions—a reputation which is certainly well deserved and which will be increased by their contribution to the Great Exhibition."

It is interesting to note that two of the artists who were employed by the firm of Jennens and Bettridge were described as "sculptors." Papier-mâché had come full circle. At first it was used as a material for framing and for making architectural ornaments. It was then developed as a material that provided a good, smooth surface for painting. Finally, it was regarded as a material that on account of its plasticity was attractive to "sculptors."

Jennens and Bettridge, as well as other makers, initially used methods similar to the Clay method to make the basic papier-mâché material. There are descriptions of paper pasted with glue, resin, and flour; dried in stoves; and then finished in lamp black, Virginian turpentine, pitch, balsams, resins, and drying oils. Up to the early years of the reign of Victoria, there was little variation in the way most makers developed their preferred ways of dealing with papier-mâché as a suitable material for making and decorating objects.

As the Victorian age and taste were eclipsing the Regency, a more immediately striking look was preferred to the poised style of the early work. Up to the 1830s, papier-mâché objects depended for their appeal on the beauty of their painted and gilded decoration. As a more ponderous fashion began to prevail in architecture, ornament, and even personal costume, the aesthetic criteria of the clientele changed. Unity of style within a room was giving way to a more comfortable cluttered look, which was inevitable given the larger Victorian families and their increasing possessions. Objects needed to "stand out."

Papier-mâché makers turned their efforts to ways of creating unusual shapes, with spectacular success. It is not surprising that Jennens and Bettridge were at the forefront of this further development. In 1847, Theodore Hyla Jennens found a way of steaming blanks, easing them into molds, and using pressure to achieve dense forms of equal thickness. This process opened the way to more "molding" and less joinery, softening angles and flat surfaces.

The process developed further, and in 1854 a method of giving shape to objects with the use of iron molds was described, as practiced by Jennens and Bettridge. At first the paper was pasted onto the mold. Four or five sheets could be pasted at any one time. The paper was "worked in" either by hand or with a trowel, and the excess paste was pressed out. Then the piece was dried, preferably in a stove. When ready, it was rasped with a coarse file so that the surface could be more adhesive to additional layers of paper, which were pasted on until the required thickness was achieved. The object was then given to the cabinetmaker, or to the "sculptor," who refined the form before it was finished. The final stages were the same as for straighter objects; that is, varnishing, painting, and rubbing. The last step was varnishing with as many coats as necessary, pumicing between each coat, and polishing.

More details of the varnishing methods were also given in the 1854 description, although by the 1850s there must have been preferences and "secrets" varying from maker to maker. In general terms, the process was as follows: The article was first coated with a mixture of fine lampblack and tar varnish and then just with tar varnish. When dry, it was planed or rubbed smooth before receiving more coats of varnish, each coat rubbed smooth with pumice. Then the article was polished with powdered pumice and rotten stone. The final gloss was achieved with finely powdered rotten stone rubbed with the hand.

Shaping sheets of paper on molds was still a laborious process, and experiments were made to find a faster method for creating interesting curvaceous forms. Thomas Jones of Bilston made trays out of pulped paper as early as 1805, but it was a man called Brindley who perfected the method of using paper pulp and dies to give objects the required shape. The two parts of the mold were pressed by using a hydraulic screw or press. The object was dried in the mold and then treated and finished in the usual way. Sculptural effects were thus created not by the chisel, but by utilizing the malleability of the material before it was dried and hardened. If more sharpness was required, tools could be used to give the work a final edge, but the whole idea was to avoid the necessity of prolonged individual work. Finally, the object was handed to the artist for decoration. Straight lines and flat surfaces were no longer necessary.

Brindley introduced the pulp method in 1836, and in 1842 he invented a way of forming sheets out of pulped paper by pressing them between metal plates. They could then be pressed into molds. The whole idea had come full circle.

The pulped paper and mold method was eminently suitable for creating both complete forms and ornamental components. During the middle years of the nineteenth century, papier-mâché boxes were made for a variety of purposes. The nature of the material was supremely suited to the period. It enabled the makers to create interesting shapes, such as bombe, concave, architectural, and Gothic, and stand them on plinths, round feet, "aprons," or even combinations of more than one uplifting device. Tea caddies and sewing, jewelry, glove, and card boxes all were very successfully made in this material. On account of its fragility, only small writing slopes were made. The main decoration on these was executed on the sloping front, giving the artist quite a large flat area on which to work.

Table cabinets were made in papier-mâché in impressive architectural designs, with doors opening to reveal drawers. They were decorated throughout and often featured an enclosed writing slope, jewelry drawer, and sewing tray.

So far, I have traced the evolution of the papier-mâché industry by following the development of a few Birmingham firms. This is because Birmingham was at the forefront of the commercial application of papier-mâché. Jennens and Bettridge did not miss a trick, and although upset when others copied their ideas, they were the first to grasp every opportunity for "innovation." This brought the work forward to its final overcommercialization during the last three decades of the nineteenth century.

*Below and right:*
Figure 143. A writing slope that epitomizes the height of papier-mâché work. The top is constructed of a scalloped, slightly rounded form finely decorated with painted floral designs and gilding. Inset in the center is a picture painted in reverse on glass and backed with metal foil. The building on the picture is the apotheosis of early Victorian achievement, the Crystal Palace, where the Great Exhibition of All Nations took place in 1851. The box is doubly significant in that the exhibition was a milestone in the promotion of papier-mâché work. The Crystal Palace was made of glass, and the glass painting with the foil behind the paint has captured the particular quality of the building. A piece absolutely of its time. It was very likely made by the firm of T. Lane, who excelled in this type of work. 11.5" wide. Ca. 1851. *Courtesy of Christodoulides Family Collection.* $8,000–12,000.

*Above and left:*
Figure 144. Papier-mâché slope in unusual sealing wax red with chinoiserie decoration. The oriental scene is executed both in raised and painted work. It depicts oriental figures acting happy in a landscape. A most unusual box that transcends the tradition of papier-mâché color and ornament. Second quarter nineteenth century? *Courtesy of Christodoulides Family Collection.* $4,000–6,000.

*Above and right:*
Figure 145. A good example of a Victorian papier-mâché slope. Note the structured frame, which gives the box an effect of depth. Note the well-executed design of flowers and the iridescence of the mother of pearl livening up the composition. $2,500–3,700.

The handful of pioneering firms grew to a staggering number by the middle of the nineteenth century. About fifty important businesses worked mostly in Birmingham and Wolverhampton, but also in London and other towns. There were also smaller concerns, workshops, and studios making and decorating papier-mâché. By the end of the nineteenth century, most of this work had ceased. The unraveling of this particular industry happened astonishingly fast. It is as if, when Jennens and Bettridge were no longer there, the whole business stagnated. M'Cullum and Hodgson took over the business of Jennens and Bettridge in 1864, a point after which the standard of the whole industry declined.

During the first decades of the nineteenth century, while Birmingham was busy "inventing," other northern towns were also setting up papier-mâché workshops. There was an abundance of free hands in the North of England, on account of mechanized processes taking over much of the work of the workers. Of all the towns, Wolverhampton emerged as the finest center for papier-mâché production. The town already had a thriving metal-japanning industry. There were competent japanners and artists, living in the area, who specialized in decorating japanned objects. The first steps were tentative, but by 1810 the production of papier-mâché was overtaking that of japanned tinware.

The train of events started with Benjamin Walton going into partnership with William Ryton. In 1770, the Ryton brothers had taken over the Old Hall Works, which had been occupied by a line of japanners. When one of the brothers died, Walton joined William Ryton in the Old Hall. In spite of the fact that the Hall, which dated from Tudor times, was a conglomerate of old, chaotic premises, for many years it became a center of papier-mâché excellence. The objects produced were of high quality, and they were decorated by artists of considerable merit. One of their employees, Edward Bird, R.A. (1772–1819), who has already been discussed in association with Clay, was considered a master at painting bouquets of flowers. He went on to become an acclaimed artist and a court painter to Queen Charlotte.

Figure 146. A stationery box of interesting form, which takes advantage of the special qualities of the material. It is inlaid in mother of pearl and painted with houses seemingly built on the side of a mountain. The color and a bare tree suggest winter. The shape of the box is complementary to the design, in that it curves upward in line with the pictured landscape. A sensitive and clever combination of form and decoration, combining the two with artistic integrity. 8.5" wide. Mid-nineteenth century. $1,000–1,500.

After a financial setback in the 1840s and a brief cessation of business, Walton's son went on to establish the very successful firm of F. Walton, which traded from 1850 to 1880, at times employing up to 600 workers.

The firm of Walton, like other firms in Wolverhampton, continued the tradition of fine painted decoration established in the late eighteenth and early nineteenth centuries. Perhaps it is because they did not invent easy ways of cutting mother of pearl, or perhaps it is that they preferred to work with real artists that the Wolverhampton makers continued to emphasize the importance of painted decoration. Another significant factor was the fact that, unlike Birmingham makers—who made both small and large pieces, including furniture—Wolverhampton craftsmen concentrated in the production of objects of art. The pieces

*Left and below:*
Figure 147. A rectangular box decorated with a scene from the Robert Burns poem *Tam O'Shanter*. Tam is riding over the bridge of the river Doon on his mare, Maggie, pursued by witches. He has just witnessed evil celebrations in the church and churchyard of Alloway. As he gallops away, one of the old hags grabs and tears off the tail of his horse. However, he and his mare make it over the water to safety. A most unusual theme, rather too raw for Victorian sensitivities. 9.5" wide. Second quarter nineteenth century. *Courtesy of Seawitchartist George Rix* $800–1,200.

that emerged from this town sustained a high quality of painted work well into the nineteenth century. Many artists were nurtured and provided for by this work. They earned 30—50 shillings a week—two to four times more than other papier-mâché skilled workers—and even more if they were "superior hands." Sometimes the Birmingham makers commissioned artists who worked in Wolverhampton to paint high-quality objects.

In 1812, Thomas Hubball of Clerkenwell took out a patent for painting with metals such as lead and bronze. In 1816, Davis, an artist noted for high-quality painting on papier-mâché, adopted the idea and began to use copper, brass, silver, zinc, and gold dust to paint pictures with religious or allegorical themes. No other pigments were used. The idea of using metal powders caught the imagination of the Wolverhampton artists, who adopted it as a complement to painted decoration. Bronze was particularly favored, since it gave a warm background glow without making the object too garish.

The use of a bronze background became a feature of Wolverhampton work. An early known example is a picture titled *The Triumph of Britannia* on a bronze ground that was painted on a tray by Illridge in 1818. Naturalistically painted flowers on a bronze background were also painted before the middle of the nineteenth century. More glamorous pictures of birds and flowers, with rococo borders, were popular during the middle years of the century, by which time the technique was also adopted by the Birmingham firms.

A decorative fashion that was gaining ground during the middle decades of the nineteenth century was what came to be termed the neo-Gothic style. Old ruins and churches replaced classical temples and edifices in the popular imagination. Church interiors soon found expression on papier-mâché ware. Metallic powders were used as a method of adding "light" to Gothic windows in paintings of church interiors. In the same way, shafts of light were created in dark scenes, adding "atmosphere" to the composition. Wolverhampton-based artist Frederick Perks pioneered the technique of painting these romantically melancholy scenes, using bronze powders to suggest light values. His initials are sometimes distinguishable on the pictures. Henry Perks, working around 1860, also made very effective use of this technique, painting clouds edged with silvery, metallic lines. This work, which was highly regarded, was done at the Old Hall Works.

Edward and Richard Perry (later Perry, Son and Co.) was another notable Wolverhampton firm, Edward Perry having learned his craft at the Old Hall. This firm soldiered on from 1829 to 1890. Shoolbred, Loveridge and Shoolbred also produced notable work, examples of which were exhibited at the Great Exhibition. This firm produced some stunning work of very precisely painted butterflies and flowers on flat ground. They were noted for their skillful use of gold.

There were many excellent firms in Wolverhampton, and generally throughout the Midlands area of England. It is impossible to list them all, or to know what each one produced. There were also papier-mâché makers and retailers in London. Notable known names were Jackson and Sons, W. Brindley (who in 1836 patented a method using pulped rag, which would have avoided paper tax!), J. Dixon, and J. J. Mechi. Among those who were also notable makers of boxes in other materials were W. and J. W. Papworth and C. F. Bielefeld.

The 1820s, 1830s, and 1840s were the most-innovative years for the manufacture of papier-mâché. Many artists were involved in its decoration, often copying works of successful painters such as Landseer and Wilkie. William Davis (the same Davis who adopted the bronze powder method), for example, specialized in painting landscapes and rural scenes by George Morland. After 1842, this was rarely done, since the "Registration of Designs Act" meant that fees had to be paid to artists whose work was copied. This coincided with, and perhaps precipitated, the vogue for more profuse mother of pearl inlay and more exaggerated curvilinear shapes not suitable for representational painting.

During the decades of top-quality painted work, struggling artists often worked incognito, painting on papier-mâché to support their purer artistic efforts. They seldom marked their work, possibly because the firms they worked for did not approve of artist identification, or possibly because they themselves did not wish to advertise the fact that their work could be bought on a piece of applied rather than pure art. Jennens and Bettridge sometimes had the name of the firm painted on the margin of pictures. "Studios" for the decoration of blanks were set up as early as the last two decades of the eighteenth century. Joseph Barney—a fruit and flower painter—Haseler, and Robert Noyes were some of the first artists working in this way. It is impossible to know whose hand was responsible for some of the wonderful painting and decoration on papier-mâché boxes.

Some additional names not mentioned in the text associated with high-caliber painted work have survived in records, and a mention must be made of their particular gifts:

Figure 148. A single caddy of subtle curvilinear form, with a bouquet of flowers painted over a surface treated with metal powder to give a gently glowing background. The type of work and the fine quality of the painting point to Wolverhampton work. 4" wide. Ca. 1825–40. $2,500–4,000.

Figure 149. A box made of cut papier-mâché board and shaped surround. It is exquisitely decorated with an oriental scene in mother of pearl and gilding. The mother of pearl is not painted but is inserted in small pieces, which glitter with iridescence as the light catches them. The quality and type of work, together with the theme, point to Alsager and Neville, or to their influence. 9.5" wide. Mid-nineteenth century. $1,200–1,800.

## BIRMINGHAM

**Samuel Raven** (1775—1847): painted small boxes such as snuffboxes, one of which featured a portrait of George IV.

**Sadler** was renowned as a "liner" and "filleter" in gilt. This work entailed fine hand gilding, using a squirrel-tail hairbrush to etch out black lines.

**C. Neville** specialized in sea shell painting.

**David Sergeant** specialized in fern painting.

**Philip and James M'Cullum** painted flower groups.

## WOLVERHAMPTON

**Edwin Haseler**, gifted flower painter, worked first for Jennens and Bettridge but defected to Walton of Wolverhamton, where he became master painter.

**Richard Steele** also painted flowers, after a period working as a painter of china. He was one of a number of notable painters of flowers and verbenas.

**Frederick Newman** was responsible for wonderful flowers and peacocks for Loveridge and Shoolbred during the 1850s.

**George Hicken** painted landscapes. **Voss** painted beauty spots.

**Robert Noyes** painted landscapes and coaching scenes, and he was one of the few artists to initial his work.

**Thomas Hamson** painted some distinguished parrots.

**Joseph Barney** (1751—1827), not the one already mentioned, studied with **Angelica Kauffmann** and **Zucchi** and specialized in classical and biblical subjects. He was a serious artist and held an exhibition at the Royal Academy in 1786.

**George Wallis** is remembered for painting Queen Victoria.

**Edwin Booth**, possibly the brother of Joseph (mentioned in association with **Jennens and Bettridge**), worked in the 1820s at the Old Hall, creating raised, painted, and gilded decoration of Indian inspiration.

**Amner, William Bourne, John Breakspear, Jockson, and Grimes** all are associated with flora.

The small Birmingham firm of **Alsager and Neville** deserves a mention, since both partners were highly skilled artists in their own right. In his youth, Philip Alsager had worked for Jennens and Bettridge and was a gifted interpreter of oriental scenes. High-quality oriental decoration is a pointer to this artist's work. George Neville trained in Paris and painted fruit and flowers. He was working from about 1830 onward. One of his "trademarks" was a blue convolvulus, with one petal turning back. Alsager and Neville set up their own business in 1846. They were noted for the fine painting on their wares, but also for the skillful use of mother of pearl inlay. The shell was carefully inserted into the surface to be decorated, so as to catch the light from different directions. It was not tinted with color varnish but was utilized purely for its iridescent qualities, both in floral and architectural compositions. In 1862, they created the "green malachite" finish. Other finishes followed, such as marbling—which a Mr. Jones was said to have set the fashion for—wood graining, small stars, faux boulle, and tortoiseshell.

Figure 150. Card box with a chinoiserie scene finely painted in gold. The roof of the building and the rocks are depicted in unpainted mother of pearl. The shell has been carefully selected to suggest striations in the stone and roofing materials. The artist shows familiarity with oriental art, since the diaper patterns suggesting land and water are the same as on oriental lacquer. A piece of exquisite quality, perhaps an early Alsager work. $2,000–3,000.

In addition to painting and hand gilding, which required both skill and talent, transfer designs were employed early on in the course of the industry. Gilding was sometimes done using this method as early as 1820. After the middle of the nineteenth century, the process was developed to the extent that designs from engraved plates could be transferred in oils, with the result that the work of artists was applied in this way to papier-mâché ware. However, this form of decoration had a rather "flat" look.

A form of design that gained popularity during the middle and later part of the century—examples of which were shown by F. Walton at the Great Exhibition—was the formal linear patterns inspired by cultures of the past. Strong colors such as blues, greens, reds, and yellows were applied in interlocking patterns of Gothic, Persian, Byzantine, Renaissance, and Elizabethan inspiration. Greek key and other geometric designs were also featured, the latter depicted mostly in gilding or bronzing.

In 1852, the process for such decoration was speeded up by a patented method developed by George Haselar of Waltons, in which the parts that were to remain undecorated were varnished and the varnish was removed when the design was complete. This allowed for precision of line, the varnish acting as a form of stencil. This method was not new; it had been employed in more than one Asian country for traditional lacquer decoration. We will never know if some traveler whispered the secret in Haselar's ear. In any case, we must not begrudge him this small triumph, since he did have a rather terrible "put down" experience during his professional life. The story goes that Queen Victoria was offered a tray decorated by him, on

Figure 151. A tea caddy of concave form, in faux tortoiseshell, probably by Alsager and Neville. The glamour of the piece is further heightened with metal mounts. Third quarter nineteenth century. *Courtesy of the Bielstein Collection.* $1,400–2,000.

Figure 152. A table cabinet decorated all over, including the interior, with geometric patterns in gold and vivid colors. The designs are inspired by Middle Eastern, Gothic, and Renaissance work. They are also reminiscent of ecclesiastical stained-glass windows. The form of the cabinet, with raised and sunk parts in shapes that resemble doors and windows of abbeys and castles, is complementary to the decoration. The domed top and the slightly bombe-shaped base are characteristic of the period and complement well the straight lines of the sides. A piece that makes good use both of the quality of malleability and the good surface for strong design of the material and combines the two in a strong handsome piece. Ca. 1850. *Courtesy of a private collection.* $3,000–5,000.

which some grapes were arranged. She took the grapes but handed back the tray! Perhaps she did not expect such a wonderful gift, or perhaps she thought it was a piece of kitchenware.

After the death of Prince Albert in December 1861, a more somber mode of decoration in mauve and grays became fashionable for a time. Even "black shell" was preferred to the white of the nautilus and the colors of the abalone shell. The papier-mâché industry was very much in tune with the feelings of the nation. Pale background colors were also experimented with, but nothing gave the successful results achieved by decoration on a glossy black surface.

A design that was tried in many forms during the second half of the nineteenth century was fern ware. In the *Society of Arts Journal,* 1854, this process is described either as soaking the leaves in acid and applying them on the material by using heat, or preparing copper plates with the fern impressions and printing the objects by using the plates. This form of rather subdued decoration was short lived in papier-mâché manufacture.

By the end of the century, transfer decoration was used on smaller, inexpensive boxes, hastening the end of an industry that had already been in decline. The Arts and Crafts movement rejected what was seen as indulgent ornament, which was in the nature of papier-mâché ware. This is in spite of the fact that the linear, strong color designs exhibited by Walton shared many common sources of inspiration with this elitist movement.

Papier-mâché has not had a fair press in recent decades. It is true that a great many boxes and other objects made during the late Victorian era are not of great artistic merit. As decorative pieces, they are true of their period. They are pretty in a comfortable, unpretentious way. They are useful. They were made to be appreciated by all, not just the sophisticated elite, and as such they reflect the rising expectations of the lesser classes of society—a comforting thought at the time.

Moreover, the plethora of lesser objects must not blind us to the really good pieces, which, as works of applied art, can stand their ground alongside any other object of virtue. The majority of the late-eighteenth- and early-nineteenth-century boxes were decorated by highly trained artists. Even in the latter years of the nineteenth century, some pieces were decorated with great skill. If such paintings were on canvas and framed, they would command much-higher prices. Boxes decorated in the best manner are of course hard to find, but they are worth searching for. Moreover, they are worth rescuing before they are "retouched" and "refreshed" by insensitive brushstrokes.

# CHAPTER 9 *Tunbridge Ware*

## BOXES MADE PRIMARILY IN THE AREA OF TUNBRIDGE WELLS AND TONBRIDGE IN KENT

The term "Tunbridge ware" is in many people's mind synonymous with pictorial decoration executed in micro-wood mosaic. This technique and style were adopted from the late 1820s onward by craftsmen who had been working within a tradition of fine woodwork for over two hundred years. Most surviving Tunbridge ware boxes were made during the nineteenth century and are decorated in the micro-mosaic method. However, the craftsmen working within this tradition were striving for a union of excellence between the material, the workmanship, and the artistic design of an object, and this they achieved most successfully during the pre-mosaic period. The term must therefore embrace the earlier work, as well as the later more substantial and definable output.

During the seventeenth century, the area of Kent in the vicinity of Tunbridge Wells, Speldhurst, and Tonbridge gained a degree of social prominence due to its "waters." Lord North is reputed to have been the first person to recognize the chalybeate springs in the forest near Eridge Castle. He noticed the metallic scum on the surface of the water, which reminded him of the medicinal waters of the European town of Spa, in present-day Belgium, where the well-to-do had hitherto sojourned "to take the cure." It was not long after this discovery that the Tunbridge area too became a fashionable resort. For the real and imaginary invalids, it was easier to travel to Kent than to

*Above and left:*
Figure 153. A striking whitewood box painted in gold and green on a cream ground, with a central print (with added painted color) of a musician and a lady. 13.75" wide. Ca. 1810. $8,000–10,000.

Figure 154. A turned and painted sewing box with attached tape measure holder and pincushion. 3" wide. Late eighteenth century. $1,500–2,000.

Figure 155. A small round box with pivot lid, painted with roses and with a printed label that reads "A TONBRIDGE WELLS Gift." 3" wide. Late eighteenth century. $600–1,000.

cross the Channel and trust to foreign conveyances to journey on to Spa. It was also more familiar and more likely to produce the right mixture of relaxation and social life.

The aristocracy embraced Tunbridge Wells with enthusiasm, especially after royalty gave it its approval. As early as 1630, Queen Henrietta Maria, the wife of King Charles I, visited the area and stayed for six weeks, despite the fact that there was no suitable accommodation and she and her entourage had to pitch camp at the top of Mount Ephraim. Drinking the waters was reputed to aid the production of healthy babies and the queen was as eager as any would-be mother to try the new cure.

The seventeenth century was a time of extremes. During the austere years of the Commonwealth, the people of England missed their festivals, their Christmas celebrations, their music, and their fun. Time was ripe for the return of the monarchy. Charles II breezed back onto the throne. He brought back more than just jolly times; he established a libertine court. He transformed the social mores from morality and respectability—at least on the surface—to the open and shame-free pursuit of hedonistic pleasure. Certain places attracted the well-to-do as centers of fun. In spa towns there was already a perfectly feasible excuse: health. This was not completely bogus. The waters were supposed to also cure melancholy. Perhaps it was not the waters, but the social interactions that could prove beneficial to persons with a propensity to introverted depression.

By the 1660s, the people of Tunbridge had recognized the potential for visitors and had taken steps to provide some rudimentary facilities. They were rewarded with the royal presence of Charles II, his family, and several courtiers, who considered a town visited by "society" a good spot for the pursuit of dissolute pleasure. The queen, like her predecessor, hoped that the waters would help her produce an heir. Unfortunately she was disappointed. Some other hitherto childless ladies did succeed in becoming pregnant, a phenomenon that the wits of the time celebrated in prose and verse, caustically commenting on the paternity of the babies.

The foul London air and the Great Plague were a boon to Tunbridge, which was perceived to be in a healthy and even therapeutic location. During the seventeenth century, the cottages around the area thronged with the world of fashion. In 1685, concerned about the welfare of their souls as well as their bodies, the courtiers built a church for their own use dedicated to King Charles the Martyr.

By the beginning of the eighteenth century, Tunbridge Wells was well established not just as a place for invalids, hypochondriacs, or people in need of rest and recuperation, but as a resort palpitating with sexual frisson. It became a place for socialites par excellence. Accommodation and shopping venues improved beyond recognition. Assembly rooms, coffee houses, and other meeting venues helped society to mingle. A Mrs. Bell Causey appointed herself as a questionable master of ceremonies; she was no better than a pander, but obviously the town was willing to pay for the services she provided. A bookshop was also opened. The proprietor was a Mr. Curll, a dubious

Figure 156. A box japanned in the eighteenth-century manner with gessoed and varnished surface. The top is painted in gold and colors with playing cards. The sides are painted in chinoiserie. Inside there are divisions for cards and gaming counters. 8" wide. Last quarter eighteenth century. $2,500–3,500.

Figure 157. A whitewood box painted with cottages in the countryside. This is an unusual example in that it is painted in colors. Boxes with rustic cottages were usually in black monochrome and were made during the first decades of the nineteenth century. 5" wide. $600–1,000.

character who among his other offerings stocked a varied selection of erotica and pornography.

As the eighteenth century progressed, Tunbridge Wells also attracted the marriage market. More people meant more opportunities for trade and paid-for services. Like in many spa towns, the waters could be marketed both for drinking and bathing. In 1805, a new bathhouse was opened on the Parade. It was built where the old cold baths had been, and offered treatments in cold and hot mineral waters. The building, which still stands, is in the grand neoclassical style that was fashionable at the time. Tunbridge Wells added the newly rediscovered pleasure of personal hygiene to its other attractions. Society thronged.

Flirtation and amusement were spreading from the court to a wider section of society. Genteel walks for the display of one's person, and socializing for the purpose of having one's clothes, jewels, and accomplishments admired, were more important than the mere pursuit of health. Gaming and other expensive diversions gave the opportunity to display the wealth and roguishness of the men about town.

By the middle of the eighteenth century, the reputation of the town was tinged with the excitement of possible impropriety. Mrs. Delany, advising her sister about the upbringing of her daughter, commented in a letter, "I think all public water drinking places *more pernicious* than a masquerade, and *that* I have *not* a *very good* opinion of." This is the reputation that attracted the world of fashion. Money began to flow into the area as freely as the springs. It was only natural that the craftsmen/traders of Tunbridge tried to transfer some of it from the visitors' pockets into their own.

In the early days of the visitor influx, especially during royal visits, tradespeople set up shop under the trees, selling their various wares. Many of these entrepreneurs were not local, but Londoners following their spending patrons to their places of leisure. This must have prompted the people of the town

both into developing superior selling establishments and producing more-distinctive local work to sell as souvenirs. As the eighteenth century drew to a close, Tunbridge ware began to acquire the characteristic qualities that gave it its unique appearance and desirability.

Up to that time, the wares of the area were very much in the general fashion of the country. The craftsmen made turned treen objects, or "toys" as they were called, both in local "white" woods and lignum vitae. The cabinetmakers' work was within the prevailing style of construction and decoration of the time. In 1749, Mrs. Montagu commented in her correspondence about items in the "Chinese goût" that she had seen at Tunbridge Wells.

The workmanship of the local makers was always admired and regarded as being of superior quality. Fine eighteenth-century wooden boxes and turned wares, especially in yew and

Figure 158. A box in the form of a sewing basket made from sycamore and painted with a floral design. 5.6" wide. Early nineteenth century. $1,500–2,000.

Figure 159. A whitewood box with a sliding lid having a topographical print of *The Marine Parade Brighton* and roses painted on either side. Note the similarity of the roses to those on the third box in this chapter. 10" wide. $800–1,000.

Figure 160. Detail: an illustration in Margaret A. V. Gill's book *Tunbridge Ware* shows a delightful scene of an elephant and other animals and people under a floral canopy on a box to which she gives a probable attribution to the Wise family of makers. The box is in the Tunbridge Wells Museum. The scene illustrated here is stylistically very similar to the one in the museum, both in the arrangement and the exotic feature of the floral canopy, although the central animal is a camel. It is executed in reverse penwork; that is, the background is painted, leaving the design in whitewood. This picture is on the top of a card box with tapering sides and standing on gilded feet. Box 11.5" wide. Ca. 1815–20.

holly, are very likely to have originated from the Tunbridge area. Box making flourished throughout England in the second half of the eighteenth century, when cabinetmaking achieved a high degree of refinement. It was therefore natural for a place specializing in small items, and thronged with visitors, to excel in the production of these transportable treasures.

There are references to boxes made in Tunbridge at the end of the eighteenth century that appear to have the same type of inlays—such as shells, flowers, ovals, and other fashionable motifs—used by makers in London and some of the other important centers. It is therefore not easy to identify eighteenth-century boxes as Tunbridge ware, although the predominant use of yew with fruitwood and holly inlays of high quality can be a pointer. Unusual figure and striation can also point to Tunbridge, in that the makers of the area had developed a tradition of incorporating pieces of local wood with distinctive qualities within their work. (See Figures 346, 435, 509, and 510)

The first types of Tunbridge ware boxes that can be attributed to the area with some confidence were made in sycamore, or other light woods, and painted in primary colors, depicting scenes with cottages or flowers. These boxes were mostly small, sometimes circular or in the shape of baskets. This kind of work was done in the late eighteenth century and continued into the early part of the nineteenth century. Although simple and relatively inexpensive, such items were made with meticulous attention. Their decoration was in the naive tradition of painting, and they made very charming gifts.

Some of the sycamore boxes were decorated with a central print—usually of a topographical nature—or with printed labels, and edged with painted lines. The trade card of William Fenner, dating from the last years of the eighteenth century, indicates that he sold, among other things, print-decorated ware. Judging from the date, these could have been decorated with neoclassical engravings not exclusive to makers of Tunbridge ware.

Edmund Nye used prints in the 1820s and 1830s; one example of his work dating from 1827 shows a picture of the Parade. The Parade, or the Pantiles (the name was changed at different times), was the most fashionable street in town, and the center of much of the Tunbridge ware trade. The Tunbridge family who harnessed the print-decorating business was the Wise family, who as early as the first years of the nineteenth century printed and supplied views to other makers, including scenes from other towns. The Wise family also produced views of their own manufacturing works in Tonbridge, and their repository (retail premises) at Tunbridge Wells. By this time, Tunbridge ware manufactures had seen the commercial opportunity of making souvenirs for other places—such as up-and-coming Bath, and Brighton— and even for the less fashionable resorts. Furthermore, the makers also bought prints depicting various popular subjects from Ackermann's and other London repositories.

Figure 161. A formidable feat of turning. Eleven tiny boxes, all fitting very tightly inside each other in sequence of size. The biggest box has an inlaid disk of geometric mosaic on the top; the smaller boxes are painted with thin circles. The third box has lost its lid and reveals its incredibly thin sides. There is a dressmaker's pin photographed next to the boxes, to give an idea of their size. The largest box has a diameter of just under 0.7". A real show-off piece. Early nineteenth century. $?

Figure 162. A Tunbridge ware writing slope with spaces for sewing tools and grooming containers. The main box is in rosewood veneer, and the interior is covered with the original blue paper. This is an excellent example of the relationship between the maker and his material. The juxtaposition of the woods both in the vandyke surround and the central parquetry is done with skill and sensitivity. Colors, figures, striations, and eccentric markings contrast or harmonize in a celebration of the natural beauty of the woods. The expertly inlaid corners form sharp fan shapes, giving the impression of an explosion of color and light. The respect for the wood is total. 14.25" wide. Ca. 1810. $3,500–4,500.

At the same time the boxes painted in the naive style were made, a more refined type of painted work emerged. Larger and often shaped boxes were produced mostly in the early part of the nineteenth century. These were decorated with penwork, painting, and hand-colored engravings, or a combination of any of these techniques. Once again, it is not easy to be certain that these boxes were definitely made or decorated in the Tunbridge area, since the inspirations for the pictures were often drawn from pattern books available throughout the country. There is evidence that the pioneering Wise family decorated such boxes in the typical exotic scenes and stylized flowers fashionable in the late eighteenth and early nineteenth centuries.

From the last part of the eighteenth century, and up to the second decade of the nineteenth century, some of the boxes made in light wood and decorated with combinations of print and painted decoration were fitted with sewing tools. These implements were superbly turned to the limit of the wood's tolerance. This is very characteristic of turned Tunbridge ware and was commented on as early as the last decade of the seventeenth century by Celia Fiennes, who wrote in her diary about "the delicate neate and thin ware of wood." The eighteenth- and nineteenth-century sewing tools were the result of centuries of experience and tradition.

Tunbridge makers also supplied boxes "in the white" for painters and japanners in other parts of the country, or ladies who wished to decorate their own boxes at home. By the beginning of the eighteenth century, the area was a true treasure trove for boxes and other small wooden items.

## PARQUETRY AND VANDYKE DECORATION

In the first decades of the nineteenth century, what happened in the Tunbridge area was exactly the opposite of the trend in the rest of the country. While certain strong stylistic influences were dictating both the type of decoration and the materials to be used in cabinetmaking throughout England, this small corner of Kent developed its style from available materials. The Tunbridge ware makers recognized the natural beauty of wood. They realized that by juxtaposing natural figure, color, and striation, they could achieve striking effects without the need of any other form of decoration. They even went a step further and sought out the strange and idiosyncratic, such as fungus-attacked twigs and peculiar growths, which could arouse curiosity and offer an element of surprise.

While the rest of England was concentrating on the fashionable timbers increasingly supplied in larger quantities, the men in Tunbridge relished the small and peculiar. In a way, the limited demand for these timbers by other makers made it possible for Kent craftsmen to keep their locally grown interesting woods for their own work. They had yew, cherry, holly, sycamore, furze, oak, birch, beech, fruitwoods, and smaller garden bushes that could yield the odd, interesting snippet. To these they added pieces of exotic timbers, such as rosewood, palm, ebony, zebra, purplewood, and many

*Above:*
Figure 163. A box almost completely veneered in parquetry and vandyke patterns. Note the variety of timbers and the particularly well-chosen figured fragments. 8.5" wide. Ca. 1810–20. $2,000–2,600.

others that were by now imported into England in considerable quantities.

Looking at Tunbridge ware boxes, it does not seem unreasonable to believe the claim that by the second half of the nineteenth century, the makers had a palette of over one hundred timbers, although thirty at any one time seems more realistic.

In addition to the natural colors, other effects were obtained by treating the wood in different ways. Nature had its way of providing a good emerald green by attacking fallen branches of oak, birch, or beech. After polishing or varnishing, the color looked more like leaf green, or yellowish green, depending on the depth of the fungus attack. These pieces of wood had to be found and used before they were destroyed by the fungus, which eventually rendered them soft and powdery. I have found such pieces in woodlands, but the usable parts are very rare. White or light woods, such as satinwood, sycamore, bird's-eye maple, and holly, were sometimes soaked

in the chalybeate water, which altered their color. After experimenting myself, I saw creamy woods turning to greenish, gray, yellow, and brownish. Some were very interesting "in between" colors. With the extra effect of varnish and polish, the variations were impressive. Holly was sometimes boiled in the water, a treatment that turned it white. It was then used for striking sharp contrasts. Barberry and nutmeg provided pale yellows, and "snake" effects were obtained by utilizing the quality of such woods as palm, which could retain a darker stain in the more tubular parts of its structure.

During the last years of the eighteenth century, driven by the wealth of the naturally beautiful timbers at their disposal, the Kentish makers developed the first highly characteristic and strikingly beautiful style of Tunbridge ware. This distinctive style depended for its effect on the juxtaposition of complementary timbers in geometric inlays. The main pattern was parquetry, which gave a three-dimensional effect, and "vandyke"—that is, elongated triangles. Combinations of both patterns were often used, as were variations of triangles, diamond shapes, stringings, and edgings. However, the outlines of the pieces of veneer that constituted each shape were cut so that their sides were straight. Only the figure within the wood was allowed to have curves and swirls.

It was the unparalleled range of woods used, and the masterly way in which the timbers were selected and combined, that makes boxes decorated in this way unmistakably recognizable as Tunbridge ware. The makers drew the patterns and then proceeded with the laying of the small pieces of veneer, using the contrasts and harmonies of the material with total respect for its natural qualities. The artistic judgment of the woodworkers in selecting and arranging these pieces created some of the most wonderful boxes ever made. They really are a *tour de force* of the craft.

The wood used to veneer such boxes was mostly rosewood or kingwood, and in most cases the part that was covered in parquetry or vandyke pattern was greater than the plain part. The finished product was either varnished or, by the 1820s, French polished, enhancing both the grain of the rosewood and the figuring of the various woods. This style of work continued into the beginning of the twentieth century, when the last struggling remnant of the industry finally gave up. Pieces made after about 1830 combine parquetry with micro-wood mosaic, resulting in a pretty but less robust effect. As the century progressed, smaller pieces of wood were used to compose the parquetry. These were prepared in bundles and cut transversely so as to form veneers of parquetry. This heralded the development of the micro-mosaic. The impact of perspective was weakened, and the strange striations within the woods became less striking.

*Below and left:*

Figure 164. A Rosewood veneered writing slope, the top completely veneered in parquetry. A wonderful cornucopia of markings, striations, and colors, juxtaposed with skill so as to enhance the quality of each piece. The three-dimensional effect endows the piece with depth. So as not to spoil the continuity of the pattern, the lock is fitted on the side of the box. 12" wide. Ca. 1810–20. $3,000–4,000.

## STICKWARE AND SQUARE MOSAIC

The next development in Tunbridge ware was based on the same principle as the parquetry work. Although the result looked like a miniature version of the earlier work, the technique of bundling strips together and rendering them into veneers was by now adopted universally. The method of preparing the pieces of wood for "stickware" and "mosaic" was basically the same, the main difference being that some blocks were rendered into "mosaic" veneers and other blocks turned on a lathe to create "stickware." In a way, wood prepared for stickware, or half-square mosaic, bridges the gap between the early parquetry and the later micro-mosaic method.

The technique of mosaic inlay was not new. Chequered, chevron, and other designs in alternating woods had been produced from laminated pieces of wood, ivory, and bone for centuries, especially in the countries of the Middle East. During the Renaissance, such inlays were adopted by Italian cabinet-makers. In the eighteenth century, such work found favor in England, and it was featured in the work of eminent cabinet-makers. A backgammon board attributed to Thomas Chippendale is inlaid with mosaic work. The *Dictionary of English Furniture Makers* lists a celebrated German cabinet-maker, Abraham Roentgen, who moved to London around 1733, where according to a family chronicle he specialized in "engraving, making mosaics in wood and producing mechanical devices and was sought after by the most expert masters." So by the time mosaic work was adopted by Tunbridge ware makers, it had already outgrown its experimental stage.

The Kentish craftsmen moreover did have the advantage of access to a great selection and variety of woods, enabling them to produce more ambitiously complex patterns. The mosaic was produced not as a form of decoration, but as the main veneer for the whole, or most of the surface of an item. This veneer was prepared in the following way:

*Triangular, diamond shaped, square, or other straight cut sticks of wood in contrasting colors were carefully assembled, glued, and bound together to a pre-designed pattern. When the design necessitated several layers of wood pieces, the gluing was done in stages. The core was allowed to dry before another layer was attached. When the pattern was complete, the glue dry, and the rod completely stable, it was sliced into transverse sections and rendered into veneers. The patterns were round, diamond shaped, or square. They were used either as single entities, in continuous lines as borders, or arranged to form other designs.*

Technically this process required expert handling. The sticks had to be glued very close together and kept in a straight line. Building up of the block often took considerable time, with each layer allowed to set before the next layer was added. Hot animal glue was used to adhere the bundles of sticks together. At least twelve hours was allowed for the liquid to be absorbed into the wood, so that the wooden components became a stable entity. Each block was kept to no more than about seven inches long to avoid wavering. To be able to apply maximum pressure, each small bundle was bound with wet string, which tightened as it dried. The slicing of the block into veneers had to be carefully done to avoid the parts separating. The block was sliced with a saw, each inch yielding, at best, eight slices of veneer and some sawdust waste. The resulting pieces of veneer were then inlaid, or simply stuck side by side on the pine carcass of the box to form the required design. The box was then carefully sanded and polished.

Figure 165. A Rosewood veneered box with geometric patterns in pieces of interesting woods. Most unusually there is also a heart pattern. The interior has spaces for two packs of cards and a cribbage board. The hearts and diamonds perhaps represent suits of playing cards. Alternatively, the box was perhaps made or commissioned as a valentine gift. 8.5" wide. Ca. 1800. $1,400–1,600.

*Right:*
Figure 166. A Rosewood veneered box inlaid with elongated diamond shapes to form a stylized flower. This is an unusual cut developed from the vandyke and the parquetry principle. The dramatic juxtaposition of color in a circular arrangement, and the way the pattern ends in well-defined points, give this piece vitality, elegance, and originality. 9.5" wide. Ca. 1800. $3,000–3,500.

*Above:*

Figure 167. A small box veneered all around with different geometric patterns of mosaic, exploding into a star design. This is a good example of the use of contrasting color. The box is labeled as the work of Edmund Nye. Second quarter nineteenth century. $600–800.

Alternatively, the prepared rods were turned to make small objects or "toys" of stickware. This was primarily done with blocks that had been prepared in the round by using end-grain sticks. The reason for end grain is that it results in more-stable rods that are more suitable for turning. It was of paramount importance that the rods to be turned were prepared with the utmost precision, so they could withstand the vicissitudes of the lathe. If the center of the "toy" was to be hollow, the stickware block was prepared on a core of wood that was then removed. Sewing implements and pens were made in stickware, and they were sold singly or as contents in sewing boxes and writing slopes. These are found in boxes dating from the 1820s to well into the nineteenth century.

The geometric mosaic was mostly, but not exclusively, used for small boxes, which can be handled easily. The fragments of the wood being small, the figure is not as striking as in the earlier patterns and can be better appreciated when examined from a short distance. This work has an almost textural appeal, and when used in a continuous line, it looks like a border of luxurious embroidery of rich natural colors.

Boxes dating from around 1830 are often decorated with parquetry, vandyke, and geometric mosaic in different combinations. Boxes from the first two decades of the century feature parquetry and vandyke patterns. The background wood in boxes dating from the 1830s and 1840s is usually rosewood. The shapes are rectangular or in Egyptian-inspired sarcophagus forms.

## TESSELLATED MICRO-MOSAIC

The late 1820s saw the development of what is the universally recognized small-wood-mosaic Tunbridge ware technique. The wood quality utilized for this form of decoration was color, not figure or markings. By the 1830s, micro-mosaic marquetry became very popular, and it remained so to the end of the nineteenth century. The mosaic was made by sticking together thin rods of wood, following a preselected pattern. The purpose was to create a pictorial representation by matching the color of different woods to the color of the design. When set, the block was sliced in veneers, all of which repeated the same picture. The veneers were then applied to the boxes singly, as central decoration, or repetitively to form borders. The result was that the box looked as if it was decorated with inlaid tesserae of wood.

This technique necessitated very accurately cut sticks. It also demanded great care in their assembly, so as to keep the design sharp from one end of the rod to the other. The patterns were drawn on graph paper and painted in appropriate colors, much like petit point embroidery. The instructions for the use of the correct woods were sometimes given in greater detail, depending on the experience of the craftsman and the complexity of the pattern. From about 1840 to 1860, floral borders were very much in vogue, and for these Berlin woolwork patterns were frequently used, causing the work to be referred to

*Above:*
Figure 168. Rosewood Tunbridge ware box of Egyptian-inspired sarcophagus form, the lid with a cavetto molding. The sides and top are inlaid with parquetry created by the stickware method. This type of inlay combines color and figure in small pieces of wood to give the decoration a rich textural effect. This subtle look, which utilized shades of brown from the lightest to the darkest, was short lived. The box stands on turned solid-rosewood feet. 10.2" wide. Ca. 1820. $1,500–2,000.

as "Berlin woolwork design." These designs were published in Berlin from about 1804 and were imported into England by Ackermann. However, it was a certain Mr. Wilks who boosted the popularity of "Berlin patterns . . . used in Decorative needlework." He sold them from his needlework shop in fashionable Regent Street, boasting a stock of hundreds of designs! The "Berlin" borders continued to be embroidered and to be made into Tunbridge ware for several decades.

The new mosaic was based on a completely different mindset from early work produced in the area of Tunbridge. Eighteenth and early nineteenth century inlay utilized the beauty of the wood; later work saw wood as a palette of color—an artistic medium, rather than a work of art in its own right. The new designs tapped into a growing Victorian need for pretty ornament. The Victorians rejected the earlier neoclassical rendition of flora and fauna and looked closer to home for their inspiration and comfort. Naturalistic Tunbridge ware representations became very popular, ranging from flowers, birds, and butterflies to children, dogs, mice, men, horses, and deer.

As the nineteenth century progressed into the Victorian era, the clientele for Tunbridge ware changed. Bath and Brighton had stolen the edge on fashion early on in the century. During the mid-nineteenth century, Tunbridge had to cater to a more general type of person and adapt its wares to suit the expanding and increasingly prosperous middle classes. The new visitors demanded more respectability and a more accessible aesthetic. By now Tunbridge had built an infrastructure for entertaining tourists, and also selling them beautiful wooden items, predominantly boxes. The townspeople had to adapt to the needs of the new, faster age, and the new fashion for familiar adornment and home landmarks.

There is no doubt as to the commercial acumen of the Tunbridge ware makers. They produced everything a good English person could want: St. George, a boy in kilt, the Prince of Wales's feathers, a spaniel, castles, and beloved Queen Victoria's head on a stamp box. And to crown it all, a picture of the Parade or Pantiles, the prestigious Tunbridge shopping street where many of them traded their wares! Imagine having the shopping mall on your precious box, or hanging on your wall!

This is not to say that the Tunbridge ware makers were letting go completely of their stronghold on excellence. It is true that the range widened, and most of the work became uninspired, but there was still high quality at the top. Early on, the people of Tunbridge had realized the royal potential. In 1826, the townsfolk subscribed to a table to be presented as a gift to the young princess, whose mother was already a Tunbridge

Figure 169. A selection of sewing tools that demonstrate how the mosaic blocks were used both for veneers and for turning. Note how the waxer and the spool are of "stickware." Note the light core wood around which the rods were built and then turned. In the case of the spool, some of the core wood was removed on the lathe, and a disc of mosaic was inlaid in the center. Such tools were made for sewing boxes throughout the nineteenth century.

Figure 170. This is either a repair or an experiment. A section of a few inches of mosaic inlay on the inside of the Indian-made box, figure 277, has been made with boxwood and ebony rather than the ivory and ebony used in the rest of the inlay. The straight cut mark showing that the ivory ebony was the original is clear. Is this an example of Tunbridge work repair (?) on an earlier Indian *sadeli* box?

Figure 171. A very fine example of the virtuosity of a talented craftsman. This box looks at first sight like a vandyke pattern in alternative triangles of light woods and ebony. However, in every ebony piece there is an inlaid design of an upside-down plume executed in micro-mosaic. A fine and most unusual touch. 9" wide. Ca. 1835. $3,000-4,000.

ware fan. Edmund Nye, Mr. Sharp, and James Friend joined in the fray. The lot fell to Mr. William Fenner, who by all accounts made a magnificent example of the local woodwork.

Mr. Nye had his day at the Great Exhibition of 1851, when he exhibited a magnificent workbox "ornamented with devices in wood mosaic" with a view of Bayham Abbey, reputed to contain 15,000 pieces of tesserae. He also exhibited a book stand and two tables, one of which featured a scene of a sailing ship "of 110,800 pieces of wood, of home and foreign growth, in their natural color." The picture was reputed to have been designed and executed by Thomas Barton. The book stand featured two butterflies, one of 11,000 pieces and the other of 13,000, again in their natural colors. The butterflies represented two distinctive species described by the manufacturer.

The Great Exhibition—the apotheosis of the Victorian era—featured other important Tunbridge ware, including a workbox and writing desk by H. Hollamby and a workbox by R. Russell.

In pictorial mosaic work, contrasting colors of wood were used carefully to create well-defined scenes or floral compositions. The wealth of timber varieties available, combined with the great skill of the Tunbridge ware craftsmen, made this possible. Unlike Italian Sorrentoware, the timbers used were mostly in their natural color. When the color was enhanced by using natural and chemical processes, the woods retained their vitality. In the hands of master craftsmen who created the best examples of the work, the medium of wood mosaic was used with imagination to create lively pictures of three-dimensional effect. Occasionally a truly masterful representation full of movement and vigor proves that even the inflexible medium of wood can acquire life in the hands of a virtuoso.

During the middle and latter part of the nineteenth century, the timbers used as background veneers for the boxes were varied. Rosewood was still predominant and walnut was a close second, with bird's-eye maple, fruitwoods, ebony, and other woods also in use.

The mosaic technique is a very interesting example of the aptitude of the Tunbridge ware craftsmen to assimilate and adapt techniques and designs from other traditions. Stone mosaics were uncovered in the much-talked-about excavations of the eighteenth century. Mosaic-covered boxes were known in England by the end of the eighteenth century, by which time exquisite *sadeli* mosaic work had already been introduced from India.

The Tunbridge ware makers must have studied and understood the principle of this technique, since geometric wood mosaic is an adaptation of the method of *sadeli* mosaic. The

Figure 172. A Rosewood veneered box with a distinctive and symmetrical enclosed design. The border design too is more stylized than most Tunbridge ware of the period. This work is characteristic of the work of Alfred Talbot, who was active between 1844 and 1858. The controlled pattern required a very skillful combination of timbers in order to emerge with sharp and clear definition. A pleasing and successful use of micro-mosaic. The base is covered in tartan paper, another feature of this maker's work. 8.5" wide. $1,000–1,400.

*Above and right:*

Figure 173. A Rosewood veneered tea caddy of very pleasing form with concave sides and slightly domed lid, standing on turned feet. The decoration combines very pretty elements in the characteristic mid-nineteenth-century tradition. It has bands of micro-mosaic, including a wide band of Berlin woolwork design, encircling the whole box in leaves and flowers. The center of the top is in light wood and features a micro-mosaic boy in a kilt, with hawk and spaniel. Speculation has named him as one of the royal children, perhaps the Prince of Wales. The fashion for wearing a kilt was promoted by Victoria's children, so this could have been a shrewd design decision. Whatever the case, he looks happy. Third quarter nineteenth century. $4,500–6,500.

later micro-mosaic is a further development, rejecting geometric pattern and adopting Berlin woolwork and naturalistic representations to create an altogether different effect.

There has always been controversy about who was the first Tunbridge ware maker to make wood mosaic. William Burrows is one of the contenders; his grandson claimed that it was one of their apprentices who introduced the new method to the Wise family. Others, pointing to the Italian names on local gravestones, support the theory that it was introduced by Italian workers who brought the technique from their native Sorrento. It is not certain that the Italian work predates Tunbridge micro-mosaic.

The truth is that the time was ripe for this method to come into fruition. There were pointers both in work imported from other countries and in the materials available. Like all innovations, it was a gradual set of steps that resulted in the final breakthrough.

The reason that in my opinion *sadeli* mosaic work acted as the catalyst is because early-period *sadeli*, which was first brought to England in the late eighteenth century, was rightly held in high regard. It was seen both as precious and prestigious. It found a place in the highest echelons of society, including the royal household. These were the very circles the Tunbridge ware makers liked to claim as their own. The natural step was to study this serious competition and come up with an alternative.

As it came to pass, Victorian taste and the patriotic spirit of the mid- and later nineteenth century favored the Kent wares over the more exotic imports. Victorians liked pretty pictures. They also liked birds and insects. Books on entomology, botany, and the picturesque were produced and perused avidly. Natural

gardens that could be sustained without the expense of designer/gardeners were becoming fashionable. A cult of flower symbolism was cultivated in greeting cards, the newfound way of keeping in touch with friends. Perhaps it was all tinged with sentimentality, but it was an accessible and human yardstick to use when deciding on taste. Victorians adopted comfort and familiarity in applied arts as a form of style.

The Tunbridge ware makers responded splendidly. The Burrows family devised the bird and butterfly motifs from the very beginning of the new micro-mosaic method. Others adopted such subjects, including of course Edmund Nye in his spectacular exhibition example. Flowers, including the very English rose, the symbol-laden pansy, the spectacular lily, oak leaves, and thistles all were transposed into Tunbridge ware.

During the second half of the nineteenth century, topographical views became fashionable. Recognizable and visited scenes fulfilled the need for high quality souvenirs. In pursuit of satisfying the desire for the romance of the Gothic past, the Kentish makers set about producing pictures of castles, great houses, romantic landmarks, and ruined abbeys. These represent accurate and painstaking work, but most of them lack the vitality of the best of the designs inspired by moving, ephemeral subjects. One early heroic effort was made by Fennel and Nye to produce a picture of Battle Abbey, graduating the size of the tesserae so as to create the correct perspective. This was a truly successful attempt, but it obviously proved too time consuming to be repeated.

Before abandoning the work in wood of the Tunbridge ware makers, a word must be said about "marbled veneer." This looks like a piece of wood with uneven, swirly lines drawn on it. It was done by first gluing veneers of wood in layers, then

Figure 174. A good micro-mosaic view of Hever Castle, attributable to Henry Hollamby. This was used on rectangular boxes as well as writing slopes. Ca. 1860–70.

Figure 175. One of the most lively micro-mosaic designs, again attributable to Henry Hollamby. Ca. 1860–70.

Figure 176. A Rosewood veneered tea caddy with an enclosed symmetrically circling design on top, and bands of controlled micro-mosaic floral patterns all around. The top is framed with a border that depicts a fine plant behind an angular pattern, suggestive of a Greek key. The whole design faintly harks back to the control of neoclassicism. The base is covered in tartan paper. Attributable to Alfred Talbot. 9" wide. Ca. 1860. $1,500–2,000.

forcing them into contorted shapes by using moisture and heat. The resulting blocks were then cut into transverse veneers, revealing thin striations of different woods. The technique was most probably inspired by the reports of experiments in papier-mâché work. This work was a short-lived experiment, probably because it did not prove very popular with customers.

In 1867, methods for applying photographs to enamel and wood were patented. A few pieces of Tunbridge ware were made featuring a central photograph with a wood mosaic border, and these, although of no great artistic merit, are interesting curiosities encapsulating that particular phase of the century.

Tunbridge ware flourished for many decades, until the introduction of boxes inlaid with pre-prepared geometric bands, which were less costly and became widely available. These boxes were produced for specific purposes and suited the needs of the middle classes, who by now had considerable spending power. Tunbridge ware continued to be made into the first two decades of the twentieth century, and from time to time, including now, there are attempts at "revivals." However, there is neither the infrastructure of wood gatherers and craftsmen cooperation nor the time necessary for such time-consuming work. Furthermore, the social structure that gave the industry its lifeline is gone. The lifeless offerings of the twentieth century, most of which are "off the shelf" machine-generated inlays, make us appreciate all the more the best of the earlier work.

The woodworkers in the Tunbridge ware area established their own distinctive identity during the eighteenth century. However, there was a small anomaly dating from the 1870s, when Thomas Barton introduced decalcomanie, a form of printed ware similar to that produced in Scotland. Presumably this attempt, together with attempts by Barton and Hollamby to promote fern ware, was in response to the increasing competition from Scottish ware, which was produced inexpensively and sold in large numbers. The Barton items were attractive, and are reminiscent of earlier Scottish ware before the advent of mass-produced Mauchline ware. Thus forced by competition, Tunbridge lost its identity once again. The end was in view.

*Below and left:*
Figure 177. A box veneered in bird's-eye maple with a micro-mosaic butterfly inlay on the top, and geometric mosaic borders and bands. The pattern on the sides is a good example of this type of work, which has an almost textural quality. The box is well designed, with the butterfly punctuating the center and breaking the austerity of the overall geometric design. 8" wide. Ca. 1840. $1,200–1,500.

# Notable Makers

It is very difficult to single out notable makers of Tunbridge ware, since the different firms often created partnerships, apprentices changed bosses, and there must have been a lot of copying of ideas. Furthermore, it is not until the more commercially minded nineteenth century that we find most labeled work, or detailed records. The early makers of fine-turned work and striking inlays must of necessity remain unsung.

Another problem is the extent of the Tunbridge ware manufacture. It was probably first made in Speldhurst but soon expanded to nearby Tonbridge, and Tunbridge Wells, where it flourished. In addition to this area of Kent, two cabinetmakers working on the south coast also made mosaic ware in the Tunbridge style. London makers too claimed to be suppliers of Tunbridge ware. It is not easy to be certain what was meant by Tunbridge ware, since the pre-nineteenth-century style was not distinguishable from other work, and until the advent of the micro-mosaic there was confusion of terms. Thus, Tunbridge ware in the eighteenth century could be used to describe professionally made wooden boxes and "toys." To complicate matters even further, London cabinetmakers also stocked other makers' wares if they thought them to be a good commercial proposition. It is therefore futile to try to produce a complete map of the industry. I shall therefore list only some of the makers who formed the core and contributed to the development of the work during the nineteenth century.

What we must keep in mind is that all these firms were highly commercial, especially during the nineteenth century, and that they produced work of varied quality. When buying, the first concern must be to consider if a box was made with artistic and professional integrity, whatever the name of the maker or the firm he worked for.

**Russell, Robert:** A maverick among Tunbridge ware makers was Robert Russell, who developed his own version of marquetry. This was reminiscent of ecclesiastical neo-Gothic patterns and was used either on its own or in conjunction with mosaic work. In an 1863 advertisement he claimed his new marquetry to be of "superior character." Either the "gentry" and "nobility" he addressed himself to were not convinced of this new departure of style, or Russell made a limited number of objects. In either case, not many pieces of Russell's specific work have survived. Russell was a successful maker, patronized by the Duchess of Kent, and as we have seen, an exhibitor in the Great Exhibition. Russell claimed to have cultivated the cooperation of local gardeners to obtain unusual snippets of wood. This may well have been true, but in my opinion it must apply to all good makers, as the work testifies.

**Wise:** Probably the oldest established family of makers, dating to the seventeenth century. Patronized by royalty, and successful traders and exporters to the United States of America. They appear to be in the forefront of the earlier white wood wares, although they also worked in the later styles. The "marbled" veneer probably originated from Wise.

**Fenner:** A firm that started in 1720 and continued until 1840, working in all disciplines of the ware. For a period of time they went into partnership with Nye. This was dissolved in 1825, after which time the two firms traded separately.

**Nye, Edmund:** Nye was very successful during the first half of the nineteenth century. He seems to have continued the tradition of Fenner, which was in turn continued by Barton after Nye's death in 1863.

**Barton, Thomas:** Apprenticed first to Wise, he joined Nye around 1836. Very talented both as a designer and business man, he continued Nye's business. He had the good sense to label a lot of his wares. He died in 1902 after a very successful life.

**Burrows:** Another dynastic family dating from the seventeenth or early eighteenth century. At the height of the work four brothers were involved: William, James, George, and Humphrey, the last named numbering Queen Victoria among his patrons. William was named as the inventor of the mosaic technique by a later member of the family, although James and George, who were in partnership, advertised it as their own invention. James Burrows is also credited with the early birds and butterflies. The brothers were not active after 1850.

**Hollamby, Henry:** An apprentice of George and James Burrows, he set up his own business in 1842 and bought the stock of his former employers when they retired. His commercial acumen was prodigious, selling wholesale and exporting the work of his forty employees. He was responsible for many of the topographical scenes of buildings. One of his most successful mosaic designs was the "hawk."

**Boyce, Brown, and Kemp:** Set up in 1873. Bought what was left of Hollamby's stock after a fire destroyed Hollamby's premises. They made much more use of mechanized processes. Continued the tradition of mosaic castles and other buildings.

**James Friend and Friend and Allen:** Second to third quarters of the nineteenth century. James must have been a noted maker, since he was one of the four contestants for Princess Victoria's table.

*Above and left:*
Figure 178. A card and cribbage box veneered in walnut. It has a micro-mosaic picture of Eastnor Castle within floral borders. The sides too are banded in a wide Berlin woolwork floral design. The escutcheon is cleverly made out of a geometric mosaic circle. The cribbage board has a fine micro-mosaic floral line in the center. This is a good typical example of a box richly decorated with a landmark and also wide floral borders. Third quarter nineteenth century. $4,000–6,000.

ortoiseshell, which is in most cases the shell of the hawksbill turtle, is a material whose many natural qualities render it ideal for the making of small precious objects, such as boxes. It was used in Europe and many of the European colonies from the seventeenth century onwards, both for inlaid decoration and for making or covering complete pieces.

Tortoiseshell was used in two forms: solid form and in thin veneers. Most tortoiseshell boxes date from the end of the eighteenth century, and these were made by applying tortoiseshell veneer onto a wooden structure.

As a material tortoiseshell is very malleable, a quality that enables craftsmen to mold it, impress it, and decorate it in different ways with a great degree of success. To shape tortoiseshell, the material was immersed in hot water with a little olive oil added, so as not to dry out its natural oils. When soft it was removed, placed between the two halves of a copper mold, and pressed. Because the shell tended to cool fast, more ambitious designs were achieved by plunging the shell into water already in the mold, and pressing the two halves of the mold together when the shell became pliable. An iron weight was then placed on it, and the whole thing was removed from the water and allowed to dry. This method required more skill and precision, but it had the advantage of enabling fine details to be impressed on the material. It was therefore used more for decorative patterns, rather than simply curving or vaulting.

A very effective way of decorating tortoiseshell was *piqué* work. *Piqué* is of two kinds: *piqué posé* and *piqué clouté*, or *point*.

*Piqué posé* consists of inlay of thinly cut designs of gold, silver, or both set into the shell. *Piqué clouté* consists of gold or silver pins inlaid so as to form delicate patterns. *Piqué posé* and *piqué clouté* were occasionally used to decorate the same piece, *piqué clouté* sometimes forming diaper patterns within border scrolls or arabesques around the main design. Mother of pearl was also used in conjunction with *piqué*, especially in European work of the first half of the eighteenth century.

*Piqué* work appeared in Italy, France, England, Germany, and possibly other northern European countries by the beginning of the eighteenth century. Naples is considered the birthplace of *piqué*, and the artist/jeweler Laurentini is credited with the development of this particular technique in the last years of the seventeenth century. It is the nature of tortoiseshell, which responds fast to heat and cold, that prompted this method of decoration. A small hole or groove was made in the shell. This incision was heated either by the fast blow of a hammer or by branding the shell with the pattern of the design. The dot of metal or the cut strip was then inserted and the shell was allowed to cool around it, holding it in place. This required speed and precision, both in cutting and the insertion of the precut pattern.

Boxes decorated with *piqué* work dating from the first half of the eighteenth century are of fine workmanship and are now rare. It is very difficult to ascertain their nationality with absolute certainty, aesthetic trends being at that time of a pan-European nature. A few pointers can help an informed

*Above and right:*
Figure 179. This is a small box with big action. In a combination of incised ivory and tortoiseshell, the craftsman/artist depicts scenes of rural life. People and animals interact, move, and run. The buildings and trees provide a background to life. Details are delineated with fine lines. I had to refer to furniture to try to place this interest-packed box. I think it is Spanish dating from the first half of the eighteenth century. 5.5" wide. $?

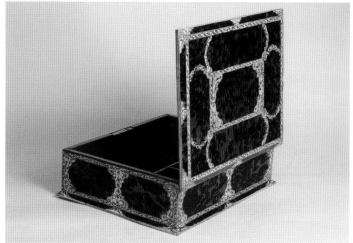

*Above:*

Figure 180. A hardwood box veneered in tortoiseshell, the panels consisting of cartouche forms framed in incised ivory. The box is of the typical early European form, but the veneering and decoration demonstrate early manifestations of exotic aesthetic. The tortoiseshell is backed with metal foil, which gives it a rich, golden glow. It is secured both with glue and tiny pins. The framing of each piece betrays the Moorish influence on Spanish art and architecture. The way the shaped ivory combines round lines that culminate in pointed peaks derives from Islamic art. The floral-incised and lacquered decoration is reminiscent of the Mughal interest in plants, which found expression in much of the designs in their art and architecture. This box encapsulates a brief moment in time in a delightful marriage of gravitas and exoticism. Indo-Portuguese. 14" wide. Ca. 1700.

guess, but certainty is elusive. Mother of pearl with *piqué* in a rococo style was most probably made in Italy, whereas grotesques or animals were more characteristic of German or Dutch work. Putti (angels) are also characteristic of Italian work. Heraldic and decorative work in *piqué clouté* could point to France, as could scenes with figures in *piqué posé*. *Piqué posé* representing legends points to Germany or England. So few examples of these have survived that sometimes we have to look at the hardware to help with our guesswork, and even this is not a completely conclusive test.

In addition to gold and silver used as inlaid decoration, gold and silver foils were sometimes applied to the back of tortoiseshell to give it an additional warm, golden glow. This was done when the shell was used as a veneer, the thinness of the material allowing the metal to shine through the lighter, more transparent parts. This method was also used when tortoiseshell was employed as one of the materials in complex structures or inlays, in conjunction with wood, precious metals, ivory, and horn. Since this was a costly way to back the shell, there are precious few examples of it surviving in boxes, and once again the origins are not easy to determine.

The *piqué* decorative work on eighteenth century tortoiseshell boxes belongs to the discipline of the jeweler's art. Hardware such as feet or handles was made by skilled silversmiths. Tortoiseshell boxes of this period and style are without exception of outstanding quality and artistic merit.

During the years between the middle of the eighteenth century up to about 1780, very few large tortoiseshell boxes were made. The precious material was saved for small objects, such as snuffboxes, patch boxes, or nécessaires.

As the eighteenth century was entering its last decade, there was renewed interest in larger items made of tortoiseshell. The

fashion for the box as a style item had already been established, so veneering in this beautifully marked shell was a natural step. Furthermore, the *beau monde*, who had already been introduced to the aesthetic delights of the East, had acquired a taste for exotic culinary delicacies such as the flesh of turtles. It was a great luxury—one portion costing as much as a week's wages for a skilled man—but in the climate of the times this proved to be part of the desirability of such fare. The turtles were kept in the water in which they had been imported for up to three months, ready to be served during the "turtle dinner" banquets of the rich. Changing the water was considered detrimental to the flavor. The popularity of such dinners must have provided additional material for tortoiseshell veneers, which were transformed into mementos of the main protagonists of the feast.

Up to the middle years of the eighteenth century, the main importer to Europe of tortoiseshell and ivory was the Dutch East India Company, which also imported cabinets and boxes already made in the colonies. By 1780, the British trading companies were becoming increasingly aggressive, and both turtles and tortoiseshell, which was obtained from species in Asian waters, were imported in larger quantities into England. This encouraged English craftsmen into making tortoiseshell-covered boxes—especially tea caddies—in ever-increasing numbers.

The boxes made between 1780 and 1810 show a total appreciation of the natural beauty of the material. They are of simple shape, with straight lines in the typical neoclassical tradition of the time. This enabled the makers to maximize the effect of the natural color, figure, and striations in the shell. The shell was used in flat pieces, often matching the figure of two panels in "book match" fashion. The wooden structure of the box was gessoed in white before the thin shell veneer was applied, so

*This whole page:*

Figure 181. A very serious boulle-work box in the manner of Jean Bérain. It is executed mainly in red tortoiseshell and brass with touches of green in two insects and yellow in two stylized flowers. The central part is in engraved silver. The composition is robust, incorporating a wealth of association and cultural reference. The central figure is that of Hercules confronting the Hydra. The work is executed both in *première-partie* and *contre-partie*, the two methods skillfully juxtaposed to strengthen the design by contrasting texture and color. The brass and the silver are engraved, but so is the shell, continuing the line of the pattern or giving more detail and definition. The feet are in the shape of harpy faces, which add to the mythical gravitas of the piece. 15" wide. Mid-eighteenth century. $20,000–30,000.

*This whole page:*

Figure 182. A box made of thick, laminated tortoiseshell with *piqué* and mother of pearl inlay. The central picture is derived from classical legend, with a girl (Persephone?) seemingly being abducted. A gold chariot is awaiting in the sky. Winged cupids hover about, as does a remarkably ethereal golden butterfly. The scene is framed in rococo scrolls executed in engraved mother of pearl, *piqué pose*, and *piqué point/clouté* in gold. The same work forms scrolls and cartouches all around the box. The gold points are very tiny and extremely well arranged in different diaper patterns. The catch is in a different-colored gold, and so are the strap hinges. There is a central division in the box, as in a tea caddy, but no lids. A very fine piece with characteristic rococo whimsical lightness of composition. 6" wide. Italian, Naples, 1740. $?

*Above and right:*
Figure 183. A tortoiseshell-veneered box backed with silver foil, which gives the surface an overall golden glow. Most of the decoration is in engraved *piqué posé*, with *piqué point* used very effectively to provide fine detail. There are hovering insects executed in tiny points of silver and also fine leaves. The main scene looks as if it is taking place on land next to water, with the impression of reflections of flora executed in *piqué point*. The scene is in the classical tradition, with suppliant women kneeling in front of soldiers. A standing soldier is leaning on a rococo shape suggesting a piece of armor. An exquisite piece of work. 9" wide. Most probably English, ca. 1750. $?

Figure 184. A large Dutch colonial box in thick, laminated tortoiseshell. It is mounted in pierced silver, with silver handles, escutcheon, handle, and feet. An impressive example of such work. The Dutch established early links with the Far East and brought some of the first tortoiseshell boxes to Europe. Such boxes were not backed by wood or metal. Seventeenth century. *Courtesy of the Bielstein Collection.* $9,000–10,000.

Figure 185. A silver, foil-backed, tortoiseshell-veneered box, with a silver decorative strip secured by small pins all around. It has both central and side handles, very fine strap hinges, and classical half-figure feet. A very attractive piece, difficult to place and date. Of European origin, possibly Dutch. Eighteenth century. *Courtesy of the Bielstein Collection.* $6,000–8,000.

that the color contrast between the light and dark markings was emphasized. The effect was beautifully subtle.

Shapes for caddies were rectangular, hexagonal, or polygonal, with a flat or occasionally pyramidal top. Since the size of the shell was restricting the size of the possible panels, thin pieces of metal were sometimes used to separate "book-matched" patterns on larger caddies. Infrequently a double caddy was made by using bigger pieces of shell to cover the entire surface of the larger panels. This presented the full sweep of the shell pattern with its exquisitely feathery effect uncut and undisturbed.

Flat sewing boxes were also made during this period, and these have four or more matched panels on the top, separated by metal lines. The larger ones also have a border, again separated by metal strips.

Basically, the larger the box, the more it needed to use decorative tricks to accommodate the natural size of the shell.

Sometimes the gesso was colored with ground powder pigment made from semiprecious stones, giving the tortoiseshell veneer a green or red color. The green can vary from blue green to yellow green and the red from red to orange, depending on the shell and pigment colors. Such boxes are rarer than boxes in natural color. These too were always made in very simple shapes with strictly straight lines. The aesthetic criteria of the late eighteenth century could not have allowed for curvature to obscure the beauty of the natural material on such small objects.

During this early period, the decoration was restricted to simple silver or silver-plated escutcheons, central plates, loop handles, or small finials. Thin ivory edging lines and facings were also used, although very early boxes have boxwood facings. Metal lines between plates of shell are not always found on the earliest examples.

Another form of decoration was a design allowing for formal neoclassical elements to be introduced with a different color, small mother of pearl dots, or both.

# 1810—1830

As the earlier Georgian period was giving way to the influence of later neoclassical forms, different shapes and styles began to emerge in tortoiseshell-covered boxes. The green color was dropped, and the emphasis was no longer on maximizing the effect of the shell pattern. This enabled shells of less distinctive figure to be used, since matching became less important. The most important feature of the shell—its natural beauty—was thus obscured.

Tea caddies were made in straight or sarcophagus shapes with such features as carved edgings, pagoda-shaped tops, stepped lids, and pediments. Unlike their predecessors, which had a flat base, these stood on ivory or silver-plated feet.

A few triple-large tea chests standing on gilded feet with gilded handles were made around the second and third decades of the nineteenth century. These are of sarcophagus, and

Figure 186. A single tea caddy veneered in blond tortoiseshell and edged in ivory. This is a good example of a Georgian piece, which demonstrates the elegance of a well-proportioned form, covered in beautifully figured shell. The center of the pyramid top is punctuated by a small, flat square of silver. Understated quality and beauty were features of eighteenth-century tortoiseshell caddies. Ca. 1790. *Courtesy of Ian Gouldsbrough.* $5,000–7,000.

Figure 187. A caddy veneered in "book-matched" shell with flat silver plaque. Another beautifully subtle early piece. Ca. 1790. $5,500–8,000.

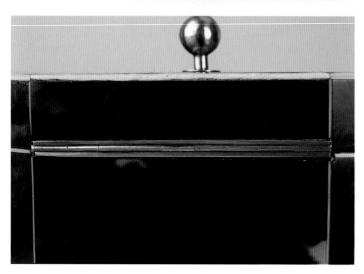

*Above:*

Figure 188. A ten-sided caddy with ivory edging and silver mounts. The central cartouche and ball finial are encircled in delicate *piqué point*. The piece is very much within the neoclassical tradition, well proportioned and with central ornament. The hinge, which is very fine, is in a continuous line. Elegant caddies of this form and proportions were made both in tortoiseshell and ivory. 6" wide. Ca. 1790–1800. $13,000–17,000.

sometimes slightly bombe shape. On account of their size, these have three panels of shell joined up at the front. Although glamorous, this design was short lived, probably because the triple joining proved difficult to achieve successfully with a material of variable figure.

Slightly later, from about 1825, the shapes and decoration of tortoiseshell boxes became more varied and complex. More stepped spreading supports were used, with serpentine, bombe, concave, sarcophagus, and other forms. The more successful examples derive from the cultural references of the time, such as combinations of pagoda tops with more "organic" bombe shapes, or architectural elements of Egyptian influence.

As the nineteenth century progressed toward the Victorian era, the shapes became somewhat detached from their design origins. The makers seemed to show off their ability to mold and polish the shell, sometimes ignoring the aesthetic justification for doing so.

The general decorative techniques introduced in the second and third decades of the nineteenth century were also applied to tortoiseshell boxes. Mother of pearl was the main medium used for embellishing tortoiseshell, and inlays of flowers and birds were popular from around 1820. Some inlays feature small pieces of pearl representing flowers, birds, and other designs interlinked with lines of silver or white metal. Larger designs in mother of pearl were engraved, giving more depth and detail to the composition. Whimsy chinoiserie designs endowed the boxes with a charming period look.

Another decorative technique that took advantage of the pliability of tortoiseshell was embossing, using the heat-and-mold method. Pieces dating from the Regency period were embossed with simple sunray designs, radiating from the center of the front and top panels. Later, in the middle of the nineteenth century, as the Gothic revival was gaining ground, patterns of ecclesiastical arches with more-complex borders were favored. These have very fine detail, which must have necessitated dexterity and mastery of this particular decorative technique.

Some pre-1840 tortoiseshell boxes were decorated in fine silver *piqué* work. Later in the nineteenth and very early twentieth centuries, tortoiseshell boxes were mounted with embossed silver decoration. During the last decades of the nineteenth and the beginning of the twentieth centuries, tortoiseshell was also used as a veneer on silver for decorative smaller boxes. Most of these have *piqué posé* swags of flowers. Tortoiseshell reverted once again to the silversmith.

Figure 190. A caddy of slightly rounded top with ball feet and finial. Still within the elegant neoclassical tradition, but moving toward a more glamorous form. Similar to an example with the label of J. Smith. Ca. 1810. $7,000–9,000.

Figure 191. A caddy showing a further attempt at a rounder shape, but still in restrained, elegant lines. Ca. 1810–20. $6,500–8,000.

*Above:*
Figure 189. A caddy veneered in tortoiseshell on a gessoed ground treated to give a green final color. The piece is in the elegant lines of the period. However, it is exceptional in that it is one of the few examples where the top is veneered in a very large piece of shell, allowing for an uninterrupted view of the beautiful figure. Note that green caddies were not made in fanciful shapes. Ca. 1790. *Courtesy of the Bielstein Collection.* $12,000–15,000.

Figure 192. A caddy with a stepped pyramid top, standing on a widening base supported by turned ivory feet. It is decorated in mother of pearl in a chinoiserie design. Very much in the whimsical spirit of the Regency / George IV, it marks a step when tortoiseshell was adopting the forms and decoration of the period. Ca. 1825–35. $8,000–12,000.

Figure 193. A caddy of curvilinear form, the lid conforming to the shape of the lower part of the box to the extent that it looks as if it is curving inward. It is decorated with mother of pearl inlay in a floral design. The decoration and the form are well matched to give the box an opulent Moorish look. Ca. 1840. *Courtesy of the Bielstein Collection.* $9,000–12,000.

*Above and right:*
Figure 194. Another caddy of curvilinear form, the lid conforming to the shape of the lower part of the box to the extent that it looks as if it is curving inward. It is decorated with engraved mother of pearl inlay in a floral design. The decoration and the form of the front is particularly complex, being simultaneously curved in two plains. Ca. 1840. $10,000–14,000.

## BOULLE OR BUHL

Marquetry of alternating metal and shell originated in Italy, but it was not widely practiced until the technique was advanced by A. C. Boulle (1642–1732), *ébéniste* to Louis XIV. This kind of work found favor in England throughout the eighteenth and nineteenth centuries. Boulle's technique involved the cutting of patterns in sheets of tortoiseshell and brass secured one on top of the other. The resulting half sheets were then used to veneer the wooden surface of the box or piece of furniture. They were fitted together, one brass sheet into one shell sheet, or vice versa. The brass into shell was referred to as *première partie*; the shell into the brass, as *contre partie*. The surface to be veneered was gessoed and usually colored red. The shell was sometimes backed with foils. In early pieces, the whole veneer was sometimes backed by canvas before it was stuck onto the wooden surface. Different makers had their own techniques and order for preparing and coloring the base before attaching the final marquetry veneer. Ivory, wood, horn, silver, mother of pearl, and other materials were incorporated in larger, more-ambitious designs. This work, which has a distinctive French flavor, is often attributed to French makers. In some cases this is correct, since boxes made in France did find their way to England, but this is not always the case.

Gerrit Jensen (1680–1715) was the first major exponent of the work in England. He was a royal maker of great repute. What is interesting for our purpose is that in the patent renewing his appointment as "Cabinet Maker In ordinary" to William and Mary, "Cabbinets Boxes" are listed as part of his work. It is therefore possible that some early-eighteenth-century boulle boxes originated in England and not in France.

However, some of the London makers did originate in France. There is evidence that Jensen employed French workers, as did other cabinetmakers during the eighteenth and nineteenth centuries. Some French cabinetmakers worked in England on their own account.

Pierre Langlois, one of the pioneers of this work, was active in London during the 1760s and 1770s. His trade card was

Figure 195. A box with a slightly rounded top pressed in a concentric pattern around a silver circle. 4.5". Second quarter nineteenth century. *Courtesy of the Bielstein Collection*. $1,500–2,000.

designed very much in the French style, complete with rococo scrolls and putti. It was printed both in English and French. He offered brass and tortoiseshell inlays "in the Politest Manner" and also careful repairs. He promised "Lowest Prices."

By the beginning of the nineteenth century, encouraged by the Prince of Wales's taste for French splendor and his purchases of French boulle work, this sumptuous decoration became de rigueur with the style gurus of the Regency. Thomas Parker (1805—1830), working in London's fashionable Piccadilly, tapped into this need for boulle cabinetwork. He described himself as a cabinetmaker and "buhl manufacturer" and attracted the royal patronage of Princess Elizabeth. By 1817, he could claim to be "Cabinet and Buhl Manufacturer to H.R.H. the Prince Regent & Royal Family." Among other items he made "Ink Stands, Portofolios, [and] workboxes." The firm of Town and Emanuel operated in London's Bond Street from 1830 to 1840. It advertised "the finest and most superb designs of the times of Louis 14th."

To determine if a high-quality boulle box is French or English, we have to look at the hardware and the interior. English makers kept up the tradition of high-quality boulle work longer than the French. By the middle of the century, some French makers did not use tortoiseshell, but a kind of lacquered

Figure 196. A caddy veneered all around in pressed tortoiseshell. The design is of a characteristic neo-Gothic pattern of arched windows sectioned in patterns reminiscent of ecclesiastical structures. 7.5" wide. Mid-nineteenth century. $18,000–22,000.

Figure 197. A box covered in boulle work of brass and red tortoiseshell. The pattern is in bold swirls forming floral designs and cusps typical of eighteenth-century work. The top is built around a stage, where a musician sits playing his instrument. This style of decoration, which was inspired from ancient Rome through the Italian Renaissance, became popular in France during the second half of the seventeenth century. One of the main exponents of this genre of design was Jean Bérain, whose arabesques foreshadowed the rococo style, while remaining formal and restrained. Like on this box, Bérain placed his figures in the center of elaborately fantastical compositions. A complex, opulent, and at the same time whimsical piece. 11.25" wide. Mid-eighteenth century. $15,000–18,000.

papier-mâché filler colored to simulate tortoiseshell. Later the lacquer was colored with light-blue, pink, or even green pigments. I have come across a number of nineteenth-century French boulle pieces marked on the lock with the name of Tahan, Paris. These are of variable quality and must be judged on their merit.

During the eighteenth century, boulle boxes were made in casket shapes, standing on ormolu feet. In the nineteenth century, they fell into the usual categories: tea caddies, desk boxes, writing slopes, glove boxes, and occasionally sewing boxes. The decoration on boxes made during the eighteenth century reflects the baroque, rococo, and, in the last decades, the classical influences of the period. The opulent quality of the materials is matched by the complex cultural references of the designs.

During the nineteenth century, designs respectful of symmetry, without excess of symbolism, were successfully executed in boulle work. However, during the last decades of the century, the designs became purely decorative. By now, the cutting of the brass/shell laminate could be done using machinery. Although the work was of excellent technical quality, the patterns became quite tight and lost the robust flowing energy of the earlier work. Late boulle pieces were retailed from prestigious establishments well into the twentieth century.

## MOTHER OF PEARL

Mother of pearl was used mostly in combination with tortoiseshell. It was mainly inlaid into the shell in decorative designs. The first step to its use as a material in its own right was made around 1800, when a "harlequin" design was developed using diamonds of tortoiseshell and mother of pearl. This was very effective and led to later tortoiseshell boxes having panels of diamond-shaped or oblong-shaped mother of pearl. Some Victorian boxes were entirely veneered in mother of pearl diamonds.

Very few boxes were covered solely in mother of pearl. This is probably because the aesthetic quality, which depended purely on the iridescence of the shell, was difficult to appreciate, and also because the process of cutting, matching, and fixing diamonds of mother of pearl is technically quite treacherous. Boxes in mother of pearl had no other decoration except silver central plates and escutcheons.

A few boxes of incredible workmanship were made in mother of pearl, inlaid with floral decoration executed in more-colorful shells, such as abalone. Good examples of such work are rare. The decoration ranges from exceedingly fine to mind-blowingly fine. It must have taken an astonishing degree of skill to inlay one hard material into another with such accuracy. Even in pieces, such boxes are worth preserving.

Very occasionally the tables were turned and a mother of pearl-veneered box was inlaid with tortoiseshell. Such boxes date from the middle of the nineteenth century. The inlays are usually of large swags.

A few carved mother of pearl boxes and tea caddies were made in China for English patrons; these are of fine quality. The carving is in openwork style, representing mostly floral patterns. They were made at the end of the eighteenth century in typical oblong forms.

*Above:*
Figure 199. A high-quality French glove box in boulle. Note how the front folds down. 10" wide. Second half nineteenth century. *Courtesy of the Bielstein Collection.* $2,500–3,000.

*Above:*
Figure 198. A good example of a writing slope in curvilinear shape covered in boulle work. The form and the design are robust and well executed. Mid-nineteenth century. $7,000–9,000.

141

Figure 200. A box of serpentine form covered in boulle work. The work is of good quality, and the pattern of floral scrolling patterns is pleasing. 9.25" wide. Mid-nineteenth century. $3,000–4,000.

*Above and right:*
Figure 201. A tea chest in tortoiseshell and mother of pearl in a harlequin pattern. It combines early neoclassical form with a design reminiscent of the Italian *Commedia dell'Arte*. An effective combination of the two materials. It is unusual to have canisters in this form of box. 7.5" wide. Ca. 1800–1810. $15,000–20,000.

# IVORY

Ivory reliquaries, bible, and other precious boxes were made in Europe as early as the Middle Ages. The material was carved either in a fretted technique, a three-dimensional technique, or a combination of both. Very few examples of such work survive, and it is reasonable to assume that such boxes were made only for royalty or church use.

The tradition for carved boxes was revived in parts of Europe during the seventeenth century. Dieppe, in France, was a center for ivory work; although craftsmen from that region were also working in England, no tradition for carved ivory boxes was ever established in any part of the United Kingdom. There were a number of cabinetmakers who advertised their skills as ivory turners. Judging by some of the tools in the English sewing boxes, this branch of work was significantly advanced during the eighteenth century.

Russia and France were the two countries that really perfected the art of the carved ivory box during the eighteenth century. These two countries were cross-pollinating each other's traditions through mutual exchanges of craftsmen and objects. It is sometimes difficult to differentiate between French and Russian work, since it was executed by using similar techniques and the craftsmen were operating within a shared aesthetic tradition. There are certain characteristics that can act as pointers, such as preferred motifs or hardware, but these are not always present.

In Russia, walrus and mammoth tusks were used for the majority of the work, while in France, elephant ivory and bone were more prevalent. It is sometimes difficult to distinguish between the different types of material, especially when the carving is in the openwork style, making it hard to look for evidence of blood vessels found in bone.

*Left and below:*
Figure 202. Details of the front and side of a tea caddy, showing the incredibly fine inlay of shell into shell. The caddy is of similar shape to the chinoiserie-inlaid example. The caddy is 7.5" wide. Mid-nineteenth century. $15,000–20,000.

In the seventeenth century, the ivory-working tradition was already strong in Russia, especially in the Arkhangelsk (Archangel) region north of European Russia. Peter the Great was so impressed by the work of the carvers invited to his court that he acquired the skill and furnished himself with a sophisticated workshop for turning and making objects in ivory. Catherine the Great was a great patron of this craft throughout the middle and later part of the eighteenth century.

In England, ivory and bone boxes were very rare until the beginning of the nineteenth century, when Napoleonic prisoners of war made some examples of this type of box while in captivity. Eighteenth-century fine examples of such boxes were known only in aristocratic circles, where they found their way as precious gifts.

Ivory was not a material familiar to the English cabinetmakers, who did not have much experience using it as a veneer. When it was introduced in the late eighteenth century as an import from Africa, the first makers to use it were probably more versed in jewelry and fine-object techniques rather than cabinetwork.

In England, the majority of boxes veneered in ivory were tea caddies made during the last two decades of the eighteenth century. Ivory must be properly dried before it is cut. It must be cut following the pattern of the growth lines. When used as a veneer, it tends to curve and crack. The first caddies were made by applying the ivory slices directly onto the gessoed carcass of the box. A technique used slightly later, probably in an attempt to compensate for the curving, was to stick the ivory slice first on a piece of thick paper and then onto the carcass of the box. Whatever the reason, technical or aesthetic, the era of the ivory tea caddy was short lived, albeit quite fruitful.

All the ivory caddies were made on the same basic grid. With flat or pyramid-shaped tops, they were hexagonal, octagonal, or decagonal, with straight sides. In between the ivory panels, strips of tortoiseshell, silver, or gold were placed, the precious metals being usually chased.

The hinges on these caddies were very fine, as were the small silver escutcheons. The tops were decorated, either with Dutch drop handles or finials delicately made by silversmiths. Such caddies did not have heavy decoration. They often featured a shield for initials or coat of arms, occasionally surrounded by *piqué* festoons, or bows. *Piqué clouté* was sometimes used for more-elaborate designs. Another form of decoration was dots in mother of pearl of the same type used in tortoiseshell work. Cut steel was also used in the form of faceted "nails." This was derived from Russian and French work, although the steel points were English made. I have also come

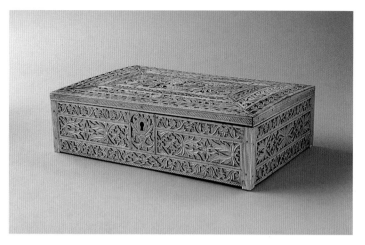

*This whole page:*
Figure 203. A very finely carved box in bone with a straw work interior. The fretted and carved bone panels are backed with gold foil. The basket design is characteristic of Dieppe work. 10" wide. Late eighteenth century. $12,000–18,000.

across panels of steel used in conjunction with ivory to form a tea caddy.

It is not surprising that similar forms of decoration were applied both to tortoiseshell and ivory caddies. These caddies were made by the same makers who advertised themselves as ivory and tortoiseshell workers. It could not have been otherwise, since both materials were used on the same type of boxes in reverse roles. The shapes of the ivory caddies mirror the shapes of the polygonal tortoiseshell caddies of the same period.

A miniature painted on ivory was sometimes inserted into the front central panel of the caddy. These miniatures depicted scenes with classical figures in the neoclassical fashion of the period or were portraits of particular people. If the miniature was inserted at the time of manufacture, it is likely that the escutcheon remained intact. (Caution to note this feature when inspecting such an item.)

Another departure from the basic design was to turn the panel of ivory into a "ribbed" surface. This was probably done to compensate for the stress on the material caused by its tendency to curl. In all other respects—shape, decoration, and hardware—the caddies were the same as the flat-surface examples, with the exception that occasionally such a caddy was made in oval form.

Ivory, except as a trim for tortoiseshell or mother of pearl, had all but disappeared by the beginning of the nineteenth century. While it lasted, it kept its integrity; it did not allow for fanciful combinations, for deviations of the size of panels, or for variations in the shapes and lines of boxes. Perhaps this is the reason for its disappearance from the repertoire; the

cabinetmakers did not know how to perfect or develop its application.

After the Regency, some Russian and French boxes of simpler designs found their way into England. These tend to have fretted, flat, geometric designs.

Chinese carved boxes, which were made for the English market, were also imported during the nineteenth century. These are carved with scenes of oriental life. The work is intricate and skillful, but only the best examples have any artistic vitality.

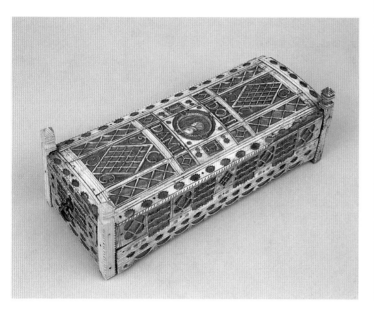

*Above and right:*

Figure 204. A carved-bone box, containing dominoes in two side drawers. It is backed with gold and colored foils. The work shares characteristics both of French and Russian work. On the top there is a carved face of a uniformed man flanked by the initials "J.F." His insignia of rank are visible on his shoulder. There are also the words "DON D'AMI," "a gift from a friend," also carved on the top. There is a speculative scrap attached to the bottom of the box, linking it to the French statesman Joseph Fouché (1763–1820). Fouché, the Duke of Otranto, was a revolutionary who was elected to the National Convention (France) in 1792 and voted for the execution of Louis XVI. In 1799 he was made minister of police. He was a political and ruthless individual, who ended his days in exile, having been banished as a regicide in 1816. The dates match and the portrait bears a likeness. 8.5" wide. Ca. 1800. $5,000–6,000.

Figure 205. A Russian carved box with the characteristic wheat sheaf motif, very similar to an example in the St. Petersburg museum. The fine lace effect was perfected by Russian craftsmen. See the example in the chapter "Sewing Boxes or Workboxes" (figure 453) for more details. 8" wide. Early nineteenth century. $1,500–2,000 (in damaged condition).

## Some Recorded Makers

The vast majority of tortoiseshell and ivory boxes are not marked, so the following is far from being a complete record; it is an attempt to paint some more of the picture:

**Daw:** Cheapside, London: Label on large sarcophagus-shaped tea chest, with gilt handles and paw feet. Two canisters and caddy bowl.

**Lund:** Thomas Lund, Cornhill, London, 1819–1839, and William Lund, Fleet Street, London. ca. 1835: a family business of high-quality box makers. They worked in all materials. They worked from various addresses within the same area. Known examples:

An octagonal tortoiseshell tea caddy and a domed tortoiseshell caddy with ivory feet bear the T Lund mark.

A slightly pagoda-shaped top caddy standing on ivory feet and a tortoiseshell letterbox bear the W. Lund mark. Darker shell than average.

Also nécessaires and needle boxes bear the LUND mark.

A characteristic of their caddies is an ivory "lip" around the inside of the caddy, which is slightly taller than the two internal lids, so when the lids are in place the container is airtight, as on a humidor.

**Powell, T.:** Leeds: Describes himself on his label as "Jeweller & Manufacturer of Desks workboxes Dressing Cases & Fancy Goods of every Description." Example: a flat tortoiseshell sewing box, veneered in four pieces, separated by metal stringing, with a central silver plaque, late eighteenth–early nineteenth century. An oblong nécessaire with silver fittings, early nineteenth century.

**Smith, J.:** describes himself as "Shell & Ivory Worker. 39 Cheapside, London." It is interesting to note that his address is on the same street as **Daw's**, in the City area of London, and quite close to the King's Head Tavern, the main depot for the unfortunate turtles destined for the Regency feasts. Example: label on a single caddy of slightly bombe sarcophagus form with silver escutcheon, ball feet, and finial. Very good quality and look, ca. 1820.

**Spriggs, William:** Old Fish St., London, b. 1746, d. 1805. A tortoiseshell veneered tea caddy was attributed to him some decades after his demise. Judging by the address, this is probably correct (I have not seen this caddy).

**Comys, William:** Late-nineteenth-century caddies and boxes with silver mounts.

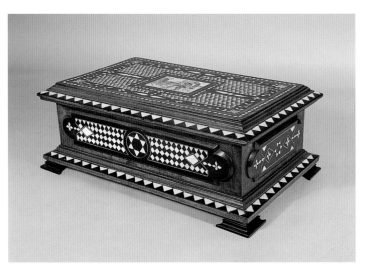

Figure 206. A box in walnut and ivory with ebony panels and feet. The ivory center is finely engraved with a classical scene. This is typical of Italian work of the nineteenth century. 15.5" wide. $2,500–3,500.

Unfortunately, as in most cases, information about the earliest and, often, most-distinguished boxes is obscure. It is only commercial awareness that made labeling more widespread. Aesthetic and quality criteria must always take precedence over a name when choosing a piece.

There are some makers listed as tortoiseshell and ivory workers, or turners, but it is not clear who was making boxes, or who was an inlayer in the boulle style. Fittings for sewing boxes and turned handles on various boxes were supplied by such specialized workers.

*Above and right:*

Figure 207. An octagonal ivory caddy in characteristic form and proportions. Such caddies were also made in tortoiseshell. Note the very fine engraved hinge. Do not trust fancy shapes and narrow strips in such caddies. Their proportions were strictly within the neoclassical tradition. End of the eighteenth century. 4.25" wide. *Courtesy of Ian Gouldsbrough.* $5,000–8,000.

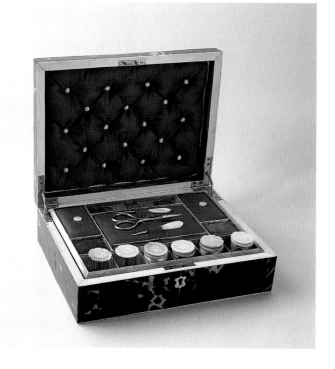

*Above and right:*

Figure 208. A tortoiseshell sewing box complete with mother of pearl spools. The facings are in ivory. Mid-nineteenth century. *Courtesy of a private collection.* $2,500–3,000.

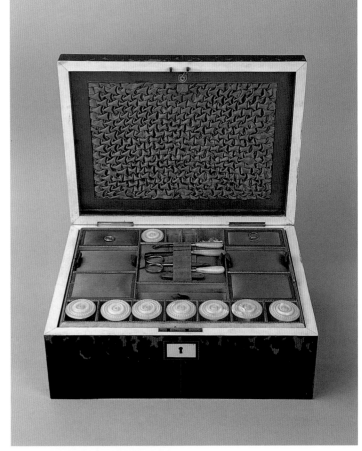

This whole page:

Figure 209. A sewing box, which bears the label of Thomas Lund. The form of the box is characteristic of this firm's work. Their caddies too were constructed along the same principles; that is, very straight side lines with tops that have subtle structural variations such as the gently concave and stepped form of this box. All their boxes are faced in ivory. In the examples I have seen, they also seem to favor very dark shell, which, combined with the straight lines, gives the impression of strength. The interior is in characteristic Regency whimsy of color surprises. The spools, like the rest of the piece, are of very high quality. 12" wide. Ca. 1820. $15,000–20,000.

# CHAPTER 11 *Filigree or Rolled Paper*

Originally filigree was the creation of delicate artistic objects by using rolled-up thin sheets of precious metals. Parchment, or paper filigree work, was an imitative decorative device adopted for less expensive and more varied work.

Paper filigree work for the decoration of boxes was fashionable for a very brief period during the latter part of the eighteenth century and the first years of the nineteenth century. This work entailed the rolling up of paper to create delicate coils, which were then attached to the surface of the box. The end of the paper was gilded, or colored, so as to give the impression of rolled metal work. Sometimes the entire surface of some of the paper was gilded. The technique as such was not new; it had been practiced for centuries within the same underlying principle.

During the fifteenth and sixteenth centuries, filigree was used mainly for ecclesiastical decoration. In the seventeenth century, it was combined with waxwork, shells, seeds, threads, metal, and hair to create pictures, picture frames, and other objects. Its eighteenth-century revival as a decoration for boxes was perhaps prompted by silver filigree work—including boxes—imported from China. Mrs. Delany called it "mosaic work" in her correspondence, but by the end of the century the term "filigree" was widely accepted.

*Above and below:*
Figure 210. Filigree-work tea caddy with central bucolic print. The condition of the inside leading is typical of what would be expected in a caddy of this type, which has not been relined. 7.25" wide. Ca. 1800. $5,000–7,000.

In 1786, the *New Ladies' Magazine* published an account of the craft and offered several designs for its execution. These were mostly stylized floral patterns and borders, palmettes, and garlands. Other manuals also gave instructions as to "paper filigree work." The craft was practiced mostly by ladies at home as a genteel amusement. The materials were purchased either from art suppliers or cabinetmakers. Already colored and gilded papers, as well as mica and mother of pearl flakes, were combined to form the selected or created pattern. Medallions and colored engravings were sometimes incorporated within the overall design, providing the work with a central focal point.

The particular accomplishment of filigree work was also taught at ladies' schools. Trade cards of the period mention the supply of cases for filigree work to boarding schools. In 1791, a royal tradesman, Charles Elliott, supplied Princess Elizabeth with "15 ounces of different filigree paper, one ounce of gold paper, and a box made for filigree work with ebony moldings, lock and key, lined inside and outside and also a tea cadde to correspond with box."

Filigree boxes were also offered by professionals. A correspondent in *New Ladies' Magazine* recommended a London shop, on fashionable Mount Street, where such work was on display. Very likely the work was done by talented, genteel ladies who had fallen on hard times. In the 1793 cabinetmakers' *London Book of Prices*, the price of the work is described as follows: "if any of these caddies are made for fillagree to be the same [price] as veneer'd."

Most "filigree" boxes were small tea caddies in the typical shapes of the period: hexagonal, octagonal, oval, or elliptical.

The undecorated boxes were made so that each side was framed by a protruding wooden line. This allowed enough depth for the paper scrolls to be stuck onto the inner wooden structure and form a surface in line with the framing wood. Sometimes the paperwork was glazed, the outer wooden structure acting as a frame. This was done to protect the delicate nature of the work and the material. To this end it was successful, but it did detract from the aesthetic quality of the box.

The fashion for filigree was short lived, possibly because the work was not suited to early-nineteenth-century forms, possibly because it was so easily damaged, or possibly because talented amateurs moved on to penwork.

Jane Austen's *Sense and Sensibility* refers to the work when Elinor offers to help Lucy Steel roll papers for decorating a basket Lucy is making for the daughter of their hostess. Although the novel was started in the last years of the eighteenth century, it was not published until 1811. It is impossible to know when the author composed this particular scene. However, it is significant that it is the vulgar, social-climbing Lucy who is initiating the work and not the cultured, refined Elinor. This points to the fashion for filigree work being already in decline.

A few filigree caddies were also made by Napoleonic prisoners of war. These are indistinguishable from English work.

The colors of rolled papers have by now faded, and the gilding on the gold has rubbed off. Expecting to find "pristine" examples is unrealistic. The often-practiced replacement and regilding of papers frequently results in garish and artificially glossy creations that are neither original, nor honest reproductions.

*Above and left:*
Figure 211. Filigree-spaced ornament on a background of mica flakes. Colored prints of classical inspiration were popular. 6.75" wide. Ca. 1800. $5,000–7,000.

traw marquetry is usually referred to as Napoleonic prisoner of war work. The reason for this is that most pieces available today were made in England in prisoner-of-war camps and prison ships between 1793 and 1815. Dartmoor and Norman Cross were two of the chief centers, but such prisons were scattered throughout England, with some of the work dating back to 1756.

Considering the living conditions in such camps and ship hulks, this extraordinarily beautiful work is a celebration of the human spirit over adversity. The technical expertise and the design sense displayed on many pieces are remarkable. Furthermore, the sensitivity of composition, color, and use of material on the best work is breathtaking. The humble materials in the hands of people brought low by circumstances were transformed into treasures reflecting a world of imagination and culture. It is as if the prisoners' intellects soared while their bodies were confined.

The prisoners sold their wares in the prison markets, where they had the opportunity to interact with the world outside and earn some money toward their keep. Work was sometimes directly commissioned, with the patron providing some of the more specialized materials, such as dyes. There are traditional recipes using chemicals and natural processes and materials for dying straw, as well as theories as to when the straw should be gathered and how it should be kept. However, by the end of the eighteenth century and in prison circumstances, the dying was done by more-direct methods.

*This whole page:*
Figure 212. A piece made to commemorate a marriage. The inside of the lid depicts Cupid standing between a couple within a domestic setting. This amatory convention was used both in the applied and fine arts. The arrangement is reminiscent of seventeenth-century Dutch painting, both in the perspective and the carefully placed elements within the work. The front of the box depicts a townscape in the background and Leda and the Swan in the foreground. This alludes to the mythical amours of Zeus, endowing the earthly marriage with divine grandeur. The lid of the box is framed by flowers, two corners ending in tulips and two in wild roses. The center has a crossed motif under a crown. The crown looks like a representation of the royal crown of the Netherlands. Judging by the implied association with the Olympian couple and the crown, this points to the box having been made in celebration of the marriage of William of Orange and Mary in 1677. In 1689 William and Mary became the English monarchs. There is incised writing in between the two figures, which (as of yet) is not possible to read. Some features of the box are reminiscent of work that was done by members of the Hering family at the end of the seventeenth century and the beginning of the eighteenth. However, it is difficult to attribute work with any certainty, since early examples are very rare and makers are not documented. For example, Andrew Renton, curator of applied art, National Museum & Gallery, Cardiff, tells me: "A Robert Wiseman was recorded as a producer of straw work in Oxford in the 1670s, though we know nothing of the character of his work." Examples of boxes made by the Hering family are in the Sankt Annen-Museum in Lübeck. Andrew Renton illustrates some of these in his article "Straw Marquetry Made in Lübeck, Leiden and London by the Hering Family," in *Furniture History* 35 (1999): 51–86. 5" wide. Ca. 1700. $?

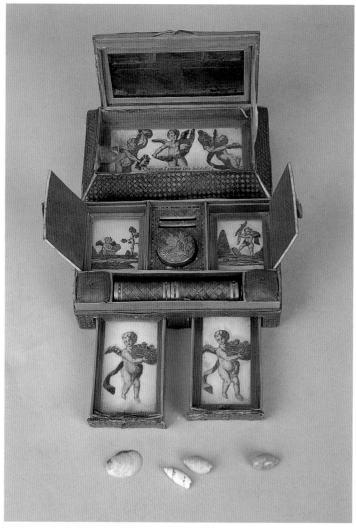

*This whole page:*

Figure 213. A delightful valentine or marriage box decorated in straw work and colored scraps pasted onto paper. The straw is used so as to maximize the quality of different light reflections to create a subtly colored checkered pattern. The top is inlaid with a rose, symbol of love, and a pink carnation, symbol of passion, in gilded straw. When opened, the box bursts into color. The straw is in vivid pink with roses depicted in gold. The pretty putti are in typical eighteenth-century style. There are small seashells in the different compartments. The main picture depicts two people on either side of a clown riding on a donkey. One of the figures looks as if he is a boy in female disguise playing both a tabor and a long pipe. The figures could very well be *Commedia dell'Arte* characters. The verse translates "though love is fickle, though you scorn my attentions, my care for you does not falter." However, the message, taken with the picture, is far from being merely an innocent declaration of love. It is full of innuendo, characteristic of eighteenth-century society courtship. A magic microcosm of its time. 4.75" wide. French. Mid-eighteenth century. $3,000–3,500.

This whole page:

Figure 214. Extremely finely executed, this box, in the form of Noah's Ark, is decorated on the top with a marquetry picture of a rural scene. The work makes use both of the sheen values of the material in its natural color and also of dyed pieces of straw. Details are engraved and darkened. The scene aims at a naturalistic interpretation, in the genre of the painting of the period. The border is formally arranged and the floral designs are flowing but symmetrical, in the manner of eighteenth-century wood marquetry. Most probably Continental, dating from the second half of the eighteenth century. $3,000–4,000.

*Above and right:*

Figure 215. A Greek straw work–decorated box in the form of a marriage chest. The patterns on this piece are different from those of other European work and are reminiscent of traditional Greek embroidery patterns. The religious inscription is in harmony with the time when the box was made. During the period when Greece was part of the Ottoman Empire, the only education available to most children was in secret schools run by the church. With the bible as the only text, religion and ethnic identity were inexorably linked. The straw writing translates "God Has" (i.e., God in his infinite wisdom will show the way, or In God we trust). Note the bright colors inside the box. The exterior has faded. 11.75" wide. Eighteenth/nineteenth century. $?

The prisoners, who were French or Dutch, brought the knowledge of straw work with them. Straw work had been practiced in many parts of the Far East and Europe for centuries. A box in the museum of Vienna dates from the Middle Ages, although it was not until the seventeenth century that such work was fashionable, especially in Italy, Spain, France, and the Low Countries. In England it was known in Stuart times, with at least one lady reported as a master of the craft. In 1703, the *Edinburgh Gazette* offered the services of a London gentlewoman willing to teach the craft. There are reports that Dunstable was one of the earliest and longest-surviving centers of such and other straw work. Later on in the century, observation of the Continental work done either by prisoners, prisoners on parole, or refugees must have cross-pollinated with English work, making it impossible to distinguish between different traditions.

The diarist Evelyn, writing in the middle of the seventeenth century, referred to work done by nuns in Milan. The laborious and exacting discipline necessary for this refined craft was suited to the contemplative life. Straw work appears to have been practiced by religious orders in many European countries. (See figure 300)

The connection with nuns also dates from ancient times, when votive objects were made in straw in many agriculturally oriented societies. It was only natural that with more leisure and refinement of splitting and gluing methods, straw began to be used as a fine decorative medium. The wonderfully light responsive quality of the straw must have spurred the artistic instinct of at first the rural, and later the urban craftsperson. As attested by the illustrated Greek example, straw marquetry tradition was perhaps developed independently in many countries at a different pace, crossing religious and worldly divisions.

In 1759, *l' Année Littéraire* wrote about "le sieur Chervain," who opened a shop in the *rue Tiquetonne*, where she stocked "boites doublée de paille, ou sont exécutées toutes sortes de sujets chinois, flamands et francais." The shop also offered "petits écritoires." It is interesting to note that Chinese, Flemish, and French designs were sold by the good sister. Decorative preferences crossed borders and continents, making it difficult to place straw work accurately. By the last two decades of the eighteenth century the work became very fashionable. There are mentions of more shops, and this time there are specific

Figure 216. Napoleonic prisoner-of-war boxes in the form of books. Note the play of light on the geometric patterns. One of the boxes has stylized motifs in watercolor under glass. This particular box is a sewing box. The bone circles on the side are pierced in the center, so that the thread can pass through without the need to take the spools out of the box. Boxes in book form were made in many sizes. The boxes here measure on the narrow "standing" side 1.6", 4.5", and 5.5" wide. Ca. 1800–1815. $1,000–2,000 each.

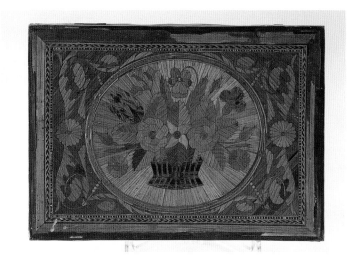

*Above and right:*
Figure 217. Another prisoner-of-war-made box with characteristic decoration. Although the flowers on such boxes are often arranged centrally in the neoclassical style of the period, many of the blooms are understandably chosen for their sentimental symbolism; for example, the love-laden rose and the pansy, which in French is a homophone of the word for thought, *pensée*. Under the two lidded compartments there are also two small drawers. Everything is completely covered in straw stripes of different colors. 10.5" wide. Ca. 1810. $1,200–1,500.

*Above and right:*
Figure 218. Ships, boats, and buildings were popular motifs in prisoner-of-war work. This reflects the importance of seafaring in the fortunes of nations during that particular period. The ribbon tied rose is typical of French work. The inside of the lidded compartments and the drawer are covered in straw work. 10" wide. Ca. 1800–1815. $1,200–1,500.

*Above and right:*

Figure 219. A religious note of love and faith on either side of the floral arrangement, an understandable sentiment for a prisoner of war. Inside the box there are two lidded compartments. Every surface is decorated in straw work. 13" wide. Eighteenth/nineteenth century. $1,400–1,800.

*Above and right:*

Figure 220. An exceptionally fine piece of Napoleonic prisoner-of-war work. The whole arrangement is in the formal neoclassical tradition. The framing ornament too is neoclassical. The lids are decorated with trophies of arms. The inside of the top breaks with the tradition of neoclassicism and is in the style of eighteenth-century landscape painting. The top too is decorated with a scene with buildings. Note the superbly fine detail, especially for the trees and the people in the boats. Note also the very subtly grated shading for land and water. A similar example is in the Peterborough Museum, which houses a considerable collection of work made in the Norman Cross prison. 9.75" wide. Late eighteenth century. $3,500–4,500.

references to *boites a jeux* and *a thé* boxes, which were very necessary for the social pursuits of gambling and tea drinking.

The technique of straw marquetry appears to be more or less universal. Basically the straw was split, flattened, sometimes bleached and dyed, and then glued onto the wood, or first on paper, which was then glued onto the object. Care had to be taken in the application of appropriate pressure to ensure the adhesion and flatness of the delicate material. Blotting paper was used to absorb the extra moisture from the glue. Sometimes, geometric shapes such as herringbone, lines, chequered squares, and other designs were cut out of long strips of straw that were first glued on paper. For example, lines cut diagonally could give long lengths of sharply defined herringbone designs. These were inspired by traditional tapestry designs, such as the Italian bergamot patterns.

Two additional techniques were also used, mostly in earlier work. One was engraving, which was done very much the way it was done for wood marquetry, by using a sharp point to incise details or outlines. The incised lines were then colored mostly in black, giving a sharper definition and a more realistic depiction of the scenes. The second technique was the building up of the design with more than one layer of straw. Sometimes molds were used to emboss and thus define and refine the pictorial representation. This technique is found in conjunction with flat work, mostly in the form of central medallions, as in the illustrated bombe-shaped tea chest.

The designs on the boxes follow the traditions of other arts. Early boxes on the whole represent scenes typical of period painting and tapestry, framed by designs within contemporaneous conventions. From the end of the eighteenth century, some boxes follow the neoclassical tradition of arrangement and ornament, although the motifs are often more realistically depicted than in similar wood marquetry. Geometric patterns are also strong within straw work tradition. Sometimes they are used as part of a complex design incorporating representational parts and sometimes as an overall cover for a complete box. Such designs make use of the particular quality of straw reflecting light according to the way it is arranged. Subtle effects of color and sheen can be achieved by clever juxtaposition of straw following different directions.

After the first two decades of the nineteenth century, straw marquetry became less fashionable. Perhaps the departure of the prisoners meant that a ready supply was no longer there. However, if the demand had remained strong, English craftsmen would have continued the work. Instead, as the nineteenth century progressed, the craft continued to decline. It is more likely that the rise of the middle classes and the demand for goods that looked more "manufactured" spelled the end of this fine craft, which allowed for more idiosyncratic and at times playful interpretations of the world.

Another factor could have been the cost. A box, or a picture, decorated by prisoners was sold for 20—40 shillings, as much as any high-quality box was sold for at the time. Free craftsmen could not have competed in a field that needed so much personal

Figure 221. A typical prisoner-of-war box with several popular motifs of boats and houses. The theme of boats continues on the inside. 11" wide. Ca. 1810. $1,400–1,800.

*Above:*
Figure 222. A very finely decorated box. Note the tiny pieces used in the composition of the inside scene. Note also the very vivid original color. 7.75" wide. Beginning of nineteenth century. *Courtesy of Susan Webster.* $3,000–4,000.

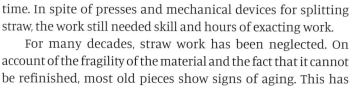

Figure 223. A tea chest of baroque form decorated with single-stem rosebuds and chrysanthemums on the four sides. The stepped top has a central embossed scene of a man sitting under a tree, and a lady holding a basket in characteristic eighteenth-century bucolic fashion. The outside colors are faded in contrast to the pink stripes of the canisters. Very few tea chests have survived, especially in such ambitious shapes. The form of the box and the skill needed to execute straw marquetry on such curvaceous surfaces points to a master of the craft. 6.4" wide. Ca. 1740. $?

time. In spite of presses and mechanical devices for splitting straw, the work still needed skill and hours of exacting work.

For many decades, straw work has been neglected. On account of the fragility of the material and the fact that it cannot be refinished, most old pieces show signs of aging. This has meant that it was sought after only by connoisseurs who had the confidence to display antiques as antiques and not as over-restored pieces from centuries past. With the recent advent of the ever more sophisticated collector who demands genuine period pieces, straw work is showing a rapid and sharp increase in price.

Prisoner-of-war work and work of the same period can still be bought for under $1,000 (US). Most such pieces are rich both in charm factor and finesse of execution. A few are rather rigid, betraying an untutored hand. Even these are attractive in a naive way. Price should depend on the work. Do not expect perfect pieces, and please resist the temptation of turning the lid inside out so that the box looks perfect from the outside. This is an insult to the integrity of the intention of the original maker and often results in the disruption of the original design. Remember, these boxes have real human input.

Exceptional prisoner-of-war work and early pieces, which are very rare, command considerably higher prices. With scholarship identifying artists and areas of work, these small treasures are fast disappearing into museums and important collections.

Above:
Figure 224. A straw marquetry writing slope. The work is very rooted in the tradition of Dutch painting of peasant figures. It is refreshingly earthly and robust. Such scenes are known on early-eighteenth-century Dutch straw marquetry boxes. A curious genre of decoration, considering that writing slopes were a totem of refinement. However, this combination of the opposing sides of human nature was characteristic of the Regency man about town. Very few slopes in straw work were made, and surviving examples are very rare. 12.5" wide. Ca. 1810. $4,000–5,000.

Figure 225. A card box for playing cards and gaming counters. This is a good example of the use of colored straw and also straw used angled to define patterns purely using light values. The pattern incorporates initials that point to a specific commission. Arabesque-inspired floral arrangements are known on identified Dutch straw marquetry boxes of the eighteenth century, although French and English work of the same period was also likely to have used this type of decoration, which was popular in all forms of marquetry. First half eighteenth century. $3,500–4,500.

# CHAPTER 13 *Scottish Boxes*

The Scottish box owes its distinction to a remarkable man, James Sandy, and its existence to another remarkable man, Lord Gardenstone. Its commercial viability was nurtured by a gifted craftsman, Charles Stiven, and promoted by the dynastic family Smith. In the earlier part of the nineteenth century, the Smiths treated box making as an art form. By the second half of the century, they transformed this particular craft into a souvenir box industry beyond the scope of this book. So although the Smiths are the best known and most prolific of makers, it is the earlier boxes and makers who deserve careful scrutiny, even though in many cases they remain anonymous.

James Sandy died in 1819, at age fifty-three, an acknowledged genius and a convivial man. This last quality must have been difficult to maintain, since throughout his life he had to fight against tremendous odds. Due to an accident and the inappropriate administrations of a quack doctor, James lost the use of one of his legs when he was a child of twelve. This infirmity did not deter him from busying himself making violins and other musical instruments, despite the fact that the only tools he had were very rudimentary. He triumphed over his primitive work conditions and achieved a degree of success early on in his life. This enabled him to furnish his workbench to a superior professional standard, making it possible for him to produce objects of high quality. He was musical himself, and his striving to understand the importance of scientific acoustic principles in the course of making instruments must have contributed to his wanderings in the realms of science.

When James was seventeen, his family house was flooded. His mother tried to move him to a higher floor. This resulted in another accident and a second broken leg for the already crippled James. This additional affliction rendered James completely unable to walk. Undaunted, he continued to make the best use of the faculties he still possessed, mainly his intellect and dexterity. Ensconced in his bed, which he adapted to double up as a workbench, he successfully tried his hand at making clocks, telescopes, tools, machines, and false teeth! He received an award for making a very serviceable false arm for a man who lost his arm in an accident!

James Sandy had a reputation as a rather eccentric genius who produced wondrous things, and who hatched bird eggs in his bed! (This was a tall story developed after James had adopted an orphaned gosling that grew up to be his pet goose and constant companion for many years.) This "artist of distinguished eminence," as he was described on his tombstone, drew many visitors to his bedside. Inquiring foreign travelers, as well as people from closer home, all admired James and his work. His room must have been a hubbub of exchange of ideas and bonhomie, since James liked to share both his inventions and his whiskey with his visitors.

In exchange, the visitors must have allowed him glimpses of the outside world, stimulating his ingenuity and rendering his activities applicable to the necessities and fashions of the time. Thus, James must have been aware of the habit of snuff taking and of the mess that unhinged snuffboxes could create in the pockets of his visitors. Furthermore, it is likely he had seen and examined handmade "blind" hinges on Scottish or other northern European snuffboxes. The crudeness of the hinges, which defeated the object of keeping the snuff dry, must have puzzled James, who set about solving the problem.

It was James's grasp both of the disciplines of woodwork and clockmaking that enabled him to develop a process for cutting hinges with impeccable precision. James lived in Alyth, Perthshire, in the east side of Scotland. News of his new hinge must have traveled quite fast to Kincardineshire, especially to Laurencekirk, which was only twenty miles northeast of Alyth, where another highly skilled craftsman, Charles Stiven, lived and worked. It is just possible that Stiven had found his own way of perfecting the concealed hinge. He certainly never claimed to have done so. However, by the time of Sandy's death, Stiven had adopted the use of this particular hinge to such an extent that any box fitted with it was described as a Laurencekirk box.

Enter Francis, Lord Gardenstone. Lord Gardenstone had a distinguished legal career; he became a Law Lord and acquired civic distinctions in his native Scotland. He had an eccentric and expansive personality that could not be satisfied within the mere confines of the law. He was one of those gigantic characters whom the eighteenth century periodically engendered and nurtured. His inspired efforts changed the social landscape of his particular country for the betterment of his fellow men. He produced literary works, was a patron of the arts, and was a philanthropist in the most positive sense of the word.

Lord Gardenstone seemed to be on good terms with people in all walks of life, appreciating the skills and insights they could offer. He had two weaknesses: the first for snuff taking, and the second, an extraordinary liking for pigs. One sow in particular he indulged to the point of allowing her to sleep on his bed, and when she grew too large, to sleep on his clothes when he undressed for the night. In this he had something in common with Sandy and his goose!

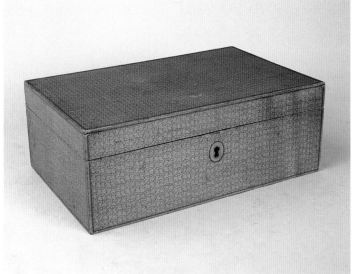

*This whole page:*

Figure 226. A box painted in yellow and decorated all over, with very fine wavy lines forming loose trefoil patterns. The decoration continues over the "blind hinge" at the back. No metal is visible from either the inside or outside of the box. The interior is lined with the original yellow silk. On either side of the lock the embossed mark of W. CRAB L KIRK is just about visible. These marks are very shallow and have become very faint with age. Caution! Cleaning can erase them completely. 12" wide. Late eighteenth century. $3,000–5,000.

In 1786, Lord Gardenstone set off on a Continental journey. His knowledge of the French language was faultless, having had cause in the past to practice his legal expertise in French. In France, probably in search of another snuffbox, he visited the workshops in Chantilly that had been established by the Duc de Bourbon Condé. He was very impressed both by the work and the whole concept of the enterprise. After France, Lord Gardenstone proceeded to the Netherlands, Germany, and Italy. He lingered in the town of Spa, in present-day Belgium, where he took the waters for the benefit of his health.

On his return home at the end of 1788, he published an account of his journey, which appeared in two volumes in 1791 and 1792. At the time Lord Gardenstone visited Spa, a thriving industry in boxes and other small items was already established in the area. Lord Gardenstone admired the quality of the finishes and artwork on these small objects. He was particularly taken with the work of lac master Vincent Brixhe, who had worked with the distinguished landscape painter Antoine Lelou for twenty years and who himself was renowned for his flower painting and marble effects on wood.

It is not clear when Lord Gardenstone conceived of his plan, bringing all the elements for a successful enterprise together, but when he returned to Scotland he had already convinced Brixhe to come and set up a similar business in Laurencekirk. For this enterprise Brixhe was offered £30 a year plus £5 per apprentice for three years. After this period, if Brixhe decided to stay, he could have a free house for life. Brixhe did stay, and in 1791, another eminent craftsman, H. Henrard, also came from Spa to work and train local craftsmen, although he did not make Scotland his permanent home.

Lord Gardenstone already had the seeds of a possible distinctive box-making industry in Laurencekirk, in the presence of the aforementioned Charles Stiven, who was a joiner on his estate. Laurencekirk was a hamlet that bordered on the estate of Lord Gardenstone. In 1779, he procured it, and with his active involvement, he transformed it into a prosperous village. He built an inn comfortable enough to accommodate the new class of travelers, a museum, and workshops for the advancement of different activities. He also founded a library for the erudition of the local inhabitants.

Stiven was born in 1753 and was persuaded to move to Laurencekirk by Lord Gardenstone sometime around 1783. He was already acclaimed as a snuffbox maker and was obviously open to new ideas and designs, as his adoption of the concealed hinge testifies. Brixhe's artistic skills complemented Stiven's impeccable craftsmanship. Together they were capable of masterminding a business of aesthetic integrity and commercial viability.

Before Lord Gardenstone died in 1793, he had the satisfaction of seeing his brainchild—a thriving box-making enterprise—well underway. The business continued successfully for about seventy years. When Stiven died in 1820, his work was continued by his son Jonathan, who had most probably been trained by Brixhe in the art of painting. By the time Jonathan took over, the firm already had the Royal Warrant, which it continued to hold until its closure in 1868. The Stivens always upheld high standards of workmanship and had the distinction of showing their wares to the royal family at Balmoral on several occasions.

Stiven's boxes usually have an embossed mark on the facing, near the lock, either as C. Stiven, Charles Stiven and Sons, Stiven and Son, or variations. The word "Laurencekirk" is also stamped. Even after the father's death, his name remained on the label.

Stiven had premises in the coach house booking office, from where he sold his wares. Travelers who bought his work must have been instrumental in spreading both the characteristic hinge and the particular quality of the work farther afield. The hinge soon reached the West of Scotland and established itself in Ayrshire. The first time the hinge was used in this area is clouded in legend. One version of events recounts how a Laurencekirk snuffbox was repaired in Cumnock by William Crawford, who, realizing the special quality of the hinge, set about trying to re-create it with the cooperation of his boss, Mr. Willie.

It is interesting to note that it was a gunsmith, and later a clockmaker, who succeeded in making the necessary tools for Crawford and Willie to enable them to make the concealed hinge. Crawford and Willie went into the box business first as a partnership and then on their own separate accounts. The secret of the hinge was thus further disseminated, possibly through employees or simply by observation. Other makers followed, and soon the villages of Old and New Cumnock, Catrine, Ochiltree, and Mauchline were growing prosperous with the income from the ingenious woodwork of their artists and craftsmen. In the 1820s, the small village of Cumnock was reputed to have an income of up to £10,000 a year from its box production. During the height of the industry, a box maker could earn one guinea a week; an artist, two guineas; and a varnisher, twelve shillings—healthy wages by the standards of the day.

In 1822, the fashion for visiting Scotland was given a boost by no less a person than King George IV. The king had been on the throne for less than two years when Sir Walter Scott masterminded this journey of good will to the north. By all accounts the king enjoyed himself and returned home bearing as a gift the knife, fork, and spoon used by the Young Pretender in 1745! Good will had been reestablished, and now that the old wounds

*Above:*
Figure 227. Another box with the W. CRAB mark. The overall design is similar to the previous box, but this box has the added central picture of a crest. This is very finely drawn in penwork, as is the black surround on the front and top of the box. 12.5" wide. Late eighteenth century. *Courtesy of Anne Brooks.* $5,000–7,000.

*This whole page:*

Figure 228. This magnificent tea chest is nothing short of an artistic explosion. The floral paintings on all surfaces are breathtakingly beautiful. The compositions, delineations, and colors are the work of a master painter; there is not one neglected petal or leaf. The work ranks among the best within the genre of flower painting, be it on a box or a canvas. On applied art, such highly skilled work is rare but not unique. It is found both on wooden and papier-mâché boxes decorated by professional artists commissioned by box makers of high repute. There is something that sets this tea chest apart. The picture on the top does not conform to any genre of decoration popular on boxes: it is not another floral composition, it is not chinoiserie, and it is not a classical scene or a visual precise representation of a scene or a building. This painting is a direct artistic vision by a fine-art artist. It belongs to the stratosphere of individual high art. There are strong pointers to this painting being Scottish. Scottish literature and art of the time are infused with the philosophical ideas of the Scottish thinkers of the eighteenth and early nineteenth centuries. In brief, for an artistic manifestation to bear cultural validity, it must celebrate the intellectual and historical context of the scene. The collective experience must dominate over the individual; man must take his place within the natural order. Looking at the work of nineteenth century Scottish artists as well as the places they painted, Horatio McCulloch emerges as the obvious candidate. McCulloch painted the area around Cadzow Castle and Forest from 1834, when he lived within easy distance of the area, in Hamilton, southeast of Glasgow. The atmospheric quality, the composition, and the treatment of the elements in the landscape, such as the trees and rocks, as well as the location and the use of light values, point to the work of McCulloch. The tiny touch of red is also a McCulloch trait. The structure of the painting frames the landscape around a central glowing part. There are shade cloud contrasts in the sky and subtle reflections on the water, but essentially the center creates a bright pattern framed by dark trees. The water flows in the midst of present time. The castle on the top is redolent of past history, which overshadows the man fishing near a contemporaneous cottage. The domestic finds its place within the sublime. The trees, the stones, and the plants are beautifully painted, but not with specific detail; they are rather the sum of the experience of nature. The painting is not there as a glorified postcard, but as a visual manifestation of the soul of the nation. Man's instinct guides his way among topography where the air is crowded with the spirit of heroes and philosophers. The past and the present harmonize in a romanticism infused with grandeur and heroism. Nothing could be more axiomatic of Scottish high art. To find such a painting on a box is nothing short of a miracle. It must have been a special commission by a patron who did not just want arguably the best painted box, but definitely the best painted box, ever. This tea chest was the only object painted by a fine-art artist featured on the BBC program on Scottish art by Lachlan Goudie, artist and art expert (2015). 15" wide. $?

of royal rivalry had been healed, things Scottish became desirable even in the South.

By the time the Smiths entered the scene, conditions were perfect for further innovation and expansion. It is possible that two of the five Smith brothers were already in business in 1810. However, it was the two younger brothers, William and Andrew, who put the family firmly on the map. Their business dates from 1821, with premises in Mauchline by 1823.

The Smiths of Mauchline were prolific makers, and it is no wonder that they are the best known of all the Scottish makers. Not only did they make boxes of local interest, but they expanded their business to embrace souvenir making for other parts of the globe, exporting their wares in large quantities. In fact Mauchline ware, as it came to be called, finally abandoned the secret hinge. The more commercial later boxes were fitted with metal hinges and no longer had the specific Scottish quality of the woodwork.

It is not easy to distinguish between the makers and painters of the late eighteenth and early nineteenth centuries. The technique and finishes used were similar in all workshops. The wood used was called plane in Scotland, which is the same type of wood referred to as sycamore in the South of England, or maple in America. This wood, with its light color, dense texture, and unfigured appearance, was very suitable for painting or penwork decoration. The designs were executed with great skill by artists of renown, such as Daniel Macnee, William Leighton Leitch, and Horatio McCulloch, to name but a few (these three worked in Cumnock).

Motifs painted or drawn on the boxes were variable. Earlier boxes were sometimes painted with neoclassical or chinoiserie decoration. The more immediately recognizable landscapes, pastoral scenes, flowers, hunting scenes, and scenes from legend and poetry are more particularly characteristic of Scottish work. One early design, which was used as an overall background, was a network of finely drawn wavy lines. This was used to frame a central picture, or a cartouche, which enclosed initials or a family crest.

Mauchline could not lay claim to the genius of Sandy, nor to the entrepreneurial spirit of Lord Gardenstone, but it could lay claim to neighborliness with Robert Burns (1759–1796), the Scottish bard born at Alloway.

This association gave the Smiths and the numerous other Ayrshire makers a wealth of possible illustrations. The bard himself, his poetry, the landscape associated with him, and his poems all were proudly painted on Scottish boxes.

The Scottish box was often decorated with an interlocking thistle design around the central decoration. This design could also incorporate the English rose and the Irish shamrock, and in some boxes this continuous pattern is the predominant or sole decoration.

The varnishing of boxes was a long albeit less artistic business. It was done either with thirty coats of spirit varnish, which took three weeks to dry, or with fifteen coats of copal varnish, which took six weeks to dry. The final product was then polished with ground flint.

*Above:*
Figure 229. A rosewood veneered box with a central panel in light wood decorated with a picture of a boy wearing a kilt and riding his horse. Very likely it is meant to be Bonnie Prince Charlie. The work is executed in pyrography, which is sometimes called "poker work." Although the box does not have the typical Scottish hinge, it has a more solid look than English boxes of the period, and it is of Scottish inspiration. 11.75" wide. Ca. 1815–20. $2,000–2,500.

Figure 230. An example of the pattern of roses, thistles, and shamrocks typical in Scottish work. This particular box is a large snuffbox, but this type of interwoven pattern occurs on all types of boxes. $1,500–1,700.

This whole page:
Figure 231. An early tartan painted tea caddy with a central picture of a railway bridge, a bridge, and a townscape. The caddy is stamped on one side of the lock: "S. STIVEN & SONS LAURENCEKIRK," and on the other side: "BOX MAKERS TO HER MAJESTY." Note that this is not one of the machine-painted, machine-printed, or paper-covered Mauchlinware. 8.5" wide. It has the characteristic wooden hinge. Second quarter nineteenth century. $3,000–7,000.

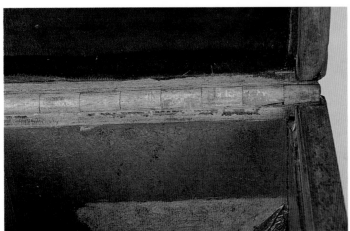

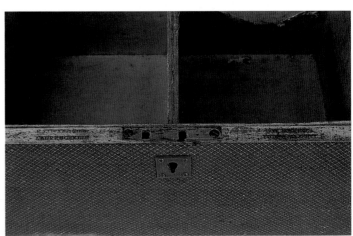

Once the Scottish makers began to look for recognizable Scottish themes, it was not long before they started experimenting with chequer and tartan designs. By about 1820, hand-painted tartan replaced the thistles and roses on some of the boxes. Tartan became very fashionable, and early tartanware had a certain quality. Charles Dickens had a tartan stamp box that he specifically bequeathed in his will. This new, preferred design gave the opportunity for the ingenious Smiths to overtake their competitors. They invented and patented a machine for painting lines that speeded up the decoration of tartanware. This machine they perfected at different stages, acquiring patents for the different processes. The Mauchline machine was described as "weaving with colors."

In 1850, William and Andrew Smith published a book describing the "Authenticated Tartans of the Clans and Families of Scotland." Other makers jumped on the bandwagon of tartanware, including James McRae and Co., which exhibited some of the work in the Great Exhibition of 1851.

However, competing with the Smiths, with their royal patronage both from William IV and later Queen Victoria, was no easy matter. The Smiths eventually swept away all their competitors and built a commercial empire for themselves.

The Smiths also experimented with transfer ware, and the first Scottish transfer-decorated boxes are of excellent quality. Viewed from a certain distance, they are hardly distinguishable from penwork-decorated objects. The engraved copper plates used for this work were copied from fine drawings by very skilled artists, and the transfer work was executed by experienced craftsmen.

Another Smith first, again executed by one of their ingenious machines, was engraving on metal-covered boxes, in imitation of damascene work. This was restricted to small items on account of the technical difficulty of applying this process to larger boxes.

The Smith boxes are marked in different ways, depending on whether the brothers worked together or separately. In 1843 they split up, and during the decades that followed, what had begun as an art form was taken over by industry. Many boxes became mere souvenirs. By the middle of the century the transfers had become simple representations of places, and the tartanware was made by simply sticking printed paper on wood. Boxes were made for utilitarian commercial use, such as for thread manufacturers. These boxes have a certain nostalgic charm, but they are a far cry from the vision of Lord Gardenstone.

Another late-nineteenth-century decorative technique was applying ferns to the wooden surface. At first this was done by a hand process, laying or printing directly from plants, and later with transfers, or even photo labels.

By far the greater number of Scottish boxes made with the concealed hinge are snuffboxes. Larger boxes are rarer. These are usually of rectangular shape, with straight sides and flat tops. Occasionally a high-quality Scottish box, decorated in thistle or other typical style, can have a non-Scottish hinge. In such cases, as also in the case of most of the larger early transfer boxes, the hinges are of good quality, usually of the "double" kind. The late souvenir boxes have thin metal hinges.

In addition to the above, there are also boxes that were made by Scottish cabinetmakers that do not conform to the mainstream of Scottish boxes but follow the stylistic developments prominent at the time in the whole of the United Kingdom. Boxes with characteristic Scottish features were made in centers that concentrated in the making of small items only and not in cabinetmaking workshops.

*Above and right:*
Figure 232. A sewing box decorated with transfers of different views. Note that the views are not the souvenir box landmarks, but rather romantic visions of the country. The interior is partitioned for sewing tools, with a lidded central compartment decorated with yet another picture. 11.75" wide. Second quarter nineteenth century. $700–1,000.

# CHAPTER 14 *Irish Boxes*

King George IV was the most suitable of all monarchs to extend the hand of friendship to the Irish. He had the right temperament to appreciate the charismatic idiosyncrasies of the Celtic character. The surreal, the myth, and the magic were close to his heart and transposed to his physical environment. So it is not surprising that in 1821, the recently crowned king decided to make the first state visit to Ireland. He entered Dublin wearing the uniform of a field marshal, which he had designed for himself, and in his hat he attached a spray of shamrock. The visit was a success. Ireland was thereafter placed on the map as a fashionable destination.

The beauties of the country had been discovered and extolled since the eighteenth century, but the difficulty of traveling and the lack of facilities meant that only very few ventured across the sea, and even fewer made the journey to the more remote and rugged area of the Killarney Lakes. This area of breathtaking beauty lies in the southwest of Ireland. The landscape, which was formed during the last Ice Age, combines the picturesque with the dramatic. It inspired many poets and artists and eventually began to attract a few adventurous tourists.

During his visit, the king was presented with a bog oak carved walking stick, which became the ignition signal for the production of such items as souvenirs of Ireland. Bog oak, a dense, dark wood, was found in plenty in the area of the Lakes, and local craftsmen soon saw its potential as a material suitable for the creation of beautiful carved objects. During the 1820s, accommodation in the Killarny area improved, and by the 1830s, there were at least two spacious inns and other houses offering rooms. Race meetings, a regatta, and most of all deer hunting were organized for the entertainment of visitors.

The makers of Tunbridge ware in England were perhaps the first to realize the potential of selling boxes with views of the Killarney Lakes to visitors and began to produce mosaic work with local views. These were supplied to local tradespeople, who sold them both to Irish and English tourists. The local cabinetmakers, seeing the demand and appreciating the wealth of their own timbers, soon began to make their own distinctive ware.

During the 1840s, rail travel made the area more accessible, resulting in the increase of visitors. In 1847, the poet Tennyson was captivated by the dramatic beauty of the place and wrote:

*The long light shakes across the lakes,*
*And the wild cataract leaps in glory.*
*Blow, bugle, blow, set the wild echoes flying.*

*(The Princess)*

Others, too, were charmed by the scenery, the clean air, the varied flora, and the charismatic people and wanted to take home some mementos of their experience. It was during the mid-Victorian decades that the most characteristic Killarney work was produced. Unlike Tunbridge ware and Scottish work, which had been influenced by other traditions, Killarney ware was made mostly out of local woods, featuring local themes right from the start.

The first timbers to be used were mostly bog oak and bog yew. Holly, laburnum, maple, sycamore, and yew, as well as wood from the arbutus bush—of the strawberry genus—were soon added to the repertoire of box makers.

The boxes were decorated with local views, such as Muckross Abbey, Ross Castle, Glena Cottage, Innisfallen, Dunloe Castle, Killarney House, and Aghadoe. Eagles, deer, ferns, arbutus sprays, oak leaves, acorns, roses, holly, and thistles represented the natural life of the area. The shamrock and the Irish harp affirmed the nationality of the objects. The motifs were executed in marquetry and pyrography. Sometimes the pyrography was used to emphasize details in the design, and sometimes it was used to execute the design or to provide a diaper pattern of background ornamentation.

Killarney ware won royal patronage both from Queen Victoria and the Prince of Wales. At the time of the Great Exhibition in 1851, Denis Connell, one of the foremost makers of the work, found it worth his while to bring and exhibit his wares in London. Arthur Jones, Son & Co., from Dublin, also exhibited Killarney ware, which by the middle of the century had asserted itself as a more widely practiced Irish style.

Although Killarney boxes continued to be made throughout the nineteenth and twentieth centuries, by the last decades of the nineteenth century, the industry was already in decline. There were, and still are, people visiting the beauty spots around the Lakes and the "Gap of Dunloe," but the traditional ways faded with the advent of the modern tourist.

Killarney never quite acquired the polished ways of Tunbridge Wells, with its parade of shops and sophisticated entertainments. Its social charm lay in the alternative view of life held by its inhabitants, which was romanticized by the urban visitors. People such as Kate Kearney, who sold her poteen and was described as one of the "mountain dew women tribe," and girl hawkers who sold boxes and other souvenirs around the streets must have been a breath of fresh air after the affectation of the metropolitan social scene.

Killarney ware has a very distinctive style and is very recognizable. The motifs and styles remained the same for decades, and it is often impossible to date boxes accurately. However, I must confess that for sheer "charm factor" I treasure two Killarney boxes above all others. They are very typical of the work, but they also convey both humanity and warmth shared by the patron and the maker at the time of their creation.

If anybody out there knows who Flo and May were, please let me know.

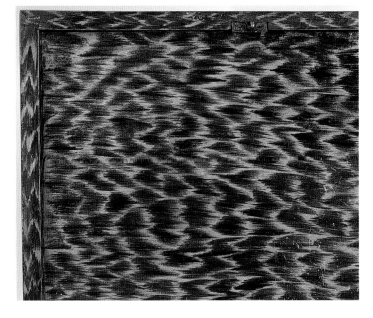

*This whole page:*
Figure 233. A sycamore box painted with a scene of Gothic ruins, with two small figures dwarfed by the size of the crumbling structures. A lake, a moored boat, and a small island with further ruins show in the background. Trees grow among the walls unchecked. A strong example of the Gothic style, well painted to convey the atmosphere of ancient mystery and legend among the decay. The sides are painted with native flowers, roses, bindweed, heart's ease, marigolds, and others. The frieze has a running pattern of the Irish shamrock. The picture is Muckross Abbey on the Killarney Lakes. It was most probably painted by one of the first travelers to the area. The boat suggests the way the Abbey was approached. The inside is treated to resemble tortoiseshell. 10.5" wide. Second half eighteenth century. $3,000–4,000.

*Above and right:*

Figure 234. A typical box with a picture of a castle in the midst of shamrocks. The main body of the box is veneered in yew wood. A very unusual feature is the writing in *piqué* work on the two strips of wood on the top and bottom of the picture. It reads "May Butler, Killarney Lakes." 5" wide. Mid-nineteenth century. $500–600.

Figure 235. A domed-top box, perhaps originally a tea caddy inlaid with an Irish harp on top, and shamrocks. The main body of the box is veneered in burr and straight yew. 8" wide. Second quarter nineteenth century. $1,200–1,500.

Figure 236. A long box, with the surround veneered in yew, the center inlaid with geometric designs and shamrocks, and the front with engraved strawberry leaves. The box has very fine *piqué* writing on the top that reads: "KILLARNEY LAKES. FROM MAY TO DEAR OLD FLO." As in the earlier example, such writing is most unusual and was probably done only in the early days, when boxes were commissioned personally. 10" wide. Second quarter nineteenth century. $1,500–2,000.

# CHAPTER 15 *Oriental Lacquer*

## GATHERING AND PREPARING

O riental lacquer is the natural sap of trees belonging to the *Toxicodendron* (formerly *Rhus*) species. It was first used in China both to protect and to beautify wooden structures and objects. There are references to Emperor Shun (2255—2205 BCE), the last of the five sages, advocating the use of lacquer to his people. It is impossible to determine the precise date of its first application; it is part of an ancient and revered tradition, interlinked with the culture of this complex, ancient civilization.

The tree that produces the best lacquer is the *Toxicodendron vernicifluum*, formerly *Rhus vernicifera* (*Ch'ichu*), which is indigenous to China. At first the trees grew wild, but later, as their value was understood, they were cultivated and even periodically protected by law.

The trees ooze the best sap when they are a few years old. Depending on weather and soil conditions, they can mature in five years and continue to yield good lacquer until they are about ten. The best time for gathering the sap is during the warmer months of the year, when the trees are actively growing and the liquid flows and rises in greater quantities. It also oozes more freely before cold weather causes it to freeze. The trees are found mostly on high ground above 6,500 feet, where temperatures are very low in winter. In earlier times, before the plains were cleared for agriculture, *Toxicodendron* trees were also grown on lower ground.

Traditionally the sap was gathered by incising the trees horizontally and allowing the liquid to trickle into cup-shaped containers of copper or bamboo tied under the cuts. When the sap first came out it was dirty white, somewhat like a grayish mushroom. Exposure to light and air thickened and darkened it.

The preparation of the sap was and still is a long and laborious process. At first it was strained to remove any impurities, such as fragments of wood and insects, that had gathered in the containers. Then the sap was heated in shallow containers. Throughout the "cooking" process it was stirred and skimmed, so it gradually became more pure and even. Finally it was filtered through cloth to make sure that even tiny particles of foreign matter were removed. Once the sap had been purified and turned to lacquer, it was stored in airtight containers, where it could be kept for years.

Inferior lacquer was extracted from the smaller branches of the trees by boiling them in hot water and then allowing the water to evaporate. The lacquer was then cleared of impurities and used for undercoating.

## APPLYING THE LACQUER

Once the lacquer was prepared, an even more painstaking and time-consuming process was needed to successfully use it for coating whatever surface was to be lacquered.

The main quality of lacquer is that it provides a hard surface impervious to insects, acids, water, and other natural and human-inflicted attacks. However, for the lacquer to harden evenly, care and skill as well as vigilance must not slacken for one second. The chemical process that combines the elements within the sap and enables the final product to harden must be carried out in strictly controlled conditions. The temperature must be between 25 and 30 degrees centigrade (77—86°F), and the humidity as high as 80 to 85 percent.

Oxygen is necessary for the process of polymerization to be successful, and humidity ensures that oxygen is easily and evenly absorbed. Added to this, a humid atmosphere ensures that the lacquer dries evenly without the uppermost layer, however thin, drying too fast, with the risk of trapping damp bubbles.

Workshops for drying lacquer were often set up near rivers. Small wooden chambers for drying objects were kept damp by moistening the walls. Vapor baths were also used for the purpose of increasing humidity.

The basic structure of objects—such as boxes—to be coated was constructed out of softwoods, mostly pines. The pieces of wood had to be selected so that they were free of knots, because the resin, which the knotty parts of timber excrete more freely, could seep into the lacquer and spoil the hardening process.

Once the wooden form was made, it was primed in inferior lacquer. On some boxes a thin muslin-type cloth was also used to cover the basic structure. This was held in place with vegetable glue or lacquer, sometimes mixed with rice paste. Looking at cross sections of damaged boxes, it is obvious that different workshops employed different techniques. The main purpose was always the same: to seal the wood completely before the final, more-decorative layers were applied. The wood sap was thus completely isolated from the final surface.

It was important to seal the underside of the wood at the same time as the top so that the drying process was uniform on both sides, avoiding the problem of uneven hardening, which could cause cracking or rippling. When the box was completely primed, it was smoothed down with ground stone or clay so that its surface was as even as possible before the more precise and arduous application of the top layers began. At this stage the required pigment was added to the lacquer. The lacquer was then applied in very thin coats. Each coat was allowed

*This whole page:*

Figure 237. A rare compendium cabinet in Chinese-export lacquer, which exemplifies and combines many fine characteristics of such work. The top opens to a sewing compartment complete with carved ivory tools. The second drawer is fitted with a jewelry tray, the third drawer is empty, and the fourth, which is double the depth, pulls out completely and folds down into a writing box. The whole piece is structured so that the cartouched centers are sunk in, giving a three-dimensional effect. The framing borders on the doors and sides are elaborately decorated with objects and creatures rich in symbolism. Among others, there are bats, symbolic of good fortune; butterflies and flowers, denoting love; and bottle gourds and scrolls, symbols of the Immortals. The central scenes are minute representations of figures in gardens and pavilions. The top of the cabinet is decorated with a detailed scene of figures on the terraces of an important structure, most probably a palace. The whole is framed by an elaborate design of a *ruyi* scepter. This does not have the meaning of a mace of office. It is a graphic device that figures in important texts, including Buddhist writings, and that symbolizes the wishes for the fulfillment of an ambition. This central cartouche is surrounded by dragons chasing a flaming pearl. The dragon was the multilayered symbol of the emperor, the Son of Heaven. The emperor was the only person allowed to have five-clawed dragon motifs. The dragons here have four claws, four-clawed dragons being the prerogative of princesses. The corners feature realistic and mythical animals. The inside lid is finely decorated with warring scenes arranged in an oval flanked by exquisitely painted grasses. The banners refer to the three armies of the Romance of the Three Kingdoms (see the chapter "Tea Caddies," figure 247). The border is painted with peacocks; the facings, with peacock feathers. The inside door panels and the back are decorated with vases. The word for vase, *ping*, is phonetically the same as the word for peace. The vase is also deeply symbolic with its connotations of the womb of deities. It is one of the symbols of the Buddha and denotes perfect wisdom. The vases are further enriched with representations of peacocks, orioles, and butterflies around flowers. The flowers are peonies, the Queen of flowers, a symbol of wealth and distinction. It was believed to be the only flower who dared disobey the order of Empress Wu to bloom at her will. The cabinet stands on dragon feet, a pearl held in the mouth of each. Pearls spat out by dragons during storms were highly significant, denoting the substance of the soul. The decorative significance of this piece is so rich that it almost provides a complete record of the work carried on export lacquer during the most important years of this art. 14.5" wide when closed. Ca. 1820–40. $?

to dry for three days or more if necessary, until it became completely hard. It was then rubbed smooth with clay or charcoal dust. Several layers were built up until a completely smooth and even surface was achieved. The final coats were rubbed with deer horn ash, the finest form of abrasive.

Examining cross sections of damaged boxes, it is obvious that different craftsmen favored different techniques. The color of the undercoats is sometimes whitish, sometimes brown, and sometimes grayish. This must be because the undercoating lacquer was sometimes mixed with clay, sometimes with fine ash, sometimes with rice flour, and sometimes with any of these in different combinations. All these materials had been used in making lacquered objects for thousands of years.

It took up to thirty coats of applied lacquer, starting with undercoats and grading up to finer layers, before a box was ready for decoration. Having gone through the hands of the cabinetmaker, who made the wooden base, and the lacquerer, who prepared it, the box then moved on to the artist, who decorated it.

# DECORATION

Lacquer decoration has always been revered in China as one of the great arts. Prized throughout the centuries above gold, it reflects the civilization that developed it, in that it is a patient and meditative process, requiring a variety of structured disciplines, as well as intellectual and artistic input.

Perceived as such a special reflection of the country's culture, it is not surprising that the art of lacquer decoration was a constant striving for perfection. This art took many and varied forms throughout the four thousand years of its known existence. Archaeological evidence points to lacquer first used as a protective coating, and by the second millennium BCE as an in-fill in bronze-incised objects, or adhesive for precious metals or stones.

Carved objects made out of multilayered built lacquer were made at various periods and are still made today, albeit new techniques have made the work simpler and the quality inferior. Shallow carving on lacquered surfaces as a decorative device on its own, or in conjunction with other techniques, was also used at different periods.

### DECORATION ON BOXES MADE IN CHINA FOR EXPORT

Europe learned about Chinese lacquer as a result of the activities of the merchants who first ventured to the East. The first examples were brought back as early as the sixteenth century, but these were mostly pieces of furniture, and although mindful of their European destination, they were still very much within the Chinese tradition of decoration. In France a Jesuit priest, Father Martin Martinius, mentioned the lacquer tree as early as 1655, and the Italian father Filippo Bonanni explained his understanding of the process in 1690.

*Above:*
Figure 238. Two lacquered boxes inlaid in ivory and semiprecious stones. This work is close to the aesthetic tradition of China and was not developed for the export market. Octagonal, 8" wide. Oblong, 6.9" wide. Nineteenth century. $1,000–1,500.

It took another century before this work was really developed in the form of boxes with a view to export. It was during the last decades of the eighteenth century, when the East India Company began to trade aggressively, that a distinctive style of lacquer boxes began to emerge. Gold leaf, gold lines, and painting in colors or gold was used in China for lacquer decoration since the first millennium BCE. The boxes decorated for export continued this ancient tradition of painting in gold. Other colors were sparingly introduced. The painting was applied to the final coat of black lacquer. A few boxes were finished in red lacquer, and in rare occasions, a box was completely coated in silver, gold, or white gold before it was painted.

In China, different ways of employing gold leaf or lines were used in lacquer decoration throughout the centuries. Examples of painting on flat lacquer exist on objects dating from the Han dynasty (206 BC–221 CE). On early objects, gold

*Above and right:*

Figure 239. An early box in terms of export lacquer, decorated in gold raised and flat lacquer, depicting landscapes with rocks. The design predates the popular decoration for export work on boxes. It is very much in the style of decoration on early pieces of Chinese furniture that were exported to Europe and rooted in Chinese aesthetic tradition. In Chinese, "landscape" was literally "mountains and water." This included the nature around these two symbol-laden elements. 8" wide. Second quarter eighteenth century. $1,500–2,000.

was used mostly as gold leaf inlay. The origins of gold painting as seen on boxes dating from the eighteenth century date from the relatively recent fifteenth century and are the result of Japanese influence on such decoration.

The art of lacquer was introduced to Japan by Chinese craftsmen, who also introduced the art of incising lacquer and enhancing it with gold lines. The Japanese were most impressed by lacquer as an art medium. They also admired the appropriateness of gold decoration on this smooth, luxurious surface. When more gold reserves were found in Japan, Japanese artists perfected the craft of powdering gold very finely and mixing it with lacquer, making it possible to paint or build layers of gold dust and lacquer on pre-prepared surfaces without the need of using gold leaf. This gave the artist much more flexibility in using gold, since it could now be applied in extremely fine lines, thus allowing for complete artistic control.

Craftsmen from both countries were sent back and forth to learn from each other. A renowned Chinese lacquerer, Yang Xuan, is said to have gone to Japan early in the fifteenth century to learn the new gold techniques from the Japanese. He not only learned from the Japanese but also invented a technique of incising and in-filling lacquer with gold that impressed his very teachers.

During the four centuries following this visit, there was a lot of cross-pollination between the two cultures regarding lacquer decoration. The sprinkled gold and other metal dust technique associated with Japanese work is also found to a much-lesser degree on Chinese objects. Although the decorative styles are on the whole distinguishable, there are overlaps to the extent of confusion.

Furthermore, there are the oriental symbols and motifs found on lacquer throughout the Far East, such as dragons, vases, insects, and diaper patterns to denote water, air, and earth,

as well as stylized borders of Greek key, or other formal designs. It is not always certain where each design originated from, although China, with its history of early cosmopolitan trading, was usually the first oriental country to add to the repertoire of lacquer decoration.

Chinese artists absorbed and translated designs from different traditions, imbuing them with a unique oriental flavor. These imported influences were added to the art, which had its roots deep in Chinese culture and spiritual attitude, and contributed to the creation of some spectacularly beautiful export boxes. These boxes encapsulate that particular moment in

Figure 240. A scalloped-shaped box containing smaller boxes in pre-export decoration. The arrangement of the designs, allowing for the ground to remain black, is characteristic of furniture pieces that gave rise to English chinoiserie decoration. 10" wide. Mid-eighteenth century. $1,500–2,000.

history when the East truly met the West. There is no way that an artist who was not steeped in the tradition of striving for perfection, however long it takes, could work in lacquer. The most important reward was the final artistic achievement.

## EXPORT LACQUER BOXES, EIGHTEENTH CENTURY TO 1820

By the end of the eighteenth century, the East India Company had its feet well ensconced in Chinese soil. Near the "factories" of this company and other European and American company headquarters, a small trading community sprang up, trading not only in commodities such as tea and spices, but also in an unprecedented wealth of eclectic goods such as silk, porcelain, paintings, and, of course, lacquer. Most of these artistic outlets were in the Old and New China Streets, which were within easy reach of the foreign traders.

The first boxes to be made in "export lacquer" were commissioned by the foreign traders or diplomats for their own use. These were of very high quality, and family crests or initials often formed part of the decoration. Such a box included in the 1774 inventory of the Clive collection at Powis Castle combines several characteristics of the period. The overall design is that of stylized plants in precise zigzag patterns, with the family crest depicted in gold within a central cartouche.

The eighteenth century boxes have several features that betray their European destination. They were made to be used for the needs of Europeans or Americans and were mostly card boxes, sewing boxes, and tea caddies. Their forms were of the type that in European countries was made mostly in wood.

The decoration was of a style instantly appreciated by Europeans. Formal floral designs, borders of linear patterns, and centrally placed cartouches predominated. There was a definite input of decorative conventions that were fashionable in England at the end of the eighteenth century. There was the symmetry of neoclassicism and the quasi-classical symbolism of certain plants.

Vines, ivy, and other stylized flora were the order of the day. Symmetrically arranged, these motifs were reminiscent of ancient Rome, although in raised gold lacquer they definitely acquired a Chinese aura. Some boxes had diapered designs interspersed with the floral designs, or had leafy patterns that formed part of a diapered background. The convention of complete surface decoration had a definite Chinese feel about it, especially when seen on the smooth lacquer surface.

Sometimes the design was executed in a mixture of flat and raised lacquer painted in gold. It had the textural quality of opulent brocades. The artists who produced this work must have been very well versed both in lacquer decoration and stoical patience in the pursuit of perfection. Each box represents countless hours of dedicated application.

The shapes of the eighteenth-century lacquer boxes were restrained. Like their European counterparts, they were made in straight lines, with flat tops. Their uses were differentiated by their interior.

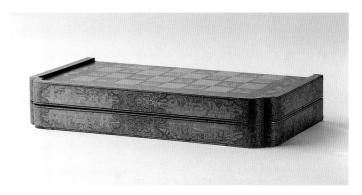

*Above:*

Figure 241. A combined backgammon and chess board in export lacquer. Gold is used for marking whole squares, for painting delicate borders, for framing the center with fighting dragons, and for painting scenes with oriental figures in alternating squares. Delicately and expertly executed, gold is used both as a pure decorative medium and as a means of subtly marking the game squares. 22.25" wide. Second quarter nineteenth century. $3,500–4,500.

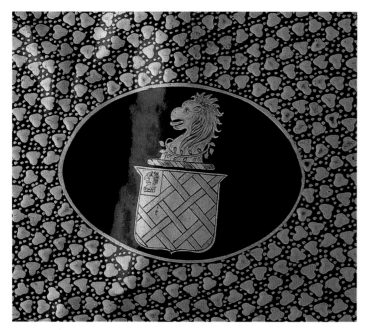

Figure 242. A characteristic design of a background of raised gold lacquer and a European coat of arms painted in the center. The decoration is very much in the European taste. This is on a flat card box, but such work was also done on other types of boxes. Ca. 1780–1800.

*Above and right:*
Figure 243. A pattern of tendrils and vines characteristic of late eighteenth century European-influenced decoration. It is found on different types of boxes, although this particular box is a very rare example of a lacquer paint box. Two boxes with similar vine patterns were shown in the bedroom of George IV at the *Chinese Whispers* exhibition at the Brighton Pavilion in 2008. It contains some china dishes for mixing pigments. 14.5" wide. Ca. 1790–1800. $6,000–8,000.

# NINETEENTH-CENTURY EXPORT LACQUER BOXES

The early nineteenth century was the golden period for the Chinese-lacquer box. The merchants associated with the East India Company were making vast amounts of money selling opium to the Chinese, albeit at times via circuitous ways. More money was available for buying Chinese treasures to satisfy the demand of the increasingly prosperous people at home.

In addition to individually commissioned boxes, a number of additional boxes were bought with a view to selling them in England. They were also sold to other European countries from the London-bonded warehouses of the Company. The Cathay style had already captured the imagination of the European *beau monde*. A whimsical oriental style had already been set in motion by such arbiters of fashion as the Prince Regent himself. This led to significant stylistic and thematic developments in the decoration of lacquer boxes during the first decades of the nineteenth century.

On boxes made during the early years of the century, the differences are subtle, often resulting in very pleasing cross-cultural effects. For example, a background of vine leaves could surround an oriental scene. A diapered dot pattern could be juxtaposed with a picture of Chinese life.

The development of the decoration followed the pattern of trade and social change. Chinese-export boxes were first made for foreigners who commissioned work for specific patrons, or for their personal needs. As in other forms of such commissions—for example, furniture or paintings—the person ordering the item supplied designs and specifications. The craftsmanship of the Chinese was admired, but the European eye was too unaccustomed to oriental art to accept it without a degree of Western mitigation. Thus, the eighteenth-century boxes have tendrils that could have been copied from Pompeii, and vines that could have grown in Greece. When such motifs were combined with lattice and abstract meandering designs that were mostly oriental, the latter were subtle and unobtrusive.

*Above and right:*
Figure 244. Details of cartouches painted with beasties, including a Buddhist lion. A typical border design of the early nineteenth century.

However, as foreigners became more familiar with Chinese art forms and the symbolism and culture expressed therein, the balance began to shift. Whereas at first the English were trying to tell the Chinese what they wanted them to know and make, by about 1820 they wanted the people back home to know what the Chinese knew and made.

The box borders became more elaborate, often depicting mythical beasts, butterflies, and birds. The vignettes within the borders began to have paintings portraying Chinese courtly scenes. These were mostly of figures in pavilioned gardens or in landscapes. Figurative painting was already part of the long tradition of Chinese lacquer decoration, so it was a natural step to apply it to the export work.

Another type of early nineteenth century decoration was the depiction of an animal or bird within a cartouche. This was done in flat paint, usually in blue, gray, and red. These creatures were stylized and glamorized and harkened back to Chinese-lacquer paintings of previous centuries. Such vignettes were executed with great skill, and each one of them is a complete artwork in itself.

By the 1820s, intertrading was very robust, and although foreigners were forbidden from living in Chinese areas, a lot of social intercourse had developed among the traders, diplomats, and the Co Hong merchants. The Co Hong merchants were the go-betweens permitted by the emperor to trade with the "foreign devils." They amassed huge fortunes and kept impressive and beautiful establishments where they occasionally entertained their foreign colleagues.

Their fairy tale homes were constructed among wondrous gardens in shapes and structures of unfamiliar curves and pinnacles. These, together with the visits to the botanical gardens, which foreigners were allowed, must have opened up a miraculous new world to European traders.

The Chinese people too, floating in their rich silk robes, must have looked pretty spectacular. Their festivals and activities tinged with fairy world magic were a breath of fresh air after living within the strict rules of European society. The Chinese had their rules too, but to an outsider they posed no threat; they could be presented as charming customs. In short, this was an exotic world that expanded one's understanding of beauty and culture. At least this was the vision the traders wanted to present to the people back home.

The artwork on the boxes began to depict more and more scenes from Chinese life: gardens, water, pavilions peopled with ladies, sages in grottoes, musicians, animals, birds, and boats. In a way the boxes became like elaborate and precious postcards of the enchanted Cathay.

Sometimes the scenes were very complex and precise. They depicted festivals, battles, the life of the harbor, or specific activities, such as the growing of tea or the treatment of silk. Boxes decorated in this way did not have borders, and the painting, which was mostly flat, was not contained within cartouches. The scenes were sharply executed in gold lines against black lacquer in a free asymmetrical fashion, like landscape painting. In very rare examples of tea-processing scenes, or battles, Chinese calligraphy was included in the decoration. Boxes with a narrative decorative theme were not made in any numbers and as a result are now rare.

Flat, freehand painting was also done on boxes covered completely with white gold or silver and decorated in black and colors. These must have been the work of one artist, since their style is very distinctive. Occasionally, such boxes also feature

*This whole page:*

Figure 245. A superb example of a tea chest in red lacquer, framed in black lacquer and decorated in two colors of gold. The central raised panels are painted with groups of different birds among very finely painted plants. Around the panels there are tendrils, vine leaves, and grapes. On the top there are animals playing among the vines. The thin black frame is exquisitely painted with stylized grasses. The base and overhanging part of the lid are painted with centipedes, butterflies, and moths. The interior is painted with butterflies; the facings, with grass patterns. The lid of the metal container is edged with figures in a garden. Both the structure and the decoration on this piece are most unusual. The box is structured along European lines using paneling, except that the cartouches are in wavy, softer Chinese lines. Birds and insects were not usually painted as the main subject on export lacquer-ware. All the creatures painted on this box have symbolic and mythical connotations in Chinese culture. Birds in particular are rich in associations, and many stories exist of bird language–speaking people who escape danger by being helped by birds. On one side there is a crowing cock, the tenth creature in the Chinese zodiac. Among his many attributes, he is supposed to ward off evil and to symbolize achievement and fame. There are also peacocks and orioles—the first standing for dignity and beauty; the second, for joy and friendship. It is very likely that this was a specially commissioned piece by a person who wanted a piece redolent of the more arcane culture of the host country. 11.5" wide. Ca. 1820. $?

Figure 246. Detail of the inside lid of a sewing box: a scene painted in raised lacquer and gold. It is particularly well preserved because it is painted on the inside of the lid of a sewing box and has escaped wear. The scene, although in this example it is larger and bolder than in most, is typical of the themes painted on most export lacquerware. It depicts an oriental pavilioned garden with elegant figures sitting and walking therein, looking as if they have all the time in the world. The box measures 17" wide, which is unusually large. Second quarter nineteenth century.

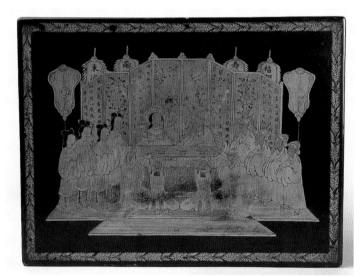

*Above, left and below:*

Figure 247. A tea chest decorated in gold on black lacquer. The theme of the decoration is steeped in Chinese tradition. It depicts the battle of the Three Kingdoms. *The Romance of the Three Kingdoms* was a fictionalized account of real events first published in the fourteenth century. This historical epic describes events that took place in the second and third centuries, when a struggle for supremacy erupted between three warring armies. The front of the box depicts Liu Bei, the legitimate Han heir, fighting with Cao Cao of Wei. The flying pennants distinguish the sides. Cao Cao, who is the final victor, is depicted with a beard, which is a Chinese convention. Important men and sages always have long beards in pictorial or theatrical representations. The top of the box has Cao Cao sitting in state. Behind him there is a screen with fine drawings and classical poetry written in a fine hand. Here is a snippet just to give a flavor of the poem: *When the cold rain became one with the waters of the river, we entered Wu. In the clear light of dawn, you will be a lone traveler to the mountains of Ch'u.* This piece would take pages to describe fully. It is so redolent of Chinese symbolism, literary reference, and culture. 11.5" wide. Second quarter nineteenth century. $?

*Below and left:*
Figure 248. A tea chest in black lacquer, completely covered in white gold and painted in very fine black lines and a few touches of color. The decoration is not in the fashion of export lacquerware, but in the ancient tradition of Chinese brush-and-ink sketches. The painting is done with assured minimal strokes. There are also poems in calligraphy. This points to the painter being a skilled and learned man. There are scenes of outdoor Chinese life and representations of flowers, fruit, birds, and landscapes, all of which carry symbolic significance. The front panel on the lid shows figures under an almond tree in bloom. The poem reads: *The color of almond flower, it perfumes ten miles.* A very fine piece that portrays both Chinese life and Chinese art. 9.25" wide. $?

verses written in fine Chinese calligraphy. Calligraphy was an art form much valued by the Chinese. The writing on these boxes expressed another highly revered Chinese intellectual pursuit: classical poetry. Very few Europeans were able to read or understand it, but the beauty of the characters and the finesse of the brushstrokes are indisputable. It is possible that Chinese-speaking foreigners commissioned some of these boxes. The Chinese artist who decorated them must have enjoyed reminding his patrons of his own ancient literary heritage. This type of box is exceptionally rare and so fine that even a fragment is worth rescuing.

Sometimes a box, which was most probably individually commissioned, included unusual decorative elements. For example, the artist combined typical Chinese decoration aimed at Europeans with very strong Chinese symbols, such as peonies, prunus, or the rare rendering of the Buddhist symbol of a vase. A European figure sneaking into the oriental landscape is equally unusual.

The earlier convention of painting within a cartouche continued, but the cartouches expanded to the point that they became the predominant element of the decoration. The borders gradually changed from tendrils of flora and diapered patterns to robust oriental motifs, such as striding dragons and giant butterflies. As the trade in such boxes expanded and more artists were employed, decoration became more varied.

By the middle of the nineteenth century, some lacquer boxes were produced, which, although very attractive, were not of equal artistic merit to the earlier examples. The scenes and

Figure 249. Another example, possibly by the same artist: this is a detail from the drawer of a sewing box. It is decorated in paint and tints over a gold background. The colors, although delicately employed, are exceptionally vivid for this kind of work. The rather melancholy verses speak of the music of the rain on the banks of the Hsiang River.

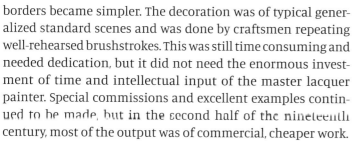

borders became simpler. The decoration was of typical generalized standard scenes and was done by craftsmen repeating well-rehearsed brushstrokes. This was still time consuming and needed dedication, but it did not need the enormous investment of time and intellectual input of the master lacquer painter. Special commissions and excellent examples continued to be made, but in the second half of the nineteenth century, most of the output was of commercial, cheaper work.

After the death of King George IV the fashion for things foreign declined, and when Victoria came to the throne in 1837 there was a patriotic spirit blowing through the English interiors. Most boxes imported after 1840 were probably sold through the Company's bonded warehouses to other European merchants and found their way to the continent.

*Above:*
Figure 250. A tea chest made in the shape of a gourd/melon. Gourds and melons had particular significance in Chinese culture. On the seventh day of the seventh month, the Feast of Women took place. Part of the ritual in central China, during this feast, was the offering of melons. On the fifteenth day of the eighth month, melon cakes were made. Because the months were divided according to the phases of the moon, the fifteenth was the night of the full moon with all its significance. The decoration is of figures in Chinese gardens. 7" wide. Second quarter nineteenth century. *Courtesy of Dr. Joseph Martin.* $6,000–10,000.

## Shapes in the Nineteenth Century

Although the decoration became more Chinese, the shapes of boxes continued to be influenced by English forms fashionable during the early part of the century. Flat, rectangular boxes gave way to what can be described as the Chinese version of the sarcophagus shape. This was quite different from the English version.

The Chinese shapes were softer and looked as if they were organically grown, rather than architecturally constructed. In fact, some boxes were gourd shaped and some were in the form of a butterfly. The most prevalent forms were abstractions of fruits and lanterns and looked quite magical.

Early nineteenth century boxes were made to stand on wooden feet that were a version of the Regency animal feet. Some very good examples had dragon, bat wing, Chinese lion, or ball-and-leaf feet that were totally oriental in feel

## Types of Boxes

Lacquer boxes made for export were primarily for cards, tea, or sewing. A few writing boxes and jewelry boxes were also produced. Some boxes were made as containers for precious things such as fans, silk shawls, and ivory Chinese puzzles. One extremely rare example I came across contained a tea service. Another was a three-tiered picnic box. Both were reminiscent of Japanese forms, although the work was definitely Chinese.

Table cabinets were also made during the nineteenth century. These were decorated both on the outside and the inside of the doors, as well as the drawers. The drawers were not usually fitted. Compendium cabinets are exceptionally rare.

*This whole page:*
Figure 251. A tea chest in the abstracted elegant form of a lantern. The main scenes are framed by elaborate floral designs, which are very well spaced, allowing for the different central compositions to be distinguished. The scenes are of figures in gardens, although one illustration is rather puzzling. It appears to be more rooted into Chinese culture than the more usual general garden and pavilion scenes. The picture portrays a man sitting under a tree. A young attendant is offering him a creature wrapped up, with only his head showing. On close examination the creature appears to be Pigsy, a character in the sixteenth century novel *Journey to the West*, which was based on the seventh century epic journey of Xuan Zang to India in pursuit of Buddhist texts. Pigsy was the companion who was consumed with earthly desires. The fact that the man is sitting under a pine tree, which symbolizes self discipline, and that Pigsy is wrapped up may be a gentle hint of advice given by the Chinese artist. Second quarter nineteenth century. 6" wide. *Courtesy of Dr. Joseph Martin.* $8,000–11,000.

Figure 252. A domed jewelry box decorated all around with scenes of figures in gardens arranged in circles. The top is decorated with a similar scene flanked by further floral motifs. The whole is framed in very fine border pattern. Ca. 1830-40. *Courtesy of Joan Kiernan.* $1,200–1,500.

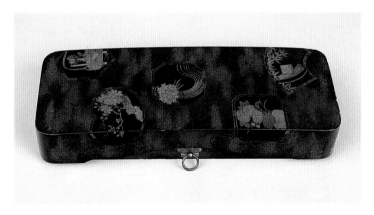

Figure 253. A black lacquer *fubako* box (a box for carrying scrolls) decorated in flat and slightly raised gold designs. 9.5" wide. Nineteenth century. $1,500–2,000.

Figure 254. Detail: a striking figure of ravens against the moon on a Japanese box. This is reminiscent of work done by the print artist Gengyo (1817–1880), whose work is said to have influenced Van Gogh. Third quarter of nineteenth century.

*Below and right:*

Figure 255. A brown lacquer *fubako* decorated in *maki-e* (gold, silver, and metal flakes and powders sprinkled on wet lacquer), *takamaki-e* (high-relief metal decoration), and *kirigane* (square flakes of gold used in the *maki-e* decoration). The *nashiji* ground (gold and bronze powder sprinkled) is further decorated with cranes flying over trees, one of them a blossoming plum. At the lower end is a picture of a *minogame*, the legendary Japanese hairy turtle. The box is of exceptional quality. Note how the decoration continues under the overlapping upper part. Eighteenth/nineteenth century. $4,000–6,000.

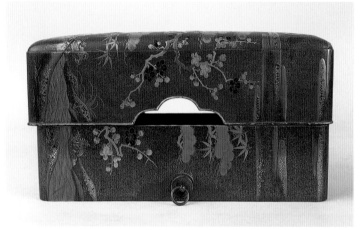

*Above and left:*

Figure 256. A black-lacquer *fubako* decorated with cranes in flight. The decoration, which is both very fine and very striking, continues on the inner part. Cranes, which are imbued with wonderful qualities and symbolism, are found in all fields of Japanese art. Here their upward flight renders them heralds of success. 17.5" wide. Nineteenth century. $4,000–6,000.

## AFTERTHOUGHT

During the latter part of the nineteenth and earlier part of the twentieth centuries, ignorance and prejudice contributed to the neglect of many of these fine boxes. Many perished or were damaged beyond recognition. Even if the boxes were not neglected, the very nature of the decoration causes it to wear with usage. The soft gold gets rubbed off with handling, and temperature extremes cause the boxes to split. Very few if any lacquer boxes have survived totally intact, and very few have survived in very good condition. Most tops show signs of wear.

This has had the effect of making available a good number of excellent examples at reasonable prices. Such boxes have escaped the mania for new-looking antiques—a phenomenon

of our times. Even if such boxes are worn, they are still very beautiful and have parts of exquisite decoration. A fragment of good lacquer represents hours of precious work.

Restoration must not be attempted, since lacquer is very toxic, and by the nature of the work is not really possible or cost effective. Consolidation is the best way of avoiding further erosion if the box is splitting. Consolidation can be done by gluing splitting parts together. This should be left to experts who are aware of the importance of reversibility to accommodate future research into materials and techniques.

Added to the quality of the lacquer work, the cross-cultural undertones of this art make it a fascinating, varied, and rewarding field of study.

*Left and below*
Figure 257. An overall *nashiji* ground decorated with separate oak leaves. This static design is very unusual for Japanese lacquer decoration. 15.5" wide. Nineteenth century. $3,000–4,000.

# Japanese Lacquer

With the exception of the Dutch, who established a trading post on the island of Hirado Shima as early as 1609, Europeans did not fare well in their trading relationships with Japan. The dislike of the Japanese toward the English was augmented when Charles II married Catherine of Braganza. Catherine, being Portuguese, carried with her the hostility felt toward the Jesuits, who pioneered Far Eastern exploration—or exploitation, depending on one's point of view. The Portuguese were expelled from Japan in 1639, and no other European nation succeeded in opening up trade routes for over three hundred years.

By the middle of the nineteenth century the wall of rejection was beginning to give way, and in 1854 a Treaty of Peace, Amity, and Commerce was signed with Japan. It was the first time that Japan gave trading concessions to the West. The first Japanese lacquered boxes were brought to England by pioneering traders who went over trying to establish commercial links with this newly welcoming country. These boxes were not made for export but were made for the Japanese market and reflected Japanese needs. The lacquer on these boxes was of exceptional quality, with built-up gold decoration depicting stylized motifs within Japanese decorative traditions.

In 1862, another great exhibition was arranged in London, and for the first time Japanese objects were seen in England. Although the popularity of Chinese lacquer was by then on the decline, the English embraced the new Japanese lacquer objects. One of the reasons was that the Japanese had not been demonized by the authorities as the Chinese had been. England was not at war with Japan. On the contrary, Japan was seen as a business opportunity, and as such it was "sold" to the people.

After the exhibition, Japanese objects were sold at the Oriental Warehouse on Regent Street. Lacquered boxes were a great favorite, judging by the fact that during the following decades many such boxes were imported into England.

Most of the boxes sold in England during the last three decades of the nineteenth century were made for export and reflected the needs of the English market. Writing boxes, workboxes, and tea caddies were arranged in the style of European wares. The quality of the lacquer work varies a great deal, with some trinket boxes painted very hastily and work and writing boxes incorporating quite garish decoration in mother of pearl slithers. Pretty though some of these boxes may be, on the whole they do not compare with the lacquer work made by the Japanese for home use.

*This whole page:*
Figure 258. A black-lacquer box decorated in raised gold with insects among vines. The very fine decoration continues on the gold-sprinkled interior. Note how the raised and flat decoration gives the insects a three-dimensional effect, without detracting from the delicacy of their limbs. 10.2" wide. Nineteenth century. $3,000–4,000.

There are some surviving export pieces that demonstrate the tradition of lacquer workmanship nurtured in Japan for over four centuries. Most of these pieces are either tea caddies or table cabinets and were perhaps the original exhibition pieces. The decoration on these is very much in the Japanese manner, with motifs depicted against a suitable background, rather than active scenes as in Chinese-export lacquer.

The Arts and Crafts movement embraced Japanese design, which was perceived as simple and striking. Some of the lacquer decoration was extremely complex and multilayered, but the whole composition could be taken in at a glance and could give the false impression of simplicity.

Japanese lacquered export boxes were imported well into the twentieth century, with their quality declining to the point of bearing no resemblance to the original work.

Figure 259. Two small boxes in innovative fun shapes made for export in the later part of the nineteenth century. The red one is a depiction of Daruma, the founder of the Chan Buddhist sect. About 3.5" wide. *Courtesy of Charleen Plumly Pollard.* $500–800.

Figure 260. A Japanese-lacquer table cabinet with decorations in flat and raised gold. The themes of stylized mountains (Fuji), clouds, rocks, and trees are characteristic of Japanese work. On this piece, they are executed in a striking manner. 14" wide. Ca. 1870. $2,000–3,000.

Anglo-Indian boxes were made in India for English expatriate residents and traders. Their forms were adapted to European needs, but their artistic input was rooted in the traditions of the Indian subcontinent. Anglo-Indian boxes were made from the earlier part of the eighteenth century onward and retained a high standard of quality well into the nineteenth century. The earliest examples—up to the 1820s—were usually commissioned pieces, and as such they were of superior quality. After the first decades of the nineteenth century, Anglo-Indian boxes were imported to England more commercially, although not in any significant numbers until the middle of the century. Anglo-Indian boxes remained highly valued throughout the nineteenth century, to the extent that inexpensive copies of their designs were copied on late nineteenth and early twentieth century tins. Due to political bias, the popularity of Anglo-Indian work declined during the middle years of the twentieth century, resulting in the neglect of many fine pieces. Fortunately, the trend has now been reversed, and good examples of such boxes are once again highly valued. Prices are rising fast.

Wooden Anglo-Indian boxes fall into four major groups:

1. Rosewood or ebony boxes inlaid with ivory

2. Sandalwood boxes veneered in ivory, tortoiseshell, horn, quills, or combinations of any of these materials

3. *Sadeli* mosaic-covered boxes on a sandalwood base

4. Carved boxes, which are of various styles and were made in different areas

The first two categories are referred to as Vizagapatam work from East India. *Sadeli* mosaic is Bombay work from West India.

There are also other types of boxes that were made in different areas of India and Ceylon, mostly from the middle years of the nineteenth century. Because these did not have a significant period of development but were made to fulfill the demand for objects in locally developed craftsmanship, I will deal with them pictorially, giving details of their special characteristics within the captions.

*Above:*

Figure 261. A hardwood cabinet covered in narrow panels of incised ivory. The designs of stylized plants are matched so that the joints in the ivory are obscured. Note the precision, control, and finesse of the line. It predates the British colonial period. 12" wide. Seventeenth to early eighteenth century. $10,000–14,000.

# 1 INLAID BOXES: VIZAGAPATAM

The rich timbers and intricate workmanship found in India in the early part of the eighteenth century caught the attention of English traders and officials. The work was not entirely unknown in Europe. It was introduced by Dutch traders during the seventeenth century and also by the Portuguese, who, before the British imposed their colonial supremacy, had already established trading links with India. Boxes dating from the pre-British period were mostly in the form of table cabinets in the typical drop-front form, which was popular in Europe and the colonies up to the middle of the eighteenth century.

The main body of such cabinets was made of hardwood—mainly rosewood or ebony—and it was inlaid with ivory. Sometimes both bone and ivory were used on the same piece. The decoration was done either by inlaying already shaped patterns into pregauged spaces in the wood, or by inserting panels of ivory already decorated with incised and lac-filled designs.

These two disciplines developed into two important categories of Vizagapatam work: the direct inlay into wood and the engraved ivory work on sandalwood boxes completely veneered with ivory. Vizagapatam workshops were established before the beginning of the eighteenth century, but very few boxes were made before the 1740s.

The work of the Indian artist-craftsman was recognized as an invaluable source for satisfying the need for furniture and boxes that would both serve and enhance the English household in India. It was not long before the English wished for their households at home to be enriched with such exotic work. India was rightly perceived in Europe as a land of immense culture. Architectural drawings of Indian buildings were

*This whole page:*

Figure 262. A hardwood box inlaid with incised and black-lacquered ivory. The work is very fine, both in its execution and conception. The design was first routed out of the wood, and then the ivory pieces were inserted in place. The details were then incised and lacquered in black lacquer before the whole was finally polished. The design emerged sharp and precise. The pattern that surrounds the top of the box and frames the sides is made up of swirling, undulating flowers. These are given definition both with lines and also with diaper patterns, which introduce an element of formality to the design. The beauty of the artwork is carried to its spectacular zenith by the central motif of an interpretation of the Tree of Life, which unexpectedly grows out of a pattern made out of feathers or leaves, suggesting both a cornucopia and a sea conch. The symmetry is deceptive, since the varying blooms rise asymmetrically to a constrained circular pattern. The spacing of the decoration is done with true virtuosity. It avoids the pitfall of overcrowding, which sometimes mars the aesthetic appeal of this type of work. There is plenty of air around the flowers. The design is redolent of many multicultural and aesthetic references and has an element of eccentric imaginings at its heart. Vizagapatam. 21" wide. Ca. 1730.

*Above and right:*
Figure 263. A rosewood box inlaid in ivory and ivory panels incised with scenes of Indian life. Although likely to date from the late nineteenth century, it is of very high quality and quite unusual in that the representations are of everyday life. 8.75" wide. $600–800.

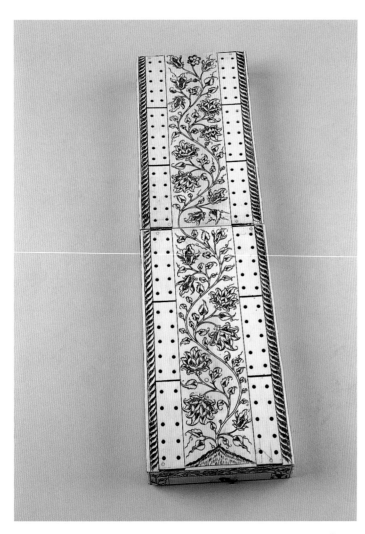

Figure 264. Sandalwood cribbage box veneered in incised ivory. The design of sinuous flowering plants robustly winding their way upward is very characteristic of Vizagapatam work. It is a version of the Tree of Life motif suggestive of the serpent deities associated with many Eastern myths. In this box the design is adapted to the form of the piece. The plant looks as if it is growing out of the earth to reach the sky. 14" wide when open. Late eighteenth century. $2,500–3,500.

already in circulation. Indian mythology, religion, and iconography fascinated the mind of Europeans at a time of intense intellectual and artistic exploration.

There are examples of Eastern motifs, such as the Tree of Life, in seventeenth century European embroidery. During the eighteenth century, an increasing quantity of chintzes and other fabrics featuring Indian-inspired designs found their way into English interiors. Textiles were produced in Dutch and English factories in India as early as the seventeenth century and were exported to England by the East India Company from British-controlled ports on the coast of Coromandel.

By the time the second wave of British traders and colonials arrived in India, they were already receptive to decorative motifs redolent of the vibrant cultures of the East. It was a natural step for the cabinetmaking workshops that had been established in Vizagapatam (on the east coast, between Calcutta [now called Kolcata] and Madras) to make furniture and boxes for the newly wealthy clientele. Later in the century, cabinetmakers working in India referred to English design books, enabling them to adapt the shapes of their objects to suit the taste of the commissioning clients. "Steward, Cabinet-maker, Bengal," was listed as one of the subscribers to Thomas Sheraton's *The Cabinet-Maker and Upholsterer's Drawing-Book*. Patrons also supplied designs, furthering the fusion of European and Indian traditions.

The first Anglo-Indian boxes were made in rosewood or ebony and were decorated with ivory directly inlaid into the wood. The ivory was incised, and the engraved details were filled with a type of black lac that gave further definition to the design. There is no definite record of how this "lac" was prepared, and like early European varnishes, it probably varied a great deal from workshop to workshop. A black powder was produced from burnt available materials, such as ivory or wood scraps. The powder was then mixed with lac and wax or other hardening and adhesive substances. The resulting black lac was melted into the groove of the design, and the excess was scraped off the surface. (Raw, unmixed lac is the secretion deposited by coccid insects on the twigs of trees in Eastern countries. For use in European polishes it is refined, rendered into shellac, and mixed with spirits. It forms the main ingredient of French polish.)

The decorated borders on the boxes were sometimes panels of ivory pinned with ivory pegs. This was a slightly later development. Some boxes were edged with a combination of ivory and wood. This served a dual purpose, both as ornament and protection. The end grain of the main wooden surface was sealed by this finishing strip and was thus protected against weather conditions.

The boxes often had silver escutcheons and drop handles in silver or tutenag (an alloy of zinc and copper). The shape of early boxes was either sloping at the front or rectangular. Boxes of this type were made until the middle of the eighteenth century; now they are rare.

The ornamentation on eighteenth century boxes was executed within a pre-prescribed tradition, yet it was flowing and robust—a perfect complement to the strength and figure of the rosewoods. Sometimes the whole surface of the box was inlaid with vigorous scrolls of looping or undulating flowering stems and leaves. Sometimes the borders were ornamented with stylized spiral floral designs—the centers, with a single motif—following a circular or oval symmetrical or asymmetrical pattern. This motif was often an interpretation of the Tree of Life found in many Eastern cultures.

The origin of the tree was said to be the Chaldean date palm. It was a symbol of religion to Zoroastrians in Persia of the last millennium BCE, and it survived as a mystic form through many centuries, traversing boundaries and religions. In Byzantine embroidery and iconography it was depicted flanked by a mirror image of a pair of animals or birds. This particular version, with the tree separating two confronting animals or birds, was executed on larger Anglo-Indian table cabinets. Sometimes birds were depicted sitting on the tree or in flight close to it. This was suggestive of the literary thread spinning from the Middle East and throughout Europe celebrating the symbolic character of the birds in spring.

The Assyrians and Persians preferred a stylized, rigid form of the design. For boxes, Indian artists transformed the traditional formal pattern into a sinuous serpentine encirclement, its winding quality suggestive of a barely constrained life force. This more vibrant interpretation was probably influenced by the fabric and embroidery renderings of the theme that were propelled toward a livelier direction on account of the greater flexibility of their material.

It is not surprising that these particular plant designs were selected by the English commissioning the boxes. The patrons

*Below and right:*
Figure 265. Incised ivory-veneered box with flat overhanging lid, protruding base, and strap hinges. The arrangement of the designs and the garlanded sides show strong neoclassical influence. However, the central panel draws its inspiration from many aesthetic influences. The ground, with the minimalist suggestions of plant life, is oriental. The vase, which is like an inverted Moorish dome, is garlanded in neoclassical fashion and is used to display controlled but asymmetrical flowers, giving it a hint of rococo. A fine example of the particular fusion of cultures that influenced the second half of the eighteenth century. 8" wide. Ca. 1780. $4,000–5,000.

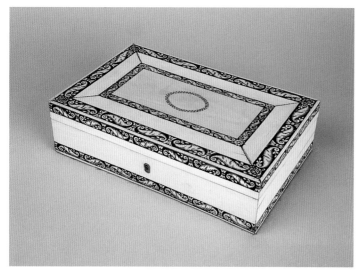
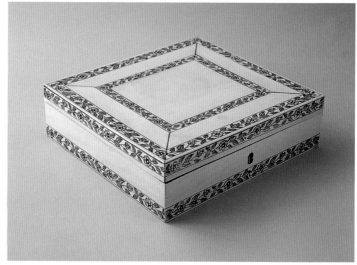

*Above and right:*

Figure 266. Two characteristic examples of ivory-veneered boxes. The central panels are quite wide. Note the clever joining of the framing panels. The decoration is incised and lac filled. The narrow but densely foliated strip design became popular from the end of the eighteenth century onwards. The longer box, with its central oval and the stylized design of a repetitive motif suggestive of leaves, is very much within the neoclassical tradition. 8.5" wide. Ca. 1800. *Courtesy of a private collection.* $1,800–2,500.

were probably unaware of the source of the symbolism, but the accumulation of cultural references could not but work its aesthetic magic. Familiar with the fabrics, they appreciated the boxes. The design had come full circle.

## 2 VENEERED BOXES

The second group of Anglo-Indian boxes was made from the last decades of the eighteenth century onwards. In 1768, a significant area in the region where Vizagapatam was located was ceded to the East India Company. This strengthened the already vigorous trading prospects of the district and attracted more settlers from England, who soon established a thriving English community. From about this time, the decoration began to be influenced more by the foreign (i.e., English) patrons, rather than indigenous artists.

The boxes were constructed in sandalwood, or occasionally in hardwood, and internally lined in sandalwood. This was not done merely as a cost-saving exercise. As any experienced craftsman knows, the layering of boards of different woods creates more stability, especially when the timbers are not predictably and uniformly seasoned. This lessens the possibility of the veneers cracking or lifting. The surface of the boxes was then veneered in ivory, tortoiseshell, horn, quills, or combinations of more than one of these materials. Sometimes sandalwood boxes were decorated with inset strips of ivory, or segments of fluted ivory, with their major part remaining uncovered.

After the middle of the eighteenth century, the East India Company was well ensconced in the Indian centers of British trade and power. One commodity this company and the Royal

Africa Company traded in was elephant tusks from Africa. These were much bigger than the tusks of native Asian elephants and yielded larger plates of ivory. There was not much demand for ivory in England. English box makers were finding ivory difficult to work with on account of its curving and cracking. Tortoiseshell gave fast and glamorous results and yielded easier profits. As a result, large tusks were transformed into Anglo-Indian furniture and boxes.

Although some Anglo-Indian boxes were veneered both in ivory and tortoiseshell, with the tortoiseshell often backed with gold, gilt, or other metal foil, the majority were covered entirely

Figure 267. A porcupine quill box edged in horn, with horn turned feet and turned and carved finial. The natural structure of the material is used to give a fluted effect and create an interesting surface. Second quarter nineteenth century. *Courtesy of a private collection.* $1,500–2,000.

in ivory. The plates of ivory were usually secured with ivory pins. Before the last two decades of the eighteenth century, the boxes were of rectangular shape. They stood on a narrowly protruding base, and the lid, which was flat, also protruded to the same extent as the base. Sometimes the larger boxes had drop handles. The hinges were mostly of strap form.

The veneering was usually done by forming a border of ivory around a central panel, again of ivory. The ivory was incised and filled with black lac to form intricate and dense floral motifs. In addition to their beauty, the borders also had a practical purpose. They disguised the joints in the ivory and tortoiseshell pieces, which were, on account of the nature of the material, of restricted size. Like the earlier boxes, the veneered boxes were mostly edged in ivory, which sealed the end grain of the basic structure and protected it from moisture.

During the last two decades of the eighteenth century, neoclassical designs, which were already fashionable in England, were added to the decorative repertoire. Linear delicate garlands, Greek key patterns, central circles, octagons, and ovals were engraved into the ivory. The lids no longer hung but were constructed with four sides and a top. Bases also no longer protruded. This was a very successful fusion of the two cultures, resulting in boxes that graced many refined neoclassical interiors.

By the beginning of the nineteenth century, porcupine quills and buffalo horn were also used as veneers on boxes, combined with ivory borders decorated in the incised and black lac technique. Because all of these techniques continued well into the century, dating objects precisely is not always possible. An understanding of the forms and decoration fashionable in England is often the best way to proceed, although shapes abandoned in Europe after about 1830 continued to be made in India up to the end of the nineteenth century.

From the beginning of the nineteenth century, all of the veneered boxes, ivory, quill, and horn were made in various shapes. One very successful adaptation was that of the English "basket" form in Anglo-Indian work. Boxes veneered in quills gave the impression of baskets made of reeds, thus utilizing the special quality of the material. Although very effective, they were not made in any numbers, since examples of early quill baskets are now rare.

The most popular "basket" box was veneered in incised ivory. It featured two sloping lids and a central handle. Horn edgings were usual, giving a defining contrasting color to the shape. The ivory baskets were decorated with floral borders in incised and lac-filled ivory and also featured a central complementary motif. "Baskets" completely veneered or made in horn are extremely rare. This is on account of the shape of the material being ideal for fluted work, which was suited to the structure of sarcophagus shapes.

Other early-nineteenth-century Anglo-Indian boxes were made in the architectural shapes of the later neoclassical phase. They often had stepped lids of radiating reeded

*Above:*
Figure 268. A monumental horn-veneered tea chest that combines fluted horn panels fielded with panels of incised flat horn. This type of work is extremely rare. The engraving on the horn is very subtle and has the quality of fine lace, which depends for its beauty on the delicacy of the work, rather than color or form. The juxtaposition of the very strong form, which is inspired by ancient monuments, and the subtle, engraved floral pattern results in a hybrid piece that defies classification. The aesthetic appeal of the tea chest is complex and sophisticated; it makes it the prerogative of the confident connoisseur. Technically too the box is made with care. The decoration, judging by the joints, was done after the pieces of horn were attached by glue and pins onto the wooden frame. The radiating and side-forming segments of horn are expertly carved. The feet are both turned and carved, harmonizing with the whole. The top is crowned by a finial, while the concentrically turned middle and segmented surround suggests a stylized flower. The interior of the tea chest is fitted with ivory-veneered canisters decorated with incised black-lacquer work. The central well retains the original bowl. 14.25" wide. Ca. 1835. $20,000–25,000.

Figure 269. A very successful use of quills to cover a sandalwood basket. The borders are of incised ivory; the handle and feet, of horn. Second quarter nineteenth century. *Courtesy of Ian Gouldsbrough.* $5,000–7,000.

Figure 270. A sandalwood basket veneered in horn and ivory. Although such baskets were a popular Vizagapatam design, this one is very unusual in that it combines both solid ivory panels incised and lac filled in traditional plant motifs and fretted ivory work. Furthermore, the central cartouches are engraved with representations of Indian deities and not floral designs, which were the normal decorations on such baskets. It stands on lion paw feet. The handle is decorated with scrolling flowers in characteristic fashion. 12" wide. Mid-nineteenth century. $6,000–8,000.

*Above:*
Figure 271. A most unusual basket made out of large, flat panels of buffalo horn. This must have been a technical nightmare. The sides are secured with silver straps. The interior is fitted in pink silk and sewing tools of early-nineteenth-century English origin. An elegant understated piece, the only one of this form I have ever seen. 10" wide. Ca. 1800. $6,000–8,000.

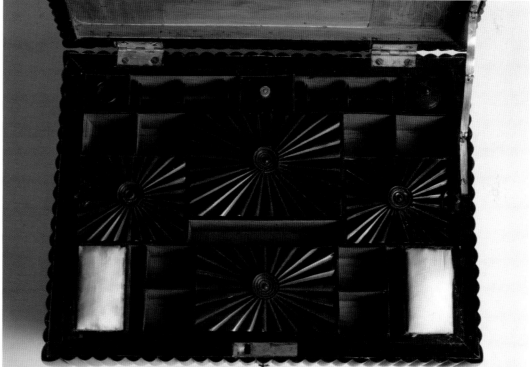

*Above:*
Figure 272. Horn veneered workbox, the interior veneered in sandalwood. This construction gives the box structural stability. The form of the box is designed to appeal to the European clientele of the era: it combines elements of neoclassicism with the exotic. The shape is in the spirit of the later phase of the neoclassical tradition, when the discovery of the ancient art and monuments of the Near East influenced the shapes of objects desired by erudite Europeans; boxes became miniature versions of ancient monuments. This box combines the austerity of ancient form with more organic exotic elements. The sides are slightly rounded and veneered in segmented shaped horn pieces radiating upward. The top is constructed in an elaborate manner with downward-rounded horn segments over a polished flat horn surface. The sides feature upward scrolls, harmoniously concluding the rounded shape and adding another classical note. The top is crowned with a finial carved to resemble a symmetrical flower. The interior of the box holds a tray fitted for sewing tools and materials. 13" wide. Ca. 1835. $10,000–12,000.

Figure 273. A very elegant combination of elements of Vizagapatam work. The box is made of sandalwood and edged in strips of finely incised ivory. The four top panels are segmented and culminate in a carved ivory finial. Second quarter nineteenth century. *Courtesy of Ian Gouldsbrough.* $2,500–3,000.

Figure 274. A charming sewing box veneered in ivory. It is in the shape of a cottage and is incised and filled with black lac to highlight the structural as well as the garden details of this idyllic English country home. Ca. 1800. *Courtesy of the Bielstein Collection.* $10,000–14,000.

segments, culminating in turned and fluted finials. Flat and fluted sections were sometimes used in alternating levels. The boxes stood on turned feet that complemented their form. These striking shapes were made well into the nineteenth century, after they had been abandoned by English box makers, who reverted to forms most suited to mechanized processes.

All materials—that is, ivory, horn, and quills—were used for veneering shaped boxes. Quill boxes were usually edged in decorated strips of ivory. A few boxes I have seen feature deep-fluted horn and ivory tops on quill-covered boxes. Although such boxes offer a complete picture of the different types of work practiced at the time, such heavy tops sit uncomfortably on the rather delicate-looking quills, making for a rather discordant whole.

Ivory, which was at first used discreetly to veneer elegant shapes, was used later in the century to cover complex and heavy forms. This resulted in the production of boxes that combine incongruous structural and decorative elements. Such ponderous structures betray the neocolonial vanity that drove their creation. There is more than a hint that the patrons who initiated their creation understood neither the material nor the grammar of the design of these boxes.

Although more varied, the decorative motifs often sat uneasily on the pieces. It is indicative of the cross-cultural messages Indian craftsmen were given at the time: that an Anglo-Indian box could be of sarcophagus shape (Egyptian influence in England), executed in ivory, with Chinese figures incised in the border, and the interior fitted with spools and sewing implements in the English fashion. There is nothing wrong with multiethnic influences, provided they are understood and interpreted as a unified whole. This results in

inspiring and often great work. This fine line between distillation of ideas and third-party imposition was occasionally lost in the uneasy relationship between patron and craftsman. Examples of such work are interesting on account of their very confusion.

More than any other Anglo-Indian work, Vizagapatam ivory veneered boxes betray the stress of the unequal relationship between client and craftsman. Sometimes the commissioning clients had their colonial buildings depicted on the boxes in incised and lac-filled ivory as mementoes of their activity in this exotic land.

The most "English" of designs must have been "English Cottage"-shaped sewing boxes, which had incised decoration in a naturalistic style, with doors, tiles, and climbing flowers. These boxes, which must have been copied from pictures or

Figure 275. Horn veneered with fretted ivory decoration. Inside it is veneered in sandalwood. Such work was done mostly in the late nineteenth and early twentieth centuries. 7.5" wide. $600–800.

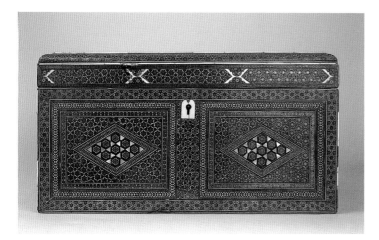

*Left and below:*

Figure 276. A very unusual *sadeli* mosaic box that, in its overall design, suggests its Persian ancestry. Different patterns of design are juxtaposed at different angles. Brass is used in varying thicknesses to bring out an uncharacteristic golden color. Another unusual feature worth noting is the use of mother of pearl as a means of separating and defining units of pattern. The box looks like a small treasure chest. 16" wide. $5,000–7,000.

painted wooden boxes supplied by the client, have an unaffected bucolic charm. It is hoped that they gratified the expatriate's nostalgia for the English countryside. All the same, a part of an African elephant being converted in India into an English cottage must have been a truly surreal experience for the local craftsman!

During the second half of the nineteenth century, boxes were produced in greater numbers. Shapes became simpler and smaller. Sometimes the boxes were domed and covered with flat horn veneer. They were decorated with fretted or incised ivory strips secured with ivory pins. This work continued into the twentieth century.

Quill boxes, which early in the nineteenth century were made in interesting shapes and were of high quality, also became simpler. In the last decades of the nineteenth century, they were framed by ebony strips pinned with ivory or bone pins. The quills were very different from those used to cover earlier boxes. They were much larger, and instead of the pale straw color with very little color variation, they featured definite color contrasts, from pale to dark brown or black. The basic wood on the late quill boxes was not sandalwood, but forms of hardwood or ebony. Much of this later work was done in Ceylon and continued into the twentieth century.

*Below and left:*
Figure 277. An early *sadeli* mosaic box. Note with what precision the expanse of the top is overlaid with mosaic. Note also how well the designs of the borders complement the main pattern and provide a harmonious visual framework for the whole piece. A similar example is in the Clive collection at Powis Castle. However, the example illustrated here is probably earlier. There is no metal within the mosaic, which makes it more difficult to make and to keep stable. This problem must have been recognized early on, since other known examples of similar form include metal within the mosaic. 17" wide. Ca. 1800. $10,000–12,000.

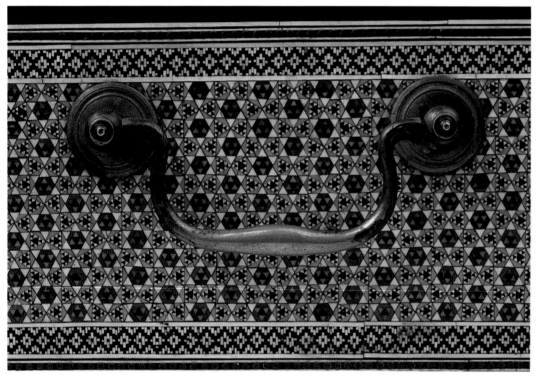

## 3 SADELI MOSAIC, BOMBAY

The ancient art of *sadeli* mosaic was introduced to Bombay from Shiraz in Persia via Sindh. This art was already known in Bombay (now called Mumbai) a long time before Anglo-Indian boxes were made. It was a technique that required a high degree of skill and patience. It was executed very lavishly, in that the frequent cuts wasted great amounts of the precious materials used. The workmanship was more than commensurable to the value of the materials.

Ivory, silver, pewter, tin, and wood were cut into faceted strips that were bound and glued together to form rods of a predesigned geometric pattern. When the glue had set, the rods were sliced in transverse sections. This gave the maker a number of angled circular pieces in the original pattern.

Several variations of patterns could be achieved by combining materials in different ways. The ivory was sometimes dyed green to give an extra color to the composition.

In the early years of the nineteenth century, pieces of pre-prepared *sadeli* were laid and glued onto the carcass of the box, so as to cover its whole surface. One pattern was usually predominant, covering most of the top and the sides, with other patterns used for framing. The different sections were separated by ivory, ebony, metal, or horn stringing in different combinations and variable thicknesses. It took incredible skill to create such expanses of mosaic without any shakes or wavering of the pattern. It is miraculous how impeccably coordinated the corners and the joints on these boxes are.

*Above and right:*
Figure 278. An example of the second phase of *sadeli* mosaic. *Sadeli* hexagons are set into a larger ivory veneer. The ivory, however, is still part of the pattern. It forms star shapes around the mosaic work, which is still predominant. It stands on silver-plated feet. 8.5" wide. Ca. 1820. $3,000–4,000.

Figure 279. A box overlaid in *sadeli* mosaic in an interesting arched design reminiscent of its Persian origins. Inside it contains silver napkin rings with *repoussé* designs of warriors. 7.5" wide. $2,000–3,000.

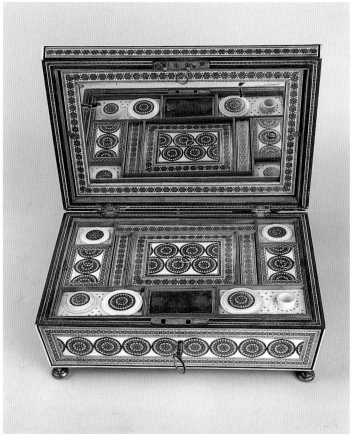

*This whole page:*
Figure 280. A box veneered in ivory, with circles and lines of *sadeli* mosaic. The form is in the Regency style. The *sadeli* mosaic predominates. Note how the corners are impeccably matched and the keyhole is fitted with exactitude between two circles. The patterns are juxtaposed with skill and aesthetic awareness. The interior, too, including the thread barrels, is veneered in *sadeli*. A true treasure. 10" wide. Ca. 1825. $5,500–7,000.

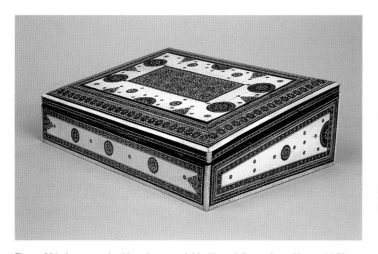

Figure 281. An unusual writing slope overlaid with *sadeli* mosaic and ivory. 11.5" wide. Mid-nineteenth century. $4,000–5,000.

Figure 282. A sewing box veneered with panels of ivory and *sadeli* mosaic. Note that the ivory forms quite a large part of the design. 12.5" wide. Mid-nineteenth century. $2,500–3,500.

The first makers of *sadeli* mosaic were Persian. The boxes made during the first two decades of the nineteenth century displayed a total understanding of the qualities of the different materials used. They combined substances that can expand and contract, according to atmospheric conditions, with other materials that are hard and unyielding. The result was a sharp definition of the lines and patterns that made up the whole design.

The designs on early nineteenth century boxes look deceptively simple. The fact is they emerged from a culture that had mastered geometry and understood how to generate a pattern from a set number of points. The patterns are so harmoniously composed that their incredible complexity is not immediately apparent to the uninitiated.

The earliest *sadeli* boxes were made in rectangular shapes with flat surfaces, which gave the makers the opportunity to create large sections of unbroken mosaic. The combination of the diverse patterns was a triumph of artistic judgment, impeccable workmanship, and deep respect for the material in hand. These boxes have an opulence emanating from the richness of the materials used, yet the total control of these materials and the cerebral nature of the overall design give this work a restrained dignity. Early *sadeli* boxes are now very rare and worth preserving, even in a damaged state.

The great difference between the artists and craftsmen who made early *sadeli* mosaic work and the craftsmen who made other types of Anglo-Indian boxes is that the former were

Figure 283. Detail of another form of *sadeli* mosaic. It is suggestive of parquetry, with sandalwood and ivory giving a three-dimensional effect.

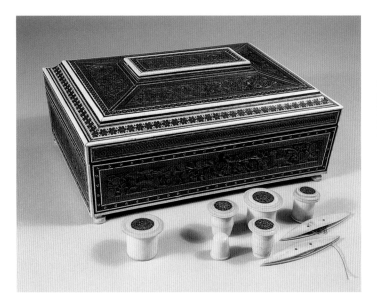

Figure 284. A well-carved box with borders in *sadeli* mosaic. It is fitted with ivory sewing tools, the tops of which are inlaid with *sadeli* mosaic circles. Ca. 1850. $1,000–1,500.

*Above, and right:*
Figure 285. A superb example of Mysore carved work. The box, which is in sandalwood, is carved all around with parrots sitting in arched alcoves amid densely carved stylized foliage. The top continues the theme. The moldings and borders are also carved in minute, repetitive formal designs. The inside has a lift-out tray that is fitted with silver and sandalwood sewing tools and two ruby glass bottles. A label on the inside cover indicates that the box was exhibited in 1857 at the *Art Treasures* exhibition. This possibly refers to the Manchester or the Madras exhibition of that date. $6,000–8,000.

treated with the respect of their clients, while the latter were working under their clients' instructions. Bombay was the first British trading foothold in India, and links were established in the area before the attitudes of the colonial era twisted the relationship between the native and the invading population. A beautiful location, with Elephanta Island in the harbor famous for the shrine dedicated to Shiva nestling in its Great Cave, Bombay was a spiritual and a trading center.

The first English settlers, some of whom had come from Surat, were joined in Bombay by wealthy Gujerati and Parsee (Zoroastrian Persian) merchants. These people had trodden the Silk Road to the East for generations. They were part of an ancient trading network the English could not yet penetrate, and they were party to the wisdom and the treasures of the Far East. No way could the newcomers sustain any pretence at superiority.

Contemporaneous opinions of Bombay work attest to the appreciation in which it was held. A letter to Lord Clive from G. Taswell dated 1802 exemplifies the respect shown for *sadeli* work. He writes: "Mosaic inlaid lady's workboxes … as being of peculiar workmanship that is greatly esteemed here and to be procured from one man, a Persee, which renders them very scarce." It is obvious that at least during the early stages of this work there was no aesthetic interference. The boxes made were such as could be used by Europeans—that is, sewing boxes, writing boxes, tea caddies, and card boxes—but the integrity of the decoration remained intact.

Boxes that were completely, or mostly, covered in *sadeli* mosaic required astonishingly high levels of skill. The precision needed to complete a design in straight lines and corners, keeping to the grid of the pattern, must have made this work incredibly expensive. Very few craftsmen could have worked to such high standards, even allowing for perfect eyesight and steadiness of hand. Such boxes found their way to the grand aristocratic houses in England. Queen Charlotte, the wife of George III, owned three.

As the demand for Bombay work increased, other methods were used to deliver *sadeli* mosaic. The workshops making the mosaic increased, employing larger numbers of craftsmen who delivered the mosaic in smaller units, which did not require the incredible skill of the early masters. During the next period, starting from about the second decade of the nineteenth century, sandalwood boxes were covered in a combination of plain ivory veneers interspersed with insets of roundels, diamonds, and other small shapes and lines of *sadeli* mosaic. Unlike English mosaic work, the corners were always impeccably matched. There was still great care taken to keep to the fundamentals of geometry, and the boxes were still executed with a great deal of skill and awareness of the principles of design.

The work spread to other centers in the Bombay Presidency, and by the middle of the nineteenth century, an enterprising Parsee (Persian) introduced the work to Calcutta and sent some boxes to the 1851 London Great Exhibition. The Calcutta work consisted of *sadeli* patterns set into wood and ivory.

As the English Regency forms began to be adopted in India, large, flat surfaces on boxes were replaced by narrower, variously shaped tapering strips that were not always suited to solid mosaic, either aesthetically or structurally. In the best examples, the various *sadeli* insets are meticulously orchestrated and cover much of the surface.

As the century progressed, *sadeli* mosaic was used more sparingly, with other materials covering larger proportions of the surface. In addition to ivory-veneered boxes with circles, diamonds, hexagons, rhombus, or other shapes and bands of mosaic, units composed of *sadeli* mosaic were directly inlaid into sandalwood or ebony boxes.

In the second half of the nineteenth century, *sadeli* mosaic in simplified forms was made by several more workshops. The strips became larger and the rods longer. There is evidence of less precision in the gluing of the strips, suggesting less control and care. The accuracy of execution and the sharpness of design suffered, although boxes from this period are still pretty and more possible to find. Bands of the mosaic were also used as framing decoration on carved boxes.

## 4 CARVED

Carved Anglo-Indian boxes fall into two very distinctive categories:

**A.** Mid to late nineteenth and twentieth century boxes in sandalwood, or less precious woods, carved in varying degrees of skill, with or without bands of late-period *sadeli* mosaic. These boxes, some of which are very attractive, have to be judged on their quality, since they were obviously made by many hands. They were produced mostly in the Bombay Presidency.

**B.** Nineteenth century sandalwood boxes finely carved with repetitive floral and bird motifs, or figures.

These boxes were made in South India, in the area of Mysore and Canara. The work, which was executed by craftsmen who were famous for their temple carvings, was considered as the finest of its type. Sandalwood was locally available, but in Mysore its availability was controlled, on account of its sale being a state monopoly. The decoration on these boxes is deeply rooted in Indian tradition. Examples found their way into exhibitions, including the 1851 Great Exhibition. The high standard of the work was maintained well into the nineteenth century and kept its traditional Indian identity throughout the period of its application on boxes.

Figure 286. An impressive carved-sandalwood stationery cabinet, Sagar, the two sloping doors on top opening to reveal notepaper compartments, set with two small drawers, the exterior relief carved with Hindu deities on chariots. A similar cabinet acquired by Edward VII during his tour of India in 1875 (and now part of the royal collection) is in the Victoria and Albert Museum. (See Amin Jaffer's *Furniture from British India and Ceylon*, illustration 20.) It is interesting to note that the museum's example is inscribed SANNA PUTTAPPA. SANDALWOOD CARVER. / SAGAR. / SHIMOGA DISTRICT MYSORE. 12.7" wide. Ca. 1875. *Courtesy of David Tomsett.* $7,000–10,000.

## OTHER ANGLO-INDIAN BOXES. THE NORTH: PUNJAB

Punjab, in northern India, was not annexed until the middle of the nineteenth century, but it soon developed a tradition of Anglo-Indian work. Timbers of rosewood varieties, such as shisham, were obtained from locally grown trees. Boxes in hardwoods inlaid with ivory continued the type of decoration abandoned in Vizagapatam in preference of all-ivory veneers. Brass bindings popular in England often replaced the intricate inlays or were used as a strengthening feature alongside the more delicate decoration. These boxes were made so as to be suitable for harsh traveling conditions. They are very handsome in their way, and the best combine strength with beauty.

## MONGHYR

From around the third decade of the nineteenth century, the people of Monghyr, in northern India, adapted their traditional craftsmanship to the taste of the Europeans traveling upstream. Noted for ivory inlay work, they produced boxes in ebony decorated with very fine floral designs. The boxes looked very striking, the ivory providing a strong contrast against the dark wood. Some of the later work included inkstands and very elaborate cabinets and boxes incorporating

*Above and right:*
Figure 287. A box in solid hardwood of the *Dalbergia* genus, inlaid with brass. Sometimes referred to as shisham, it is not always easy to differentiate between rosewoods and blackwoods from the subcontinent, especially since there was no consistency in naming such woods. The box is rather unusual in that it has a trick opening that does not correspond to the obvious exterior signs of usual construction. North Indian. 16.5" wide. Ca. 1875. *Courtesy of Pradeep Chakravarthy.* $1,000–1,500.

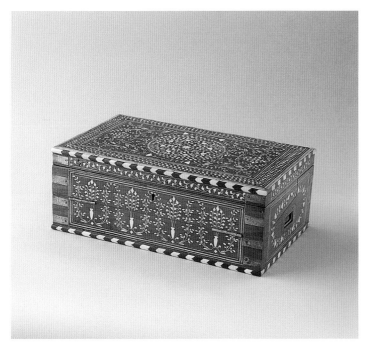

*Above and right:*

Figure 288. A writing box in the form of English triple-opening boxes. It is bound in brass and has brass carrying handles. It is made of a *Dalbergia* species wood and is profusely inlaid in ivory. Although not incised, the patterns formed by the ivory pieces are derived from eighteenth-century decorative conventions. There is a predominant circular motif in the center of the top, among other symmetrical but freer-flowing formal floral designs. The sides are inlaid with stylized repetitive foliage. North India. 15.25" wide. Ca. 1875. $3,000–3,800.

stands and ornaments. These are impressive, but so laboriously heavy both in design and actuality that the delicacy of the inlay is completely overshadowed. Monghyr work also found its way to the Great Exhibition.

During the second half of the nineteenth century, other boxes were produced in India for the colonial trade. Shallow carved-ebony boxes from Nagina, in eastern India, featured repetitive geometric designs. In northern India, carved ebony and ivory boxes were made and mounted with topographical ivory miniatures. Boxes painted and varnished in similar ways to English japanned work of a century earlier were made in eastern India. Sporadic examples of other types of work using native woods and designs also exist.

## CEYLON

In addition to Indian boxes, there are boxes that were made in the Galle district of Ceylon. The quill-covered boxes have already been mentioned. In addition to these, there are workboxes and writing boxes of coromandel and ebony featuring ivory-inlaid interiors.

Deeply carved boxes, both in ivory and ebony, were also made, the work on these being particularly robust.

Ceylon also produced silver-mounted boxes, both in wood and tortoiseshell.

## AFTERTHOUGHT

Unfortunately, the attitudes of the nineteenth and most of the twentieth century allowed many Anglo-Indian boxes to deteriorate. It is only in the last two or so decades that the wonderful workmanship of these boxes has been appreciated and treasured. *Sadeli* mosaic boxes, which to my mind are the most precious of all, are practically impossible to restore. Nevertheless, even in fragments, the early examples should be preserved in honor of the artists who infused them with so much of their ancient culture.

Judging by how few early Anglo-Indian boxes have survived, it is reasonable to assume that a very limited number were made for "general trade" before about 1820. The earlier ones must have been too expensive for most people and were therefore placed directly with the final customer. Some very small boxes were also made, mostly in *sadeli* mosaic. It is likely that these were tokens of Anglo-Indian work. Jane Austen kept an ivory alphabet set in just such a small box.

Many nineteenth-century Anglo-Indian boxes found their way into prestigious European showrooms and exhibitions, and subsequently homes. Today they are once again displayed in museums and serious collections.

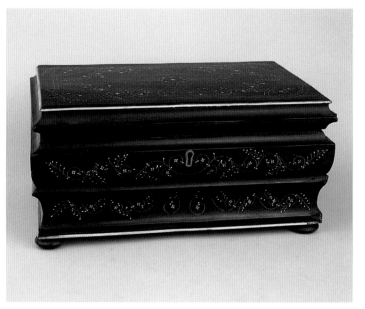

*Above and right:*

Figure 289. Two examples of Monghyr work. Note the amazingly fine inlay into the very hard ebony. The design on the larger box is reminiscent of eighteenth-century fabric designs, but here only a faint outline is executed, swirling and curling all around the box. 12" wide and 12.5" wide. Second quarter nineteenth century. $600–800, and $2,000–2,500.

*Above and right:*

Figure 290. A very good and characteristic example of Ceylon work. The box, in solid coromandel wood, is inlaid on the inside with incised ivory filled with lac in different colors. Note the circle of specimen woods in the center of the lid. This is a trademark of the Galle district area of Ceylon. Second quarter nineteenth century. *Courtesy of a private collection.* $3,500–5,000.

Figure 291. A very deeply and richly carved ebony box from Ceylon. Inside the lid there is a characteristic carving of an elephant. The sharpness of the work, considering the hardness of the wood, is breathtaking. Mid-nineteenth century. $600–800.

Figure 292. A group of small Anglo-Indian boxes from Vizagapatam and Bombay. $300–500.

Figure 293. A basket of finely fretted ivory framed in sandalwood overlaid with *sadeli* mosaic. It stands on ivory feet. 8" wide. Second quarter nineteenth century. *Courtesy of Ian Gouldsbrough*. $2,500–3,000.

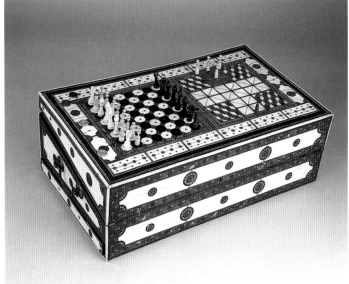

Figure 294. A most unusual multipurpose box. One half of the center of the top is inlaid in the form of a board for playing the games of chess and drafts. The other half is inlaid for playing the game of fox and geese. On the front and back of the top there are two ivory long panels, configured for cribbage. The drawer opens into a backgammon board. Ivory and horn pieces for playing the games are stored inside the box. The box folds down into a writing surface like a regular writing box. The whole is veneered in sandalwood, ivory, and *sadeli* mosaic. 15" wide. Mid-nineteenth century. $6,500–8,500.

*This whole page:*

Figure 295. A box that defies categorization. It is veneered in ebony framed in *sadeli* mosaic and ivory. The inlay is in incised and lac-filled ivory. Although technically this work is within the tradition of Indian craft, the design does not exactly correspond to the designs of any particular region. The sides are inlaid with flowering plants symmetrically scrolling from a central vase. The front is punctuated with butterflies. The top is framed with similar fine foliage. Note the clever joining of the corners. The delightful central picture is rooted in the chinoiserie tradition. A mother monkey sits on a man-built edifice, feeding her baby with the help of a very large exotic bird who is bringing her berries. Other birds and huge butterflies hover and perch among strange trees. A Sino rococo element permeates the whole composition. The inlaid ebony panels are most probably of an earlier date, with the *sadeli* bandings added later. The ivory inlay is similar, although finer than an example now in the Victoria and Albert Museum, which was a present given by Princess Charlotte of Wales and dated 1720–30. The design on this box is considerably more ambitious than that of the museum piece, which is attributed to Vizagapatam (See Amin Jaffer's *Furniture from British India and Ceylon*, illustration 36). The form of the box and the *sadeli* bands suggest that the box in its current form was constructed in the early part of the nineteenth century. The box stands on silvered feet. A very individual piece. 9" wide. $?

# CHAPTER 17 *Tea Caddies*

amellia sinensis is a many-stemmed bush with small, frost-resistant leaves. This unpretentious, pretty plant gives us our tea. The dried leaves are now packed in containers and are even powdered and squeezed into tea bags. This is no way to treat a piece of flora that played such an important part in the cultural and political history of the world, especially England, China, and India. The role of tea in shaping the destiny of so many people is unrivaled by any other species of plant, barring perhaps the biblical apple.

In the fourth century CE, the Chinese made medicine from the green leaves of the tea plant. By the seventh century, during the T'ang dynasty (581—907), *Camellia sinensis* was already seriously cultivated. In 780 CE, the scholar Lu Yu addressed it with appropriate reverence in his *Tea Classic*. During the Sung period (960—1279), tea houses were establishments of cultural entertainment, which in oriental terms incorporated the services of refined courtesans.

Buddhist priests, who used tea for religious rites, introduced it to Japan before the end of the T'ang dynasty. In the Far East, tea remained for centuries a much-respected beverage served with ceremonious meticulousness and deference.

It took almost another millennium before tea was introduced to Europe. Within three hundred years of its introduction, it was transformed from something arcane and sacred—first into a social ritual, and finally into a domesticated drink much abused and poorly prepared.

In 1559, the secretary to the Council of Ten in Venice wrote how a Persian told him that an infusion of tea leaves was good

Figure 296. Caddies in many shapes and materials.

Figure 297. A small tea chest used for the transportation of tea. It is japanned and inlaid with mother of pearl, depicting oriental figures in gardens. 12" wide. Eighteenth century. $1,200–1,500.

for the stomach and that it also alleviated gout. The merchants of the Middle East had established land trade routes to China centuries before European ships sailed to the Far East, so it is natural that they were the first heralds of the new beverage.

It was during the seventeenth century that Europeans ventured in any numbers to the Far East. The pioneering Dutch set up a trading base in Java in 1596, and by 1606 they had brought a small quantity of tea to Europe. The Dutch and other European merchants who traveled to the Far East as servants of the various East India Companies were arguably the first Westerners to sample the delights of tea. They were soon followed by fellow traders from the rest of Europe. A Mr. R. Wickham, who was an agent of the English East India Company, wrote in 1615 to a Mr. Eaton at Macao, asking him to forward a pot of "the best sort of chaw." Macao, which had already been ceded to the Portuguese as a trading base, produced tea that enjoyed a high reputation, since it was grown there for the Japanese shogun.

The English East India Company merchants brought small quantities of tea back home, and by 1658 the "Sultaness head, Cophee-house in Sweetings" advertised that it served "The Excellent and by all 'physicians approved,' China Drink, called by the Chineas, Tcha." This was not the first coffee house to serve tea. The distinction goes to "Garraways," an establishment in Cornhill, London, opened in 1639 by Sir Henry Garraway, who was at the time a governor of the East India Company. Garraways both served and retailed tea.

Tea was also served at the Company's headquarters, where Mr. Harris was the beadle and his wife was the housekeeper. Mrs. Harris was responsible for brewing and serving tea to the members of the Company and must be awarded the title of "First Tea Lady."

Figure 298. *Lady*: plate 3 in Mathias Darly and George Edwards's *A New Book of Chinese Designs*, 1754.

Figure 299. An oak tea box veneered with a geometric pattern in very thick pieces of veneer, which have undulated with time. Appropriately, the interior is lined with yellowed paper covered in Persian writing. 7" wide. Ca. 1760. $1,600–2,000.

*Above and right:*
Figure 300. A metal jar-shaped tea caddy, covered in straw work. The particularly fine work in geometric patterns is characteristic of early Continental work. Such work was executed both by nuns in Catholic orders and lay craftsmen and women. The front and back are decorated with watercolor and, I think, ink pictures and writing, both under glass. The back picture depicts a heart with a crown of thorns. The front is of particular historical significance. The female figure is that of H. Ioanna (i.e., Jeanne de Valois), daughter of Louis XI of France and Charlotte of Savoy. Born sickly and deformed, Joanna was married off at nine for political expediency. The marriage was annulled when her husband became King Louis XII. She devoted herself to religious works, one of her lasting legacies being the founding of the Order of the Annonciades. The writing on the caddy, in old Dutch, is a dedication and a plea to her for protection: "Holy Joanna queen of Vranckriyck and Fendatersse of the holy order of our dear ladies of the Annunciation. Pray for us. Grant us the favors we ask of you especially for Florecyn and Grainol." Joanna died in 1505 and was beatified in 1738. In hagiography she is depicted in the same colors as on the caddy, with a small, haloed boy by her side. On the caddy, however, she wears a crown, and the shield at her feet bears three fleur-de-lis, the symbol of the kings of France. On the inscription she is given the secular title of Queen, which dates the caddy to before her beatification. Taken with the style and the mention of specific names, this caddy must have been an individual commission executed in the Low Countries sometime during the seventeenth century by Annonciades nuns. Significant. 5" wide. $?

At first, tea was sold in coffee houses in liquid form. The tea was made in large urns and remained stewing and waiting for the excise man to come and levy his duty on it! This was not perhaps the best way of serving it, but it did not deter the patrons of coffee houses, who were happy to drink it among the hubbub of ideas, financial deals, news, and scandal. During the seventeenth and eighteenth centuries, coffee houses were the haunts of intellectuals, businessmen, and "chancers." They were the financial and political heart of the city of London. Lloyds owes its existence to its coffee house origin, where news of ships was exchanged, which in turn led to marine insurance. Tea could not have had a better introduction to the business world than through the coffee house. In spite of disgruntled rumors that tea could make men "as unfruitful as the deserts," the men took to it with gusto.

The marriage in 1662 of Charles II to the Portuguese infanta Catherine of Braganza introduced tea to the English court. The Portuguese and the Dutch, who had already established trading posts in the Far East, stole a few decades of tea drinking on the English. However, it was the English who took on all aspects of the new beverage with zealous enthusiasm.

The English East India Company was swift to see the potential of the new trend, and in 1664 the Company placed a specific order for tea. Shrewdly, the Company presented the king with a gift of tea. Tea was quickly taken up by "pothecarys," who, according to Samuel Pepys in 1667, assured their customers, including Mrs. Pepys, that it was "good for cold & defluxions" ("defluxions" were supposed to occur due to the maladjusted flow of "humours," an all-embracing medical theory of the time).

Tea was imported in large quantities by the Company from China and auctioned to merchants in London "by the candle," with the hammer falling every time a candle burned away. In turn, buying merchants sold it to retailers, who by today's standards belonged to a strange and varied assortment of trades. In 1725, Twinings had only one grocer on their

Figure 301. A rare Portuguese colonial tea box of hardwood with insets of tortoiseshell and ebony. 14" wide. Early eighteenth century. *Courtesy of Anne Brooks*. $6,000–8,000.

books, with the bulk of their tea distributed through more-specialized establishments.

Coffee houses bought tea, both for selling already brewed and in leaf form. Apothecaries, snuff shops, confectioners, and ladies' shops such as drapers, milliners, and mercers also sold tea. The potential of the female market was recognized by Thomas Twining, who opened the first tea shop for ladies in 1717.

For many decades tea remained an expensive commodity. Thomas Garway advertised it in 1665 at 16 shillings to 50 shillings a pound. In 1728, Bohea was advertised at 13–20 shillings and Green at 12–30 shillings. This is when a skilled man earned an average of 20 shillings (£1) a week.

Tea was pivotal to the fortunes of the country because it provided much-needed revenue. As discussed in the chapter "Trade and Taste," tea importation was inextricably linked with the opium trade, which was to give England its colonial advantage. It suited the authorities to present it and promote it as something very special. At the time of its introduction, tea was believed to be therapeutic as well as delicious. The health benefits of tea were known in the East for thousands of years. In England, people accorded it time and space, and this alone must have had the effect of producing a sense of well-being. The fact that water had to be boiled before it was used for making tea, together with the antibacterial qualities of tea, must have contributed to improved hygienic drinking. Tea was enveloped into a miraculous aura, and the price was commensurate to its high reputation.

In Henry Fielding's *Joseph Andrews* (1742), the eponymous Joseph is carried—badly injured, and looking as if he is about to expire—to an inn, where he asks the landlady for "a little tea." The landlady would not hear of such an outrageous request and offers instead "a little beer," beer being modestly priced in comparison.

It is very difficult to be exact about prices, since we have no way of discriminating between boasting and truthful advertising or of checking the quality of what was sold. We cannot even be sure of the exact mixture of what was sold as tea. Adulteration was rife. Green tea was mixed with dried elder buds, thorn leaves, and other flora; sometimes, nearly lethal substances were added to improve its color. Prussian blue and verdigris were popular color enhancers, although, to be fair, the danger was not always fully understood. After all, pickles and fruit were often cooked in copper pans to "bring out the greenness" of the produce. Black tea was mixed with dried ash leaves or other leaves, and in extreme circumstances—allegedly—with dried sheep droppings and cow pats. Black lead and gum were known to be used to enhance both the color and texture of the leaves. This was especially necessary when the leaves were bought by unscrupulous merchants "secondhand" from servants who worked in wealthy households.

The ups and downs of tea pricing and quality are extremely complex, especially since this was a government-manipulated commodity; the people were always trying to get the better of the system. Markets were controlled through granting of monopolies and by taxation. Lack of information due to the difficulty and slowness of communications allowed the exchequer to extract vast amounts of revenue from the buying public.

Tea could be as much as three guineas per pound (£3 3s), when a bottle of wine was two shillings. In the late part of the eighteenth and the early part of the nineteenth centuries, a servant had only 1½d (1 shilling = 12d) a day for beer. In 1777,

Parson Woodforde paid 10s 6d per pound for smuggled Hyson tea; much less than if he had bought it legally. A Christmas goose or turkey could be bought for 2s 6d.

It was understandable that people preferred to buy their tea from smugglers. Early in the eighteenth century, Daniel Defoe was already commenting on the smuggling of commodities, including tea, along the Kent and Essex coasts. He observed that people had "grown monstrous rich by that wicked trade." Even respectable, God-fearing people wrote in letters and diaries of buying smuggled tea as a matter of course. Rumor had it that members of the Board of Trade bought their tea from smugglers!

Finally the government got the message; in 1784, William Pitt tried to address the problem in his Commutation Act. Taxes on tea were reduced and the official tea price was halved. Legitimate imports quadrupled, making legitimately bought tea more accessible to a wider section of society. Smuggling still continued, albeit the fact that it was less profitable. By today's standards, tea was still expensive.

In the home, tea was drunk in the morning and at first as an after-dinner beverage. At the beginning of the eighteenth century, breakfast could be around ten in the morning and dinner in midafternoon. By the end of the century, meal times became gradually later, with dinner at around six o'clock. During the first years of the nineteenth century those moving in the more fashionable echelons of society were beginning to dine later. By the second half of the nineteenth century the time between the midday meal and dinner had extended for all, including the middle classes, whose male members had to accommodate different working hours. As a result, tea was introduced as a regular light repast in the afternoon to breach the gap between main meals.

Tea was also drunk in varied social situations. Before the end of the eighteenth century, tea drinking had woven itself into the very fabric of English society.

*This whole page:*
Figure 302. A mid-eighteenth-century japanned tea chest with chinoiserie decoration, containing three metal canisters. The decoration is flat painting mostly in gold. There is an attempt at being less angular than the Stalker and Parker designs, but still not quite as rounded as the Darly work. One or two figures may have been inspired by the depictions of oriental trades in *The Ladies Amusement*. Interestingly, there are two figures smoking long pipes, obviously an early attempt at giving figurative expression to the Chinese opium smoking (see chapter 3, "Chinoiserie," and chapter 5, "Trade and Taste"). A rare and early example of this form of decoration and arrangement. 11" wide. $7,000–9,000.

Figure 303. An oak tea caddy that uses subtle juxtaposition of the timber grain. The structure, although quite complex, looks quite simple, a characteristic of early, understated, high-quality work. Ca. 1780. *Courtesy of Kevin R. Kiernan.* $1,600–2,000.

Figure 304. A fruitwood-veneered caddy with inlay directly into the wood. The two branches of leaves are very fine indeed. Although stylized in a neoclassical manner, they are most likely depictions of branches of the tea plant. There are subtle variations in the color of the inlay, from brown to golden to shades of green. Because the green tones are not uniform or even, they were done by selecting fungus-attacked wood, which was turning green without further chemical treatment or staining. Exceptional work. 7.25" wide. Ca. 1780. $4,500–6,000.

Everybody drank tea. The poor often replaced a meal with a cup of tea. In the eighteenth century, curious nutritious concoctions were made with tea. One such was purely tea slowly poured into a basin containing a beaten egg. Another was tea caudle, made with green China tea, castor sugar, nutmeg, egg yolk, and white wine.

Primarily tea was drunk in its pure form, out of the newly discovered beautiful china "dishes" or cups. "Dishes" were small bowls without handles that were first imported from China. By the second half of the eighteenth century, there was a plethora of elegant utensils especially designed for the ritual of tea drinking.

Tea was drunk even by those who could not afford the china. Dr. Deering, a Nottingham doctor, was complaining in 1730 that "almost every Seamer, Sizer, and Winder will have her Tea in the morning." If poorly paid people could not afford to buy good tea, they used secondhand leaves from the local inn or bought "pinches" of tea from the local shop for ³/₄d each. A gentleman's family, on about £10,000 a year, could afford to buy decent tea and also employ a housekeeper, one of whose duties was to prepare the tea accessories in the parlor.

The making and taking of tea developed into a social art that required several accoutrements and demanded a certain level of dressing up. It was not long before tea gowns were worn between morning and evening dress.

Tea even captivated such paragons of level-headedness as Dr. Johnson, who found that it cleared and quickened his mind. He admitted to being "a hardened and shameless tea-drinker" (*Literary Magazine*, 1757) and spoke in favor of tea drinking, although his balanced thinking saw the reasoning behind the concerns of those set against the new habit. Throughout the eighteenth century, the perceived fiscal drain on the private and public purse alarmed many public figures. In 1797, Sir Frederick Eden voiced his concern about "poor families drinking tea in their cottages." His was one of many such voices. It was not until the nineteenth century that the true fiscal position regarding tea was understood, and then only by a few. As far as most people were concerned, precious English coin was exchanged for tea leaves.

Jonathan Swift was caustic in his remarks about tea and called it "water bewitched." His friend, the very correct Mrs. Delany, saw it as something only the rich had the right to enjoy. In the middle of the eighteenth century, when she herself had reached middle age, she was commenting in correspondence about the people in Down, Ireland:

*I am very sorry to find here and everywhere people out of character and that wine and tea should enter where they have no pretence to be and usurp the rural food of syllabub . . .*

On the other hand, she took great delight in reporting how she was entertained at Windsor Castle:

*This whole page:*
Figure 305. A most unusual caddy with a double picture: one showing a Chinese scene with writing; the other, a Russian scene complete with samovar and kettle. The caddy is of a single compartment, so it could not hold both Chinese and Russian tea. 6" wide. French, nineteenth century. $1,000–1,200.

*At eight the king came into the room with so much cheerfulness and good humor; ... the band of music playing all the time under the window. When they returned we were summoned into the next room for tea and the royals began a ball....*

It was reported that at times King George III took only one slice of bread and butter and a "dish" of black tea between breakfast and dinner.

Figure 306. A mahogany-veneered caddy with inlay of boxwood, the pattern further defined by incised and inked lines. The design of this caddy is highly symbolic in that it intertwines the Scottish thistle with the English rose. The thistle was adopted as the Scottish emblem by James III (1460–88), although its origins may go back to the thirteenth century, when the Scots gained advantage over an invading Norwegian army: an unwary invading Norwegian soldier trod on a thistle, cried out, and betrayed the position of his camp! Judging by the date of this caddy, it could be that it symbolizes the end of the civil war and the return of amity between the two sides of the border; that is, Scotland and England. It could also be that its symbolism is more subversive and that the rose is not the English rose, but the Jacobite symbol of the Old Pretender (James Francis Edward) of the House of Stewart as the full-blown flower, with his son Bonnie Prince Charlie (Charles Edward) represented by the rosebud. A very rare and significant caddy redolent of Scottish history. Aged with dignity. 7" wide. Third quarter eighteenth century. $?

Figure 307. A dome-topped straw work caddy with geometric designs. There is some green, but otherwise there is not a great variety of color in the straw. The effects are achieved by subtle use of the direction of the grain, which catches different light values, giving dark and light patterns. Possibly early Napoleonic prisoner-of-war work. 9" wide. Ca. 1800. *Courtesy of a private collection.* $4,000–5,000.

Figure 308. An interesting tea chest veneered in specimen woods, forming specimen patterns. The interior is very unusual in that each canister's container part is made of metal, but the lids are in wood in a pattern conforming to the outside. 12.5" wide. Second half eighteenth century. $2,200–2,700.

## Tea Gardens

The aristocracy took their cue from the royals, and the middle classes followed. The Duchess of Marlborough received her guests in her "Italian garden," where tea tables had been laid. For those who did not possess large private gardens, public gardens had to suffice. Gardens were already *de rigueur* as places for indulging the Cathay fantasy. Tea drinking was an added bonus. The most-fashionable gardens in London were Vauxhall and Ranelagh, attracting the well-to-do, the ambitious, and the better class of demimondaine, or demirep, as high-class courtesans were then called. Smaller gardens also offered tea, some with special attractions such as the delicate pastries at Marylebone Gardens, or the syllabub sold at the "Adam and Eve" made from the milk of the in-garden cows!

In 1742, the admission to Ranelagh was half a crown (2s 6d), which was a vast sum for the ordinary worker. By the beginning of the nineteenth century, Ranelagh was already declining in popularity. In 1803, the Ranelagh lights went out. After the first decades of the nineteenth century, Ranelagh was already declining in popularity. It was referred to as frequented by riff-raff and Cits. (Cits were people living in cities who did not possess country estates but who had recently made their money out of "trade." The upper classes still held the belief that gentlemen never worked.)

Vauxhall, on the other hand, went from strength to strength until well into the nineteenth century. Its popularity lasted from 1720 until its closure in 1859. Vauxhall was more than a garden; it was a veritable entertainment complex. There was a concert hall, a picture gallery, pavilions, temples, and various rooms for the indulging of fashionable activities. One of its strongest points was its lighting. When gas light was discovered, Vauxhall was lit in the most spectacular manner. Gas lamps were positioned in the trees together with revolving mirrors. At a time when most people had access only to candle light, this phantasmagoric spectacle must have seemed nothing short of miraculous.

*This whole page:*
Figure 309. A sycamore-veneered tea caddy, painted all around. The front of the caddy is painted with a Martello tower. Looking at the picture, this looks very much like the tower built in Sandycove, Ireland, in 1806, with the Dublin hills in the background. Such towers were built to defend the country from the French. At the beginning of the nineteenth century, Ireland was prosperous and Dublin was considered the second city of the British Empire. The tower is now the James Joyce Museum. The back of the caddy is painted with shells, continuing the theme of the sea. These were probably a mixture of observation from nature and inspiration for their arrangement from the plates in *The Ladies Amusement* (see the "Chinoiserie" chapter). The top and lids are painted with naturalistic flowers, and the rim is painted with wreaths in the neoclassical tradition. The sides are a superb interpretation of neoclassicism. They are painted with urns, which end in a base that features an acanthus leaf motif. The two-headed eagle handle is placed centrally on the painted urn so as to look part of the design. The eagle motif is carried further in the talon-and-ball feet. An ingenious Regency composition, the caddy blends naturalism and classicism with incredible panache. The wreath design binds the two elements in complete harmony. When opened, the back of the lid is lined in velvet with silk-rounded tufts. Note the original leading to the interior and the peeling later-nineteenth-century foil. Probably Irish. Rare and significant decoration. 11.5" wide. Ca. 1810–20. $10,000–12,000.

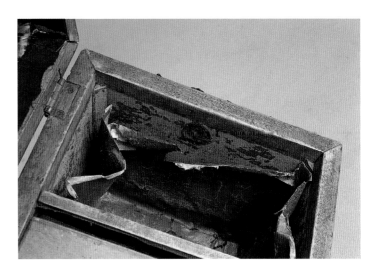

Figure 310. A single tea caddy in harewood with an oval medallion of peculiar growth, framed by a formal design of delicate foliage, suggesting the Grecian laurel or myrtle wreath. This evergreen plant was symbolic of victory, achievement in the arts, immortality, and love. Sacred to Venus, it was adopted by the exponents of the neoclassical style. An Adam drawing in Sir John Soane's Museum library (London) shows this motif on a chair designed "for the Right Hon. Lord Stanley." An excellent example of an altogether classical composition, surviving in original condition. 4.5" wide. Last quarter eighteenth century. $3,500–5,000.

*Ah I loves life and all the joy it yields,*
*Says Madam Fussock, warm from Spittle Fields,*
*Bon ton's the space twixt Saturday and Monday,*
*And riding in a one-horse chair o' Sunday:*
*'Tis drinking tea on Summer's afternoons*
*At Bagnigge Wells with china and gilt spoons.*

Fashionable resorts such as Brighton, Bath, and Tunbridge Wells all had their tearooms that offered tea and refreshments. It was customary in Bath to retire to the tearoom at nine after dancing; in Brighton on Sundays, tea was taken at the Public Tea Rooms. Even inns were offering tea and coffee to weary travelers.

Tea was a social phenomenon during the whole of the eighteenth century and the early part of the nineteenth century. Hardly any diarist, letter writer, novelist, or chronicler failed to mention tea drinking. The habit, together with its political and social baggage, was made fun of by cartoonists, satirists, and playwrights. As early as 1693, William Congreve in his play *The Double Dealer* expresses through Mellefont the idea of ladies retiring "to their tea and scandal." Tea and scandal as an interconnected notion turns up in literature and art repeatedly, especially in verse, plays, and prints. Edward Young (1683—1767) writes in his *Love of Fame* "Nor take her tea without a stratagem," while Henry Fielding (1707—1754) in his *Love in Several Masques* declares that "Love and scandal are the best sweeteners of tea," echoing the distant murmur of the Chinese tea house.

In prints, tea scenes are often crowded with putti, exotic birds, dogs, cats, and mischievous monkeys. Perhaps it is this element of social mischief that enhanced the lure of tea. When it was served at home, sometimes in a person's private boudoir, it was an excuse for intrigue, gossip, and waggery, activities that were not quite proper for the dinner table. The round, small tea tables afforded an intimate stage for communication, where all persons present could join in conspiratorial conversation or injurious tittle-tattle.

In public, tea was served where life could be witnessed at its most socially chaotic. In fact, tea was sometimes served in quite bizarre circumstances, hosted by the most fascinatingly shady characters of the period. Fanny Burney, the eighteenth century writer, diarist, and royal *protégé*, records how "We . . . drank tea at Lady Dalston's," which was quite proper. However, Miss Burney also gives an account of another lady who offered tea. This was Mrs. Cornelys. Teresa Cornelys was one of those larger-than-life personalities who strode boldly through the social structure of the eighteenth century. She was an opera singer of Italian origin who in her youth had enjoyed an amorous relationship with Casanova. She moved to London in the middle of the century and set herself up in "Carlisle House." She set about transforming the interior of her establishment with lavish furnishings and decorations. Thomas Chippendale was commissioned to make several pieces for her, attesting to a level of wealth.

Vauxhall Gardens also offered food of high quality, as well as special entertainments such as firework displays and circus acts. Particular events, such as the victory at Waterloo, were also celebrated at Vauxhall. The fêtes in these gardens, which were often hosted by members of the aristocracy, were legendary. Only the Prince Regent got it wrong, by inviting so many people to his "do" that there was a veritable crush.

Vauxhall was definitely the place to go for tea if one was, or aspired to be, a member of the "beau monde": the "haut ton," "bon ton," or simply "ton," as it was colloquially termed. For ordinary people the cost was prohibitive. At a time when a cook could be had for £5 a year and the main employment for a poor girl was domestic service, it was impossible for workers to spend so much on one outing. Even for skilled workers the entrance fee to the fashionable venues could be a quarter of a week's wages. People whose work allowed the rich to live in splendor did not presume to airs above their station in life, but they did aspire to drinking a cup of tea in style. To this purpose they thronged to less genteel spots and devoured with gusto the exquisite delights on offer. One such place was Bagnigge Wells, in what was then a rural part north of the city of London and what is now an inner city area. This city spa and garden, together with White Conduit House, offered classic tea entertainment every Sunday. By all accounts it was the highlight of many a modest person's week. Colman's prologue to Garrick's *Bon Ton* (1775) puts it in a nutshell:

*This whole page:*

Figure 311. It is difficult to place this tea chest with total confidence. The decoration is so surprising that it is most probably a unique creation resulting from the cooperation between an eccentric commissioning client and his cabinetmaker. The wooden structure of the chest points to mid-eighteenth century. The box is made of dense mahogany veneered in kingwood. The molding and the mitered molded feet are in mahogany. It points to Dutch work of the period, or possibly English. Unfortunately, the lock, which would have given us another pointer, is missing. The feature that makes this chest such an extraordinary piece is the decoration. Within the wooden framing there are panels of reverse-painted glass depicting oriental figures in a landscape. Reverse painting on glass was practiced in China during the eighteenth century, when Europeans would have been introduced to such work in Canton. The work on this piece lacks the representational precision of Chinese reverse glass painting done as work of art. Could it be chinoiserie done by a European hand? This is a tempting theory until one looks at the treatment of the plant life. The pine trees especially point to Chinese work. Flowers and rocks too remind me of oriental work, but not reverse-painting work, but instead work on applied arts, such as china or export lacquer. My guess is that the panels were brought from China, and the chest was constructed around them. Alternatively, they were commissioned in advance for the purpose. Whatever the origins, this is a striking object. The figures in vibrant colors look happy in their exotic setting. Even though they are delineated only in a few skillful strokes, their movements, and especially their expressions, have a spontaneity and vigor often missing from more refined work. The couple on the small panel at the front looks absolutely delighted with their recent encounter. As he walks away, her smile and starry eyes say it all. Inside the chest there are three silver canisters, each 43.4 troy ounces. They bear the crest of the Tufnell family; Samuel Tufnell spent some years at Antwerp during the eighteenth century. The hallmarks on the silver date from 1977. Another conundrum: Were the canisters made in another country and hallmarked years later, or, being a private commission, were they not hallmarked at the time to avoid duty? Or are they a replacement made by Jane Penrice How of How of Edinburgh, whose sponsor mark the caddies now bear. How was one of the most important figures in this field (see bibliography). Being such an exotic, eccentric, and extraordinary piece, it is not surprising that the chest holds some of its mystery. 9.75" wide. Mid-eighteenth century. $?

Figure 312. Detail: a small souvenir box with a print pasted and varnished on the lid. Inside the lid, a contemporaneous label reads *Ranelagh Gardens*. 8" wide. Ca. 1800. $800–1,200.

Figure 313. Eighteenth-century tea chest veneered in shagreen, containing three silver caddies. *Courtesy of the Bielstein Collection.*

Figure 314. A tortoiseshell box, fitted with two trays of silver gilt teaspoons and a caddy spoon. 6.75" wide. Dutch, early nineteenth century. $5,000–7,000.

By the year 1770, when Fanny Burney was writing about her, Mrs. Cornelys had created in her London house caves and grottoes, as well as two Chinese tearooms. Each room had tables for forty sets of parties. Fanny thought it too crowded, but others seemed to enjoy the close proximity of the strange *mélange* of people dressed in various degrees of formality that this intriguingly glamorous hostess attracted. Her guests paid to attend her *soirees*, which she sometimes graded, holding different events according to the class of the patrons. However, the social barriers were very lax at establishments such as Mrs. Cornelys's, especially at times of financial opportunity.

Mrs. Cornelys offered many attractions and entertainments, including singing and staging of operas! In fact this was part of her downfall, since she eventually brought upon her the wrath of the opera house. In addition to the formal entertainment, a major enticement of such "salons" was the opportunity to rub shoulders with people outside one's own social stratosphere. The upper classes were fascinated by more-worldly individuals. There was a frisson in mingling with adventurers and even conceivably raffish characters. For their part, the opportunists liked the idea of elevated and potentially useful acquaintance. The entrance fee maintained Teresa Cornelys's lavish theatrical "home," and for a few decades this peculiar business thrived. Disaster struck in 1772, when poor Teresa was declared bankrupt and was unfairly treated by astute business people. Regrettably, Mr. Chippendale was one of the syndicate who contrived to ring the auction of her assets. Miraculously she soldiered on, and an account by Samuel Curwen, an American traveler, tells us that she was still serving tea and chocolate as late as 1780! Eventually her star did fade and she died in poverty.

Unlike the eighteenth-century hostesses, the passion for tea did not fade; tea continued to be the beverage of fantasy. Even as late as 1865, Lewis Carroll led Alice's footsteps to the Mad Hatter's tea party, a social occasion perfectly suited to a fantastical world. Tea drinking was part of Cathay and the

*This whole page:*

Figure 315. A caddy painted blue, with an overall design of fine black lines interwoven in what may be an abstraction of seaweed. Different views of the Brighton Pavilion are pasted around. The caddy must have been made soon after the completion of the restyling of the Regent's Summer Palace by Nash, in the first years of the nineteenth century. Although small boxes with Pavilion views were made as mementoes of the building, which epitomized the Regency style, these seldom had more than one or two views. This caddy is a rare example and was possibly made as a special gift. The treatment of the background too is most unusual. Although the coloring is very different, the pattern is reminiscent of eighteenth century Scottish work. An artist from the North, perhaps working in Brighton, or a caddy made in Scotland in recognition of the 1822 royal visit by George IV in the first years of his reign. 8" wide. $7,000–10,000.

dream of freedom from the social straightjacket. A person was allowed to drink it, even in dubious company. When it was drunk in the relative privacy of the boudoir, a lady usually had an audience, however small. This sharing of experience entailed a display of finery for the purpose of asserting one's aesthetic awareness and one's wealth. Fine china and silver were employed as part of the ceremony. But most of all, the tea caddy was the pivotal prop of the whole performance. After all, the precious leaf was kept safely locked in this curious little container.

As tea "connoisseurship" developed into an art, more than one type of tea was necessary for the fastidious of palate. Double chests could hold two types of leaf, usually one green and one black variety (green tea, such as Hyson and Singlo, is dried unfermented, while black tea is fermented before it is dried). The patrons preferred to mix their own blend, according to their own preference, so they needed more than one tea container. Tea poys—from Hindu *tin* (three) and Persian *pae*

(foot)—which were large, self-standing chests, could hold four or even six types of tea. These were not made until late in the eighteenth century, and they were too cumbersome to move around. The most elegant solution was a collection of caddies and chests.

Real aficionados, such as the Regency dandy Lord Petersham, could match the character of the box to the character of the tea. His walls were said to be covered in shelves "upon which were placed the canisters containing congou, pekoe, souchong, bohea, gunpowder, Russian, and many other teas, all the best of their kind." Single caddies were sometimes referred to as canisters, and vice versa.

# Tea Chests of the Early Eighteenth Century

Wooden tea caddies—or, rather, tea chests or tea boxes as they were first called—were made from the first decades of the eighteenth century. In the 1720s, Jonathan Swift mentions in his satirical *Directions to Servants*, "small chests and trunks, with lock and key, wherein they keep the tea and sugar."

Paintings of families at the tea table were beginning to feature tea boxes as one of the necessary domestic accessories. In William Hogarth's *The Strode Family*, a tea box stands on the floor by the tea table. It is of plain rectangular shape, with a simple escutcheon and what looks like a brass carrying handle on the top. It is difficult to be sure of the type of wood the box is made of, but it was most probably walnut.

Sir Henry Gough, a first baronet who was a director of the East India Company, had his family painted at tea by William Verelst in 1741. Their tea chest was placed open on the oval tea table, revealing three identical domed containers. The front of the box is inlaid with a simple oval, an early use of a neoclassical motif.

Tea chests partially replaced seventeenth-century tea containers, which were jars in china, glass, silver, enamel, and metal. These were not made by cabinetmakers, but by craftsmen working in various disciplines outside the scope of this book.

One of the first areas where tea chests were made by craftsmen specializing in small wooden items was Kent, where the Tunbridge ware tradition was already very strong. In fact, Tunbridge ware became synonymous with fine wooden articles, which in the early days were not so easy to distinguish from other "ware." The term was used by makers outside the area—many in London and the South-East of England, but also as far as the North of England. In 1762 Samuel Derrick, the indomitable chronicler of the area, sent from Tunbridge Wells "the prettiest tea chest" he could lay his hands on.

Many eighteenth-century cabinetmakers advertised tea chests or tea boxes, and several drawings of such boxes appear on trade cards. Moreover, tea chests made by cabinetmakers working on a variety of projects are mentioned on invoices and inventories dating from the early part of the eighteenth century. I will list a few significant entries to give a flavor of the development of the work and the word.

The London and later US maker James McClellan advertised "Tea Boxes" among his wares prior to 1732. George McKinder (1739–1744), who modestly called himself a "carpenter," invoiced the Duke of Gordon in 1739 for what appears to be an ambitious piece of work, "A Fine Mahog. Tea Box with an inside Spring Drawer." The Duke must have liked his tea, since in the same year he was also billed by Richard Fielder, a Portsmouth cabinetmaker, to the tune of £1.10s for another tea box.

A few early tea chests were made in walnut. One such was labeled as the work of "Benjamin Crook snr.," who worked between 1732 and 1750 in the center of the hubbub of cabinetmaking, St. Paul's Churchyard in London.

This is not to say that mahogany and other woods were not used early on in the century. Around 1731–1733, William and Richard Gomm, who worked in London between 1698 and 1794, invoiced Richard Hoare of Barn Elms "for a fine mahogany tea chest." Joseph Cooper, of London, ca. 1760, who described himself as a "wood and ivory turner," offered on his trade card "Dressing Boxes & Tea Chests of the most Curious English and Foreign Woods."

Tea chests and tea boxes were mostly designed to contain canisters in wood, or other materials, for holding tea. Noted London cabinetmaker John Cobb (1715–1778) invoiced the famous actor David Garrick at Hampton for work he carried out for him during 1766–1772. Included in the items listed was a manila wood "Tea Chest with 3 Tinn Canisters £1.15s."

In 1766, Thomas Chippendale invoiced "A very neat Mahogany Teabox with 2 wood Cannisters lin'd with lead £2.2s.0d" to Sir Lawrence Dundas Bart. It is not clear if this is the same box described by Samuel Norman as "A Very Curious Mahogany Tea Box with inside lin'd wt lead Top cover to do lin'd wt Green Velvet and Mahogany Canisters," but the later description gives us further information about the interior-lining practices of the period. This box may have been made by James Cullen.

The canisters, if made of wood, were lined so that the wood was sealed and the tea was unaffected by dampness and air. Edward Rigg, who worked in Liverpool (1750–1765) and prided himself in following the new designs of Chippendale, advertised "Mahogany Tea Chests," but also "tin Foyle." Sometimes the lining foil was referred to as "tea-pewter." It was made mostly of a tin-lead alloy.

The wood of these early boxes was undecorated, or sparsely decorated, with perhaps a chevron fine banding, or herringbone or half herringbone. I have found a reference to a "Dutch tea Chest" made by William Bradshaw for Holkham Hall, sometime between 1740 and 1747, which may refer to Dutch-style marquetry, but on the whole, it was the quality of the wood that gave these early boxes their distinction. Nicholas Cross's (Liverpool, 1754–1780) advertisement was typical of the period; he claimed to supply "best Jamaica or Hispaniola mahogany…tea chests."

These eighteenth-century boxes are shaped like small trunks, or occasionally they are of rectangular form with flat tops. In most examples, both the form and the decoration are subtly interlinked. The decorative elements are usually part of the structure, or sparsely employed. Mostly the boxes stand on bracket feet, or on a plinth support base. The edges are frequently molded. The odd rare example is known to have tracery carving in the manner of Chippendale, banding the box just above the base.

*Opposite page:*
Figure 316. *Tea Chests*: plates CXXVIII and CXXIX, T. Chippendale's *The Gentleman and Cabinet-Maker's Directory* (1754), engraved by M. Darley Sculp.

*Tea Chests.*

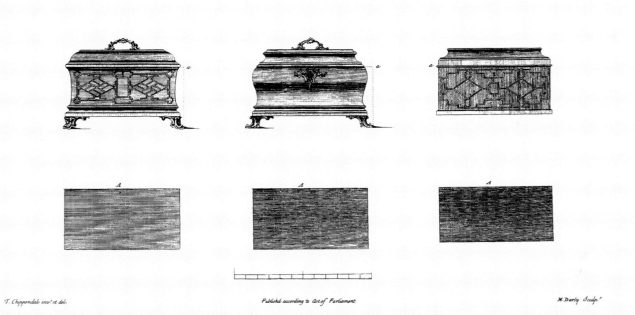

T. Chippendale inv.t et del.

Publish'd according to Act of Parliament

M. Darly Sculp.t

N.º CXXIX

*Tea Chests.*

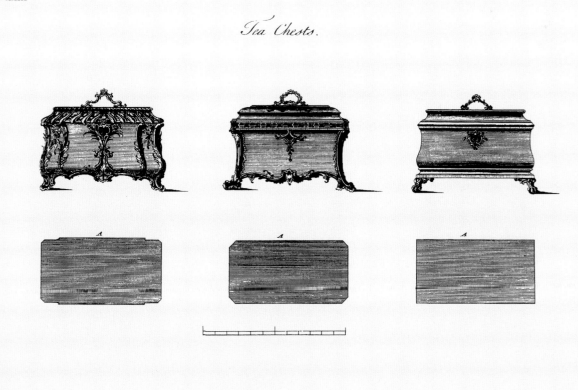

T. Chippendale inv. et del.

Publish'd according to Act of Parliament

M. Darly Sculp.

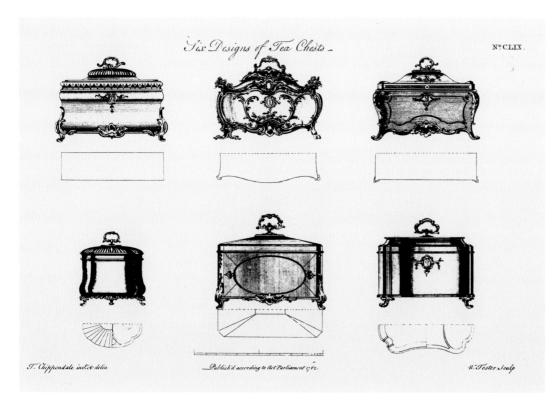

Figure 317. *Six Designs of Tea Chests*: Plate CLIX, T. Chippendale's *The Gentleman and Cabinet-Maker's Directory*, published in 1762, engraved by W. Foster Sculp.

*Above and right:*

Figure 318. A mahogany tea chest with a most unusual internal arrangement of four canisters, one of which is double. 7.9" wide. Third quarter eighteenth century. $15,000–20,000.

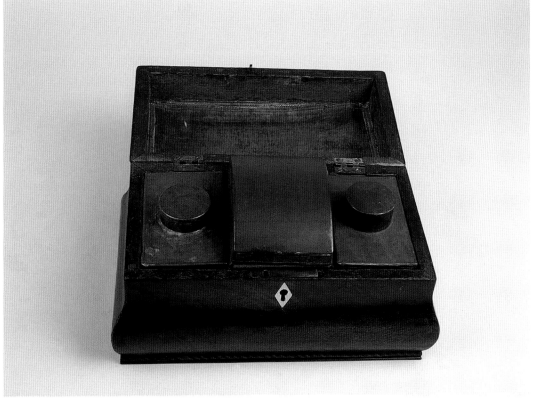

*Above:*
Figure 319. A mahogany-veneered tea chest of bombe shape with rope twist banding, containing three metal canisters. Note the exceptionally good patina. A tea chest of similar form was auctioned in 1984 bearing the label "Braithwaite." This name is consistent with recorded makers in London and York at the correct date. Note the surviving traces of leading on the sides of the wooden lid. 10.25" wide. Ca. 1760–70. $8,000–10,000.

*Above:*
Figure 320. A mahogany-veneered tea chest, containing two canisters. This is an unusual arrangement. Third quarter eighteenth century. *Courtesy of Robert A. Erlandson.* $4,000–5,000.

The trunk-shaped boxes have stepped lids, sometimes incorporating concave elements or, more rarely, domed tops. The structure of the main body of the box is predominantly straight. Bombe forms were rarely made. A mahogany caddy bearing the label "Braithwaite," with a bombe lower part and stepped lid bearing a simple escutcheon and an unusual one-stemmed handle, could have been made by one of three makers who shared this name and who were active during the third quarter of the eighteenth century.

The style of these tea chests roughly falls into two categories: the austere and the rococo with baroque undertones. The

rococo style was fashionable for a brief period in the middle of the eighteenth century. Both styles share certain characteristics, and both allow for metal mounts, handles, and escutcheons. Inlaid escutcheons were sometimes used, either as an outline of the keyhole or in a diamond shape.

Where the two styles differ is that the rococo boxes have more-elaborate, mostly gilded brass mounts that also form the feet. An unusually elaborate tea chest is in the Victoria and Albert Museum in London (W.11 1965). It is of bombe shape, made of mahogany, crossbanded, and inlaid in engraved brass, and it stands on paw feet. It has a possible attribution to the leading cabinetmaker, John Channon. It is reminiscent of the more complicated eighteenth-century French designs.

A few of these chests have a secret space or drawer, which is revealed by sliding upward one of the sides of the box. The inside of the lid is lined with velvet, or baize, or even lead. Occasionally there is a space for caddy spoons on the lid, or on the back part of the box.

Such chests were made to hold canisters that were predominantly made of metal. The lids of such containers could be removed and the tea measured out into them before it was poured into the tea pot or tea urn. Wooden canisters were rarely made, but the examples that have survived are of very high quality.

In addition to the mahogany boxes in the chest style, there were also boxes veneered in shagreen, tortoiseshell, or ivory. These were made to house silver canisters, and their metal mounts (escutcheons, handles, feet, and other decoration) were mostly of silver or gilded brass. Although beautiful in their own right, such chests were subordinate to the work of the silversmith who made the inside containers, and their value depends more on the worth of the silver work than the cabinetwork.

I have come across only one early reference to a japanned tea chest. Eminent cabinetmaker William Vile billed Lady Caroline Bridges in January 1755, "For a Japann'd Tea Chest £1.15s." Most japanned boxes and furniture of the eighteenth century are predominantly black, with rare examples in other colors. Examples of red japanned caddies are almost unheard of. The illustrated example has three containers that show signs of green enameling.

Before abandoning this period, a word must be said about the "Shakespeare" tea chests. These are reputed to have been made from the mulberry tree that grew in the bard's garden, which was reported to have been bought by cabinetmaker George Cooper. These boxes are stamped "George Cooper Stratford upon Avon maker 1759." An example with provenance at the Victoria and Albert Museum in London has a carving depicting Shakespeare's tomb, with the bard's torso placed between two pillars. Inside there are three removable canisters with sliding lids, decorated with carved mulberries. The box stands on lion paw feet. Several pieces were made from this tree, not all of them tea caddies or boxes. Caddies claiming this origin appear in sales rooms from time to time. Not all of them are identical or genuine, although they all feature a carving of Shakespeare.

Figure 321. A tea chest in burr walnut and mahogany inlaid with a star design in mother of pearl with central carrying handle. Although now empty, the fine quality of this box points to its original purpose —holding silver canisters. Ca. 1760. *Courtesy of Kevin R. Kiernan.* $3,500–4,000 (empty).

Figure 322. A mahogany-veneered tea chest, with an unusually elaborately constructed top. This is formed of a concave-stepped lid that follows the curved line of the side of the box and the uppermost domed part with central handle. 10" wide. Ca. 1770. $6,000–7,000.

*Above and right:*
Figure 323. A mahogany tea chest of traditional form, mounted with central handle and rococo escutcheon. Note the strength of the lines, and the carefully constructed upper part. Despite their restrained look, such boxes are in fact quite complex and meticulously made. Third quarter eighteenth century. *Courtesy of Elizabeth Fuller.* $3,500–5,000.

Figure 324. Mahogany tea chest with detail of the secret compartment. Very few chests were made with this particular extra feature. It required precision of execution and meticulous seasoning of the timbers for the side to line up imperceptibly when closed. Ca. 1770. *Courtesy of Berry and Marcia Morton.* $5,000–6,000.

*Above and left:*
Figure 325. A japanned chest in rare seal wax red with very finely executed raised chinoiserie decoration. The reclining figure may have been inspired by Stalker and Parker (see "Chinoiserie" chapter). The interior is fitted with three canisters, which are enameled in green. 8.5" wide. Ca. 1770. $?

Figure 326. A mahogany-veneered tea chest, showing the internal back arrangement for tea spoons. End of eighteenth century. *Courtesy of the Bielstein Collection.* $2,500–3,000.

## LATE-EIGHTEENTH-CENTURY TEA CHESTS AND CADDIES

Although during the last two decades of the eighteenth century tea was still seriously expensive, more households were drinking it and more containers were needed to keep the precious leaves fresh and safe. Tea chests became serious business, with some cabinetmakers even making them for export. The London firm of Richard Holes was advertising as early as 1781 "Tea Chests for Exportation."

The cabinetmakers saw the opportunity of introducing new designs, woods, and shapes to their clientele. More arrangements for the inside of the tea box were also experimented with. In 1793, the firm of Ireland E. and Hollier C. W. supplied Gertrude, Dowager Duchess of Bedford, with "a neat inlaid case with a bottle & place for sugar & tea spoon."

The next generation of tea chests no longer had metal canisters. They either had two wooden canisters, or two wooden canisters and a central space for a crystal bowl. Thus, both the canisters and the outside of the box could be completed in the same workshop. Rarely were both canisters and bowl made of glass.

By the 1770s, the mood of fashion was changing. The aesthetics of neoclassicism and of unified design were gaining ground. The cabinetmakers of the eighteenth and early nineteenth centuries were highly sophisticated and had perfect control of the art, science, and craft of their profession. They designed their tea chests to fit in with the new interiors in a harmonious and complementary manner.

The lines of the tea chests became straight; the tops, flat. The handles, if used at all, were flatter and finer and were placed on classically shaped, thin, metal backplates. Other mounts and ornaments were replaced with flat decoration, mostly in wood. John Folgham (London, 1750–1803) billed Stourhead, Wilts, in 1783, for a "neat Satinwood Tea Chest banded with tulipwood."

Figure 327. A tambour top caddy, rendering the use of hinges obsolete. An unusual, rare piece. Feet and handles date from the first decades of the nineteenth century, although the tambour form was used for writing boxes in the last quarter of the eighteenth century. *Courtesy of the Bielstein Collection.* $?

Figure 328. An unusually shaped mahogany-veneered caddy inlaid with a marquetry oval of musical instruments. 8.5" wide. Last quarter eighteenth century. $3,500–5,000.

A tea chest made by Seddons of Piccadilly between 1793 and 1800 also conforms to the straight rectangular shape with a recess for a bowl. The design and combination of woods inside and outside are harmonious.

While the shape of tea chests was undergoing transformation, tea caddies were beginning to appear in greater numbers. The term "tea caddy" was used when describing boxes that did not have inner canisters but served as containers in their own right. It is not certain when the word "caddy" was first used, or when the first wooden caddies as distinct from chests were first made. According to Thomas Sheraton, the term was already in established usage by 1803, by which time several caddies had already been made. The word derives from the Malay "*kati*," a measure of weight about $1^1/_3$ lb. Now, "caddy" is used to describe both chests with removable containers and caddies with lids. In the eighteenth century there was a clear distinction between the usage of the two terms.

Richard Copeland Jr. worked in Liverpool between 1761 and 1779 and was already advertising tea caddies. John Evans (Bristol, 1774—1801), a cabinetmaker, billed John Pinney—whose house is now the Georgian House Museum—18s for a tea caddy in the early 1790s. By the last decade of the eighteenth century, the caddy had gained in popularity, although a fair number had already been made in the previous two decades. William Allin of Newark, Nottingham, was advertising in 1776 that he was selling off his stock, including "Caddies plain or inlaid." John Best of Cornwall, "Cabinet-maker, Upholsterer, and Auctioneer" (1798—1839), featured a list of items on his trade card, including "plain, inlaid, and varnished tea caddees."

Figure 329. Oval caddy veneered in harewood. The inlay on this piece is in a very pure neoclassical style. It is executed in subtle contrasts and combinations of woods. The front features a lyre, the instrument favored by the god Apollo. The lyre is formed of two acanthus leaves growing out of the abstract interpretation of a tree trunk transformed into the base of a classical pillar. This particular formation of a lyre was expounded by Robert Adam. A drawing by Robert and John Adam, now in Sir John Soane's Museum in London, shows this treatment for the back of a chair. Chippendale used this motif for carving. It is also found in a less pronounced form in late eighteenth century designs. On the caddy, on either side of the lyre there is a symmetrical, mirror image branch of laurel, the plant of triumph. The top is inlaid with an oval medallion of fiddleback sycamore inlaid with a small central oval of a flower center with inverted, slightly green leaves, which in turn is surrounded by an oval arrangement of acanthus leaves forming an elongated sunflower. This metamorphic interpretation of neoclassicism was a distinguished characteristic of some of the most celebrated cabinetmakers of the second half of the eighteenth century. This caddy exemplifies this particular work. It has patinated to perfection. An outstanding piece. 6.2" wide. Ca. 1780–90. $8,000–10,000.

Figure 330. An octagonal caddy veneered in harewood, and inlaid with oval marquetry panels. Although the arrangement of the decoration is in the neoclassical manner, the flowers in these particular panels are unusual in that they are an attempt at more-familiar country flora. Perhaps bluebells? 5.5" wide. Ca. 1790. $2,500–3,500.

Many of the caddies were inlaid more elaborately than the chests. John Cooke (Chester, 1765—1789) disposed in 1782 of "Neat inlaid Caddies and Tea Chests." In addition to inlaid decoration, cabinetmakers experimented with different shapes. Samuel Tilt (1787—1791) sold in 1788 an "Oval Cadie 15s and a Cadie ladle 6s."

Caddies and chests continued to be made until the end of the nineteenth century, both forms conforming to the prevailing stylistic fashions of the time.

To illustrate the change of style in the last decades of the eighteenth century, we can compare Thomas Chippendale's designs for "tea chests" in his *Gentleman and Cabinet-Maker's Director 1762* and George Hepplewhite's designs in his *Cabinet Maker and Upholsterer's Guide* of 1788, in which he offers both chests and caddies. Comparing the chests in the two design books, we notice similar use of straight, concave, and convex shapes, but in the Hepplewhite boxes the rococo ormolu mounts are replaced with inlaid decoration in the neoclassical style, resulting in more-controlled, symmetrical compositions.

The decoration on the three Hepplewhite caddies is also in the neoclassical style and mirrors many of the motifs that were currently in use: paterae, stylized flowers, festoons of flora, and urns.

The Hepplewhite caddies are in the three prevailing shapes of the late eighteenth century: square, oval, and oblong, all with straight sides. Their surface is flat and they have no feet or other support. Two have small drop handles on the top.

In the last two decades of the eighteenth century, the prevailing forms of tea chests and caddies made are as follows:

Figure 332. Mahogany-veneered caddy with shell medallion and star inlay. A typical period piece retaining its original patina. Ca. 1790. *Courtesy of Joan Kiernan.* $1,000–1,200.

Figure 333. Oval caddy veneered in harewood. The top is inlaid with an excellent example of an oval shell marquetry. The design is gently scalloped and shaded, offering no great color contrast. The front is decorated with a directly inlaid design of a stylized acanthus leaf branching evenly into the two sides and curling into two flowers, out of the center of which emerge two strands of formally bound laurel leaves. The leaves are shaded in a soft green, harmonizing rather than contrasting with the background. The acanthus was thought to be the origin of the Corinthian column capital. Legend has it that this came about when the artist Callimachus saw an acanthus plant growing around a tile-covered basket that had been placed on the grave of a dead girl. A caddy with a very strong period look. Original finish. Excellent patina. 6" wide. Ca. 1785–95. $6,000–8,000.

Figure 331. Burr chestnut–veneered caddy of typical form. End of eighteenth century. *Courtesy of Janice Walls Interiors.* $1,000–1,200.

## Single Caddies

The shapes of the single caddies are varied. In addition to the shapes already discussed, they can be square, polygonal, or elliptical. Tops are mostly flat, sometimes with a small loop handle or finial in the center. Escutcheons are inlaid and are made of ivory, bone, or boxwood. Inside they have a freestanding lid.

Sometimes the tops are of pyramid shape, continuing the proportions of the side panels. This is mostly, but not exclusively, the case with ivory- or tortoiseshell-veneered caddies. Concave and domed tops dating from this period are rare.

## Double Caddies or Tea Chests

Double caddies are usually rectangular, sometimes octagonal, or oval. They have two lids, or two removable canisters with hinged tops. Sometimes they have one lid and a recess for a glass bowl. There are references to "sugar bowls," although later, when sugar bowls were supplied with the tea service, it was thought to be a bowl for mixing the required blend of tea.

## Triple Caddies or Tea Chests

Triple caddies have either two lids, three lids, two canisters, three canisters, or two lids or canisters flanking a space in the center for a glass bowl. Very rarely they contain two glass jars and a bowl. Rectangular shapes are prevalent.

The tea chests in this category are really the aristocrats of tea containers. The woods used are of very high quality and the decoration is very subtle and fine. Although deceptively simple looking, these chests are in fact constructed in a laborious and meticulous way. Facings, linings, and canisters all were crafted with impeccable accuracy. Attention to detail did not falter, even in areas not immediately visible.

The inside canisters were mostly hinged. Sometimes the tops of the canisters had an extra level with oval structures topped by hinged lids. A chest in the Victoria and Albert Museum in London made by Thomas Miniken, or Minikin, in 1804 has such canisters. The chest is in the typical eighteenth-century form, which continued to be made up to the end of the first decade of the nineteenth century.

Another feature of these early chests is their bowls. The eighteenth century exploited the quality of brilliance and luster in glass as it was never possible to be done before. Glass was a luxury item, and as such it was heavily taxed. On top of the price for a heavy crystal tea chest bowl, there was the duty to pay. The bowls were therefore used mostly for boxes deemed to be of special quality. Many bowls, even in English chests, were of Irish origin, since at the time Ireland was producing some of the finest examples of cut glass.

However, there is a small afterthought regarding the bowls. Some tea chests of extremely high quality were made without a space for this accessory. This may be because they were commissioned by patrons who objected to the use of sugar, on account of the employment of slaves in its production. Although few people allowed such views to interfere with their personal comfort, the anti-sugar voice was sufficiently distinctive to prompt both serious debate and caricature. So a two- or three-canister chest was not necessarily thought to be of inferior quality on account of not having a bowl recess.

Structurally, the late-eighteenth-century tea boxes were constructed following rules both for stability and style. The basic structure was made of pine, oak, or mahogany and then veneered in different woods. This enabled the manufacturers to make the best use of rich figuring in the wood, since many veneers could be cut from the most-beautiful pieces of timber. Native fruitwoods, as well as imported exotic woods, gave the cabinetmakers and their patrons a rich choice of designs within the aesthetic scope of the period.

Cutting veneers by hand using a saw was a highly skilled job. This was done in a "saw pit" with two workers working together. The veneers were much thicker than later machine-cut veneers. This created structural problems, such as the edge of the veneer (end grain of the wood) allowing moisture to be absorbed if it was not sealed. This problem was further exacerbated if the box was structured by using an already veneered flat piece of timber. An elegant decorative solution dealt with this problem. The boxes were edged in strips of contrasting plain wood—usually holly or boxwood—or in strips of pre-prepared herringbone, or similar designs.

*Opposite page:*
Figure 334. *Tea chests*: plates 57 and 58 from George Hepplewhite's *The Cabinet-Maker and Upholsterer's Guide* (1786).

*Pl. 58*

*Tea Chests.*

*Plans*

London, Published Sept.r 1.st 1787, by I. & J. Taylor, N.º 56, High Holborn.

*Pl. 57*

*Tea Caddies.*

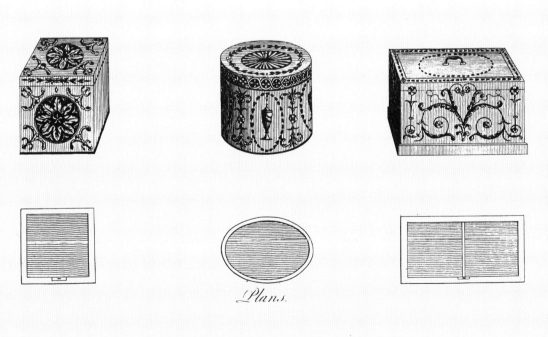

*Plans.*

London, Published Sept.r 1.st 1787, by I. & J. Taylor, N.º 56, High Holborn.

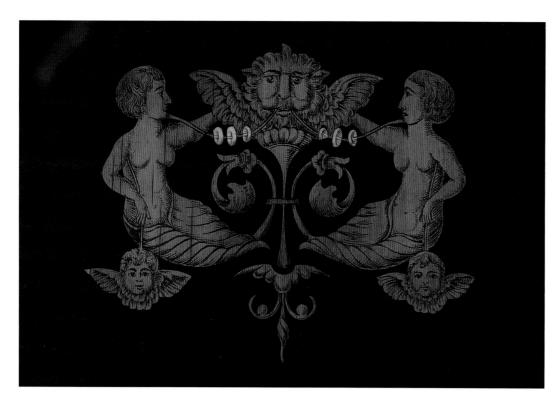

*Left and below:*
Figure 335. A mahogany-veneered caddy with inlay of holly and ivory, enhanced with "engraved" lines. The design on the caddy is derived from neoclassical motifs that were adopted by leading cabinetmakers during the second half of the eighteenth century. George Hepplewhite's *The Cabinet-Maker and Upholsterer's Guide* contains a tea chest inlay design of a half-human creature trailing into flora, but such elaborate compositions were primarily reserved for pieces of furniture. The inlay on this caddy is more robust than the Hepplewhite example and is executed with mastery and precision. A strong piece, highly representative of its period. 10" wide. Ca. 1790. $?

*Above and right:*
Figure 336. An unusually shaped tea caddy veneered in rosewood. This is an early use of rosewood and points to an important maker. The top is inlaid with an excellent example of a shell within an oval. The shell is slightly shaded and is further enhanced by fine engraved lines. The front is inlaid with the more formal classical design of a festoon, further engraved with a symmetrical design. This type of festoon inlay was favored by Robert Adam and is found on furniture executed by Thomas Chippendale and other leading exponents of the neoclassical style. 7.5" wide. Last quarter of the eighteenth century. $8,000–10,000.

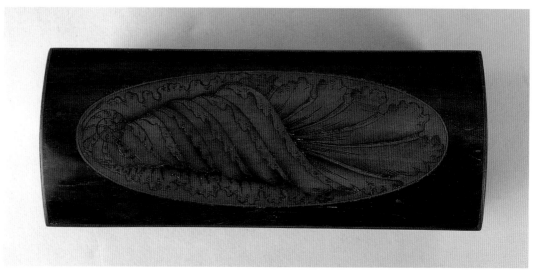

Figure 337. Oval caddy veneered in a particularly fine piece of amboyna, which shows the sudden transition from a satin figure to a burr. The oval panels of marquetry are almost identical to a caddy of the same form and proportions in the collection of the Victoria and Albert Museum in London and featured in Gillian Walking's book *Tea Caddies*. The museum example is stamped *Gillows of Lancaster*. 6" wide. End of eighteenth century. $5,000–7,000.

Figure 338. A caddy of elliptical form, veneered in mahogany, with medallions inlaid with baskets of flowers. The designs are finely engraved and the flowers have a more robust movement than often found on such compositions. Original finish, good patina. 6" wide. Ca. 1790. $5,000–7,000.

*Above and right:*
Figure 339. A harewood-veneered tea caddy with marquetry medallions featuring birds. Although the birds are subjects drawn from nature, they are represented in a stylized pose conforming to the neoclassical form of the whole piece. The details of the well-defined design are enhanced with the hot-sand shading technique. Note that the caddy was finished with a varnish, which has survived unrestored. 7.4" wide. Ca. 1800. $5,000–7,000.

*Above and left:*
Figure 340. Double satinwood-veneered tea chest with two lift-out hinged canisters, the tops of which are veneered with rosewood crossbanded with satinwood. The box is in the neoclassical tradition with controlled Greek key ornament and central handle. The interior is lined with rosewood, with the outside decoration repeating in reverse colors. 8" wide. Ca. 1790. $5,000–7,000.

*Below and left:*
Figure 341. A Georgian tea chest of typical oblong shape, with the arrangement of two canisters and a bowl. These chests usually had a centrally placed top handle. They were made to a high standard and were veneered in a variety of woods. Mahogany was the most popular, but rosewood, partridgewood, satinwood, harewood, and fruitwoods were also used. Such boxes were subtly decorated and look deceptively simple, when in fact they are a feat of craftsmanship. They were popular from the last two decades of the eighteenth century to about 1810. This particular box is veneered in rosewood. The box retains its original finish. Note how the outside has faded. 12" wide. $2,000–3,000.

Figure 342. Yew wood–veneered caddy in the classical design of the end of the eighteenth century and early years of nineteenth. The central handle in simple, elegant lines is typical. This particular box has lids and bowl, although this structure was also favored for chests containing canisters. Last decade eighteenth century. *Courtesy of Cathy A. Crim.* $1,500–2,000.

Figure 344. Detail of a partridgewood-veneered tea chest of rectangular form with two canisters and a glass bowl. The top with a central oval handle. Note the continuous hinge on the canister. Note the very fine lines of stringing framing a thicker line of green both around the canisters and the frame of the box. The same decoration continues on the outside. The subtle detail and quality of this chest is characteristic of this type of tea chest. Ca. 1790–1800. *Courtesy of Anne Brooks.* $2,500–3,500.

Figure 343. Detail of the side and the canister of a chest in the same typical form. This is veneered in rosewood and has side handles rather than a top handle. Note the incredibly fine inlay on the base of the box, and the subtle feature of the inlay on the base of the rosewood canister. This could not be seen unless the canister was taken out of the box. A real connoisseur touch. Ca. 1800. $1,800–2,500.

Figure 345. The canister top of a mahogany tea chest of rectangular form. The box has the usual canisters and central bowl. Note the construction of the lids of the canisters: The oval part is raised. The flat part is made of four mitered pieces. The whole is edged with boxwood. This form of canister is reminiscent of the earlier metal canisters. Ca. 1790–1800. $2,500–3,500.

*Left:*
Figure 346. A tea chest with domed top veneered at the back and sides with mahogany and the front and top with cherry wood. The box is decorated all around with formally arranged ovals and leaf patterns. The ovals at the back and sides are of burr yew framed by thin lines of stringing. The front and the top ovals are of book-matched wood cut from the center of a small branch. They are also cross-banded with kingwood and fine stringings of boxwood and ebony. A leaf-and-berry pattern follows the line of the top and front ovals. A similar formal pattern is inlaid into a band of boxwood that frames both the top and the front of the box. There are fine stringing lines separating the framing from the main wood. The oval theme continues on the canisters, which have raised oval lids decorated in the manner of the outside. Although the chest is inlaid in profusion, the precisely arranged decoration belies the complexity of the work. A very strong example of neoclassical work and superb workmanship.

Although this piece would not be classified as Tunbridge ware, I have a strong suspicion that this work was done in the area of Tunbridge. My reason is that the variety and treatment of very carefully selected timbers, mostly local, taking special advantage of the minutiae of figure, fungal attacks, and other peculiarities, was a tradition among Tunbridge ware craftsmen during the Georgian period. There was a respect for the beauty of the particular that could be used in small objects. There is also affinity of design between this tea chest and the Georgian writing slope (see figures 349, 509, 510), which in turn can be attributed to Tunbridge work. Note other boxes with similar work, which points to a shared tradition. Exceptional. 11.75" wide. Ca. 1780–90. $20,000–30,000.

*Right and below:*
Figure 347. Tea chest framed in the neoclassical tradition with fine geometric pattern and lines. Inside it contains three wooden canisters, similarly edged, and also inlaid with medallions decorated with colorful marquetry of strawberry plants. An unusual feature in a box of neoclassical design. 10" wide. Last decade eighteenth century. $6,000–8,000.

*This whole page:*

Figure 348. A mahogany-veneered caddy inlaid with three oval medallions. The rectangular structure and the centrally placed ovals give this piece a strong neoclassical appearance, but in fact there is an unexpected element of surprise in the design of this box. The front medallion is of a piece of well-figured darker mahogany. The top medallion of boxwood has a marquetry of a stylized vase. When opened, the last medallion is revealed on the inside lid. This is inlaid with a lively and delightful composition of a mother bird feeding her chicks. The green background has not faded. The definition of the birds is reinforced by hot-sand shading. This is an exceptionally complex representation of such a subject on a box. 11" wide. Last decade of the eighteenth century. $5,000–7,000.

# DECORATION OF WOODEN LATE EIGHTEENTH-CENTURY TEA CADDIES AND TEA CHESTS

Although not specifically categorized as Tunbridge ware, many pre-nineteenth century caddies must have originated from the Tunbridge Wells area, which already had an established reputation for small wooden objects. As mentioned in the chapter "Tunbridge Ware," certain wood combinations are characteristic of the work carried out in this particular region. An oval caddy illustrated in Dr. Brian Austen's book *Tunbridge Ware and Related European Decorative Woodwares* bears the label "Joseph Knight, Tunbridge Ware Maker to Her Majesty, Tunbridge Wells." The caddy is veneered in harewood, with a floral swag directly inlaid into the wood. Examples of inlays by the same hand, or within the same stylistic genre, combined with known types of locally grown and used woods, such as yew, holy, natural green, and other fine timbers, indicate a Tunbridge origin.

By the last two decades of the century, there are mentions of oval inlays with preset marquetry used to decorate Tunbridge ware caddies. Both the inlaid medallions and the boxes are difficult to place, since they share characteristics of work executed in different areas. Sometimes, although made elsewhere, beautifully inlaid boxes were called "Tunbridge Ware." The name conjured up a type of work and a standard of workmanship.

Wood inlays, painted, filigree paper, straw work, and chinoiserie all feature on boxes dating from this period. If the wood was particularly well figured, it was sometimes enhanced only with an outline of contrasting wood, or simple chequer design and a small silver-plated handle in the center.

Stringing and crossbanding were effective and elegant decorative devices used both for overcoming structural problems and for subtle visual results. We find deceptively simply decorated boxes in well-figured veneers, such as partridgewood, satinwood, yew, burr yew, harewood, flame or fiddle back mahogany, and fruitwoods. The variations are endless. Sometimes different woods were juxtaposed, giving a three-dimensional effect that heralded the next phase of shapes that were decidedly deliberately architectural.

The firm of George Seddon, the largest cabinetmaking firm in London at the end of the eighteenth century, is known to have used veneers to create the effect of depth. Labeled pieces include an amboyna tea chest banded with satinwood, and a satinwood tea caddy with yew wood panels.

Boxes veneered in plain or figured mahogany, sycamore, or fruitwood and sometimes even boxes veneered in strongly figured woods were inlaid. Inlays fall into two main categories:

1. Pre-prepared medallions, mostly of oval form, of marquetry, or engraved and penwork-enhanced marquetry, were inserted into the surface of the box by cutting the required shape out of the veneer. The prevalent designs were in the neoclassical style of flora, urns, garlands, paterae, lyres, stylized baskets, birds, and mythical beings. The Prince of Wales feathers and an amusing Britannia sitting on her lion were also occasionally used. By far the most-popular designs were representations of conch shells executed in fruitwoods shaded with hot sand or lead. Marine motifs were popular at the time, one theory being that they were a tribute to Lord Nelson.

2. Inlay directly inlaid into the surface veneer. Each small element of the design was inserted into the equivalent hollowed-out space of the wood. This was a more time-consuming and difficult process. It allowed for more individual expression, and as such, in addition to the neoclassical designs, we also find more naturalistic and idiosyncratic compositions.

There were specialist inlayers who worked at different workshops, and also suppliers of "ovals." This explains why the same designs are sometimes found on boxes from different

*Above:*
Figure 349. Octagonal caddy veneered in fiddleback sycamore. Every side is framed with delicate lines, herringbone, and minute chequer lines in subtle shades of green and golden woods. The front and the sides feature formal neoclassical decoration. The canted corners are inlaid with the fluted pattern inspired by classical pillars. The top is inlaid with a free-flowing floral pattern. In his book on Tunbridge ware, Dr. Brian Austen features an oval caddy with a similar design of a thin stem with delicate flowers, bearing the label of *Joseph Knight, Tunbridge Ware Maker to Her Majesty, Tunbridge Wells*. The combination of woods, the effective use of yew for the ovals, and the general quality of such pieces can point to early Tunbridge work. 4.75" wide. End of eighteenth century. $7,000–9,000.

Figure 350. Top of a two-compartment octagonal caddy with similar distinctive free-flowing flower pattern inlay. Ca. 1790. $7,000–9,000.

Figure 351. A pyramid-shaped burr yew caddy featuring the early influence of Egyptian-inspired structure. The caddy is constructed with perfectly proportioned sides, separated by boxwood stringing. Ca. 1800. *Courtesy of the Bielstein Collection*. $4,000–5,000.

Figure 352. A single caddy of neoclassical design, unusually veneered in ash. It bears a central medallion of floral marquetry. 4" wide. Ca. 1790–1800. $2,000–2,500.

workshops. The boxes were priced according to the wood, shape, and decoration.

Wooden caddies and chests of this period were either varnished or finished in wax and turpentine. Good examples, with original finish, have built up a mellow, rich patina. Running one's hand across the wood, one notices minute unevenness on the edges of inlays and edgings. Restoration must be done with the utmost care. Refinishing with later glossy, hard polishes destroys the particular beauty of this early wooden surface.

Unfortunately, very few caddies have survived to our day with their original finish. Many were French polished in the nineteenth century, when French polishing superseded varnish and wax. The new finish was applied with necessary care, and many such boxes have mellowed and patinated with time. These are acceptable alternatives to the earliest finished boxes, and realistically, they are possible to find. Recent attempts, which have glossed over the undulations, and subtleties of the inlays should be avoided, unless the work is rare and of particular merit.

Another form of decoration very rarely used was the insertion of fine wood carvings glazed and framed in ebony ovals. Such a caddy exists in the Victoria and Albert Museum in London and is attributed by Gillian Walkling in her book *Tea Caddies* to the Dutch craftsman Cornelius Bavelaar. The designs are either of neoclassical or rural inspiration. Although the work is fine, it is rather lifeless, and to my mind inappropriate for the purpose.

*Above and left:*
Figure 353. A well-patinated satin-birch caddy inlaid with a fine rendition of the Prince of Wales feathers above a crown. The design is sharply defined and subtly shaded on a background of green. 4.5" wide. Ca. 1790. $4,200–5,500.

Figure 354. A birch-veneered caddy with ovals of floral marquetry. Characteristic period composition, unusually light-colored wood. 10" wide. Ca. 1800. $2,000–2,500.

Figure 355. A mahogany-veneered caddy with interesting outlines of contrasting woods, forming stringings and geometric patterns. The top is inlaid with a marquetry oval. 7" wide. Last decade eighteenth century. $1,200–1,800.

Figure 357. A mahogany-veneered tea caddy with robust shell inlay. Note the green background of the oval and the skillful hot-sand shading on the shell. A good typical design of the last decade of the eighteenth century. 9" wide. $1,200–1,800.

Figure 356. An octagonal, partridgewood-veneered caddy inlaid with oval medallions decorated with characteristic floral designs in marquetry. 5.5" wide. Last decade eighteenth century. $2,500–3,500.

*Above and right:*
Figure 358. Oval caddy decorated both with a large marquetry oval and a directly inlaid floral composition. The work is "engraved" in the best practice of the period. The design on the top is of a floral arrangement in a vase, standing on what looks like grassland. It is very lively, with the stems stretching almost to the edge of the background. The front design is of flowers tied with a ribbon, almost struggling to break loose. The motif of a bouquet with ribbons was very much "in the French taste." It was favored by Pierre Langlois, an eminent French cabinetmaker who worked in London from 1759 to 1781. Although the shape and the arrangement of the decoration are within the neoclassical tradition, the inlay is imbued with natural vitality. The box retains its original finish, which has darkened slightly and has mellowed into a beautifully patinated surface. 6" wide. Ca. 1780–90. $6,000–8,000.

Figure 359. Examples of tea caddies turned to look like fruit. Iron hardware points to a Continental origin. These caddies are typical of genuine examples of the work. Although the forms vary, they are always quite solid looking, without too-much top thinning for pears. Care must be taken to examine the finish of such caddies. *Courtesy of the Bielstein Collection.* $6,000–12,000.

Figure 360. An example of a genuine painted caddy in the form of a house. Note the color and the finish, which has none of the peculiarly shining or "sticky" qualities of the many fakes. Ca. 1800. *Courtesy of the Bielstein Collection.* $20,000–30,000.

## TURNED FRUIT CADDIES

In addition to caddies and chests constructed by cabinetmakers, there is another type of caddy that dates from this period and which continued to be made well into the nineteenth century. These are single wooden caddies made by turners, both in England and Europe, in the shape of different fruits, mostly but not exclusively apples and pears. I have been unable to find any references for any such caddy being supplied or made. These were turned rather crudely, and it makes me wonder how many were made by grandfather when the family apple tree was felled. Early examples have iron or silver hardware.

A few such caddies have survived with a good patina or traces of old color. These have a certain rural charm, and, like other "treen" objects, they have mellowed into a comforting folksy tactile familiarity.

Another type of folk art caddy was made in the form of a painted cottage. These caddies were gessoed and painted in ochre. Features such as windows and plants were painted in a direct, naive manner. Unfortunately, like the fruit caddies, these are very susceptible to faking. A yellowing gooey surface is a usual giveaway.

Occasionally, a cabinetmaker tried to create something very complex, such as the miniature model of Carlton House made by William Potter of Cornhill in 1786 and presented to George III for inspection. The king did not jump at the opportunity of buying such an object, but he tactfully suggested that it should be raffled. It allegedly raised 880 guineas and was won by the maker, who kept the unsold tickets! (Reference: *Directory of English Furniture*)

This box is a veritable work of love and must have taken hours of meticulous and arduous work to complete. It is also proof of the maker's understanding of the architectural grammar of the late eighteenth century. Whatever its artistic merit, it is certainly a tour de force of craftsmanship.

An object that represented something else was not condoned as good taste during the Georgian period. George Hepplewhite, in his preface to *The Cabinet-Maker and Upholsterer's Guide*, condemns "such articles, whose recommendation was mere novelty and perhaps a violation of all established rule, the production of whim at the influence of caprice." The cabinetmakers looked to the stylistic influences of the time as repositories of inspiration to be adapted to articles relevant to the lifestyle of the period, always mindful of the rules of proportion. Many of them subscribed to books dealing with the orders of architecture. Gimmicks were not what they aspired to create.

Caddies in the shape of urns, knife boxes, pieces of furniture, and even buildings have of late appeared with increasing frequency on the market. While some of them date from the Georgian period, entirely convincing examples with original finish are elusive. At best they seem to have an Edwardian feel, and at worst they are brand new. Mindful of

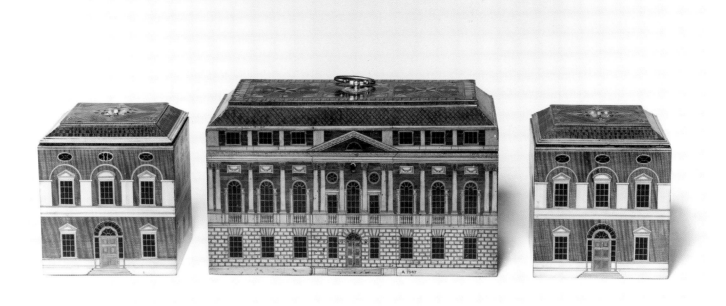

Figure 361. Tea caddy fashioned after Carlton House by William Potter of Cornhill. Ca. 1786. *Courtesy of Museum of London.*
See text for the story of this piece.

the rules of proportion adhered to by eighteenth-century
cabinetmakers, most of these boxes do not seem to make the
grade. This is not to say that there are no exceptions to this
observation, such as the Carlton House, or the chest described
in 1754 in *The World*, which was made to resemble a pile of
books (the box was made of carved wood, with the hinges
and lock "artfully concealed").

## PAINTED DECORATION

Eighteenth-century caddies were painted in the styles fashionable at the time. Hepplewhite recommends for tea chests and
caddies: "The ornaments may be inlaid with various colored
woods, or painted and varnished." The boxes were veneered in
maple or other "white woods" and painted or decorated in penwork with neoclassical motifs, chinoiserie, stylized flora, Gothic
ruins, pastoral scenes, or naturalistic designs. This style of decoration continued and became more prevalent during the
beginning of the nineteenth century. A few caddies and chests
were veneered in satinwood and decorated in the neoclassical
style in the manner preferred by Adam, with Angelica Kauffmann—style vignettes and with floral swags and putti. Small
caddies were sometimes covered in paper and then painted and
gilded. On account of the fragility of the material, these are now
very rare.

Figure 362. An octagonal, harewood-veneered caddy, the canted corners with fluted
inlay, with a central medallion inlaid with a rosebud, executed in a more naturalistic
manner than the stylized convention of the period. The top features a loop handle
placed in the center of a classical patera motif. 4.5" wide. Ca. 1790–1800.
$3,500–4,000.

Figure 363. Mahogany-veneered chest, in an interesting shape, containing silver canisters. Mid-eighteenth century. *Courtesy of the Bielstein Collection.* $?

Figure 364. An unusually small caddy veneered in harewood. The caddy is decorated with prints framed in chequer inlay circles on the top and a chequer inlay oval at the front. The top prints represent Eros (or Cupid) in infant manifestations, and, on the front, a girl holding a squirrel. Original varnish with slight pitting. 3.4" wide. End of eighteenth century. $2,000–2,500.

*Above:*
Figure 365. A very rare example of a genuine miniature caddy; it measures only 2.75" in width. It is made of sycamore, the top veneered with burr yew. It is constructed to the high standards expected of full-size caddies: the base with appropriate facings, the lid knob turned, and the hardware solid and well fitting. The top is decorated with a hand-colored print depicting classical figures; the base, with a strip of stylized design. A little gem. 2.75" wide. Ca. 1790. $?

## Rolled Paper or Filigree

Wooden frames in mahogany or oak were supplied undecorated during the last part of the eighteenth and the first part of the nineteenth centuries. These were decorated with "filigree" work, mostly by ladies of the house.

## Papier-Mâché

Eighteenth century papier-mâché caddies in original condition are rare. They were made mostly by Henry Clay (see pgs. 96—101) in small oval or rectangular shapes. They were gilded or painted (or both) in the traditional style for landscape painting of the eighteenth century, or in the neoclassical and other fashions of the time. (See Figures 133, 134.)

## Straw Work

The first straw work caddies known in England were tin "jars" covered in straw work and brought most probably from Holland or Italy during the seventeenth century. During the eighteenth century, straw work—covered wooden boxes were also made in England in very small numbers. (See Fig. 223) Such boxes are now so rare that very few collectors have even seen one. The intricacy of the work and the way that straw color mellows make successful restoration impossible, and thus surviving examples have escaped the abuse of "refinishing." These caddies should be treasured for what they are, even in distressed condition.

## Japanned Chinoiserie

Very few caddies or chests of this type survive from this period. (See Figures 302, 325)

## Caddies from India and China

Anglo-Indian ivory and Chinese-lacquer chests were brought to England from the last decades of the eighteenth century. However, serious importation did not start until the beginning of the nineteenth century (see chapters 15 and 16).

The Chinese chests had removable soft-metal containers engraved with floral or oriental designs. They were larger than the English caddies and wider than the English chests—almost square rectangular shapes. The sides were straight and the tops were flat. The quality of the decoration was of a very high standard.

*This whole page:*
Figure 366. Filigree tea caddy decorated with curled paper in characteristic designs (see "Filigree or Rolled Paper" chapter). There are traces of the original gilding on the edge of the paper. There is a colored print in the center of the back and front panel. The back depicts two classical figures, who, judging from their sparse garments, are lovers. On the front, Cupid and Psyche. Ca. 1790. *Courtesy of Charleen Plumly Pollard.* $3,000–4,000.

Figure 367. Straw work caddy, with neoclassical decoration, dating from the end of the eighteenth century. *Courtesy of the Bielstein Collection*. $3,500–4,500.

Figure 368. Straw work caddy. The floral motif, as well as the swirling treatment of the surrounding foliage, are characteristic of Continental work. 6" wide. Second half eighteenth century. $4,500–5,500.

Anglo-Indian chests were ivory veneered, with incised decoration and hardware reminiscent of the English wooden caddies, although mostly in silver or silver plate. They were designed to contain metal, sometimes silver, or crystal canisters.

## EARLY-NINETEENTH-CENTURY TEA CADDIES AND CHESTS—REGENCY

The period often referred to as the Regency has a distinctive stylistic flavor, indulged in, encouraged, and promoted by the Prince of Wales, who was later to become the Regent and, in 1820, King George IV. This flavor was well suited to the design of tea caddies and chests. The best boxes dating from this period are incredibly well structured. Furthermore, they look dramatic in a splendidly opulent way, without straying into vulgarity. The box makers were so cognizant of their art that they balanced their creations on the pivotal point where design reaches the limit of its potential and achieves maximum strength without inappropriate diversions.

By the last decades of the eighteenth century, the philosophical, stylistic, and financial certainties of the mid-eighteenth century were already undermined by the widespread exposure to diverse cultural influences. Improved transport, trade, and publications changed both aesthetic perceptions and social structures. The neoclassical designs of the last two decades of the century were only the beginning of a natural progression to even stronger departures from old accepted forms.

The neoclassical influence of the eighteenth century, which in the case of tea boxes translated itself into straight shapes and stylized ornaments, developed in the early nineteenth century to embrace the adaptation of more complex classical architectural forms in the construction of tea chests and caddies. Egyptian-inspired classicism, which was the next step after Greek- and Roman-influenced traditions, was pivotal in the creation of the new shapes, which rejected straight lines and adopted forms derived from the architectural grammar of temples and ceremonial structures.

Decoration too became more robust, aiming at suggesting depth either with painted, inlaid, or structured ornament. Parallel to this, the inspiration from China and India was shaking the roots of classicism into the realms of the exotic and the magical.

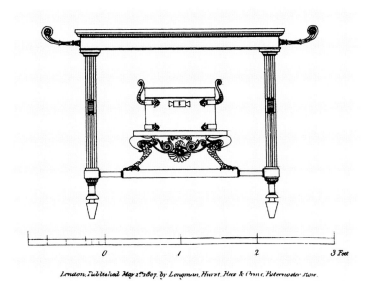

Figure 369. A design for a tea chest by Thomas Hope from his *Household Furniture* (1807). It is described as such: "Under this tea-table, on a tablet supported by pheasant's feet, ending in a scroll, stands a tea chest with perpendicular handles."

*Above and below:*
Figure 370. A Rosewood veneered tea chest of very superior quality, featuring early Regency decoration. The brass inlay is restrained and at the same time robust, featuring straight lines and separate ornament of the Irish shamrock. The box is also edged in brass, strengthening the outline both aesthetically and practically. The feet and handles are of strong neoclassical form. The chest is fitted with heavy crystal canisters and matching bowl. The back is lined in leather, punctuated with silk tufts. This interior arrangement, which was very costly at the time, is rare. 13" wide. Ca. 1810. $16,000–20,000.

During the eighteenth century, excepting Tunbridge ware makers, most caddies and chests were generally made by cabinetmakers who were engaged in general furniture production. In the nineteenth century, box makers were beginning to appear as a separate discipline. This is not to say that all boxes were made by specialized makers. Far from it; wonderful boxes have survived bearing labels of makers who did not even mention boxes on their trade cards. The significant fact for the box maker was that boxes became such a fashionable accessory that a cabinetmaker could make a living by specializing in such a narrow field.

Specialized inlayers also targeted the now fashionable boxes. John Jones, who worked in London from 1818 to 1829, advertised himself as "a tea chest and cabinet inlayer," not just as "an inlayer." In addition to wood, inlaying in brass, metal, and mother of pearl was offered by specialists in different fields of work.

Tentatively at first, tea box makers began to experiment with new shapes. Some caddies and chests made in the first decade of the nineteenth century have "pagoda" or pyramid tops or tapered sides or both. The lines are still reminiscent of the classical purity of Greek structures.

Before long, the shapes became more robust. The sarcophagus- and temple-shaped box predominated in its many variations. The simply tapered form, with perhaps a stepped top, gave way to forms combining shaped structural elements, including concave and convex lines. Sometimes the whole of the main body of the box was curved. Some boxes were made with domed lids, three-dimensional paneling, gadrooning, or any combination of architectural elements then in vogue.

The shape of caddies and chests was often enhanced by standing them on turned wooden feet or on feet made of pressed brass; the brass feet were sometimes gilded. The metal feet were inspired from the ancient world and took the form of animal paws or bird talons. Sometimes they were in the form of clustered formal flowers. Side handles in a complementary design to the feet were often added, such as lion masks, two-headed eagles, or baskets of flowers. When the feet were made of turned wood, so were the handles, which were either in the form of a turned circle or looped rings.

*This whole page:*
Figure 371. A tea chest incorporating both inlay and carved elements of decoration. The separate ornament and brass line are typical of early Regency. The carving is more characteristic of late eighteenth century work. The form of the box too is exceptional in that it combines the Egyptian-inspired tapering sarcophagus lines with three-dimensional effects interpreted through carving and slightly curving lines. The interior features heavier brass ornament, completing the sense of weightiness that permeates the whole composition. A truly monumental-looking piece, very much in the spirit of Egyptian neoclassicism. 13.5" wide. Early nineteenth century. $?

As the shapes of boxes became more complex, inlaid wood decoration became less popular. Early sarcophagus-shaped caddies in mahogany veneers depended for their aesthetic appeal on the form of the box and the richness of the figure of the wood. Some were built with fielded panels, the frames edged with gadrooning. The whole structure was managed on architectural principles, and the final result was strong and impressive. In the first years of the nineteenth century, the use of mahogany veneers was still predominant. Burr yew, yew, bird's-eye maple, harewood, partridgewood, and satinwood were sparingly used.

By the beginning of the second decade of the century, especially after the Napoleonic Wars, a new impetus was given to box design with the importation of varieties of exciting hardwoods from Africa, the Far East, the Americas, and Australia. These, especially rosewood, had been used in high-quality cabinetmaking since the early part of the eighteenth century but had not been available in any significant numbers. Furthermore, such timbers were not easy to finish with the varnishes and waxes available during the eighteenth century. Dark, richly figured woods such as rosewood and kingwood were quickly adopted as new favorites. The depth of color and richness of figure rendered the new arrivals eminently suitable for the strongly structured forms of the Regency.

Firms such as Seddon's were now using the new timbers; a caddy with their label dating from about 1825 is veneered in rosewood.

Interesting combinations of woods allowed for striking, yet subtle effects within the rules of the grammar dictated by the new shapes. The label of James Hicks (1809—1837), one of the pioneering London cabinetmakers specializing only in the production of boxes, has been found on a domed-top rosewood tea chest banded with amaranth and containing two mahogany and satinwood canisters and a central bowl. The juxtaposition of darker and lighter woods added effectively to the depth of perspective without the necessity of excessive deviation from straight lines in the construction of the box.

Rosewood is an open-grained wood, and the full advantage of its figure can be justly appreciated when it is highly polished. French polish, which was first introduced by French workers, was thus adopted as the universal finish for early-nineteenth-century caddies. This was made of shellac dissolved in fine spirit and applied in many thin coats on an already grain-filled surface. By 1815, every cabinetmaker had perfected his own way of polishing. The methods were more predictable and the results more uniform than with earlier varnishes. The final product presented a glossy finish and a very even surface.

We have another, rather sad record of two boxes in the new shapes. These were unfortunately stolen from the maker, C. Jones of Liverpool, in 1824. It is interesting to note the price difference: "a handsome black rose-wood tea chest, banded with tulip wood hollow round the top with two canisters & a basin place in the middle, £2.14s . . . a mahogany tea caddie with bevelled top, 16s." By 1832, Edward Thomas (London,

Figure 372. Caddy veneered in skillfully juxtaposed mahogany to create geometric patterns. The shape is a subtle departure from the strict straight lines of earlier neoclassicism. Early nineteenth century. *Courtesy of Christopher and Catharine Hughes*. $1,000–1,200.

Figure 373. A mahogany and fiddle maple (interior) chest of subtle design and superb quality. This piece is important in that it typifies the brief moment in time when the early neoclassical taste was just beginning to give way to the Egyptian phase of influence. The box is slightly sarcophagus shaped but still retains quite pure lines. The top part does not follow the line of the lower part, but straightens up, giving the box an air of strength. The crossbandings in kingwood and the boxwood stringings are very subtle and still within the neoclassical tradition. The inside of the box, which is in golden-colored sycamore inlaid with rosewood, contrasts with the outside. This creates a dramatic effect, but the lines suggestive of Greek key are untussy and precise. The escutcheon and handles are made of pressed gilded brass in formal designs within the neoclassical tradition. 11.5" wide. First decade nineteenth century. *Courtesy of Kevin R. Kiernan*. $4,000–5,000.

Figure 374. A mahogany-veneered caddy that combines several stylistic elements in its small form. The bombe shape harkens back to the early eighteenth century and foreshadows the late Regency. The concave top is reminiscent of oriental ceramic pillows and was perhaps influenced by the fashion for things Chinese. 5.5" wide. First quarter nineteenth century. $2,500–3,500.

Figure 375. This is the archetypal Regency, George IV, William IV, and early Victorian tea chest. Sarcophagus shaped, with feet and handles and given depth with gadrooning. The form in all its variations remained popular for many decades, although the veneers became thinner as the century progressed. Earlier versions such as the one here tend to have well made canisters and carefully finished interiors. Furthermore, they are structured with care. Note the gadrooned base, the well turned feet, and the complex loop handles. 12.25" wide. Second quarter nineteenth century. $800–1,200.

Figure 376. A concave-shaped, Rosewood veneered tea chest, a more complex form than the straight sarcophagus shape. Curving the thick veneer used at the time needed a certain amount of skill. The result was a robust and attractive shape, combining formal architectural elements, with forms that looked as if they had been molded by nature. Ca. 1825. *Courtesy of Kevin R. Kiernan.* $1,800–2,500.

1832—1839) was invoicing John Arkwright of Hampton Court, Leominster, " £4.4s for a rosewood tea chest." It is not possible to have a complete understanding of prices, since financial structures were very different, but tea caddies and chests were certainly items of value. (A note of interest: Thomas Brooks of Yorks, a cabinetmaker, described himself in the early 1820s as a tea dealer!)

Rosewood, kingwood, species of ebony, and other exotic woods popular in the early part of the nineteenth century are very distinctively figured woods, often featuring strong striations of dramatically contrasting color. Inlays in wood cannot be effective on a background of such strong natural figure. The type of ornament suited both to the timbers and to the new shapes had to be vigorous enough both to complement and enhance their robust forms.

The new structured shapes, standing on their metal paws and claws, demanded commensurable ornamentation. Many of the ornaments included in Thomas Sheraton's *Cabinet Dictionary* (1803) and following publications that were originally suggested for furniture were also adopted for tea boxes. In fact, the animal monopodia, brass motifs, brass inlay lines, and strikingly contrasting wood marquetry had been used on sarcophagus-shaped wine cellarets during the second half of the eighteenth century. Tea boxes followed the same lines in smaller proportions.

The most exciting new material for inlay was brass. Caddies and chests in well figured mahogany, rosewood, or kingwood were often decorated with brass stringing, stars, and roundels. Brass escutcheons in more complex shapes replaced earlier diamond-shaped bone/ivory ones.

Heavier floral brass inlay was promoted by eminent architect Thomas Hope, who advocated brass-inlaid borders. The decoration on boxes dating from the first two decades of the nineteenth century tends to be made up of separate ornaments inlaid into the wood. These ornaments are neoclassical in inspiration, such as anthemion and Greek key patterns.

Figure 377. A bombe-shaped Regency caddy veneered in rosewood, with feet and handles in early-nineteenth-century style. The shape on this caddy is pushed to such an extreme that it looks almost like a friendly living creature. 8" wide. Ca. 1820. $3,500–5,000.

*Above and below:*
Figure 379. An example of the use of fielded panels and gadrooning to create a sense of structural depth. Note the exceptional use of the rosewood veneer. The maker had total respect for the particularly good figure on his piece of veneer and used its natural striations to create natural sweeps of light and darkness. The "frame" of the box is veneered by using slanted book-matched veneer, which gives a gentle emphasis to the subtly upward-augmenting form. At first sight the box looks simple, but it is in fact a very intricately and skillfully constructed piece. 12" wide. Ca. 1825. $4,000–6,000.

Figure 378. A bombe-shaped, Rosewood veneered tea chest with brass inlay. The pattern of the line is suggestive of a classical Greek pattern. The box stands on classically inspired simple feet, which enhance its form. Both the decoration and the mounts are formal, in contrast to the form, which tries to break into more "organic" lines. This is characteristic of the successful fusion of ideas during the first decades of the nineteenth century. 12.5" wide. Ca. 1815–20. $3,000–4,000.

Figure 380. A serious example of the best use of material and technique to create a deceptively uncomplicated shape. The tea chest is veneered in richly figured rosewood, giving a large expanse of natural material. The flat top is joined to the lower part by a wide piece of carved rosewood. This harmonizes with the body of the box and the large feet on which it stands. A box made in bold strokes. An impressive construction, conveying the fashion for monumental design. 13" wide. Ca. 1825–30. *Courtesy of a private collection.* $3,000–4,000.

Figure 381. A trunk-shaped and strapped tea caddy veneered in mahogany. The caddy is inlaid in ebony and mounted in steel. As a decorative device, steel was favored by French cabinetmakers, who were influenced by Russian work. This particular caddy is French and shows the skillful and effective way that steel and wood could be combined to create unusual pieces. Under the lock there is a small drawer that has a "trick" opening method. 5" wide. A most unusual caddy dating from the early nineteenth century. $3,000–4,000.

In deference to the Regent, the *fleur-de-lis* motif was employed in conjunction with straight brass lines. Hybrid fleur-de-lis/anthemia were also created in a fusion of ancient and topical reference. Slightly later swirly floral motifs, more in the boulle style, replaced severe earlier designs. These became more naturalistic during the 1820s, sometimes covering the whole surface of the box. The composition remained controlled, even though the elements within it were more recognizable. Meticulously executed, such inlays retained the dignified gravitas of classicism.

Rosewood brass-inlaid caddies of this period usually feature a rosewood-lined interior, sometimes also inlaid in brass. In tea chests, the canisters are of high quality, sometimes with a central brass-inlaid motif similar to the exterior decoration and sometimes with G and B (Green and Bohea tea) inlaid in brass, one letter on each lid. Bohea was a popular type of black tea.

Mother of pearl, with its glamorous translucence and its brightness of color, is another material that looks well against the dark and glossy background of rosewood and ebony. Previously it had been very occasionally and sparingly used in conjunction with wooden inlays. It is possible its use in papier-mâché boxes alerted woodworkers to its potential as an accompaniment to the exotic dark woods. This combination produced some fine and striking boxes.

The caddies decorated in this material fall into two categories. The first category consists of simple rectangular or sarcophagus-shaped boxes decorated in pewter stringing with mother of pearl circles in the corners and mother of pearl escutcheons, or just mother of pearl escutcheons.

The second category includes caddies and chests in sarcophagus shapes with fine designs of birds, animals, and flowers. These sometimes have escutcheons incorporated within the design. They invariably stand on turned feet, and sometimes they also have flat or loop-and-ring wooden handles. The inlays are very fine, the result of skilled and careful craftsmanship. Like the brass inlays of the early nineteenth century, the designs are formal and symmetrical. One firm specializing in such work was that of Dalton, who operated from different addresses in London during the first half of the nineteenth century. I have found labeled pieces of extremely high quality both in workboxes and tea chests.

This form of decoration continued into the era of William IV (1830—1837) and the early years of the Victorian period.

During the 1830s and 1840s, marquetry was revived as a decorative device, but unlike earlier examples, where the design was made up of different colors, now it was made up mostly of two contrasting woods, such as rosewood with bird's-eye maple or satinwood. This work, although executed mostly in the form of formal borders, strived toward a more naturalistic representation of flora and fauna. It continued into the first decades of the Victorian era.

Figure 382. A fruitwood and steel-studded caddy, featuring cut-steel dots. This was a more usual form of steel decoration (see the "Palais Royal" section in the "Sewing Boxes or Workboxes" chapter). 7" wide. Continental, ca. 1820–40. $800–1,000.

*Above and left:*

Figure 383. This tea chest has the monumental quality of a truly magnificent piece. It is veneered in kingwood on mahogany and accented with a discreet classical ornament in brass. Although its label has not survived, the combination of wood, ornament, and specific hinging suggests a piece made by one of the top firms of the period. Its superb quality and the use of kingwood with the distinctive decoration, which I have come across in another labeled box, made me suggest that it was made by Edwards. However, the particular hinges were patented by another distinguished maker, E. Wells. It could be that the same craftsman/journeyman worked as inlayer for both firms. The distinctive, probably unique, feature of this chest is its square bowl. It must have been a bespoke piece made for a particular customer. I have never seen a square bowl in a tea chest before this one. It is of very heavy crystal, with deep and sharp cutting in a formal restrained pattern. The bowl fits very snugly, and it fits only one way around, which makes me think that the well was made to measure for this bowl to sit securely between the canisters. This is a bespoke piece of supreme aesthetic and technical quality. 13.75" wide. Ca. 1820. $10,000–12,000.

Figure 384. A Rosewood veneered tea chest of very superior quality, featuring early Regency decoration and shape. The feet and handles are of strong neoclassical form. The chest is fitted with heavy crystal canisters. The back is lined in leather, punctuated with silk tufts. This interior arrangement, which was very costly at the time, is rare. The chest is without a central sugar bowl. The use of sugar was associated with the slave trade, and a chest such as this was a subtle way of communicating your attitude toward the issue. 8" wide. Ca. 1810. $9,000–11,000.

Figure 385. A Rosewood veneered caddy that opens like a drawer. This must have been an experiment aiming to avoid the necessity of hinges. However, it created other problems, such as the difficulty of pulling the whole drawer out while keeping it steady. An interesting thought. Perhaps a unique piece. 12" wide. Second quarter nineteenth century. $2,000–3,000.

*This whole page:*

Figure 386. A Rosewood veneered tea chest that combines all the best elements of early Regency work. This use of brass inlay demonstrates the early phase of separate distinctive ornament set into the wood. In this case the ornament is an interpretation of the palmette motif, which was already introduced during the eighteenth-century neoclassical period. The palmette was a popular design in ancient times, especially in ceramic decoration. Thomas Hope, in his *Household Furniture* (1807), gives examples of such classical ornaments as the palmette, the anthemion (honeysuckle), acanthus, and star motifs. The differences between the palmette and anthemion motifs, especially when abstracted, are not always easy to define. A general rule of thumb is that the palmette usually branches outward, while the anthemion curls inward. Designs similar to the ones on this particular box are found on Regency furniture, including a table executed after Hope's designs and now at the Victoria and Albert Museum in London, dated 1807. The ornamental inlay on the outside of the box is continued on the interior canisters. The escutcheon is skillfully incorporated within the design. The interior facings of the tea chest are also inlaid with a brass pattern, which continues over the lock plate, rendering it indistinguishable from the surrounding structure. A rare feature, most skillfully executed. The box has lion face handles, which are typical of the period. 12.5" wide. Ca. 1810. $16,000–20,000.

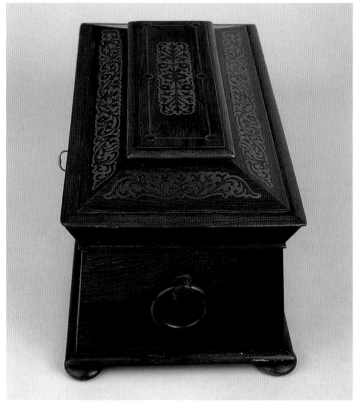

Figure 387. A tea chest veneered in rosewood and inlaid in brass. What is special about this box is the increased use of brass inlay to suggest architectural construction. Although of sarcophagus form, the box features canted corners that are inlaid with tapering brass lines. These have the effect of drawing the line of vision upward, like columns in a temple. The strong feet emphasize this sense of grandeur. The separate brass ornament and side handles are characteristic of the period. Ca. 1810–15. *Courtesy of the Bielstein Collection*. $7,000–9,000.

Figure 388. Tea caddy veneered in particularly well-figured rosewood. The inlaid brass ornament is of separate form but more flowing and expansive than earlier examples. Inside it has two lids with inlaid floral star motif. 8" wide. Ca. 1815–20. $4,000–5,000.

*Right from top:*

Figure 389. A significant tea chest. This particular piece is distinctive in that its inlaid decoration is very deliberately used to create a structural architectural effect. Unlike the chest in figure 387, where the canted corners draw up the vision with the tapering brass inlay, this box is actually structured to be redolent of a temple. The symmetrical brass inlay on each side of the front tapers inward, as if one is looking at a temple entrance and the perspective makes the top of the pillars look smaller. The inlaid lines reinforce the impression of the perpendicular diminution in width. The whole box tapers inward, and then it is crowned by what looks like an angularly constructed roof. The design is the result of a sophisticated and well-informed mind, able to transfer the rules of one discipline to another without resorting to inappropriate, slavish copying. 13.25" wide. Ca. 1815–25. $5,000–7,000.

*Above left and right:*
Figure 390. A tea chest that exemplifies the period of transition between separate ornament and free-flowing naturalistic design. A good George IV shape, combining sarcophagus and pyramid elements, it is edged in ebony, which adds definition to the horizontal lines. The decorative design is carefully worked to give an impression of controlled symmetry. The stylized flora incorporates the shamrock design. The box retains its original finish in remarkably good condition, and with careful examination it is possible to see the continuation of the line of the design engraved onto the wood. Often this is not visible, either because it was never there or because it disappeared with over cleaning. 12.75" wide. Ca. 1820–25. *Courtesy of a private collection.* $4,500–6,500.

Figure 391. A truly glamorous use of brass inlay. Although still a controlled pattern, both the shape of the box and the pattern have become more elaborate. Note the main panel of inlay. In the very center, the pattern is formed by the wood framed by the brass. This grows outwardly in reverse, with the brass defining the shape of the stylized leafy design. This creates an impression of exploding unfurling richness, characteristic of the mature George IV period. 12.5" wide. Ca. 1825–30. *Courtesy of Mark DiPaolo.* $4,500–7,000.

*Above and right:*
Figure 392. A Rosewood veneered tea chest with mother of pearl decoration. The box is shaped following the late neoclassical phase of monumental-inspired design. It is of exceptionally high quality, both in terms of construction and inlay. The mother of pearl is inlaid with precision, forming a clear, sharp pattern. The piece bears the label of "Dalton's" on the base, under one of the canisters. 13" wide. William IV. $6,000–7,000.

*Above:*

Figure 393. Rosewood veneered tea caddy with boxwood inlays. The design represents scenes of classical inspiration. The nude figures betray an attempt at representing the ancient Olympic games. It is unusual to find inlaid human figures that are meant to be realistic rather than metamorphic or mythical beings. Although rather stiff and hardly athletic, the figures and the whole box have a certain naive charm. Difficult to date accurately, since it does not conform to any tradition of cabinetmaking. 8" wide. A guess would be 1830–50. $2,500–3,000.

## TUNBRIDGE WARE

A very important group of tea caddies and chests produced in the first three decades of the nineteenth century are the Tunbridge ware boxes. Shapes are similar to other caddies and chests of the period, with the exception that the nature of the decoration precludes extreme bombe or concave shapes. In the first thirty years of the nineteenth century, caddies were usually made in rosewood veneer with vandyke (elongated triangles) and cube pattern parquetry decoration.

This is the first time that Tunbridge ware began to acquire its distinctive style, and caddies and chests dating from this period are of very high quality and aesthetic excellence. They are a celebration of the natural beauty of the woods combined in multiple variations never before available to the craftsman. The clientele was still both discriminating and curious, and the makers produced items of strength and subtlety with total respect and understanding of the grain and nature of their timbers.

The earliest boxes do not feature micro-mosaic inlays, which appear in the 1830s mostly as borders. Turned feet were usual, but not handles, which would interfere with the all-around pattern of decoration.

## PENWORK

Penwork and painted caddies from this period reflect very strongly the often conflicting influences of the time, which gave it its particular vibrancy and charm. Shapes are the typical shapes of the day. Feet and handles are usually of gilded brass. Decorated both inside and out with oriental, classical, English romantic, or naturalistic themes, they are a joyous celebration of the excitement created during the early part of the nineteenth century with the explosion of such diverse cultural influences.

## PAPIER-MÂCHÉ

Richard and George Bill (1818—1839) of Birmingham advertised among their wares "Tea Chests and Cadees." This was quite unusual, since most papier-mâché makers did not make chests. The nature of the material is not particularly suitable for sliding containers. The boxes made during the first two decades of the nineteenth century were painted, gilded, or both. After about 1825, mother of pearl decoration was introduced and was used mostly in conjunction with painting and gilding. The double caddies were of curvilinear, sarcophagus, or rectangular forms. They had two lids inside.

*This whole page:*
Figure 394. A Tunbridge ware tea chest veneered in rosewood and a variety of native and exotic woods. The sides are in a vandyke pattern; the top, in marquetry. Note that, unlike slightly later pieces, this box does not have bandings of micro-mosaic marquetry. The patterns created by the skillful juxtaposition of the varied timbers are striking. The box is a true celebration of the natural beauty of the woods and the respect with which the craftsman treated his material. A strong, dignified example. Second decade nineteenth century. *Courtesy of a private collection.* $6,000–7,000.

*This whole page:*
Figure 395. A penwork tea chest, true to the spirit of the Regency. Its shape is of pure Egyptian inspiration. The top is decorated in designs of neoclassical derivation. The center features a pattera pattern slightly suggestive of a flower. The lower surround and the wide triangular panels feature acanthus leaves. The narrower sides have leaves enclosing either a stylized pine cone (ancient symbol of fertility) or a pineapple (a fruit of the East). The main body of work is in chinoiserie. The figures and landscapes have a light element, which was introduced in the second part of the eighteenth century but did not find true expression in England until the advent of penwork. Much of the design is inspired by Mathias Darly and George Edwards's *A New Book of Chinese Designs*. For example, the book gives illustrations of "Indian" islands, bits of land somehow floating in the universe. Such islands were earthly manifestations of the "Islands of the Blessed." Furthermore, there are "dragon

boats," dragons, roofs with hanging bells, fishing figures, pointed hats, bridges, and railings. Dragon boats are used in South China in festivities during the fifth day of the fifth month. Such boat races were most probably witnessed by the Europeans who were stationed in Canton. The people in the peculiar conveyance carried by two bearers could have also been inspired by designs showing fantastical vehicles with rococo curves and cusps. Specific designs for buildings were also illustrated in this book and were repeated in *The Ladies Amusement*. For example, the building on the left of the back with the large bells may be a Royal Garden Seat. Both the composition and the execution of the artwork is a sheer delight. Note the formal woven design, again a mixture of the classical and the oriental. Unusually, the feet too are decorated in penwork. The box retains much of its original varnish. A superb piece of its period. 11.25" wide. Ca. 1820. $15,000–20,000.

Figure 396. A delicately fanciful tea caddy, defying categorization. Maple veneered, with painted, formal, scrolling leafy designs, it is inset with cut and colored panels of glass. For sure the caprice of a Regency dandy, it carries its glamour with panache. 1820s? *Courtesy of a private collection.* $2,000–3,000.

*Right and below:*

Figure 397. A polychrome tea chest with scenes of oriental life. The pictures are skillfully painted in the manner of the Company school of painting. This particular genre was developed by English artists who went to China and India and painted exotic scenes and people from these countries. They were influenced both by Chinese painters who were executing commissions for the East India Company traders, and by Indian artists and book illustration. The precision of line, the application of color, and the professional nature of the work display many character-istics of this artistic genre. The figures are sometimes tilted toward Indian prototypes and sometimes toward oriental. This is in keeping with the artistic intention of producing scenes from the vague magical place, Cathay. Around the top rim of the box there is a line of dragons chasing each other. This was probably inspired by Mathias Darly's drawing of these creatures. The birds and flowers with their precise blocks of color are very much in the genre of the Company school of painting. The floral patterns share characteristics with fabrics produced in India both in the English and Dutch Company factories. The original varnish survives, albeit understandably cloudy. Exceptional. 13.6" wide. Ca. 1815–20. *Courtesy of Anne Brooks.* $?

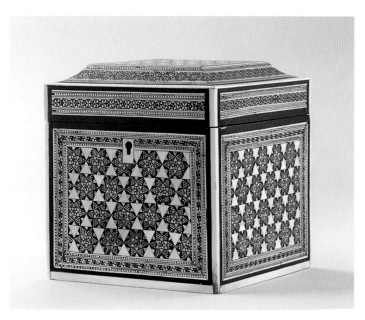

Figure 398. An example of an Anglo-Indian caddy in *sadeli* mosaic; very few caddies were made in this work. 4.75" wide. Second quarter nineteenth century. *Courtesy of a private collection.* $6,000–8,000.

Figure 399. This is an Anglo-Indian tea chest that combines European neoclassical influence with the organic exoticism of India. The form is of sarcophagus derivation but is rounded in a softer shape, formed of segmented horn and culminating in a finial representing a formal flower. The top of the chest is stepped with alternating flat and segmented horn parts, the fluted sides scrolling slightly inward in ridged semicircles. The whole, albeit its derivation from classical monumental architecture, is reminiscent of Indian buildings with complex curvatures and magnificent roofs. A true example of its time and place. 13" wide. Ca. 1830. $10,000–12,000.

*Above:*
Figure 400. A Chinese-export lacquer tea chest with metal canisters. This particular box is decorated with scenes depicting different processes in the preparation of the tea plant, making it particularly significant in the history of tea. Such scenes would have been observed firsthand by the artist who painted it. Even the patron who commissioned it may have been able to observe some if not all the stages of the production of this precious leaf. 7.75" wide. Ca. 1825. *Courtesy of Dr. Joseph Martin.* $6,000–8,000.

Figure 401. A Chinese-export lacquer tea chest in an interesting shape, reminiscent of English Regency but imbued with a more organic quality. The painting, which depicts figures in gardens, is of extremely fine quality. 6.5" wide. Ca. 1825–1830. *Courtesy of Dr. Joseph Martin*. $6,000–8,000.

*Above and right:*
Figure 402. A Chinese-export lacquer tea chest with a single canister interior. The decoration on the top is rubbed but the sides are painted with fine scenes of warrior horsemen. There is a label inside the canister lid that reads "*Hipqua Lacquered Ware.*" A Hipqua label identified in Carl Crossman's book *The China Trade* gives Hipqua's address as New China Street. This is consistent with the location of traders supplying quality work to members of the East India Company. The name of the merchant could just be Hip, with Qua standing for "mister." 9.5" wide. Second quarter nineteenth century. $2,000–4,000.

## ANGLO-INDIAN

Anglo-Indian caddies and chests of this period are very rare. In chests made of horn, the sarcophagus theme has the dimension of texture and depth given by lids constructed in reeded and radiating pieces of horn. (See Figures 268 and 399.)

*Sadeli* mosaic caddies are in simple shapes with exquisite patterns, and they are even rarer than the horn examples.

Chests in earlier rectangular shapes with stepped tops continued to be made in engraved ivory.

## CHINESE LACQUER

The Chinese-lacquer chests of the late eighteenth and early nineteenth centuries are in a way the focus of the whole tea and tea caddy culture. They are symbolic of the introduction of tea, the culture whence it came, the trading and the human relationships of the European and oriental merchants, and the whole magic of the Cathay dream. No collection can be complete without at least one of these reminders of the birth of tea drinking in the Western world.

Some caddies depict scenes of oriental activities, including the processing of tea; some show the ceremonial and leisurely life that suited the drinking of this aromatic infusion. It was the magic of this life that promoted tea as the new panacea and inspirational elixir.

The same people who traded in tea, introducing it to their compatriots, also commissioned tea chests. It was their vision of the tea country and of the tea people. The artists who made and decorated boxes tried to interpret the flavor of their culture on the containers destined to preserve the flavor of their tea. I can think of no other object that encapsulates so completely the moment of history that gave it birth.

Figure 403. A Chinese-export lacquer tea chest of complex curvilinear form. The finely painted central scene is enclosed in a cartouche set into a diapered design. 9.5" wide. Ca. 1835–40. *Courtesy of Dr. Joseph Martin.* $3,000–5,000.

## MID- TO LATE NINETEENTH CENTURY

Although when tea was first introduced it was seen by some as an alternative to drinking gin, and therefore in some way beneficial, this virtuous side of the argument was applied only to the poor classes. Nobody suggested that the rich or the rising middle classes should also give up their favorite tipples. This attitude was beginning to change by the time Charles Dickens was writing. In his *Pickwick Papers* (1836) he mentions "Tea Meetings" for the purpose of promoting temperance. Drink was still seen as a problem of the lower classes, but with the expansion of the middle classes the problem was creeping upward.

As the apparent propriety of the Victorian era fogged the dazzle of the Regency, tea became domesticated. It was still served in the drawing room and parlor, but also in the kitchen. It was no longer part of a flamboyant gesture in salons and pleasure gardens. It was a comforting hot drink to be shared with friends of one's own class.

The first half of the nineteenth century saw great social and economic changes. Medical improvements contributed to the increase of the population of the United Kingdom to eighteen million—double what it was fifty years previously. Trading with other countries gave opportunities to more people to increase their wealth and their social standing. Country towns almost unknown a hundred years previously developed their own class structures. The potential for tea drinking was reaching new heights.

The government, being aware of the pressure to reduce prices, took a major step in 1833, by withdrawing the monopoly of the East India Company to import tea. Excise duty was abolished, which reduced prices considerably. In 1838, another major development happened in the history of tea. Up to that date, tea had been imported only from China. In 1838, the first consignment of tea from Calcutta reached London. The India trade was encouraged and developed, and tea became much more accessible. After 1875, Ceylon too was developed as a tea-producing region, its coffee plantations having been destroyed by disease in the late 1860s.

Tea caddies to house everybody's tea were by now in even-greater demand. New mechanical processes made it easier to cut thinner veneers, although superior timbers continued to be cut in thicker slices for the production of high-quality pieces. By the 1840s, New Zealand was added to the list of countries exporting timbers to England, and together with timbers from the Far East, Africa, and the Americas, there was a wealth of choice. What is interesting at this time is the dichotomy of quality between the caddies made for average citizens and caddies made for those who aspired to a superior style and could pay for it.

In the second half of the century, a great number of caddies were made of pinewood veneered with walnut and decorated with strips of geometric inlay in different woods. The quality of this marquetry varies a great deal, although the positioning of the inlay, either as two perpendicular strips or a surround, makes for a sameness of effect.

These caddies are double, with two lids on the inside. They occasionally have a domed top and are of a modest size. Occasionally a more special one was made in a more curved shape.

*Above:*
Figure 404. A domed-top tea chest veneered in coromandel and edged in brass. The interior is fitted with glass canisters and bowl. A rare example of a tea chest of this period, in that it contains all glass fittings, which was a rare feature even in Georgian chests. The veneer is thick cut and the whole box is finished with meticulous care. The dark wood and brass make for a strong and handsome container for the heavy cut containers. Ca. 1830–40. *Courtesy of Alan and Joanne Tausz.* $8,000–10,000.

These caddies were made without any pretensions, and they were retailed from several outlets. They are still relatively easy to find, and they make pretty additions to the home. Other caddies made inexpensively were caddies in the earlier simple shapes, but using thinner veneers.

In 1848, England saw a major influx of French craftsmen who fled France because of political troubles. They probably suggested some of the decorative techniques developed at this time. French caddies in ebonized wood and rosewood with "THE" inlaid in brass or white metal were made in the earlier part of the nineteenth century. These were translated into inexpensive English caddies in combinations of rosewood and light-colored wood, with "TEA" inlaid on the top.

Caddies and chests of superior quality were made in the Regency forms. The structures were less dramatically architectural, although they were of recognizably sarcophagus-like shapes. The veneers were mostly of walnut and coromandel, or in some early examples amboyna. If decorated with inlays, the design was in a much more fluid and naturalistic style.

A pure Victorian style was the neo-Gothic caddy. The patriotic sentiment that swept England after the Napoleonic Wars was translated in architecture in the neo-Gothic revival of the 1830s and 1840s. This influenced the production of furniture and home accessories during the second half of the nineteenth century. In terms of wooden caddies, it was translated into boxes veneered in dark coromandel wood or walnut and embellished with brass-applied ornament. These caddies were mostly double, with rounded or pointed tops. They had brass strap decoration (gilded in the best examples), either with engraved or cutout Gothic-inspired motifs.

Firms such as Betjemann's and Lund were known for skillful usage of luxurious timbers in combination with brass decoration. Betjemann's especially specialized in strap decorative work and engraved hinges, and caddies of this type have survived with the name of this firm engraved in the brasswork or the lock plate.

Another firm that supplied caddies of exceptional quality in the neo-Gothic style was T. A. Simpson and Co., 154 Regent St. (London). One caddy I have seen was made of burr wood with gilded brass straps finely pierced and engraved and a matching handle in the center of the domed top. The two lids inside were also dome shaped, with labels in gilded brass engraved with the words "Green" and "Black" and small gilded brass knobs for easy lifting. I have also seen this work labeled as Simpson, Piccadilly. It may very well be the firm of the Piccadilly retailers who commissioned such work. Whether there is a relation to any of the earlier listed Simpson cabinetmakers is not clear.

A new decorative style probably influenced by French work was the combination of brass and mother of pearl inlay. This combination had been previously tried in England in more formal motifs, but in France it had already moved to more-naturalistic interpretations. The English versions of this work were not copies of French work, but a use of the technique for the creation of more free-flowing and strong designs. Tea caddies

*Below and right::*
Figure 405. An unusual, deeply carved caddy depicting hunting scenes. Difficult to place and date. Judging from the hardware and the quality of the carving, it could date from the end of the eighteenth century to the beginning of the nineteenth. Perhaps made in Scotland in honor of the royal visit of George IV in the early 1820s. 6.5" wide. $3,000–4,000.

*Below:*
Figure 406. An oak caddy in Gothic form marked on the underside "*A Relic of York Minster From the Nettleship 4 Blake St York.*" This inscription survives research: York Minster was burned down on 20th May 1840—the date on the caddy. Mumby Joseph (clerk to the magistrates) is recorded at 4 Blake Street as "Fire & Life Offices 'Eagle Life.'" In 1877, Joseph Mumby is also recorded as contributing half of £1,500 to the church in Osbaldwick, about two miles east of York, where "The pulpit was a piece of ancient oak work, and was formerly in York Minster." This caddy may be from the same oak source. $?

Figure 407. A carved caddy with trailing oak leaves, with a hint of the Arts and Crafts movement. 5.5" wide. Late nineteenth century. $800–1,000.

Figure 408. A Chinese-export lacquer chest with bold painting of oriental scenes. Although effective and decorative, the patterns are considerably simpler than on earlier examples. 8" wide. Mid-nineteenth century. $1,500–2,000.

Figure 409. A caddy veneered in sycamore and darkened bird's-eye maple. It is inlaid with pairs of carp fish all around. The fish and the water details are enhanced with fine lines of incised penwork. This is a very remarkable combination of European work and Chinese symbolism. It is of course most appropriate since tea came from China, but the oriental symbols were not widely understood, never mind applied, by Europeans. Phonetically, "carp" and "advantage" are the same in Chinese, the first word taking on the weight of meaning of the second. This fish is also said to jump over the rapids of the Yellow River, symbolizing success. Its beard was thought to denote supernatural power. 4.75" wide. Possibly French, mid-nineteenth century. *Courtesy of Susan Webster.* $2,800–3,500.

were made of coromandel or dark rosewood, and the front and top were inlaid with flowers, or floral arrangements in urn-shaped vases. The stems were made of brass wire; the flowers, of mother of pearl, abalone shell, and brass. The shape of the box was a simple sarcophagus standing on turned feet. The veneers used for these, although mechanically cut, were much thicker than the veneers cut for inexpensive boxes. The finished caddies were French polished to a high standard. I have seen boxes of high quality with this form of decoration bearing labels of the firms of Woolfield's of Glasgow, Geo. Austin of Dublin, and Lunds of London.

## PAPIER-MÂCHÉ

I have come across two caddies that bear unusual makers' labels from the earlier part of this period: one being Parkins and Gotto, 24 and 25 Oxford St., London; the other, R. Holt, French Court, Crystal Palace. The Parkins and Gotto caddy was of a typical nineteenth century design, double with lids and floral decoration. The label of this firm has been identified on high quality wooden boxes, so it is not clear if the papier-mâché items were bought in. The Holt caddy has some very distinctive characteristics: the front form consists of two semicircles flanking a central pointed shape. The two lids inside follow the shape of the exterior, and they are decorated with gold leaf abstract floral motifs. The outside of the caddy is painted with flowers, some of the painting over mother of pearl, and is of exceptionally high quality, both in choice of colors and the execution of the composition.

Figure 410. A Japanese Edo-period chest made of wood veneered with different parquetry designs. The canisters are lacquered and decorated with delicate gold designs. 9" wide. Ca. 1870. *Courtesy of Karen Ann Richardson.* $1,200–1,700.

Jennens and Bettridge caddies have been identified in a wide range of designs, since this firm marked most of their work.

Papier-mâché caddies of the early part of this period tend to have high quality mother of pearl decoration and, in the best examples, fine gilding. In the later years of the century the quality of the decoration declined, together with the rest of the papier-mâché industry. Transfers and prints were used in place of hand decoration.

## TUNBRIDGE WARE

Tunbridge ware caddies flourished in the middle of the century until the 1870s. They came in all the shapes already mentioned, but with very elaborate decoration in micro-mosaic marquetry. There are caddies with castles, flowers, birds, butterflies, and persons decorated both inside and out. Sometimes, earlier cube designs are also incorporated in many happy and not-so-happy combinations.

## CHINESE-EXPORT LACQUER

Chinese export lacquer from this period also seems to come in two qualities. The shapes are similar to the earlier caddies, but the inexpensive examples are in simpler shapes and the decoration is not so detailed, although in good examples it is still effective.

## ANGLO-INDIAN

Anglo-Indian caddies of the middle nineteenth century and later are made of carved wood with strips of later period *sadeli* mosaic.

Caddies in segmented horn continued to be made in the same shapes as the Regency caddies.

## THE FINAL PHASE

Prepacked tea was first sold in 1826 by John Horniman, who was eventually swallowed by Lyons & Co. By the 1880s, prepacking became almost universal. Tea by this time was mostly retailed through grocery stores. The era of the craftsman-made tea caddy was coming to an end.

Tea caddies were recognized as fine pieces of craftsmanship, and reproductions of eighteenth century work continued to be made—sometimes as part of an apprentice's training—well into the twentieth century. Even today, such caddies are being made, although unfortunately often presented as the genuine thing.

The late Victorian and Edwardian eras saw fine examples of caddies made in earlier styles. I have seen a tea chest made by Edward Barnsley featured in an antiques show that was a replica of a partridgewood box of a hundred years earlier. It featured the central handle and characteristic rectangular shape of the 1790s. Only by examining the finish could its age could be determined. Another Edwardian forte was the making of caddies in the form of Georgian pieces of furniture, knife boxes, and buildings. This has been revived in recent years, together with the revival of genuine designs. The last word on caddies must be caution.

Figure 411. A pine caddy covered in painted and appliquéd cloth. The back is painted with an oriental building; the sides and top, with flowers. On the front there are two figures of mandarins constructed with padded and painted silk. Unfortunately their faces have not survived the ravages of time. There is a central gilded handle on the top, in the Regency style. There is a stamp in Russian on the underside. Difficult to date. On account of the fragility of the material, such boxes do not usually survive. 6.25" wide. Nineteenth century. $800–1,000.

Figure 412. A walnut veneered tea caddy with geometric band decoration. Mid- to late Victorian. $600–900.

*The CLUB's Bon Ton. Bon Ton's a constant trade*
*Of rout, Festino, Ball and Masquerade!*
*'Tis plays and puppet-shews; 'tis something new!*
*'Tis loosing thousands ev'ry night at lu!*
*This Bon Ton, and this we call the world.*

—Prologue from David Garrick's play *Bon Ton*, 1775

T he Restoration of King Charles II in 1660 brought about the restoration of the freedom to indulge in pastimes that had been forbidden to the English gentry during the austerity years of the Commonwealth. Samuel Pepys remarked on the "deep and prodigious gaming" at court, which was already spreading into the social life of every grand house in town and country. As early as 1685, John Evelyn remarked on courtiers playing the Venetian game of basset and the king toying with his concubines while playing cards. Basset, together with Faro—a similar game—was fashionable early on in the eighteenth century. Wisk—or Whist as it was later called—gained ground from the 1740s onward.

Portraits of stately interiors focusing on scenes around the card table proliferated throughout the period stretching from the late seventeenth to the early nineteenth centuries. In several instances, the tea table and the card table were painted side by side, thus demonstrating the complementary social coexistence of tea drinking and card playing during fashionable gatherings. Tea boxes of the period share the same decorative techniques as card boxes, and it is very likely that matching sets were commissioned by the style-conscious families of the day.

When balls were given in the great houses of the rich, the young people danced while their chaperons, parents, and older guests sat down to a game of cards. Public assembly rooms in the fashionable resorts and spa towns featured card and gaming rooms alongside tearooms and ballrooms. As early as 1697, Celia Fiennes reported that there were two rooms for "the Lottery and Hazard board" in Tunbridge Wells.

Figure 413. A group of Georgian card boxes.

The Tunbridge ware makers John, James, and Ann Sharp decorated card boxes that they made with paintings and drawings of playing cards. The name of the firm was sometimes discreetly incorporated into the ace of spades. When, in 1777, new spectacular entertainment rooms were opened in Bath, the card room was said to be almost as splendid as the ballroom. Physicians recommended card playing as another form of therapy! It was taken up with great enthusiasm both by holidaying men and their ladies.

Card playing at home, or in respectable public places, continued into the early decades of the nineteenth century, without any hint of impropriety. Jane Austen set up card tables in the most correct of her fictional houses for the amusement of her middle-aged characters while her young people got on with their flirtations. Even children were allowed to play with cards, as demonstrated by the numerous portraits showing youngsters building card castles.

During the eighteenth century, in the world of the country house, card games became grown-up play, helping to while away the evenings with some skill and a little conversation. Everybody of a certain social standing was expected to have mastered the rules and moves of card games as part and parcel of genteel living.

In his poem *The Rape of the Lock*, Alexander Pope was so secure in his belief that his readers would be able to follow the nuances associated with the language of card playing that to drive his satire home, he constructed whole passages as gambling metaphors. Here is a characteristic snippet:

> *The Knave of Diamonds tries his wily Arts,*
> *And wins (oh shameful Chance!) the Queen of Hearts.*

> *(Canto III, 1714)*

Card imagery had entered literature, and card slang had entered language. A widow, for example, was referred to as the ace of spades; "sharps" were professional gamblers, while "flatts" and "pigeons" were their victims, who were usually from a higher social class than themselves.

By the second half of the eighteenth century, boxes were becoming indispensable accessories for the well dressed interior. Playing cards needed their own beautiful containers, especially if they were to be featured as part of a society soiree. Card tables were set up in wealthy and aristocratic households, where hospitality was generous and manifold. Card boxes were viewed by the fashionable and the eclectic. It is no wonder that,

Figure 414. A box japanned and painted with a chinoiserie landscape. The strong design, which is executed with an excellent sense of color, incorporates raised parts. The decoration has survived in original condition remarkably well. The interior is partitioned for cards and counters. 10.8" wide. First decade nineteenth century. $2,000–2,500.

*Above and below:*
Figure 415. A surprising box that has to be turned upside down in order to be opened. Under the sliding lid there is a compartment for playing cards, and a small section for cribbage pegs. The top of the box is covered by an oval cribbage board. The whole box is decorated in penwork. The main picture is very much in the neoclassical style, depicting two griffins flanking a vase with acanthus leaves. 8" wide. Early nineteenth century. $?

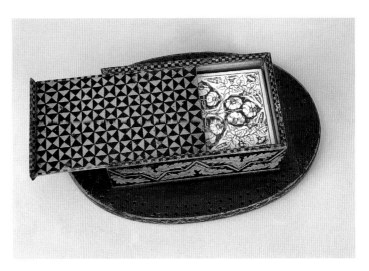

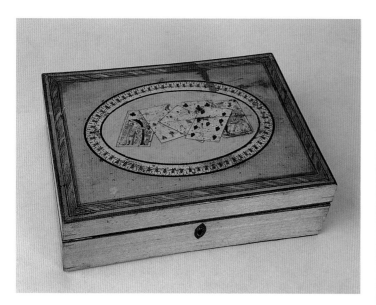

Figure 416. A sycamore-veneered box with a hand-colored print of playing cards. Most probably from the Tunbridge area. 8" wide. Ca. 1815–25. $1,500–2,000.

Figure 417. A sycamore-veneered box exquisitely decorated in penwork. The lines are very fine and the pattern is well thought out and arranged. The scrolling flora is redolent of embroideries and fabrics of the seventeenth and eighteenth centuries. The central picture is a delicately drawn chinoiserie seascape. Note the dragon boat, the flying pennants, the fantastical feathers on the head of the man at the front, and the small boats in the sea. The scene has the refinement suggested by the visual representations of China, which circulated from the middle of the eighteenth century. Dragon boats were featured in the work of Mathias Darly. The belief was that by racing such boats, which were representations of dragons, real dragons were drawn into fights, and this brought heavy rains (see "Chinoiserie" chapter). 9.10" wide. Ca. 1815–20. $6,000–7,000.

*Above:*
Figure 418. A sycamore-veneered box of striking form. It is decorated both outside and inside, including the lids, with penwork. The box is a delightful cornucopia of chinoiserie drawing. There are exotic buildings, "Indian islands" (as Darly called the little floating snippets of land), spindly surreal bridges, boats, birds, and beasts. There are also wonderful vignettes of people going about their business, or engaging with each other in social or professional repartee. A box full of the flavor of its period. 10.5" wide. Ca. 1820. $7,000–9,000.

*Above and right:*
Figure 419. A Rosewood veneered box decorated with a print of an interesting view of the Brighton Pavilion. Inside there is a label that informs us that the print was supplied by Wise, the firm of Tunbridge ware makers. There is a sycamore cribbage board and two scoring discs inside the box. These are painted and varnished like Tunbridge ware sewing tools. 8" wide. Ca. 1815. $1,500–2,000.

as a group, card boxes dating from the period of George III and George IV are a tour de force of style. They are fewer in number than tea boxes, which were made for more households and embraced a wider social catchment, but every single card box was made to high aesthetic standards.

As the eighteenth century progressed through its last two decades, George, the Prince of Wales, was beginning to tilt the balance of the ethos of the fashionable socialites toward exuberance of style, in contrast to the rather somber criteria of his father's court. The prince gambled with panache, as he did everything else in his life. The society luminaries who thronged to his parties were willing participants in his games. There are references of playing *ecarté* and other card games at the Royal Pavilion in Brighton. Card boxes of excellence must have often come into the royal presence. The prince must have commissioned a few himself.

Many Regency card boxes betray the most extrovert and daring nature of their owners. Such boxes were, after all, part of the most risqué social activity that could be carried out in company. They are often on the edge of taste, with a vibrancy and brilliancy that lifts them above acceptable rules and renders them the perfect totems of the age of devil-may-care-inspired style.

For many, card playing remained an innocent or, at the most, slightly roguish pastime. For the swaggering Regency dandies it was a different story. It is not possible to say exactly when the scales tipped toward dangerous gambling rather than harmless pleasure. The two were going on in parallel throughout the Georgian period. Finally gambling became a social problem, an obsession that engulfed many men and women irrespective of their social and financial standing. Jane Austen allows us a glimpse of this problem in *Mansfield Park* in the character of Tom, the oldest son of the house, a typical upper class Regency rake.

During the seventeenth century and following into the eighteenth, card playing for money was indulged in coffee houses and public houses to the annoyance of many upright citizens. Jonathan Swift, who thought that cards were "the devil's books," used to shake his fists outside the windows of such establishments when he caught a glimpse of gambling going on inside. Eventually legislation outlawed gambling in public places, with the result that the activity continued at best in clubs, and at worst in the unsavory haunts of the underground world.

White's chocolate house became a club patronized by the aristocracy and the men of fashion, including Beau Brummell, who used to hold court in its bay window. As early as 1743, White's kept a betting book for private wagers; this has provided us with a wonderful social record. Brooks's Club, which started life as the play nursery of young "macaronis"—rich young men of extravagantly affected dress and manners—developed into a breeding ground for Whig politicians, the favored party of the Prince of Wales. The poet Lord Byron frequented the Cocoa-Tree Club, which had been a Tory chocolate house and originally the headquarters of the Jacobites. Politicians, high society, and the rich gambled and lost their money to each other in the splendid surroundings of fashionable private clubs.

Not everybody enjoyed the privilege of membership of high society clubs. Much gambling went on the flip side of respectability, in what came to be called "the Gaff" or, very

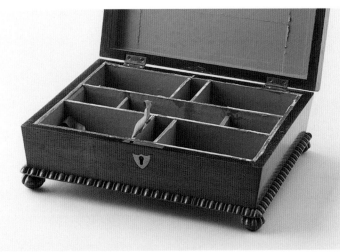

*Above:*

Figure 420. A gently tapering box veneered in well-figured Brazilian rosewood and decorated with a band of cut brass, which separates the crossbanded section from the central panel of the top. The center is inlaid with a brass plaque surrounded by a foliage design in brass. The edge and base of the box are gadrooned. A box of similar work with four crowns inlaid in the corners with royal provenance was auctioned for charity in 1982. 10.5" wide. Ca. 1825. $1,200–1,500.

Figure 421. An ebony-veneered box decorated with cut steel. The center has the word *ECARTE* engraved in the steel. This was a favorite game, and there are references to playing it at the Brighton Pavilion. The inside of the box is lined in satinwood. Quietly beautiful. 6.5" wide. Early nineteenth century. $800–1,000.

appropriately, "Hell." By the end of the eighteenth century, serious gambling was becoming an epidemic in all walks of life. Naval officers were eager to chance their "bounty," and army men even gambled in the field. Hardened criminals saw gambling as an opportunity to increase the range of their activities; young men from aristocratic families were eager to experience the frisson of gambling in bad company.

Patrick Colquhoun, a Scotsman who in 1792 became a stipendiary magistrate, enumerated the criminal activities in London and the number of persons he estimated were engaged in them. According to him, "Persons called Black Legs and others proselytized to the passions of Gaming, or pursuing it as a trade: 2000," "Foreigners who live chiefly by gambling: 500."

Provincial banks had been given the right to print their own notes, and to an extent they were responsible for fanning the gambling habit by offering easy credit. Credit was also available through sharp moneylenders eager to pounce on the estates of the landed gentry. England had lost America, and the turbulent years that followed did nothing to stabilize society. Wars against the French and precarious new trading routes bred a kind of exciting instability, a fertile ground for adventurers and gamblers. The city of London was gripped by the ethos of daring, especially as business chancers were seen as the new controllers of power.

It is not surprising that some of the most spectacular card boxes were brought into the country from China by East India Company traders. These men were carving a new social and financial status for themselves by providing new exotic accessories, objects, and culinary delights to the gentry. They dazzled the beau monde with previously unseen artistic works from far-off cultures imbued with magic and mystery.

In the early part of the nineteenth century, social boundaries were being torn down by new money. Notable politicians, traders, and the aristocracy had to support each other to maintain civic structure. Opportunists bridged the gap between the aristocracy and the underworld, which had become formidable on the back of new loose money. Regency rakes found the new licentious style of living glamorous and fascinating. It thrilled their extrovert nature to join the tables not only in high class clubs in St. James's, but also in the gambling "hells" often just a few yards away.

By 1829, John Wade wrote in his *Treatise on the Police and Crimes of the Metropolis*: "The crimes and vices now most rife in London are gaming among the higher and more opulent classes."

Estates were gambled away, and with them sunk good names and reputations. It was a curious phenomenon that although persons of rank and even royalty were often reluctant to pay tradesmen, even if this behavior resulted in the latter's bankruptcy, it was a question of honor to pay one's gambling debts.

There were plenty of warnings during the eighteenth century that card playing for high stakes was likely to develop into a social quagmire. In 1760 John Montagu, the fourth Earl of

Figure 422. A most striking and extraordinary box. It is veneered in palm woods of different density, forming symmetrical patterns. This is the largest box I have ever seen completely covered in this wood. Such exotic timbers were usually reserved for small items, or elements in parquetry. The interior is fitted with a chess/drafts board and four boxes for cards. These are made out of bird's-eye maple chemically darkened to a gray/brown color. Each box has a central inlaid motif in ebony, depicting the four suits: a heart, a club, a diamond, and a spade. The box retains much of its original thick varnish, which adds to its strangely fascinating appearance. Difficult to date, although there are pointers to the second quarter of the nineteenth century. $3,000–5,000.

Sandwich, was so obsessed with his game that he called for his meat to be put between two slices of bread so he could eat without needing to leave the table, thus inventing the "sandwich"! Not only gentlemen, but also ladies of rank disgraced their family names with reckless and unsuccessful gambling. The most famous, or rather infamous, of these women was Georgiana Spencer, who became the fifth Duchess of Devonshire, a celebrated Whig hostess. After a life of unbridled gambling, she died and left her son a legacy of £100,000 in gambling debts.

As long as the habit was contained within a certain class, there was a tacit acceptance of it. The government showed complete incompetence in dealing with the problem, and society displayed total inertia. The situation began to change when the unsavory and criminal elements of the population began to take control of the playthings of the aristocracy. Understandably, the moneylenders moved into the scene. In 1816, style luminary Beau Brummell had to flee to Calais to avoid his creditors. Lord Alvanley remarked with dry humor: "It was Solomon's judgment"; Solomon was the name of a shrewd Regency moneylender.

Alarm bells rang loudly when speculators and professional gamblers began to siphon too great a proportion of the wealth of the aristocracy into the coffers of the lesser classes.

The balance of influence was already shifting with the changing financial patterns of the world. The lemming style of behavior indulged in by the reckless highborn sons and daughters of the aristocracy literally demolished family estates. For the first time for generations, the confidence of the landed gentry was shaken.

The "gentleman's game," which was frequently oiled with heavy drinking, often degenerated into brawls and accusations of cheating. Duels, which occasionally culminated in death, became more frequent. Cheats were ostracized. Suicides too became a feature, being preferable to penury and dishonor. Watier's, a club whose existence was inspired by the Prince of Wales himself, was said to have lost all its members by 1819, because they all had been ruined! Card playing had descended a long way down the social scale from the elegant private drawing rooms of the eighteenth century.

The final blow was dealt by a Mr. Crockford. An expert gambler who had risen from the depths of the fish trade, Crockford became the club owner par excellence. Several gambling "hells" were already more decadently comfortable and plush than the clubs of St. James's, but Crockford's was a cut above them all. In 1827, this upstart had the audacity to build a most luxurious club in St. James's, a stone's throw from the haunts of the

*This whole page:*
Figure 423. A Chinese-lacquer box painted with an exotic landscape. The sides and the frame of the central picture are in the late-eighteenth-century style of such work; that is, repetitive patterns of European origin. This box features bunches of grapes interwoven within a pattern of fine crossing lines. The main picture is in the manner of early export lacquer painting; that is, of a large uninterrupted scene. There are only three figures in the composition. These are very small, and unlike the rest of the work, they are painted without much detail. By the look of their legs, they are probably meant to be Europeans; a most unusual touch. The scene is beautifully painted in silver and gray-blue colors as well as gold. Inside, the box is fitted with four card boxes and a long counter box, all painted with exotic flora. 11.5" wide. Ca. 1800. $5,000–6,000.

aristocracy. What is more, he enticed the gentry over to his establishment by offering food prepared by a charismatic French chef. He catered for every whim and luxurious requirement, down to high-quality ivory dice that cost a guinea per pair. Even the Duke of Wellington was won over and became a member. As Capt. Gronow put it, Crockford "won the whole of the ready money of the then existing generation."

By the third decade of the nineteenth century, card playing had entered the twilight world of social confusion. The papers and periodicals, fast becoming more widespread, loved to report the mishaps and misdemeanors of the rich. The rising middle classes, especially those of dubious origins, enjoyed feeling morally and cerebrally superior to their "betters." Lady

Susan O'Brien remarked that at assemblies, "No cards are admitted . . . Music in which all are proficient has taken their place."

By the 1820s, George had turned from the glamorous Regent surrounded by dazzling society into a fat, gouty king sitting at home with his aging mistresses. The sparkle and the lure of the Regency had gone. The wars were at an end; it was time to put the country and society back in order. People who for a brief time in history had been shuffled themselves like a pack of cards from class to class had to be rearranged into the neat social strata that ushered in the Victorian era.

The Metropolitan Police was established in 1829 and took over control of criminal activities, including irregular gambling, from the "Charlies"—the watchmen who had become totally ineffectual and who were often drunk.

*Above and left:*

Figure 424. A lacquer box painted with scenes that are very rooted in Chinese culture. This is quite extraordinary for an export box, although such work is found on gouache paintings that were aimed at Europeans. The scene is of a procession headed by a man who is returning in honor after passing his civil service examinations. The placards proclaim that he has passed the middle exam and is now a master. He may even have gotten the highest mark of all the candidates. Entering the civil service was considered a great honor in China, and the highest earthly attainment a man could wish for his children. In addition to other advantages, such a position saved a man from being caned! The other special feature of this box is the coordinated card and box decoration. The top of the box is painted with playing cards. These cards are copies from a set of actual playing cards, which are in the box. The four of cups refers to the maker, "F. De Juan Jose Macia, en Barcelona 1823." One of the trays features a European head in profile, within a circle flanked by flags and with a crown on top, in the manner of a trophy. This is a copy of the ace of coins in the pack. The style and date of the cards are consistent with the date of the box, which is of very high quality. It stands on carved dragon face feet. 12.75" wide. Ca. 1823. *Courtesy of Anne Brooks.* $?

Figure 425. A very finely painted Chinese-lacquer box in a scalloped shape. The scenes, which depict idealized oriental life and gardens, are enclosed within cartouches. 11.75" wide. Ca. 1830. *Courtesy of Anne Brooks.* $4,000–6,000.

*This whole page:*

Figure 426. A Chinese-lacquer box that is decorated with raised and painted lacquer in alternating patterns of bold representational forms, and fine background and border stylized patterns. The central cartouche depicts figures dwarfed by mythological phoenixes, which are significant creatures rich both in earthly and occult associations. The phoenix was also the symbol of the empress. There are also bursting pomegranates overhead, symbolizing abundance. Around the innermost part, there are "lionesque" creatures playing with coins and an embroidered ball, butterflies, and phoenixes. The border is decorated with boldly executed dragons pursuing a flaming pearl. A piece of extraordinary workmanship, rich in symbolic representations. The interior is fitted with boxes for cards and counters. The decoration on these is very precisely arranged in alternating designs, all impeccably lacquered and painted. There are also trays for holding the counters when playing and for using for the game of Pope Joan. Note the wonderful expression on the queen of diamonds. Note also that the cards are depicted in the pre-two-faced form. There are also several original mother of pearl counters in the box. These are very finely edged with figures in various trades. Early nineteenth century. 14.4" wide. $8,000–10,000.

*Above:*

Figure 427. A sycamore-veneered box decorated in penwork with a blackbird on a branch reaching for its nest. The sides of the box are decorated with what looks like stylized marigolds. The shape of the box is complex in that it incorporates gently concave lines, which soften its tapering form. It stands on gilded feet and has side-gilded handles. A piece with many Regency characteristics, it combines neoclassical features with naturalistic decoration. The workmanship, hardware, and penwork are of excellent quality. A delight. 11.9" wide. Ca. 1820. $6,000–7,000.

*Above:*

Figure 428. A box decorated in the most unexpected way. The designs are cut out of linen cloth and pasted onto the surface. The central oriental figures are gathered under a tree in front of a Chinese railing. All around there are birds, flowers, and butterflies. The escutcheon is ingeniously placed between two exotic buildings and looks just like another peak. All around the box there are vignettes of oriental figures, buildings, and flowers. The box stands on gilded lion paws emerging from fruiting vines. It has gilded side handles in a daisy/star design. A wondrous example of Regency chinoiserie. 14" wide. Ca. 1820. $8,000–10,000.

Antigambling societies began to spring up. Sermons against this particular evil were preached. Thinkers and writers took up the cause. Dickens exposed the link between the decadent gambling aristocracy and poverty in his novel *Bleak House*. It was no longer the done thing to play cards. The middle classes took the lead in dictating the social agenda. A confused aristocracy had lost its way during the dizzy days of the Regency and allowed the children of the upstarts to regulate social equilibrium. Desperate for outward respectability, the recently enriched banned cards.

The era of the stylish card box came to an abrupt end.

Some playing-card boxes were made during the latter part of the nineteenth century in typical Victorian forms, but as to style, they hardly ever rose above the mediocre. A few luxurious examples were made, mostly in combinations of dark wood with brass mounts. I have handled a good-quality box with a central jasperware plaque and bearing the label of Edwards and Jones, 161 Regent Street, London, which was probably made in the 1870s or 1880s.

Card boxes reemerged as game compendiums during the last decades of the nineteenth century. They had nothing of the pizzazz of their Georgian and Regency ancestors. They were very well made, using the manufacturing processes that had become available during the intermitting years, and were finished to a high gloss. They were of simple rectangular form with straight sides, veneered mostly in walnut or coromandel. They contained a chess set, dominoes, board games, and cards—enough to keep a family entertained for hours. Such boxes had no pretensions of style but reflected the sensible marriage of utility with obvious high-quality workmanship of the Victorian era. If embellished at all, they were edged or mounted in brass.

*This whole page:*
Figure 429. A dazzling box that must have graced the salon of a true Regency extrovert. On the top there is a wonderful painting of roses, pansies, honeysuckle, and cornflowers, with a white butterfly resting on a leaf. The four corners are punctuated by cutout patterns of stylized leaves in gold paper. The painting is protected by glass, which is edged with a strip of embossed gold paper. The slightly concave surround of the top part is decorated in a scrolling pattern of daisies/wild roses in decoupage. The design is enhanced with dark-brown painted lines and gold leaf application on some of the flowers. The sides are covered in a decoupage of daisies and thistles among scrolling foliage. The top part of the sides features a pattern of narrower leaves and tulips. The center part above the escutcheon and the side handles features a posy of trefoils or shamrocks. It is probable that the box is making references to King George IV's visits to Ireland and Scotland in the early years of his reign, or simply to the union of the three countries. The box stands on gilded feet bursting with leaves, flowers, and fruit. The handles too are elaborate in a sunflower-and-daisy pattern. The interior is lined in bright-pink paper edged with gold. There are paper-covered flat pieces with attached silk ribbons inserted in the card spaces so that the cards can be easily lifted. The facings are covered in gold paper. A fabulous individual piece. 13" wide. Ca. 1815–25. $?

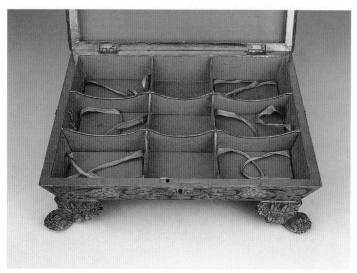

S ewing, embroidery, and its sister arts date from time immemorial. Containers for needlework tools were made in accordance to the prevailing customs of the period and place.

Embroidery was a serious art practiced both by professionals and ladies of a certain social standing, who saw it as an important outlet for their artistic creativity. During the seventeenth century, boxes completely covered in stump work embroidery were made, mainly in the form of small table cabinets. These are a celebration of needlework, rather than the craft of the cabinetmaker; they are mostly the preserve of fabric collectors, since they need special conditions of conservation.

During the eighteenth century, a wealth of inspiration hit the drawing rooms of Europe. Botanists who had accompanied travelers and explorers were disseminating their knowledge of exotic flora among the aristocrats, who in turn were setting up great gardens and zoos on their estates. Early in the nineteenth century, the Duke of Devonshire commissioned the gathering of exotic flora and fauna from the Far East and South America. This led to the building of his great conservatory by Paxton, who went on to become the architect of the Crystal Palace. The new plants were scrutinized and copied in many art forms, the medium of embroidery offering scope for the interpretation both of color and texture.

Figure 430. A group of eighteenth- and nineteenth-century sewing boxes in wood, ivory, leather, and papier-mâché

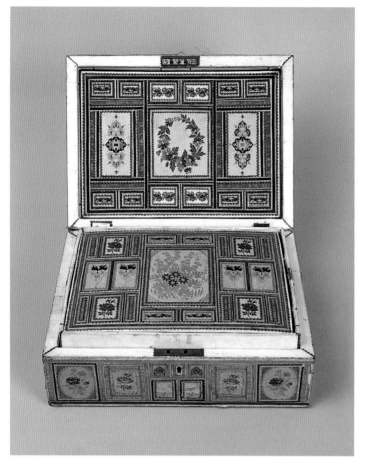

*Above and left:*

Figure 431. A most unusual sewing box that is covered all over on the inside and outside with finely embroidered cloth. The outside is understandably yellowed and a little worn on the top, but the inside still retains the vibrant colors of the silk threads. The designs are of flowers both European and exotic. Centrally, on the top, there is an embroidered design of an enclosed cornucopia made up of small floral motifs. This type of ornament, where every component furthered the development of the prevalent pattern, was characteristic of the designs on fabrics and embroideries that were produced in India throughout the eighteenth century. A pretty, unique piece, difficult to date with precision. The form, hardware, and style place it sometime around the end of the eighteenth century or the beginning of the nineteenth. 11.75" wide. $?

Chinese and Indian fabrics and embroideries, which during the eighteenth century were imported in some quantity, also contributed to a revision both of techniques and designs. Great embroiderers were respected and admired. A Miss Knowles made a reputation for herself in this field, and a Miss Linwood even held an exhibition of her work in 1798. Young girls were encouraged to master the art early on in life, and many a sampler that was worked on by tiny hands survives from this period. "Ounce Thread" was beginning to be manufactured in England during the eighteenth century, and this further stimulated domestic embroidery.

Mrs. Delany, whose hands were kept busy for the greater part of the eighteenth century—according to her husband even "between the cooling of her tea"—has left us a legacy of comments on needlework and the serious nature of the art. The needlewoman of the time was responsible not just for the execution of the craft, but also for the design and the composition of the complete work. A skilled and talented person could manipulate her thread with a degree of freedom the way a painter uses pigment. Describing one of her projects, Mrs. Delany wrote: "My pattern a border of *oak-branches and all sorts of roses* (except yellow), which I work without any pattern, just as they come into my head." Even if a lady followed a pattern from a ladies' magazine, she was expected to add her own input to the interpretation.

There are references in letters, diaries, and literature of cloth "worked" for personal or domestic adornment. Keepsakes were embroidered with loving care, and beautifully worked pieces were regarded as heirlooms. Exquisite christening gowns were treasured for many generations. The range of work extended from the public, such as pictures, tapestries, upholstery, and screens, to the personal, such as garments, handkerchiefs, and needlework accessories. Human hair, gold thread, and tiny beads were sometimes worked into the designs. The embroiderer's as well as the receiver's personality were expected to be represented in the work.

An extreme example of personality-impregnated work, typical of the eccentric indulgence of the early years of the nineteenth century, is the case of Lord Petersham. This gentleman had fallen in love with a certain Mary Brown. He immersed himself, his carriage, and his servants in brown and ordered a brown silk coat to be made for himself, embroidered with dead leaves! This was indeed designer mood embroidery aimed at striking the right note of affected melancholy.

The work was often carried out in different parts of the house, or even in different houses. The eighteenth and early nineteenth centuries were a time of long visits. Transport had developed enough to enable a certain degree of comfort, but it was still too slow and tiring for day visits. A culture of gatherings in grand houses for days at a time developed as

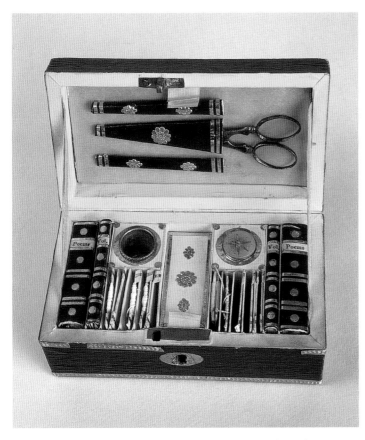

Figure 432. A leather-covered box exquisitely fitted in gilded leather and paper, containing some steel tools and paper-covered cardboard needle cases. Ca. 1800. *Courtesy of Susan Webster*. $1,600–2,000.

Figure 433. A small sewing box veneered in burr yew, crossbanded in kingwood, and edged in boxwood. There are also lines of stringing and further geometric inlay. Subtle complex work. 9" wide. Ca. 1810. $600–800.

the eighteenth century progressed. This was a way of whiling away the days, exchanging society news, and furthering desirable alliances. Ladies would often take their work with them, even if only to provide an excuse for not participating in the conversation.

There are numerous portraits and sketches of women bending over their work, drawing the flax, knotting, or working on an embroidery frame. There are also pictures of interiors featuring sewing boxes and baskets.

Up to about 1770, woven baskets were the main vehicle for carrying the essentials for embroidery. However, as the stature of the cabinetmaker increased and constructed accessories by such craftsmen became the height of fashion, boxes replaced baskets as receptacles for the work in hand.

The sewing box, or workbox, became a much-loved personal accessory where the lady it belonged to kept her embroidery tools and materials. Ability to compose and embroider designs on fabric was regarded both as a major accomplishment and an indication that one was *au fait* with the aesthetic influences of the period. The boxes associated with the work had to be of the expected artistic standard. They reflected both the personality and the social standing of the user.

There are many references in literature to sewing, embroidery tools, and boxes. In Jane Austen's *Mansfield Park* (1814), the heroine Fanny Price finds solace in "the room . . . most dear to her . . . [where] [t]he table between the windows was covered with work-boxes and netting-boxes." It is interesting to note that Fanny's boxes were given to her principally by Tom, her firstborn cousin, a veritable Regency bon viveur, and not by the more modest Edmund, although the latter was her special friend. Evidently the boxes were regarded as luxuries.

By the time Jane Austen was writing, the workbox had reached the height of its stylistic development, both in boxes crafted in England and those imported from abroad. Jane Austen herself had a large Chinese-export lacquer box/table on stand, complete with fitted tray, which can still be seen in her house in Chawton.

The stylistic development of the workbox mirrors that of the tea caddy. The main difference is that tea caddies are on the whole taller and narrower. The shapes and decoration follow the same pattern, except that workboxes revert to rectangular shapes after the middle of the nineteenth century. The interiors of the two types of boxes differ dramatically, reflecting the purposes they served.

Because workboxes were very much a single person's possession, rather than a household accessory, some of the eighteenth and early nineteenth century examples are wonderfully idiosyncratic, allowing a glimpse into the owners' special interests.

*This whole page:*

Figure 434. A Chinese export lacquer sewing box of complex form, with fine decoration of oriental scenes framed within cartouches. The background is filled with diaper designs of stylized flora. The tools are made of carved ivory. The thimbles in such boxes are usually tiny. Perhaps the carvers thought that European women had tiny fingers, like the oriental ladies they knew. This type of shaped box was imported from the beginning of the nineteenth century, although some wonderful pieces were made later. Because the nature of the work is traditional, it is not absolutely possible to date such boxes with complete accuracy. However, such fine work is more likely to have been imported during the period when Chinese work was most valued; that is, before ca. 1840. 14" wide. $5,500–7,000.

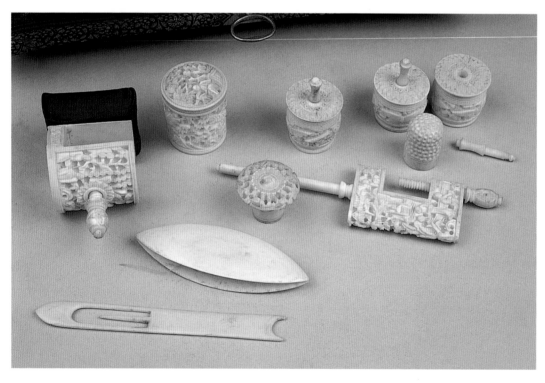

*Below and left:*
Figure 435. A box veneered in a variety of woods, mainly mahogany, pollarded oak, and yew. The sides are veneered with a diamond pattern of ebony and mahogany, very like the Tunbridge ware vandyke pattern. The central inlay is an interesting departure from the neoclassical motif of a patera. The scalloped cut pattern is defined both with hot sand shading and green wood edging. A strong design that utilizes the quality of the timbers typical of the last decades of the eighteenth century. There is a deep tray inside, but there are no sewing tools. Ca. 1780–90. $1,800–2,000.

## GEORGIAN BOXES

There are basically two categories of sewing box dating from this period:

1. Rectangular boxes in various woods

2. Decorated boxes in whitewood

### RECTANGULAR WOOD-VENEERED BOXES

Rectangular boxes of this period have wooden lift-out trays over an empty space. Sometimes instead of a space there is a drawer. The tray, the drawer, or both are usually divided into compartments. The interior, if lined at all, is lined with simple paper in pink, blue, green, or yellow. Seldom are these boxes made of solid wood. Usually they are made in mahogany, pine, or oak and are veneered in saw-cut veneers of mahogany, oak, yew, harewood, partridgewood, satinwood, or fruitwoods, such as cherry, plum, pear, or applewood. The decoration tends to be restrained, featuring simple edgings, crossbandings, or both.

Ambitious patterns were sometimes achieved by juxtaposing different timbers, bringing to attention the striking features of the figure and grain of the wood. This is sometimes called specimen parquetry. When several patterns were used on

Figure 436. This example is veneered in a parquetry design of well-figured pollarded oak, rosewood, and mahogany. The base is of solid rosewood, and the bun feet are turned. The thick veneers have patinated well. A well constructed box, the decoration contributing to the stability of the whole. There is a deep lift-out tray inside the box. Ca. 1800–1810. *Courtesy of Mrs. I. Finn.* $1,400–1,600.

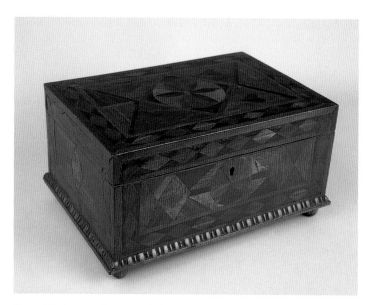

Figure 437. An example veneered with a variety of thick veneers in geometric patterns. Like the previous two examples, this contributes to the stability as well as the look of the box. It stands on turned feet and on a base that is covered in later gadrooning. It is an early experiment in juxtaposing several colors and figures of wood. 11" wide. Ca. 1790–1800. $800–1,000.

one box, the work is referred to as "sample" parquetry. The sole use of the beauty of the wood to enhance an object can be seen as the forerunner of Tunbridge ware parquetry. Many of these boxes were probably made in the Tunbridge area before the specific label was attached to the work. They were sold without matching sewing fittings; their trays are sturdy, and if lined at all, they are lined with paper.

Inlaid decoration of neoclassical or more naturalistic design is sometimes found on boxes that have trays fitted with sewing tools. Such examples are now extremely rare.

Wooden boxes dating from this period were finished in wax or varnish; the ones that have escaped insensitive restoration have built up a rich patina.

### PAINTED AND DECORATED BOXES

Boxes belonging to this category were made of light-colored wood, usually sycamore. Some were lightly gessoed before the decoration was applied to the surface of the box. Such boxes were made mostly in the Tunbridge area, or within the early Tunbridge ware tradition. Many of these boxes are unique and wonderfully idiosyncratic—real period gems.

The subjects of the decoration vary from flowers to human figures, shells, butterflies, bees, or whatever the particular person was interested in at the time of painting the box. Many were bought "in the white" and decorated at home by accomplished and dedicated ladies eager to prove their gifts as competent and inspired artists, both with the brush and with the needle.

Originally such boxes were fitted with Tunbridge ware early sewing tools. The tools were turned in sycamore and decorated

with simple lines in primary colors. They consisted of small thread barrels, tubular small boxes, tape measures, wax holders, and thimbles. The barrels were made with a central spindle inside, on which the thread was wound. The thread, which was originally bought in skeins, was pulled out from a small hole on the side of the barrel. The small boxes had screw-on lids and were used for holding beads, gold thread, or other precious embroidery necessities.

The tape measure holder was a small tubular box with a central spindle and a fissure on the side. This enabled the silk tape measure to be wound in and out when necessary without needing to be handled. The tape measures were marked in "nails," a unit of measure equal to about two and a quarter inches. The unit of the nail was established in England since the days of Henry I. Ladies would take their tape measures with them when going to the haberdashers or cloth sellers.

The waxer consisted of two circles of wood holding a piece of wax between them. This was used to wax the as-yet-unmercerized thread as it came out of the barrel, rendering it smooth.

Additional tools, such as wooden reels, rollers for lace, and ratcheted winders, were also made for use in early workboxes. Occasionally, small glass bottles with silver tops or glass stoppers were fitted in specifically cutout holes on blocks of wood within the tray. These were probably intended for hand-sprinkling powder, aromatic vinegars, or oils. I have found traces of all of these substances in such bottles.

The tools mentioned were very skillfully turned to a very thin tolerance. The skill of the Tunbridge ware turners was celebrated since the birth of the wood-turning craft in the area. The pieces found in these boxes are exceptionally fine and light. The most extreme example are the thimbles, which make one wonder if the turners were running competitions as to who could turn the finest thimble without it exploding on the lathe. Very few thimbles, or indeed other tools, have survived in the boxes. Some have perished with use, and some have found their way into thimble and tool collections, separated from their natural homes.

One or more sections of the lift-out tray often contained removable pincushions made up of a light wooden frame, stuffed with bran and covered on the top with silk. Other sections were left empty or were fitted with removable small boxes. Individual needs and preferences make for a variety of arrangements.

Because needles were precious things and likely to rust, small "emery" cushions for keeping rust off needles were also kept in workboxes. Emery grains were enclosed in fabric—usually silk or velvet—held by two small wooden circles. The points of needles or pins were inserted into the cloth when they needed sharpening or cleaning.

Boxes dating from this period are now seldom found, especially with any surviving tools. Even in incomplete condition they are extremely rare.

*This whole page:*

Figure 438. A burr yew veneered box with oval inlays all around. The side and back ovals are of rosewood edged in an inlaid line made up of slanting pieces of various woods. The front ovals are made up of small fruitwood burr ovals, framed in a fine band made up of slanting woods and a line of stringing. These are set within larger ovals of fruitwood, edged in a chequered and a thin line. The box is edged on all sides with lines and stringing, including a zigzag line in maple. Centrally there is a hand-colored print of a classical scene. Inside the box there is a label explaining the theme of the print: *SOPHONISBA receiving her Nuptial present from MASSINISSA*. The symmetrical arrangement of the decorations on this box places it firmly within the neoclassical tradition. On the lower part, there is a drawer, which is secured in place by a turned wooden rod. The rod is lifted from the main part of the box when the drawer is to be opened. The construction of the drawer is very skillful. The sides are secured to the wider front part by quite an ingenious mitered, dovetailed joint (see also the basket below in figure 448). The interior of the box is fitted with beautifully turned wooden barrels, containers for silver and gold thread, tape measure holder, ribbon reel, a thread reel and a multiple reel, and a turned thimble. There are two small, square boxes with burr yew veneered covers and a wood framed pincushion. The containers and tape measure holders are varnished; the other tools are not. The box is in original condition and has patinated beautifully. The interior is of Tunbridge ware work. The exterior also points to early Tunbridge work, with its particular woods. A very special piece. 10.75" wide. Ca. 1780–90. $8,000–12,000.

Like in other types of boxes, early nineteenth century workboxes were made in the shapes typical of the Regency. There are examples of sarcophagus and more complex architectural forms that incorporate more than one tradition dating from the first four decades of the century. The eighteenth century basket was revived in a new interpretation; that is, as a box. The basket-shaped boxes were sometimes tapered, domed topped, with double lids, or simply quite flat with a lift-up lid. These boxes always had a shaped wooden handle straddling the box from one side to the other and fixed with turned wooden pegs. There is such a box in Mrs. Fitzherbert's room in the Brighton Pavilion (George IV's summer palace), although whether the king's morganatic wife ever used it is a matter of conjecture.

Most workboxes were veneered with the exotic woods popular at the time, such as rosewood and kingwood. If veneered in mahogany, it was usually of the richly figured kind. They were then decorated with inlays in brass, wood, and mother of pearl and were often edged with gadrooning. Sarcophagus shapes were enhanced with feet and handles typical of the late neoclassical period.

In the early 1800s, the tools in these boxes were of the same form as those of the eighteenth century, but increasingly they were made of ivory, bone, or rosewood rather than painted white wood.

By the third decade of the nineteenth century, the open spool had on the whole superseded the closed barrel. The first spools consisted of turned and carved circles of ivory or bone screwing onto a bone tube supported by another plain circle on the base. Soon the top carved circle was made in mother of pearl rather than ivory. The screw on design did not last for long. It was soon modified so that the two circles joined each other by the top circle being attached to a metal tube that slid over a metal pin attached to the bottom circle.

The other tools—tape measure holder, waxer, and emery cushion holder—followed earlier patterns, but now they were primarily made in mother of pearl or vegetable ivory. The emery cushions changed their form and became tubular containers with a round opening covered in cloth in which the needle could be inserted for cleaning. As needles began to be sold in packets, emery cushions were no longer necessary. Thimbles were occasionally in ivory, but these were mostly superseded by silver and steel thimbles placed in prearranged grooved spaces on the tray. Unlike the French, English boxes did not contain mother of pearl thimbles.

The tray itself, as well as the inside of the lid, became more elaborate. Silk and gold-tooled leather were used to line the lid and to create small pincushions and covers. The center of the tray contained a cover over an empty space. This cover had loops that held small scissors, stilettos (tools with a sharp, round pointed piece of steel), hooks, flat needles, pencils, folding knives, and other implements. These had mother of pearl or ivory handles. The ratcheted winders were no longer part of the tray arrangement.

*Above:*

Figure 439. A box painted in blue-green, the varnish giving it a stronger shade of green than the original pigment. It is decorated with seashells and roses. This is an excellent example of an individually decorated piece, which was designed and executed to the particular interests of a lady. Very likely it was painted by the lady herself. The interior retains some of its original fittings, including Tunbridge ware wooden barrels and containers, a continuous reel, winders, and two glass bottles. The box reflects the taste of the period, both in gardens and in shells. Shell collecting became quite a pursuit with eighteenth century ladies, who studied, catalogued, and used shells for embellishing objects and spaces, even artificial grottoes! The indomitable Mrs. Delany promoted both the growing of roses and the collecting and working with shells. A piece that encapsulates the spirit of eighteenth-century genteel living. Likely to be unique. 10.5" wide. Ca. 1790. $10,000–14,000.

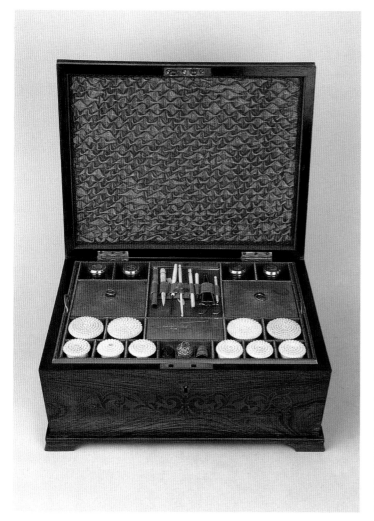

*This whole page:*

Figure 440. A superb quality, rosewood veneered box of gently tapering form standing on a rosewood base and rosewood square feet. The top has a gentle pyramid shape. The brass inlaid ornament is well defined and complements the form of the box. The inside is luxuriously lined and fitted. It is lined in pink silk and is fitted both with silver-topped small bottles and ivory spools of outstanding quality. The spools, which are of ivory with screw-on shafts, are very deeply carved both on the bottom and top parts. They are in the form of stylized chrysanthemums. It is not surprising that the box bears a large and a small label, of D. Edwards, one of the foremost early nineteenth-century makers, whose clientele included the king and other members of the royal family. 13.25" wide. Ca. 1820. $14,000–16,000.

Figure 441. A rosewood box of tapering form with continuous inlaid-brass ornament. It stands on brass feet and has gilded side handles. Inside it has a lift-out tray, but no tools. A good-quality example of a typical George IV box. 9.5" wide. Ca. 1825. $1,000–1,200.

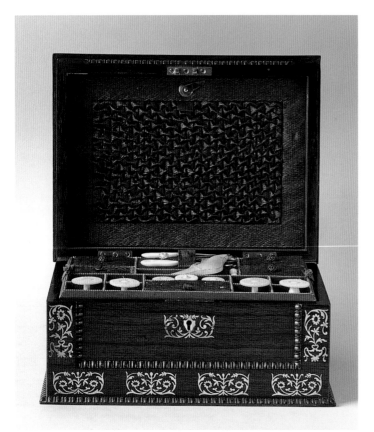

*Above and right:*
Figure 442. A rosewood veneered box constructed with fielded panels, the higher parts joined to the sunken sections with gadrooning. The box is constructed and decorated with meticulous care, still within the neoclassical tradition. The veneer is well figured, and the ornament in mother of pearl complements the dark color and striations of the wood. The floral inlay is designed and executed within the rules of classical symmetry. This finely controlled work demanded a high degree of skill. The interior is lined with pink silk and contains a set of matching spools, tape measure, and waxer in turned and carved mother of pearl. The spools are of the earlier (screw-on shaft) variety. The shafts are bone, not ivory. Note the distinctive markings. The box also contains some other sewing tools, a shoe-shaped silk pincushion, and samples of fine embroidery. A little treasure. Ca. 1835–40. *Courtesy of Lana McLain.* $3,000–4,000.

## RECTANGULAR BOXES

In addition to the very handsome shaped boxes that combine many of the design elements associated with the Regency period, there are also boxes dating from the early part of the nineteenth century made in more-restrained rectangular forms. Such boxes were veneered mostly in rosewood and were sometimes decorated with simple metal lines and ornaments.

Other rectangular boxes veneered in a variety of woods with simple crossbandings or edgings were also made. These boxes feature the same type of lift-out tray, and although their decoration is sparse, they were still made to a very high standard of craftsmanship and have the subtle appeal of understated quality.

Occasionally, rectangular boxes were made with elaborate brass or mother of pearl decoration. These were presumably made for people who were not partial to the new shapes but appreciated the new decorative styles. These boxes herald the next period, when the rectangular wooden sewing box was back in fashion.

By the end of the Regency, many sewing boxes, especially the plainer ones, were supplied without tools.

## LEATHER COVERED

A material used at this time to cover workboxes made in pine was leather. These boxes were made in exaggerated Regency shapes, often with segmented tops, concave and convex elements, animal monopodia, and gilded drop handles. The interiors were lined in paper, silk, and leather. The inner part of the lids was covered in pale silk, printed with classical scenes. Most of these boxes have been battered by age, but they still retain an excellent period look.

*This whole page:*

Figure 443. A box veneered in Brazilian rosewood and inlaid in mother of pearl. Note how the inlay follows and enhances the form of the box. The design of a deer and a peacock among undulating stylized plants is an early attempt at naturalism. It is, however, precisely and meticulously executed. The interior is lined in blue silk. The tray is fitted with tools with mother of pearl handles and a set of six matching spools carved from mother of pearl. The spools have metal pins attached to the bottom bone discs and metal tubes attached to the mother of pearl tops. A box of superior quality, it bears the label of George Johnston of Glasgow. 12.25" wide. Ca. 1830. *Courtesy of Mrs. Elizabeth M. Convis.* $5,000–6,000.

## Penwork, Painted

Such boxes were made in the Tunbridge ware tradition. Painted and penwork boxes combining different types of decoration come in all shapes. The interiors of these boxes are very similar to the interiors of the earlier ones; that is, they have lift-out trays or drawers fitted with turned wooden tools. Although many of the boxes were still supplied "in the white," a great number were professionally decorated, especially in Tunbridge Wells.

Some of the boxes that do not conform to any tradition and were in all probability decorated at home are wonderfully eccentric. Some were decorated by using an amalgam of techniques, including decoupage, cloth, and even feathers! The interpretations of exotic scenes in penwork and paint are exquisitely idiosyncratic. Such boxes are time capsules of a very personal nature and have a quality not found in less private types of boxes.

## Tunbridge Ware

Wood-decorated workboxes dating from this period that can definitely be classed as Tunbridge ware feature cube and vandyke patterns, usually on a rosewood background. They are fitted with stickware sewing tools. The sycamore barrels are either replaced with rosewood barrels or with stickware-topped open spools. (See Fig. 168) The tape measure holder, waxer, winders, and other tools all are in stickware or plain rosewood. Rosewood or unpainted wooden barrels were made only for a very short period. Soon they were replaced with open-sided spools. In 1826, the firm of Fenner made a table for Princess Victoria that included a side-drawer workbox. The reels and runners were made of sandalwood; the silk winders, of fine specimens of native and foreign woods.

Often, Tunbridge ware boxes contain an assortment of wooden tools: thimble cases, rosewood thimbles, needle cases, clamps, shuttles, and small circular boxes. If there is a set of

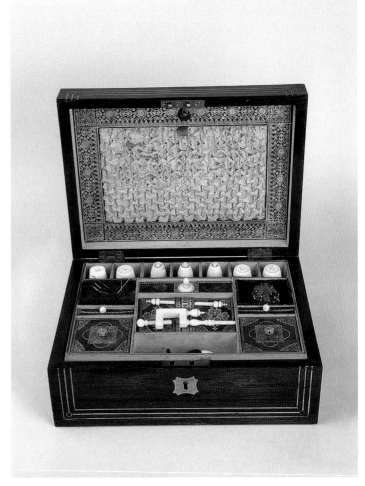

*This whole page:*
Figure 444. A box veneered in Brazilian rosewood inlaid with brass lines. The interior is lined in yellow paper, pink silk, and gold-embossed green leather. It is fitted with ivory tools and turned ivory thread barrels. The subtle exterior belies the interior of the box, which is in really exuberant Regency style, executed with impeccable attention to detail and quality. It bears the label of Wm. Dobson. 11.1" wide. Ca. 1820. $4,500–5,500.

*This whole page:*

Figure 445. A pine box covered in red leather; the domed top, feet, escutcheon, and ornament are in keeping with the style of the Regency period. The interior is lined in blue paper and yellow leather. The inside of the lid is further lined with a scene printed on cloth, which is usual in leather boxes of this period. The scene is in the classical bucolic genre. It depicts a shepherdess, complete with crook in hand, listening to her seated swain playing the bugle. A dog and a sheep sit contentedly on the grass. It was a favorite game among the Georgian aristocracy to dress up as shepherds and shepherdesses and frolic in the landscape. There are two sets of reels fitted in two of the top sections. These are in turned wood with painted lines. They are typical examples of Tunbridge ware work. A strong period piece. 9" wide. Ca. 1810–20. $2,500–3,000.

*This whole page:*
Figure 446. A large, rosewood veneered box decorated with penwork and a hand-colored print of a classical scene. The shape of the box is characteristic of Regency forms. Note the additional feature of the bombe section in the middle in sycamore, which is decorated with a band of stylized flora executed in penwork. The concave section on the top is similarly decorated. The interior is fitted with thread barrels, tape measure, waxer, ribbon reel, glass bottles, a superb clamp, and other tools. The box, which is of exceptional quality, has survived with its original varnish. It stands with justifiable pride on its Regency feet. 14.5" wide. Ca. 1815–25. *Courtesy of Anne Brooks.* $14,000–16,000.

stickware spools in the box, the tops usually feature different patterns. It is very likely that the owner added more Tunbridge ware tools after purchasing the box. The spaces in the tray are not so precise that the fittings have to be of a very particular size.

Both the boxes and the tools were beautifully made and are excellent examples of the richness of the woods and the skill and judgment employed by the Tunbridge ware makers during the first decades of the nineteenth century.

## PAPIER-MÂCHÉ

This is a period of fine papier-mâché workboxes. Both the decoration and the shapes are characteristic of the Regency. Chinoiserie is rare, but when found it has the spirited exquisite quality of the period. Skilled and talented artists were employed both for painting and gilding.

When fitted, the trays contain mother of pearl spools and tools, or, in early examples, ivory or bone fittings. (See example in Papier-mâché figures 135 and 138)

## ANGLO-INDIAN

This is the period of very fine Anglo-Indian workboxes, in *sadeli* mosaic, ivory, horn, and quill work. All Regency Anglo-Indian workboxes are now rare.

The *sadeli* boxes contained *sadeli*-topped barrels and tools. The earliest *sadeli* boxes, which date from the turn of the eighteenth to the nineteenth centuries, were made in flat rectangular forms and were completely covered in the mosaic. Slightly later, the shapes conformed to the English Regency forms, and the mosaic was used more sparingly as inset decoration in an ivory surface.

This is by far the best period for *sadeli* mosaic, but unfortunately, past ignorance and prejudice have allowed many of these boxes to deteriorate beyond repair, or even conservation. The nature of the original work required such skill and patience, as well as expensive materials, that it is beyond modern financial possibilities. Workboxes in reasonable condition dating from this time are veritable treasures. (See Figures 277, 280)

Figure 447. A sycamore-veneered box painted all around as a basket of flowers. This is an unusual treatment of the basket theme. The top is painted with an informally arranged bunch of roses. The painting is executed with professional skill and with a real eye for color and composition. There is a sewing tray inside. No sewing tools. 10.5" wide. Ca. 1815–20. $3,500–5,000.

Figure 448. A box in the form of a sewing basket, with the wood stained to resemble rosewood, and the center with a colored print of Brighton Pavilion. Note the joint on the front of the drawer. This box could be from the Tunbridge ware workshop of Wise. $1,500–2,000.

Figure 449. A shaped sewing box with a print of Sussex Place, Regents Park, and further gold painting on a gessoed background. In the Tunbridge ware tradition. 8.5" wide. Ca. 1820–1825. $700–1,000.

*Left and below:*
Figure 450. A shaped box veneered in ivory inlaid with *sadeli* mosaic. The lower drawer is fitted as a writing box. The interior is fitted with *sadeli*-decorated spools and other sewing tools. See Anglo-Indian chapter for more details of the work. 17" wide. Ca. 1850. $3,500–4,500.

## CHINESE-EXPORT LACQUER

This is the best period for workboxes in this material. Each box represents countless hours of skilled work. Sometimes they are rectangular, but mostly they are in rounded sarcophagus shapes with very fine gold decoration depicting oriental scenes. Most have lift-out trays containing turned and carved ivory tools, barrel thread containers, circular boxes, thimbles, waxers, tape measures, and sometimes clamps and other tools. These are larger than most other workboxes of the period. Most have a drawer on the lower part, opening to reveal a small writing surface. This was to be used when painting was incorporated into an embroidery design—a popular practice of the time, both in China and Europe.

## STRAW WORK

Fine, small Napoleonic prisoner-of-war boxes for holding thread were made at this time. Other workboxes with a drawer at the base and two lift-out lids inside were also made. These were supplied without tools. They are on the whole very beautiful, in spite of their often-distressed condition.

## IVORY

The last years of the eighteenth century and the first years of the nineteenth saw the greatest importation of foreign boxes and foreign traditions. Ivory sewing tools from Dieppe, in France, found their way into workboxes made in England. Dieppe is a seaport on the English Channel, and Dieppe carvers were recorded working in England as early as the seventeenth century. This exchange of skills must have stimulated the working of ivory in England when the material became increasingly available through the efforts of the Royal Africa Company. Although the English-made thread barrels are less ornate than Dieppe work, some of the other tools have similarities with the Continental work.

Whole workboxes in ivory or bone were not made in England, although those made in India and China were aimed at the English market. A few boxes made in other countries were brought back to England by travelers, diplomats, or traders.

One extraordinary category is the Russian carved box, which, although bearing a striking resemblance to French work, retains its own distinguished character. Embroidery in

*Above and left:*
Figure 451. A Chinese-export-lacquer box with carved ivory tools and a lower drawer for holding drawing and painting implements. The black lacquer is painted with a continuous scene of the growing, gathering, and processing of tea. Decoration with a narrative thematic subject is much more unusual than vignettes of oriental scenes. This particular box is painted exceptionally well, with a robustness of line, attention to minutiae, and skillful use of bright gold contrasted against black expanses. The figure sitting on the deck receiving the tea consignment is long nosed (European?). 14" wide. First half nineteenth century. $6,000–8,000.

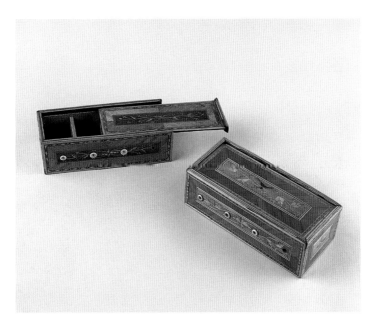

Figure 452. Two Napoleonic prisoner of war straw workboxes for holding reels of cotton. The thread was pulled through the holes on the side. 6" and 6.5" wide. Ca. 1800–10. $1,000–1,400.

*This whole page:*
Figure 453. The largest and by far the best example of a Russian sewing box I have ever seen, including museum collections. 10.75" wide. (See figure 205.) Ca. 1800. $?

*Below and right:*
Figure 454. A fine example of a Palais Royal sewing box veneered in satin wood and studded with faceted cut steel. The box is very unusual in that the tools are arranged on two levels, the top tray fitting snugly over the lower part. A little extra space is provided on the top by folding down the velvet flap. When the box is closed, it is a complete, compact cylinder. 5.4" wide. Ca. 1800–1810. $8,000–10,000.

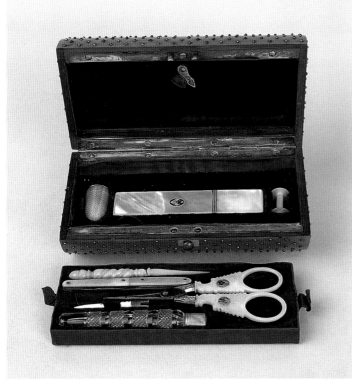

Russia had developed a long and rich tradition. It was seen as a precious art, often employing costly gold and silver threads—a practice still continuing in the adornment of church vestments. The Kieff workshops were a center of excellence, and were renowned throughout Europe for the great merit of their embroidered work.

If embroidery was undertaken by a great lady, the box for her work was naturally commensurate to the respect such work demanded. During the eighteenth century, ivory work was given a great boost by the efforts of Catherine the Great (1729–1796) of Russia. Catherine had embraced the ideas of the French philosophers and embarked on a concerted effort to stimulate and patronize the arts. St. Petersburg became the hubbub of creativity, with local and foreign artists cross-pollinating ideas and skills.

During the second half of the eighteenth century, the aesthetics of the applied arts in Russia developed to a great degree of sophistication. Regional crafts had been practiced over centuries, but it was not until the Russian nobility began to create important country estates that local production was stimulated. Works and workmen imported from abroad regenerated both the skills and designs of imperial and private workshops. One of the areas to benefit was Kholmogory, in the province Archangel, where bone, mammoth tusk, and walrus ivory work reached new heights of accomplishment.

Russian boxes were not commercially exported but were given by dignitaries as precious gifts. High-ranking Russians enjoyed cordial relationships with the English aristocracy.

Figure 455. A Palais Royal box veneered with bird's-eye maple with an inlay in boxwood of a bird sitting on a blossoming branch. The inlay is delicately executed and is aiming at a naturalistic representation. Fittings missing. 7.5" wide. Ca. 1825–30. $800–1,000.

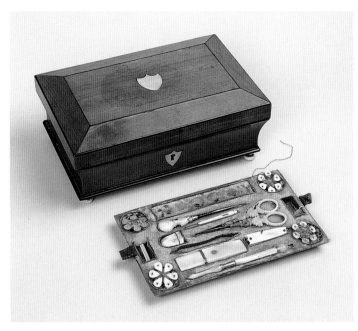

Figure 456. A pearwood-veneered Palais Royal box of conventional form. The fittings are on the top tray, which lifts out to reveal an empty space. 8.5" wide. Ca. 1815–25. $2,500–3,000.

By the middle decades of the nineteenth century, the work became simplified and much more commercial. Examples of fine openwork can be seen in the Hermitage Museum in Leningrad.

It is a privilege to see fine Russian boxes, which must be acknowledged as the most complementary containers of the work for which they were made. If a needlewoman could embroider or make lace in ivory, surely the result would resemble the work on such a box. The central motif is characteristic of Russian work of this period. The wheat sheaf carries both romantic bucolic connotations and classical links associated with Demeter/Ceres: the perfect emblem punctuating the point in time between the eighteenth and nineteenth centuries.

## PALAIS ROYAL

Sewing boxes sold in the Palais Royal area of Paris were justifiably exchanged as precious gifts at the end of the eighteenth century and the first part of the nineteenth. During the short period of peace in the early nineteenth century, and after the permanent peace of 1815, the English aristocracy rushed to France and indulged in shopping for high-quality goods. The Palais Royal shops were a great attraction to visitors. These establishments occupied a wing built in the eighteenth century by Louis Philippe d'Orléans when he inherited the palace and gave it the name Palais Royal. Originally the palace was built for Richelieu, and it was called Palais Cardinal.

The setting of the shops was splendid, and the area became the epitome of fashion both for promenading and spending money. The boxes sold through the shops of this luxurious arcade were fitted with exquisitely made sewing tools, mostly in mother of pearl but also in silver, gold, silver gilt, and ivory. The blades of the scissors and other tools were of steel. Additional implements, such as small clumps in steel, were occasionally incorporated within the fitted trays. The mother of pearl handles of the tools were joined to the steel implements with gold or gilt bands and embellished shafts. A characteristic of the work was the insertion in the mother of pearl of a gold oval featuring an enameled pansy. The pansy was not set in all tools, and it was not of uniform design—sometimes it looked like a blue forget-me-not. *Pensée* being the French word for thought, the flower was full of symbolism. Occasionally the word "*A MOI*," meaning "of me," was enameled under the pansy.

The handles of the tools were carved with great skill out of solid pieces of mother of pearl—a difficult and dangerous material to work with. The thimbles were turned out of thick pieces of shell. This is a process requiring great control of the material, which is prone to explode. Even after they were made, thimbles developed cracks, and very few have survived in reasonable condition. Both the thimbles and the other tools were snugly fitted into recessed spaces cut out in exact shapes into the lift-out tray. The trays were covered in velvet, and in some boxes they featured small pincushions, occasionally

Princess Lieven, the wife of Russian ambassador Count Lieven, was one of the formidable "patronesses" of Almack's, the most exclusive Regency club. This establishment was a bastion of female control, where an oligarchy of seven ladies guarded its reputation with an iron hand directed by unmitigated snobbery and aristocratic insolence. Unlike male-dominated clubs, at Almack's the standards of propriety were strictly observed at the expense of excitement. Madame de Lieven was also a close friend of the Prince Regent and one of the frequent visitors to the Brighton Pavilion. Indeed, we owe our knowledge of much of the social intrigues of the period to her shrewd observation and her witty and often-caustic tongue.

In 1814, Czar Alexander and his sister, the Grand Duchess Catherine of Oldenburg, came over to England for a royal visit. The idea was to boost the popularity of the British royals. This backfired, the people being much more interested in the foreign visitors than in the homegrown crowned heads. All the same, the visit provided the crowds with diverting spectacle, and the Regent with an excuse for banqueting and pageant. There was obviously significant social repartee with highborn Russians during the early decades of the nineteenth century, necessitating the exchange of costly gifts of a national character.

The Russian-carved openwork in ivory reached the zenith of perfection as the eighteenth century was drawing to a close. By the early years of the nineteenth century, it had transcended its folk roots and acquired the sophistication demanded by its new patrons. Nikolay Vereshchagin—a renowned master of openwork carving—produced his best work, including carved caskets, during this period.

*Right and below:*
Figure 457. An excellent example of a piano-shaped Palais Royal box. It is veneered in well-figured mahogany edged in boxwood. The keys are of ivory and ebony. The silver tools are fitted in the top tray, which, when removed, reveals a musical movement in the lower part of the box. First quarter nineteenth century. *Courtesy of a private collection.* $8,000–10,000.

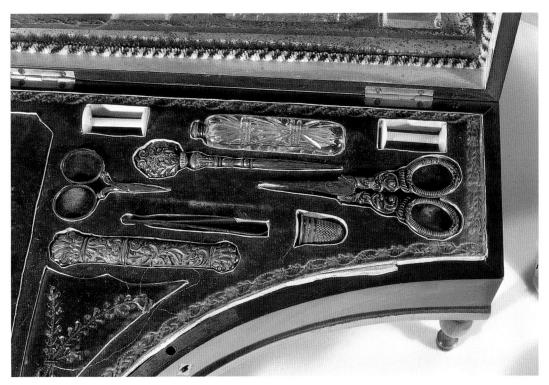

Figure 458. Two typical, small Palais Royal boxes with cut-steel pinhead decoration. Note the word *Souvenir* written in cut pinheads. Note also that the patterns on the two sides are representations of the anthemion motif (top) and the palmette (lower). These boxes were just as fine as their larger cousins but contained fewer tools. 7.5" wide. Ca. 1815. $800–1,000 (empty), $2,500–3,000 (fitted).

This whole page:
Figure 459. A box veneered in coromandel with metal stringings and mother of pearl escutcheon. The interior is fitted with a lift-out tray containing a set of carved mother of pearl spools with bone screw-on shafts. The box is of very good quality. The spools are turned and carved in a circular design that at first sight looks simple. It does however require considerable skill and control to execute a continuous design without wavering. The whole piece is of superior subtle quality. The box bears the label of *To The Queen, Turrill, 250 Regent St.* under a crown. Ca. 1840. $5,000–6,000.

embroidered or printed with a floral design. Some of the boxes incorporated a musical movement into their lower part, under the tool tray.

The Palais Royal boxes were not made primarily as useful sewing boxes, but as precious gifts—totems of an age of refinement. Sometimes the tools suggest various activities; for example, the box could contain a seal, a seal knife, or a perfume bottle. There was not sufficient room in the lower part of the tray to keep cloth, or even any meaningful quantity of thread. The winders could hold very little, and even then they are hardly ever found with any thread attached.

The boxes were very much toys for the rich and, as such, were impeccably made. They were made in various shapes, including some in the form of a piano, complete with ivory

keys. The woods used to veneer the mostly pine carcasses were satinwood, amboyna, mulberry, and pearwood. Simulated rosewood, the ultimate in artificial elegance, was also used, as were other burr or figured woods. The piano-shaped boxes were usually veneered in rosewood or mahogany.

One of the reasons for using light-colored woods was the preferred decoration on Palais Royal boxes. Cut-steel decoration was inserted in the form of faceted small pins, creating different designs, including the very apt word *souvenir*. The use of steel as a medium of applied art was developed in Tula, Russia, which already had a long tradition of metalworking, mainly for the armory. Under the auspices of Catherine II, steel became a medium for fashioning both domestic and personal ornaments. In sewing it was used both for chatelaines and tools. The

*This whole page:*

Figure 460. Another box made by Turill, although this time the name of the maker is engraved on a plaque inset into the back facing of the lower part of the box. The structure of the box and the coromandel veneer bear a resemblance to the previous example, although this piece is considerably more ornamented. The top is inlaid with three classical figures in mother of pearl. These are perhaps meant to represent the three goddesses who competed for the apple of Eris in the judgment of Paris, although the symbolism of the totems they are carrying is somewhat confused. The interior of the box is luxuriously fitted, the top unusually edged with embossed leather in colors. The spools are of similar construction and quality as in the previous example, with the surprising addition of painted butterflies in the center. A high-quality piece with unusual features. 11" wide. Ca. 1840–45. $6,000–8,000.

diamond-faceted, jewellike steel pins were adopted by French workers for the fine Palais Royal boxes and to a lesser extent for other boxes.

This form of decoration was sparingly adopted in England, although, ironically, the steel heads were exported to France from the northern English towns of Wolverhampton and Birmingham, and from Woodstock in Oxfordshire. Perhaps it was the expressed realization of how much an old nail was worth once it was converted into a cut-steel ornament that put off the English; they preferred to sell their old nails to the French.

## Mid-Nineteenth Century

By the second quarter of the nineteenth century, sewing materials became available in forms that were easier to obtain and use. Commercially produced spools of thread could be bought after 1825. Machine-twisted thread made waxers and barrels unnecessary. As the century progressed, good packaging made pre-prepared tools redundant. However, as embroidery was taken up by more women, workboxes became even more popular. Together with popularity came a desire for usefulness as well as beauty. Thus, the workbox of the middle nineteenth century changed both internally and externally.

Shapes reverted to the rectangular, allowing for a useful amount of space underneath the lift-out tray. Earlier whimsical decoration went out of fashion. Mother of pearl and brass inlays were still the most favored style of embellishment, but the earlier classically derived, repetitive formal scrolls gave way to motifs of naturalistic fluidity. Mother of pearl, abalone shell, and brass were used together to form flowers, birds, and butterflies.

Mother of pearl inlays without brass became cruder, or simpler, sometimes no more than diamond designs in alternating colors of shell. Occasionally, a prettily engraved central panel of mother of pearl or brass inset into the box was the only decoration. Wood marquetry, when done, was in naturalistic designs, mainly of flowers. Natural wood contrasts, sometimes enhanced with stains, were skillfully juxtaposed to form borders, or mostly central decorative panels.

Coromandel and walnut were preferred to rosewood for veneering the main body of the box. Veneers in walnut were cut very thin. The coromandel veneers were thicker. After about 1830, all the boxes were finished in glossy French polish.

Only the trays of the better quality boxes were fitted with tools. The ones that were contained mother of pearl-topped spools and steel implements with mother of pearl handles. After 1855, the Imperial Standard Yard was universally adopted, having been authorized by Parliament. Tape measures were marked in uniform standard inches. Trays became increasingly simpler, covered in silver paper with silk-topped covers. The inside of the lid was covered with padded silk, opening into an envelope-type compartment. Very few boxes had gold-tooled leather.

Many makers advertised "ladies workboxes" as part of the wares they offered. Some also advertised refurbishing services for the trays. This is symptomatic of the time when the workboxes were expected to be used, and therefore the fragile silks and papers of the trays to tear and stain. The great uniformity of the trays indicates that certain businesses must have specialized in this particular part of the work; that is, covering sewing box trays. The trays were made of thin pine.

A workbox decorated with a scrolling floral design and fitted with a typical tray with silk covers bears the label of C. Baldwin, who describes himself as "Ladies Workbox Fitter and Liner." His address was given as "23 Weymouth St. Marylebone." The bottom line of the label states, "Old Work Repaired."

During the last three decades of the nineteenth century, walnut veneered boxes, with bands of geometric inlay, were made in great numbers. Pretty and useful, they won the commercial battle over the more ambitious Tunbridge ware. The trays of such boxes were very standard and were never supplied with tools. (See Figure 102)

### Tunbridge Ware

Tunbridge ware workboxes of the period are decorated with characteristic mid-nineteenth century Berlin woolwork mosaic motifs. It is not unusual to find identical motifs both in woodwork and woolwork. Flowers, animals, and figures, as well as the popular borders of vines, feature on boxes, tapestries, embroideries, and beadwork. I must confess to preferring the Berlin borders in needlework for which they were designed. A continuous border avoids the problem of mismatched corners, which is inevitable on boxes.

The trays of Tunbridge ware workboxes dating from the 1830s to the end of the century are covered in paper, which is often in dark colors and patterned. If they contain any tools, these are mostly in stickware.

### Papier-Mâché

Good papier-mâché boxes with mother of pearl and painted decoration continued to be made well into the Victorian era. There was not much change from earlier boxes, except perhaps a tendency for larger sizes.

In addition to well-formed and painted boxes, a quantity of boxes were made for the ever increasing market of less discriminating clientele. These boxes, although pretty, feature standard decoration of mother of pearl and flowers.

Tools were supplied only with the best boxes and were in mother of pearl. As the century progressed to its last quarter, the boxes followed the decline of the whole industry.

### Anglo-Indian

Anglo-Indian workboxes from this period follow the forms of the Regency. Segmented horn and ivory boxes in sarcophagus shapes continued to be made, even though these shapes had been superseded in English work.

*Above:*

Figure 461. A monumental coromandel ebony compendium table cabinet of architectural form, having turned and carved feet and handles. The form of the cabinet is inspired by the archaeological discoveries of the late eighteenth to early nineteenth centuries. The top is constructed with sections redolent of ancient pediments and pyramids. The piece has a strong, assured presence, rooted strongly in the neoclassical tradition. The profuse inlay in mother of pearl introduces a note of softness without destroying the neoclassical effect. The inlay is symmetrical and within straight, defined lines. The decoration is totally controlled and executed with impeccable precision. The compendium is the personal space for the owner and has a fully fitted sewing tray complete with its original filigree silver and bone thread spools and other tools. There are two drawers for jewelry, and a folding writing box. 15.2" wide. Ca. 1850. $5,000–6,000.

*Above:*

Figure 462. A box of a very complex shape. It makes use of concave forms not just in the central bombe section, but also within the stepped top. The whole stands on a scrolling, flaring apron. It is most effectively inlaid with controlled mother of pearl designs. The interior is fitted with commensurate luxuriousness to the outside. It is lined with pink water silk and contains a set of matching spools, tools, tape measure holder, waxer, and emery circle, in silver. A luxury piece. Mid-nineteenth century. *Courtesy of the Bielstein Collection*. $5,000–6,000.

*This whole page:*

Figure 463. A fully fitted sewing box in almost black coromandel ebony, profusely inlaid to the top and front with engraved mother of pearl, abalone, green parkesine, and brass. It is very unusual to find parkesine used as a material for inlay in this way. It introduces a vibrant color that adds drama to the decoration. Inside the box there is the lift-out tray with its original purple velvet coverings and supplementary lids. The box has mother of pearl-handled sewing tools and turned and carved mother of pearl spools. Parkesine was the invention of Alexander Parks of Birmingham and was manufactured in his factory in Hackney. It is generally accepted as being the first plastic and was the predecessor of the American invention of celluloid, which was similar, but about ten years later. 12" wide. Ca. 1860. *Courtesy of Susan Webster* $3,000–4,000.

Carved sandalwood boxes were also made, the earlier examples being of very fine workmanship. These contain Indian silver tools and, occasionally, glass perfume bottles. (See Fig. 285)

Most other boxes in this category dating from this period are in a combination of carved wood and strips of later-period *sadeli* mosaic. The trays are fitted with *sadeli*-topped barrels. These boxes were made in great numbers for the English export market, and although they all are attractive, the quality of the work is varied. (See Fig. 284)

### Chinese-Export Lacquer

These are similar to earlier examples. By now the Chinese market was open to all and was no longer the monopoly of the East India Company. The fashion for all things oriental had passed its heyday, and lesser quality work was produced with an eye to the price conscious rather than aristocratic clientele.

Very few good examples with very fine decoration date from this period. By the last decades of the century, Chinese lacquer was no longer appreciated.

Figure 464. A box veneered in bird's-eye maple and rosewood forming a marquetry of stylized flora. The interior with a lift-out tray covered in paper, with silk tops over some of the divisions. There are no fittings in this box. Although of nice quality, such boxes were not supplied with tools. 11" wide. Third quarter nineteenth century. $600–1,000.

Figure 465. A box veneered in very well-figured burr walnut and further decorated with mother of pearl. Inside is a paper-lined tray with silk-covered tops. 11" wide. A typical pretty mid- to late Victorian box. Walnut sewing boxes were also inlaid with parquetry made up from many woods. See chapter 6, "Victorian." $500–600.

The portable personal dressing box was popular from the end of the eighteenth century to the third quarter of the nineteenth century. Increased mobility for social reasons, which gathered momentum as the century progressed, made this personal accessory indispensable. Before 1800, very few dressing boxes were made except for commissioning clients.

In 1680, a London cabinetmaker, Charles Bland, supplied Charles II with a "barber's case, covered with purple velvet and edged with a gold gallone, with scissors and razors tipped with silver, fine ivory, and tortoiseshell combs, horn with a gilt lock." Throughout the eighteenth century, cutlers and razor makers listed small grooming cases and separate grooming items on their trade cards.

Larger boxes were not common, although some very spectacular japanned boxes were made in the town of Spa—mostly for royal or aristocratic persons—in the earlier part of the eighteenth century. In 1762, Samuel Derrick recorded sending to a friend a dressing box and set of toilet boxes of Tunbridge ware inlaid with highly polished yew, cherry, holly, and other woods, of which "the neighborhood yields great plenty." This sounds more like a set of boxed smaller boxes and quite unlike nineteenth-century dressing boxes.

During the eighteenth century, very few women undertook serious traveling. On the other hand, men had to travel for business, education, war, or pleasure. It is therefore not surprising to find that provision for gentlemen's grooming needs in boxed containers preceded the needs for ladies' dressing boxes. Men already had writing boxes that accompanied them on their journeys. Some of these boxes doubled up as dressing boxes, with trays or drawers fitted with razors, jars, combs, shaving brushes, and anything else needed for the particular person's toilette. The alternative for the traveler was a smaller box containing just grooming essentials.

In 1745, Thomas Taylor of Huntingdon billed the Duke of Gordon "£1.1sh. for a dressing box." Since this was the same price he charged for a writing box, this must have been an unfitted box. Such boxes were fitted by cutlers, razor makers, and perfumers.

A few ladies of high social status and means did travel and, as a result, required dressing boxes. Thomas Sheraton has an illustration for a lady's traveling box in his *The Cabinet-Maker and Upholsterer's Drawing Book* that shows a compact multipurpose box with a large section devoted to personal-grooming

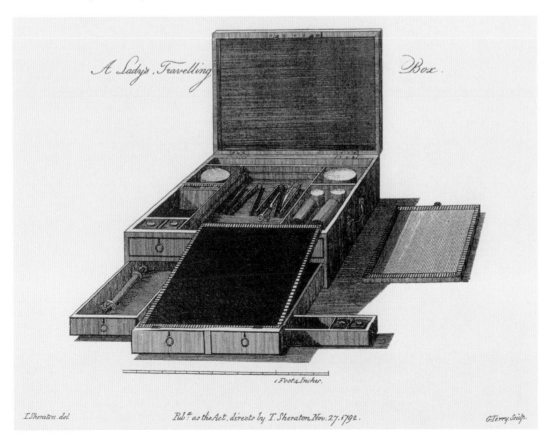

Figure 466. *A Lady's Travelling Box*, PL 39, Thomas Sheraton's *The Cabinet-Maker and Upholsterer's Drawing Book* (1793), engraved by G. Terry.

accessories. However, very few such boxes or other dressing boxes for ladies were made before the nineteenth century.

The male dressing box developed quite rapidly in various forms. Men were in fact very particular about their beauty preparations, which they often "lay on with a trowel." Mistress turned memoir writer Harriette Wilson, writing at the time of the Regency, complained how the thick makeup worn by men fell down their faces in great blobs when they got overheated. Pomatum, rouge, and powder were *de rigueur* for both sexes. Robinson, a Tunbridge Wells trader of the end of the eighteenth century and the beginning of the nineteenth, advertised no fewer than twenty-four varieties of hair powders and twenty-five varieties of French pomatums, and this is on top of waters (twenty-seven varieties), perfumes, soaps, cosmetics, and all sorts of other preparations that were obviously fashionable at the time.

Personal hygiene, a habit that had been neglected in Europe for many centuries, was given a boost in the 1770s, with the advent of cotton. Cotton was easier to wash than silk and wool, which up to that date were the predominant clothing fabrics. At about the same time, the use of "*Eau de Cologne*" was becoming increasingly widespread. This preparation, which was originally called "*Aqua Admirabilis*," was first devised by Italian perfumers the Farina brothers, who had settled in Cologne at the beginning of the eighteenth century. Ironically, its original purpose was to disguise the stench of battle.

Having been reintroduced to bathing by the Indians, by the first years of the nineteenth century, persons of good breeding were expected to cultivate a clean, pleasant personal smell. Beau Brummell was said to have always washed before dressing. The Regency saw the rise of the effete vain dandy, and every dandy who could afford it bought himself a dressing box. Thomas Raikes, a veritable nineteenth-century Narcissus, was said never to move without his gold dressing case, which was so heavy that it took two men to carry it! The gold presumably referred to the fittings.

In 1814, F. Benois supplied to the "Prince Regent a small toilette box £50" (Royal Household accounts, PRO, LC11/18). This was an extraordinary amount of money at the time. The fittings within the box must have been of royal quality indeed. The London firm of Bayley, Blew & Chapman claimed—at the time when George was King George IV—to have been dressing-case makers and Perfumers to His Majesty and HRH Duke of York. High-class dressing-case makers must have also supplied the contents of the bottles.

*Above:*

Figure 467. A dressing and traveling box very much in the style of the Sheraton illustration, with a pullout drawer and spaces for jars, bottles, and dressing tools. The box is veneered with rosewood and decorated in the neoclassical manner with Greek key patterns inlaid into the rosewood. Note the elegance of this box. 15" wide. Ca. 1790–1800. $12,000–15,000.

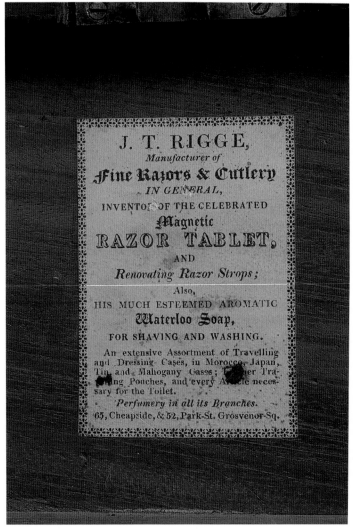

*Above:*
Figure 468. A small dressing box in mahogany, bearing the label of J. T. Rigge. Note that Rigge was the manufacturer and "inventor" of the accessories. He makes no claim to be the maker of the cases or the boxes, although he is obviously supplying fitted boxes. He also sold "perfumery" so that his clients could fill the bottles with their own choice of perfumes. 7.5" wide. Ca. 1820. $800–1,000.

During the first decades of the nineteenth century, it was not just the men of mode who acquired dressing boxes. Ladies were catching up fast and overtaking the men. Long house visits made dressing boxes necessary both for holding grooming accessories and perfumes and for showing off one's wealth. A dressing box was after all an item of pure luxury, a high-quality container for holding a plethora of costly and exquisite jars and tools. As such, the dressing box had to be both strong to protect the treasures within and beautifully fitted in keeping with its social purpose.

After about 1810, most dressing boxes were made for ladies and not for men. By the second half of the nineteenth century, very few men had dressing boxes. They had razor boxes or shaving boxes, but the cult of the vain man had passed. The Victorian culture expected men to be tough and sensible and women to be pretty. The dressing box became a girl's best friend, and not just the rich girl's friend. Alongside the luxurious boxes fitted with silver-topped bottles, a whole industry developed producing more ordinary boxes, complete with silver-plated-topped items, for the women of the middle classes. These were taken on holiday to the new seaside resorts that were opening up to crowds of new tourists who could now travel on trains easily and in relative safety.

## EIGHTEENTH-CENTURY FEATURES

Dressing boxes dating from about 1780 were made in solid mahogany, with or without brass bindings; these boxes were not usually longer than ten inches. They were wax finished and had a robust, unfussy look. Inside they had a lift-out tray with spaces for flat jars and dressing tools. The tray covered part of the inside of the box. Taller bottles were fitted at the back or the side, where the box was not covered by the tray and was therefore deeper. Under the tray there was room for brushes. The inside of the box was partly or fully covered in leather. An "envelope" flap in leather dropped down from the lid, exposing a mirror in a recess of the wooden top. This arrangement sometimes varied, but the principle of spaces for grooming jars and accessories was always respected.

Most of the bottles had silver-plated tops. These were tougher than the silver equivalent. Because these boxes were taken on arduous journeys and military expeditions, Sheffield plate, which was much more expensive to make than the modern electroplate equivalent, was preferable to the softer silver. Occasionally a box was fitted with silver-topped bottles. The decoration on the silver was restrained and of very high quality. The silver tops of the long, flat glass containers were decorated with perforated and engraved designs. The tops of the bottles and the round, flat jars were simpler, without perforations.

Most eighteenth-century dressing boxes followed the general military style of the writing boxes of the period. There are a few exceptions dating from this time. These are very fine boxes in the Sheraton style. The interiors are fitted with snuggly

Figure 469. Two very similar traveling boxes. The closed example is a portable writing desk; the open example is a combined "dressing case" and writing desk. The lift-out dressing tray is fitted for holding a man's grooming accessories. 12" wide. Ca. 1800. $3,500–4,000 (with tray) and $2,000–3,000 (without tray).

fitting containers and bottles. The trays feature leather-covered lids and boxwood edgings. Such boxes are now very rare indeed.

Tunbridge ware boxes, in the painted or inlaid style and featuring a combination of smaller boxes and spaces for bottles, are extremely rare. Henry Clay made papier-mâché dressing boxes that, on account of the strength needed for the fittings, required a thickness of ten sheets.

In addition to the full dressing boxes, a few shaving boxes were also made, presumably for the few men who kept their vanity in control.

### REGENCY FEATURES

During the Regency period, dressing boxes had the dual purpose of showing one's taste and of holding one's beauty accessories. They had to be truly glamorous. They were made in exotic woods and were often decorated with brass inlays in the prevailing period styles. They were glossily finished with French polish. The Regency dressing boxes were made both for men and women. There is not much difference in their internal arrangements, although some of the accessories were adapted to the needs of the sexes.

The interiors were lavishly lined in velvet or gold-embossed leather. The glass bottles and jars were frequently of heavy crystal, which was sometimes cut. The tops were in finely and subtly worked silver. Occasionally, a high quality box had bottles topped with Sheffield silver plate, which was considered a more robust alternative. A mirror was usually fitted on the inside of the lid. Sometimes a tray was fitted for holding jewelry under the jar tray. Other arrangements, such as small drawers or flat trays holding personal tools, were also accommodated in the most elegant manner. Everything had its own neat and precise space.

By the third decade of the nineteenth century, the jewelry tray was generally replaced by a drawer. This was lined in velvet

*Above:*
Figure 470. This dressing box is made from solid rosewood. Although the hardware and form of the box are English, such work in solid timber points to a Chinese piece made for an English client. Heavy and impeccably constructed, it inspires a solemn shave. 11" wide. Ca. 1810. $3,000–4,000.

and divided so as to hold items of jewelry in different sections. The first drawers had a separate lock and key, but soon ways were found to open them from the main part of the box, using catch and spring mechanisms.

### Victorian Features

During the Victorian era, some of the most prestigious box makers turned their attention to producing very glamorous dressing boxes. Some of these makers, who also made other types of boxes, including writing boxes, seemed to concentrate their ingenuity regarding tricks and mechanisms on the dressing boxes. As the design for secret drawers in writing boxes became standardized, more patents were taken out for different dressing-box arrangements.

Machines had become standard features in workshops, and wood could be cut with incredible precision. Joints were predictably uniform, as were the cuts for hinges, locks, and other hardware. This allowed the maker to produce boxes of impeccable accuracy in terms of matching parts. Such boxes could be fitted with catches and springs that worked smoothly and efficiently. Drawers popped out, fronts swung open in "butterfly" fashion, and tops parted with screw mechanisms to reveal extra trays. Dressing boxes became full of surprises. (See Fig. 94)

This is not to say that every dressing box became a box of tricks. Many high-quality boxes were made in more-restrained and traditional forms. Top-quality silver was perhaps safer in less mobile trays. One feature that seems to have been adopted by most Victorian makers of dressing boxes is the mirror arrangement at the back of the inside flap. The mirror became larger and could either click in place on the inside lid or swing out on an "easel" hinge. If the mirror was held behind the flap, as in earlier boxes, it was now a hand mirror.

The most-popular woods for veneering Victorian dressing boxes were walnut and coromandel, polished to a glossy finish. The boxes were on the whole quite plain on the outside. Most had a rounded brass edge that protected the surround of the box, brass escutcheons, and central plates. Most were fitted with Bramah or other good-quality locks.

The silver tops on the bottles of Victorian dressing boxes were decorated with engraved, engine-turned, or *repoussé* work. Unlike the Georgian boxes, the Victorian boxes had both jar and bottle tops decorated the same way.

By the mid-Victorian period, a considerable section of the middle classes had acquired enough wealth to be able to buy

*This whole page:*
Figure 472. Carved out of solid mahogany, this box has hollowed out spaces where bottles and accessories fit precisely. On the top is a small mirror. Incredibly compact. Back to front, 9" wide. French, ca. 1790–1800. $3,000–4,000.

fashionable luxuries. "Fashionable" is the key word here, and fashionable meant up to date in terms of design. It is therefore not unusual to find a Victorian dressing box containing earlier fittings. It is also not unusual to find matching fittings with different silver date marks. The box maker would often make a box to accommodate the customer's bottles and jars. After all, the fittings were not made by the box maker, but by silversmiths, glass workers, mother of pearl and ivory carvers, and cutlers. The trays were lined by specialists in leatherwork. Dressing boxes were a cornucopia of beautiful things and skills that required many disciplines.

High-quality dressing boxes were often supplied with an outer leather case to protect them when traveling. This was rarely done for other boxes.

Dressing boxes with silver-plated-topped bottles were made for the less well off. Unlike Georgian dressing boxes, which were fitted with plated-topped bottles, the Victorian boxes were, on the whole, of lesser quality. They were made in greater numbers, although in fewer designs. They were veneered mostly in thin Indian rosewood or plain walnut. Very few had brass surrounds or expensive locks. The jewelry trays and other lined parts were lined mostly in plain velvet. Occasionally a box of equal quality to the silver-fitted boxes

was made for silver-plated items, but this was an exception to the general rule.

By the end of the nineteenth century, wooden dressing boxes were no longer in great demand. They were replaced by leather cases that had fitted compartments on the sides for jars and bottles.

Few papier-mâché boxes were made, perhaps on account of the fragility of the material. Jennens and Bettridge made one for the queen of Spain, and Richard Turley exhibited a lady's and a gentleman's box at the Birmingham exhibition. Examples I have seen had rather uninspiring decoration of mid-Victorian fashion.

## FRENCH DRESSING BOXES

French dressing boxes were bought by the fashionable ladies, mostly from the shops in the Palais Royal area of Paris. Unlike the English boxes, which had drawers for jewelry and sometimes other spaces for personal items, the French boxes were fitted with tray upon tray, containing every tool a lady of the world would require on her travels. The trays were covered in the same way as in the Palais Royal sewing boxes. The glass in the French boxes was thinner, and it was decorated with fine, rather than heavy, cut designs.

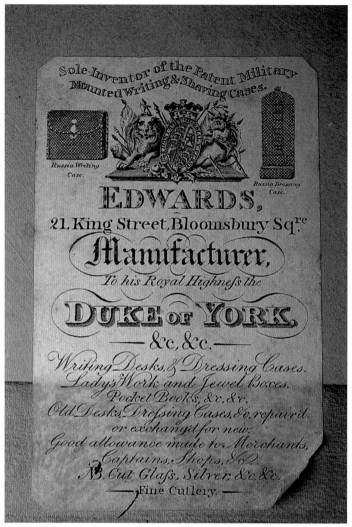

Figure 473. Rosewood veneered with subtle brass accents, this box typifies the understated quality of the early nineteenth century. The interior is lined in velvet and leather in a color combination that is again typical of the period. The bottles have silver-plated tops. It bears the Edwards label. 12.75" wide. Ca. 1810. $3,000–4,000.

## JEWELRY BOXES

In previous centuries, jewelry caskets and cabinets were made for royal and other high-ranking persons in a variety of materials. Ivory, tortoiseshell, wood, and spectacular stump work embroidery all featured as materials for jewelry boxes.

During the latter part of the eighteenth century and most of the nineteenth century, very few boxes were made especially for holding jewelry. The general dressing box always had a drawer, or a space, for keeping jewelry when traveling, rendering a separate box unnecessary. In the few instances when a box was made for jewelry, it was fitted in the same way as the dressing-box drawer. Leather-covered jewelry boxes were made late in the nineteenth century. These were utilitarian, without pretensions to style.

## GLOVE BOXES

These were long, thin boxes decorated in the fashion of the time. In France they were made with a hinged front panel, allowing the box to open both upward and downward.

## MIRROR BOXES

These are compact boxes that open up to reveal a hinged mirror and an arrangement of drawers. They were made in the Far East during the eighteenth and nineteenth centuries and were brought to Europe by merchants of different trading companies. They were made for the home market and not for Europeans, as attested by the many pictures of oriental ladies in front of such boxes. Mirror boxes were made in high-quality hardwoods and feature metal hardware. Some are inlaid in mother of pearl. The "butterfly" opening of the drawers may have been the inspiration behind Betjemann's slicker and more-mechanized patents. These oriental dressing boxes have a strong dignified quality, making them seem more like miniature furniture than boxes.

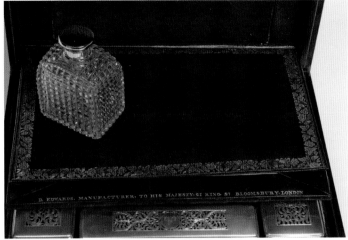

*Above and left:*

Figure 474. A very fine and rare brassbound-figured rosewood fully fitted traveling/dressing box by D. Edwards, with working Bramah lock and countersunk carrying handles, the inside lined in velvet and gold-embossed leather and containing hallmarked silver-topped, cut-lead crystal bottles and jars by Archibald Douglas and having a document wallet and lift-out mirror in the lid. The silver is decorated with pierced designs in stylized symmetrical leafy patterns around a circle designed for the engraving of the owner's initials. Two of the containers have tops secured with screw-down mechanisms. Ca. 1829. 13.6" wide. $5,000–6,000.

*Above:*

Figure 475. The style of this box and the silver are what we would expect to be commissioned by an aristocratic patronage in the first years of the Victorian era, before the elegance of the Regency gave way to the opulence of the mid-nineteenth century. The workmanship that created the box is of impeccable quality. The veneer is saw-cut kingwood, a costly timber rarely used for whole boxes on account of its narrow width. The subtly beautiful figure of the wood is accented discreetly with brass lines, the thicker edge piece featuring an engraved line that softens the austerity of the brass. The design incorporates the quiet grace and subtlety characteristic of an age steeped in the quiet dignity of neoclassicism. A piece of paper in the box claims it was owned by Daisy Countess of Warwick, whose most significant admirer was the Prince of Wales, later Edward VII. The gilded silver is of thick gauge. The decoration combines pierced and chased patterns of stylized flora, executed with controlled fluidity in the best tradition of the time, which accepted the beauty of natural forms but interpreted it through the prism of neoclassicism. The gilded silver is hallmarked London 1839 and has the maker's or sponsor's mark for Charles Rawlings and William Summers. This form of decoration predates the engraved or repousse decoration found in later dressing boxes. The surviving crystal containers are superbly and elaborately cut. Ca. 1839. 14.2" wide. $4,000–5,000.

Figure 477. A Rosewood veneered gentleman's dressing box. The tops on the jars and bottles are of high-quality engraved silver. The space at the front is for holding a watch and chain. The silver has the London hallmarks for 1851. 12" wide. $2,500–3,000.

Figure 476. A high-quality Victorian dressing box. It bears the label of Halstaff. The box is veneered in thick coromandel and edged in brass. The arrangement of the mirror, which can click into place on the back when the box is open, and the jewelry drawer are characteristic of the period. The interior is luxuriously lined in velvet and gold-embossed leather. The heavy crystal bottles are topped with robustly formed and engraved tops. The tops bear the London silver mark of 1857/8. They are engraved with elaborate floral patterns framed by rococo cartouches. Both the box and the fittings are of superior quality. Note that at this date the silver stands "proud." The interiors were designed to hold the bottles so as to create the most glamorous effect. The box has an outer protective leather case. 14" wide. *Courtesy of the Bielstein Collection*. $7,000–9,000.

*Right:*
Figure 478. A coromandel-veneered and brass-edged dressing box. Opulently fitted, the silver tops bear witness to the finest work of the Victorian silversmith. Each piece, including the small tools fitted in the fold-down front, is decorated with a different motif. This diversity of design is most unusual. The designs were inspired by Japanese work, which had been recently introduced to England. They are exquisitely executed in silver and gold of different colors. Some are engraved and some are raised in three dimensions. A costly and inspired cornucopia of Eastern plants and creatures. The silver has the London hallmarks for 1877–78. 15.75" wide. $?

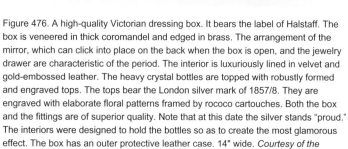

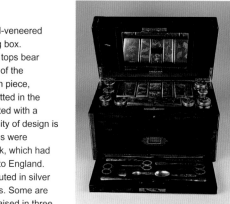

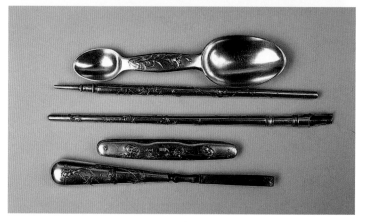

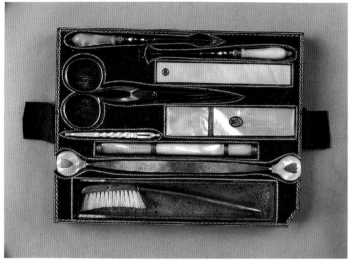

*Above and left:*

Figure 479. A French box typical of the refined quality and arrangement of boxes sold in the Palais Royal area of Paris. Note the trays, which neatly fit on top of each other, filled with precisely fitting tools in mother of pearl, steel, silver, and gold. The glass is thinner than in most English boxes and is delicately faceted and cut. Some of the fittings are particular to French boxes, such as the vessel, which can be used for warming up liquids, with its inverse-screwing safety handle. The French marks are not as precise or clear as the English. The box dates from around 1820. 11.75" wide. *Courtesy of Anne Brooks.* $?

Figure 480. An unusual box for its time, in that it is fitted just for jewelry. Made with care, it is veneered in burr walnut. The interior is fitted in silk and gold-embossed leather. 10" wide. Ca. 1850. $800–1,000.

Figure 481. Veneered with stained bird's-eye maple and ebonized wood, the box is elaborately inlaid with brass and mother of pearl. The interior is luxuriously lined in silk. A glamorous glove box befitting its glamorous purpose. Ca. 1850. $1,000–1,200.

*This whole page:*

Figure 482. A Chinese hardwood mirror box. This is an example of a robust and yet elegant compact item of small furniture. Such boxes are seen on illustrations of traditional oriental interiors, often with ladies kneeling on the floor in front of the open mirror. The lacquer work detail here, which shows such a box, is from a Chinese-export-lacquer sewing box. European cabinetmakers must have derived their inspiration for folding devices from examples of such boxes brought to Europe during the eighteenth and nineteenth centuries (see the "Victorian" chapter, figure 94). 10.25" wide. Early nineteenth century. $3,000–5,000.

Knife boxes were first made during the second part of the seventeenth century, but they were not really seen as necessary household accessories until well into the eighteenth century. When invited to dinner, guests were expected to bring their own cutlery, so sets of knives and forks were not deemed necessary dining-room items. The first record of a knife case dates from 1649. It is a drawing in Randle Holme's *Academy of Armory*, showing a standing box for holding knives and forks. However, it was not until Charles II presented the Duchess of Portsmouth with twelve golden knives and forks that sets became fashionable and began to be made in any numbers. The sets were kept in the dining room, and knife cases evolved to provide an elegant storage solution.

At first, knife cases were made singly, and the early ones were covered mostly in leather or shagreen, or they were japanned. Thomas Porter (London, 1749—1768)—upholsterer and cabinetmaker—specifically advertised "shagreened knife cases" as one item offered by his business. Some knife cases were veneered in wood, the earliest veneers being in walnut. Seventeenth century shapes were quite narrow, with flat, canted, or gently rounded fronts. Inside, the cases were fitted with a slanting piece of wood with symmetrically spaced cutout holes, so that each piece of cutlery could be stored without touching the other pieces. Knives and forks were placed with their handles upward.

Gradually the shape changed to a deeper and more elongated shape with storage space for spoons, which were stored with their bowls up. Two slope-top knife boxes ca. 1800, at Came House in Dorset, bear the label of Thomas Dobson. By the last three decades of the eighteenth century, the longer shape, which was also more complex, became the preferred form.

The interiors of the earlier cases were lined in velvet. In 1738, Peter Faneuil, ordering from London for his house in Boston, stipulated "a shagreen case . . . lined with a red velvet." However, by the last three decades of the eighteenth century, the perforated wood that held the pieces in place inside the box was left uncovered and embellished with inlay. In Gillows's letter book, there is an entry for the "22nd of January 1776" that explains the practice of the time: "fine mahogany within and without, strung with a little inlaid work around each knife, fork, etc. and also on the inside." The inlaid work was mainly of a simple chequer design in ebony and boxwood. By this time, mahogany was the preferred wood both for the outside and inside of knife cases.

During the last decades of the eighteenth century, the shapes and decoration of such boxes varied a great deal, allowing for personal preferences. Although Sheraton in his 1791 *Drawing Book* claims that knife cases were not "made in regular cabinet shops" and recommends the specialist John Lane, this claim cannot be entirely true. Although some

*This whole page:*
Figure 483. *Knife Cases*: plates 38 and 39 from George Hepplewhite's *The Cabinet-Maker and Upholsterer's Guide* (1786).

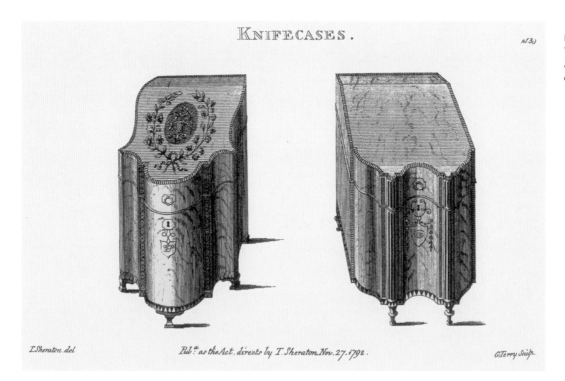

KNIFECASES.

*I. Sheraton del.*    *Pub.ᵈ as the Act. directs by T. Sheraton.Nov. 27. 1792.*    *G.Terry Sculp.*

Figure 484. *Knifecases*: PL 39 from Thomas Sheraton's *The Cabinet-Maker and Upholsterer's Drawing Book (*1793), engraved by G. Terry.

makers—for example, Allen of London (died 1809)—advertised themselves specifically as "knife case maker," others offered knife boxes as one item in a wider repertoire. William Colsey (London, 1802—1829), for example, described himself as "knife case, portable desk and tea caddy maker." Knife cases were featured on trade cards together with other items; they were also mentioned on invoices and inventories together with other cabinetmakers' work.

Furthermore, the diversity of design is such that it betrays the work of several makers. Although shaping veneers by using pre-prepared molds to produce the curved shapes of knife boxes was skilled work, it was not beyond the expertise of reputable eighteenth century cabinetmakers. Using moisture and heat to bend timbers without producing cracks was a traditional and well-mastered discipline.

What Sheraton's observation tells us is that by the time he was writing, knife cases were so popular that whole workshops could be kept busy just making such boxes. Certain workshops, especially in London, did offer this specialization, but this is not to say that the work of other cabinetmakers in this field was inferior.

Knife cases were also offered through cutlers, who sold items in steel, silver, ivory, and other accessories relevant to personal grooming and culinary needs. It is not possible to know how much of the work was done in one workshop and how much of it was commissioned. For example, John Brailsford, whose trade card featured a flat-fronted knife case surrounded by smaller items, advertised that he "Maketh & Selleth all Sorts of the Best LONDON WORK." Knife cases were also featured on trade cards of razor makers, who also made knives and forks, without being offered as part of the stock. In such cases it is

reasonable to conclude that there was cooperation between cabinetmakers and the makers of the contents to produce appropriately cased articles for the client.

During the second half of the eighteenth century, convex and concave shapes were most favored, sometimes standing on silver feet, sometimes with silver mounts of pierced or engraved silver. The trade card—dating from about 1760—of John Folgham, a London cabinetmaker, shows knife and dressing cases and lists items of stock, including knife cases and writing desks "Mounted in silver or Plain." Between 1776 and 1780, Nathaniel Dudley, a Birmingham cabinetmaker, commissioned silversmiths Boulton and Fothergill to make sets of silver mounts for knife cases. The silversmiths in turn ordered from this maker a chest for silver objects in 1774. It is easy to see how cabinetmakers on good terms with silversmiths may have gotten more than their fair share of orders for knife cases.

During the last two decades of the eighteenth century, the fashion for mounts and feet gave way to new neoclassical designs. Knife cases were crossbanded and inlaid with classical motifs. The keyholes were mostly discreetly inlaid, although smaller, plainer silver or silver-plated mounts were still in use. Satinwood, as an alternative to mahogany, was occasionally used during this period for veneering knife cases, which were then painted in the neoclassical manner.

The fashion for pairs of knife boxes was promoted after the Adam-inspired sideboard was firmly established in the dining room. The neoclassical demand for symmetry favored a knife box at each end of the elongated sideboard, with a wine cellaret placed in the middle, under the board. The Georgian sideboard stood on elegant legs, like a long, narrow wall table. The space under it was not filled with drawers and cupboards. As guest

*Right:*
Figure 485. A mahogany-veneered and king-wood-crossbanded knife box. The interior is fitted with the slotted panel designed to hold cutlery. Silver or silver-plated mounts provide one of the usual decorative devices. Ca. 1780–90. *Courtesy of a private collection.*

Figure 486. A mahogany-veneered knife box with an oval marquetry inlaid panel depicting a *Commedia dell' Arte* figure. Marquetry panels were often inlaid into the tops of knife boxes, but they were mostly in the neoclassical tradition of decoration, with motifs similar to those on tea caddies. This design is most unusual, although a similar clown figure is illustrated as a pattern for an inlay on a piece of furniture, featured in Thomas Chippendale's *Director.* 9" wide. Ca. 1790.

Figure 488. A pair of knife boxes that continue the tradition of the earlier type of velvet-lined interior. They are most unusually inlaid with robust marquetry in the Dutch style. First quarter nineteenth century.

Figure 487. A mahogany-veneered knife box with characteristic silver mounts. The figure of the wood is exceptional. Ca. 1780–90. *Courtesy of Berry and Marcia Morton.*

lists grew, three and even four matching knife cases were commissioned. Sometimes two were smaller, allowing for dessert cutlery to be stored alongside larger main meal pieces.

Neoclassical inspiration gave rise to an additional knife case form: the urn shape. Urns had already been established as inlays, designs for garden ornaments, wine coolers, and cellarets. It was a natural progression for knife cases to also be made in the form of urns. Hepplewhite, in his 1788 *Guide*, mentions that these urns were "usually made of satin or other light woods." Gillows, in his cost book for 1796, illustrates a knife urn with pineapple finial and carved elongated acanthus leaves. The whole box is divided into facets by stringing. Faceting was one way of getting over the problem of structure, and this was exploited to create fine proportion and appropriate decoration.

The urn's interior was arranged around a shaft that rose from the center, with concentrically arranged partitions for knives, forks, and spoons. A spring held the lid open. The lid was complementary to the rest of the design, sometimes continuing the segmented structure with fine stringing in between the wider sections of the main wood. Sometimes the lid was shaped and decorated or was carved in an alternative appropriate fashion.

As social gatherings became larger, with extended families and house parties, knife cases fell out of favor. They were not large enough to hold enough pieces of cutlery, and their form could not be modified further. The decor of the Victorian dining room had also changed, and the cutlery was not necessarily kept on the sideboard, which had become heavier.

Knife boxes were made in any really significant numbers for only about forty years, from 1770 to 1810.

## Price Guide

Knife boxes retaining their original interiors: pairs $10,000—20,000; singles $3,500—5,000

Knife boxes without their original interiors: pairs $5,000—8,000; singles $2,000—3,000

*Above:*
Figure 489. A very early example of a cutlery box in the conventional box form. Veneered in kingwood, with separate brass ornament, it has two levels of fitted trays. 10" wide. Ca. 1810. $2,000–3,000.

# CHAPTER 22 *Writing Boxes and Slopes*

## WRITING BOXES, EIGHTEENTH CENTURY

During the eighteenth century, writing boxes were a pointer to a gentleman's status. They were about being an officer in the army or the navy, or about being rich enough to seek mind-broadening adventure. They were about being able to read in an erudite manner. Yes, they had to follow the fashion too, but first and foremost they were about the inner man. During the whole of that century they were primarily a male accessory, a symbol of the social and cultural standing of the owner.

Portable boxes for facilitating writing had existed for many centuries and in many cultures. They were the prerogative of a few educated people, often linked with the church or the state. In Europe, portable desks, or lecterns, were used from the time of the Middle Ages by scholars and clerics. Royal persons and aristocrats also possessed boxes for writing, which they took

with them when moving from one of their residences to another. Writing was not just a medium for communicating information; it was also a form of high art. From the sixteenth to the nineteenth centuries, books on calligraphy were written by respected writing masters, and the whole performance of writing was executed with care and decorum.

Writing boxes were originally referred to as desks, since they were the only form of furniture for holding writing requisites and for writing on. Before the eighteenth century they were made mostly of oak and decorated with carved designs. Their usage incorporated a religious element, since religion and education were perceived to be inextricably linked.

Portable desks became less popular with the advent of the more complex and larger desk/bureau. However, during the

Figure 490. Writing boxes and writing slopes from the eighteenth and nineteenth centuries.

Figure 491. A rare mahogany portable desk constructed with fielded panels. A single inlay line of boxwood gives further definition to the structure. The flat front surface (not visible) is inlaid with a circular line framed by straight lines of inlay in the same wood. This is characteristic of the style of early-eighteenth-century boxes, such as Queen Anne flat lace boxes. The raised part forms a separate compartment. Rare. First half eighteenth century. $?

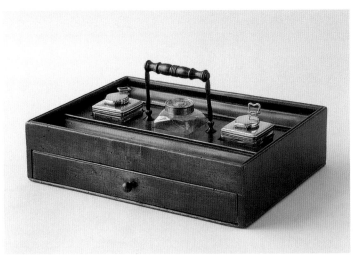

Figure 492. A portable "standish," with inkwells, pounce pot, and pen well, over a drawer for writing paper. Last quarter eighteenth century. 12" wide. *Courtesy of Christodoulides family collection.* $2,500–3,000.

second half of the eighteenth century, socioeconomic circumstances in England necessitated the wide use of a portable desk in the form of a box that could be used on a table, or on one's lap. The purpose of such a box was not to replace the piece of furniture in the household, but to provide the owner with a peripatetic accessory he could use while away from home.

Although quality, ornament, and form did play an important part in the selection of this type of box, it is the purpose for which it was used that gave prominence to the writing box at a time of expanding intellectual curiosity, communication, literacy, and increased commercial activity. The writing box was both an item of style and an item connected with intelligence, commerce, and world awareness.

From the last quarter of the eighteenth century to the end of the nineteenth, the writing box featured prominently on military expeditions, travels, libraries, and in drawing rooms. Great literature, as well as dispatches, contracts, letters, and postcards, were written on its sloping surface. The Brontë sisters were said to sit around their dining table writing on their respective writing boxes. Portraits were painted featuring writing boxes as a symbol of the sitter's status or literary achievement. Dr. Johnson tells us that the poet Alexander Pope (1688–1744) "punctually required that his writing box should be set upon his bed before he rose."

On a lighter note, writing boxes were featured on prints and caricatures, hinting at the personal power of the *word*. In 1825, S. W. Fores of Piccadilly printed a caricature by H. Heath titled *La Coterie Debauché*. This print depicted Harriette Wilson writing her memoirs on her open writing box. Harriette was a courtesan of class who numbered many members of the aristocracy among her lovers. When her best years were over, she decided to increase her income by writing about her *amours*. She gave her lovers the choice of paying her large sums of money to keep her liaisons with them out of her book. One of

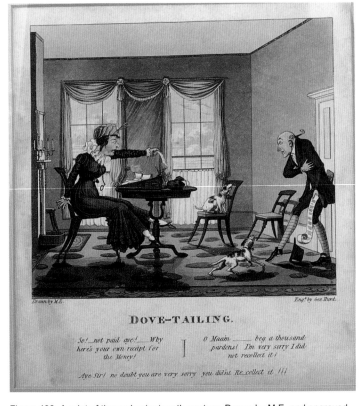

Figure 493. A print of the early nineteenth century. Drawn by M.E. and engraved by Geo. Hunt, it is titled *Dove-Tailing*. It depicts a formidable lady putting a tradesman, trying to claim an unpaid bill, in his place. From the secure position behind her writing box she exclaims, "Aye Sir! No doubt you are very sorry you didn't Re-collect it!!!"

her lovers was the Duke of Wellington, the hero of Waterloo. Furious at Harriette's audacity, the duke replied: "Publish and be damned," a phrase that found its way into the heart of the language ever since. The print shows the ex-lovers, including the duke, gathering up in a suppliant manner in front of Harriette's writing box, which stands between herself and the men, marking the line of battle.

The writing box witnessed war, business, and personal relationships. Unlike the writing desk or table, it was a personal—not a household—possession.

## WRITING BOXES AT THE TIME OF GEORGE III

The stylistic development of the writing box from the middle of the eighteenth century can be traced back to portable inkstands, writing sets, oak boxes, and sloping writing desks. The few made before 1780 were rectangular, mostly with sloping tops that were less steep than on earlier portable desks. They had side drawers for paper, and spaces for inkwells, sand boxes, or pounce pots. These last containers were for keeping a fine powder, such as chalk, which, when shaken over the ink, would act as a blotting medium. Poet, playwright, and novelist Oliver Goldsmith possessed such a box, which has survived to this day.

In addition to rather austere writing boxes, a few boxes in the more flamboyant French-influenced style were also made, mostly for use in the interiors of grand houses. In a description of Horace Walpole's mansion, Strawberry Hill, dating from 1763, there is mention of an inlaid writing box by Langlois. Langlois excelled in inlays of floral marquetries incorporating ribbons and musical trophies. He was also one of the main exponents of boulle work.

*Above:*
Figure 494. A large japanned writing slope with a side drawer, designed to be used on a table. The top of the box is not hinged and is simply removed to the side when the inner writing surface is in use. The chinoiserie decoration consists of raised and painted figures in a landscape and was executed in the manner practiced during the eighteenth century. Since japanning was a style favored by ladies, who at first did not use writing boxes to the same extent as men, it is unusual to find such a piece, especially in a large size. 16.4" wide. Third quarter eighteenth century. $4,500–5,500.

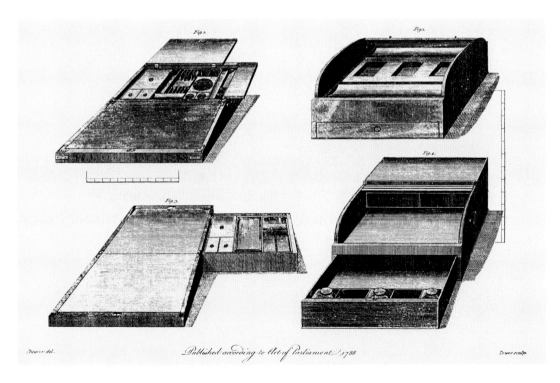

Figure 495. Designs by Thomas Shearer from *The Cabinet-Maker's London Book of Prices* (1788). The box on the top right has a "standish top." The box below (see figure 497) has a drawer operated by the "tambour" method: as the rolltop of the box is opened, the drawer emerges.

## A PORTABLE WRITING DESK, No. I.

ALL folid, eighteen inches long, ten inches wide, and fix
inches deep, lap-dovetail'd together, with a bevel drawer,   £. s. d.
the drawer partitioned off for ink, fand, and wafers  - -   0 10 0

### E X T R A S.

| | £ | s | d |
|---|---|---|---|
| Each inch more in length or width - - - - - - - - - - | 0 | 0 | 3 |
| Ditto in depth - - - - - - - - - - - - - - - - - - - - | 0 | 0 | 4 |
| Square clamping the flap - - - - - - - - - - - - - - - | 0 | 0 | 6 |
| Each miter, extra - - - - - - - - - - - - - - - - - - - | 0 | 0 | 6 |
| Veneering outfide - - - - - - - - - - - - - - - - - - - | 0 | 1 | 6 |
| Plinth round the bottom - - - - - - - - - - - - - - - | 0 | 0 | 6 |
| Lipping round the bottom or flap to receive the cloth - - | 0 | 0 | 4 |
| Putting a black or white bead up the corners and round the top - - - - - - - - - - - - - - - - - - - - - - - - - | 0 | 0 | 8 |
| Lining the writing part of the defk with cloth - - - - - | 0 | 0 | 4 |

F F 2                                      Ditto

Figure 496. The listed prices were not the selling prices but the prices paid to craftsmen and journeymen cabinetmakers for specific work. It is interesting to note all the different combinations of features possible in the construction of one box. The customer could decide what he, or she, specifically required. Note the designs of the writing boxes, which incorporate dressing sections. This option was taken by very few. Also note that the glass/silver fittings are not shown, since these would not have been made by cabinetmakers.

Figure 497. This is an exquisitely elegant, real-life example of the bottom right-hand side illustration of Thomas Shearer's book. It is made of harewood, cross-banded on the top with kingwood and decorated with a fine burnt-sand-shaded shell on the top. The tambour section is made up of unstained maple and a darker wood, probably mahogany—it is too thin to be identifiable with absolute certainty. The contrasting shades give the rounded surface a pleasing striped effect. A geometric inlay provides an elegant frame to the tambour. The interior, in mahogany, follows the design of the drawing. 10.5" wide. Ca. 1785–90. $3,000–3,500.

This period was really the beginning of the writing box as a serious trend. It was no longer the prerogative of just the aristocrat and the scholar. By the last decades of the eighteenth century, writing boxes were necessary in many nondomestic situations. Because they were necessary in activities involving traveling, their tops became flat to facilitate transportation.

The increased popularity of the writing box toward the end of the eighteenth century can be attributed to two main reasons: the onset of the Napoleonic Wars and the popularity of traveling. Officers in the army had their own boxes, using them both for army business and for writing home. They were stylistically complementary to the other campaign furniture that followed high-ranking army officers on their military adventures.

Robert Wyer, a London cabinetmaker, described his business as the "Original Military and Naval Trunk Manufacturers" on a label found on an early nineteenth century brassbound writing box. Given the stylistic similarity of early writing boxes to military furniture, it is very likely that the same cabinetmakers were responsible for the making of both.

Traveling—mostly to Italy—was the second main reason that necessitated a writing box. Tourism was an altogether more complex business than it is now. Traveling was planned and undertaken as a very serious passage to adult life, or as an earnest professional voyage of discovery. People seldom traveled alone. There were whole entourages moving slowly and clumsily, loaded with luggage covering every need. On the return journey there was even more to carry: heavy mementoes of the tour, including fragments of marble, stone, bronze, shells, and whatever else the eager travelers decided to plunder or buy. For those who could sketch or paint, there were their drawings and watercolors to bring back, and for others prints by Piranesi and other exponents of the "Classical."

By the last decades of the eighteenth century, apathy and stagnation of thought had caused the education system in England to disintegrate. Schools and universities were establishments whence the ruling classes, who had hitherto held the wealth and privilege of the land, came out to rule the country and the world. Secure in their social position, they treated educational institutions as playgrounds. Academics were not much better. The satire of the period, both in literature and prints, savages the intellectual bankruptcy of academia. Undergraduates are depicted dissolutely drunk among classical prints. Dons are shown gambling. The Earl of Chesterfield's "scholar and a gentleman, Doctor Carbuncle," typified the don of the day: he contracted all the evils a long sojourn at college could induce.

Yet, the eighteenth century was a time of great thinkers. George III actively encouraged education among the poor. He wished that every poor boy could "read his bible." Academies run by dissenting intellectuals for the education of youngsters who did not belong to the established church, and therefore were not admitted to the universities, flourished and saved the country from total stagnation of thought.

*Below and left:*
Figure 498. A mahogany writing box that opens into a writing surface that extends to the whole depth of the box. Unusually, the side drawer follows the slanting line of the box and provides storage space for writing and grooming implements. The metal shaving containers are original and very unusual. The round pot bears a patent number. The patent specifies the temperature at which the water should be kept for a successful shave!!! "A.D.1782.Nov.28. No 1345. PLAYFAIRS" specification. Judging from the patent date and the similarity to Shearer's figure 3 drawing, the box must have been made in the middle 1780s. 17.5" wide. $?

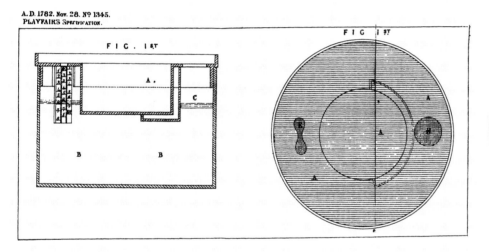

At the same time, exciting things were happening abroad. News of excavations in Europe and North Africa stimulated the imagination. Books and periodicals on different subjects became more widely available. Circulating libraries and reading clubs offered knowledge for those who wished to acquire it. Scientific and medical thinking was given a new impetus, especially in Scotland, through alternative educational establishments set up by the progressive thinkers of the time.

For the well-to-do young men who had concluded their time at Oxford or Cambridge, there was an easy way to accumulate knowledge if they so wished. They embarked on the "grand tour" of Europe, complete with servants, tutors, and even doctors. Some came back wiser; most just had a good time. Many seasoned observers disapproved of the behavior of their compatriots. Lord Chesterfield was most unflattering in his comments on young Englishmen. As early as 1758, Lady Mary Wortley Montagu, who had made Italy her home since 1739, wrote of the English youths who had arrived in her adopted

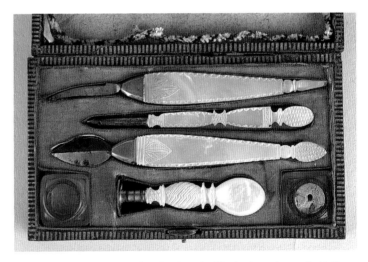

Figure 499. Exquisite mother of pearl and steel writing implements, supplied in the Palais Royal area of Paris, which was the favorite shopping playground of the aristocracy from the 1780s to the early decades of the nineteenth century. *Courtesy of Anne Brooks.* $1,400–1,600.

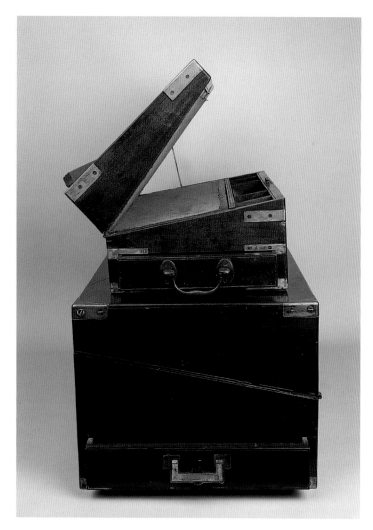
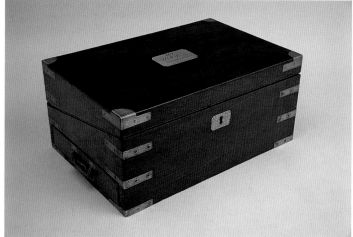

Figure 500. Profile of two typical Georgian writing boxes, both in mahogany with brass corners and side handles. Note the difference in the handles: the top box has drop handles; the bottom box has handles that are countersunk and fold-in flush with the surface of the box. Note how the top box is transformed into a reading stand. The box on the top is of a standard large size of 20" in length. The lower box is exceptionally large: it measures 26" in length. Ca. 1790–1820. $1,200–1,600 (upper), $3,000–3,500 (lower).

country; she stated that they had "acquired the glorious titles of Golden Asses."

Some commentators even thought that the young men had acquired more than shameful titles. Adam Smith, who traveled as a tutor to a Scottish duke's son, was of the opinion that the young returned home "unprincipled and dissipated." There was always a suspicion of the morals of foreign shores! On their return home, many rich young men joined the Society of Dilettanti for the appreciation and the exchange of ideas on the arts. Most adopted an air of Italianate superiority without really understanding the fundamental principles of classicism. It was not long before these youths acquired such manners of exaggerated affectation that they were reduced to the ranks of the "Macaronis." Their enthusiasm for their adopted posture was soon deflated by a plethora of caustic satires and caricatures, such as Hogarth's *Five Orders of Periwigs . . . Measured Architecturally.*

Most of the young men had not mastered the mental discipline that would have enabled them to acquire much knowledge. As Dr. Johnson put it in 1778, "He, who would bring home the wealth of the Indies, must carry the wealth of the Indies with him." However, the great man was also aware of the importance of acquainting oneself with the classical world. In 1776, he wrote to a friend, "A man who has not been to Italy, is always conscious of an inferiority." In the following decades the exodus to the Continent for months or years at a time continued and increased. The travelers needed strong writing boxes to help them record and store their memories.

By the standards of the day, traveling became easier and safer. Those who could afford to even brought their coaches to Calais or hired conveyances there. The new aesthetic awareness encouraged architects, artists, and thinkers to travel more extensively and bring back impressions, drawings, objects, and sculptures. Their knowledge was disseminated through publications and through professional application, and this in turn encouraged even more travel.

Men with entrepreneurial leanings went off to India, China, Africa, and wherever there were trading opportunities, traveling on English ships that were establishing their supremacy on the oceans. The mobility of a substantial section of the population became part of the social ethos.

*Above and left:*
Figure 501. This box bears two labels of N. Middleton. What makes this particularly interesting is the personal instructions on one label regarding the name to be engraved on the copper plate. On the other label there is another human note recording the giver in 1810. The extra-secret drawer under the nib tray, which springs out under the pen tray when the separating thin division is lifted up, is unusual. 15" wide. $?

Figure 502. A solid-mahogany writing box bound in heavy-gauge brass in the traditional military style, which remained popular for about five decades. Note the steel screws securing the heavy brass strips and corners. Ca. 1810. 20" wide. $3,800–4,500.

*Above:*
Figure 503. A mahogany-veneered box crossbanded in kingwood and decorated in the neoclassical style. Note the green background and the skillful shading on the exceptionally fine marquetry. 16" wide. Ca. 1780. $4,800–5,500.

## Features of George III Writing Boxes

Both traveling civilians and the army officers needed compact and strong writing boxes that could withstand the rough and tumble of strenuous journeys. This gave rise to the most popular type of eighteenth-century writing box: the military style, or campaign box. In look this is similar to the military chest.

The typical characteristics of writing boxes of the period are the following:

1. They are made of solid mahogany in rectangular shapes with a flat surface. Sometimes they are veneered with thick-cut veneer. The structure is almost a laminate, and this could have been done to increase stability. They are approximately eight to twenty inches long, ten inches deep when closed, and seven inches tall.

2. They open up to a sloping writing surface consisting of two flaps with space under them for paper, etc.

3. When open to the writing position, there is a space for inkwells and sand/pounce wells, pens, and quills on the top part of the box. In some early examples these are accommodated in a side drawer that follows the line of the slope.

4. They have a side drawer—occasionally two—for storing writing materials or correspondence. Sometimes they also have "secret" small drawers. The secret drawers were probably inspired by the work of German cabinetmakers who had encouraged experimentation with mechanical devices. By the time Sheraton's *Drawing Book* was published, little tricks were de rigueur. The secret drawers were usually concealed by a strip of wood that looked like part of the structure. The covering wood was released by various ingenious mechanisms that connected catches and springs by pulling or pushing on specific spots of the box. Benjamin Winter, a cabinetmaker working in London around 1799, made a point of mentioning secret drawers on his trade card. Some writing boxes have a prop-up hinge and a strip of wood that when fixed in place enables the outside to be used as a reading stand.

5. The inside of the box is made of unpolished mahogany, and the writing surface is covered in baize. The covering of the writing surface followed the customary cover of writing tables. Chippendale supplied a mahogany writing table to Paxton House in 1774. It was described as having "the middle part covered with Cloath … and drawers for papers, pen, ink, sand etc."

6. Most of the boxes are "bound" with thick brass corners screwed with steel screws. These are structurally important, in that they strengthen the joints and prevent "bruising" of the wood.

7. The earliest boxes have drop brass handles on the sides. In slightly later ones the handles are set in.

8. The outside wood, if in original condition, is finished with wax.

There are variations to the basic designs; sometimes specially commissioned boxes took care of the client's preferences. In 1774, Chippendale billed "The Right Honble Lord Irwin To a mahogany Traveling Strong Box with private partitions, drawer etc. compleat £2.18s.0d."

Very occasionally a writing box of this period was not made in the military style but was inlaid in the neoclassical tradition. Few such boxes have survived and are now very rare indeed. These were not made in solid mahogany but were veneered in saw-cut veneers in the manner of other types of boxes made during this period.

The solid-mahogany, brassbound writing boxes look good even when battered by usage. Restoration, which destroys their patination and gives them a later glossy look, is inappropriate and detrimental to their character.

Strong boxes for traveling continued to be made and used well into the nineteenth century. Oliver Goldsmith in the eighteenth century and Charles Dickens, Lord Byron, and Jane Austen a little later are just a few of the notable people whose sturdy writing boxes have been recorded.

By the beginning of the nineteenth century, many cabinetmakers specializing in boxes were offering "portable writing desks" with claims to patents and improvements.

Another style of writing box made during the late eighteenth century was influenced by French work. It had a tambour back section that rolled back when a front drawer was opened to reveal the pen-and-inkwell section. The front folded down into the writing surface over the drawer. This design was short lived, presumably because it was difficult to transport. (See Figures 495, 497.)

Figure 504. A solid-mahogany writing box stamped Gillows of Lancaster. The deceptive simplicity of the box belies the expertise and effort that were employed in its construction. The joinery is impeccable, as one would expect from a company renowned for its attention to quality. Inside the box, the wood is cut to a double-blind dovetail joint, which allows no room for inaccuracy. A box such as this would have gone on to arduous travels or wars. It had to withstand the vicissitudes of the road, the seas, and the battle ground, as well as climatic variations. Inside, the writing surface retains the original green cloth; there are spaces for pens and inkwells and an unusual secret space. There is a drawer on the side that is pulled out by one of the brass carrying handles. The long side drawer was the preferred feature for boxes that were expected to be used for necessary paperwork. Unusually, the box is edged with stained oak, which acts as a strengthening and tidying device while retaining the subtle unfussy look. 16" wide. Ca. 1790. $1,600–2,000.

## Exceptional Writing Boxes of the George III Period

These are stylistically the same as the writing boxes described previously, but they are made to perform extra services for their owner.

**1.** One type of such a writing box incorporates personal grooming items that a gentleman would require on his travels (e.g., shaving and general hygiene containers). The glass jars in such boxes had tops in Sheffield plate.

**2.** Another type incorporates a machine for printing. This comprises a heavy brass cylinder turned by a handle over a sliding surface, enabling the fast copying of maps, dispatches, etc.

**3.** The third type is what is now generally referred to as a ship captain's writing box, although such a box could have been used by other military men and travelers. Mechanically, these are the most complex and intriguing of all portable writing desks. Each one seems to differ in its arrangement of secret compartments and drawers. In some there are spaces for candlesticks and a reading stand. Their most remarkable feature is that they have a mechanism enabling them to be screwed down, thus achieving some stability on stormy seas. Furthermore, when secured in place and locked they are also protected from thieving hands. John Bradburn appears to have made such a box for George III. It is described in the Royal Accounts as "3 bottles to turn out at the ends with a Lock to suit the Hings, Key and 2 Brass Stops to stop it from sliding on the table."

**4.** The last unusual type is the triple-opening writing box. These were made to open in two directions: one part upward and the other down. The middle and down part form the two sections of the normal writing box. The upper part opens to an upright position. Inside, it has an attached fold-down board covered in leather. These boxes are most impressive when opened into the writing position, as they take care of the aesthetic view in front of the user. They also offer the added advantage of partially shielding the writing person from the heat of a fire, strong light, or prying eyes.

These four types of writing box are now rare, as are all such boxes with extra features. The rarest is perhaps the printing type. Triple-opening boxes can still be found if one looks hard enough.

## Writing Slopes, George III Period

Because writing slopes are more delicate and less travel worthy than flat boxes, not many were made during the eighteenth century. The ones dating from this period must have been commissioned by society ladies and men of certain refinement.

Figure 505. A rare, small-sized mahogany traveling box of dovetail construction, the compartmentalized interior with a Watt's patent copying machine ca. 1790. The box retains many of the accessories, including the crank handle and a special tool for adjusting the tension of the rollers. The roller mechanism of machined brass and steel is particularly interesting, in that the pressure and alignment of the rollers can be adjusted; the rollers are connected to each other by cog wheels. Watts was granted a patent in 1780. The patent covered not only the roller press, but also the ink, which had to be semisoluble in water. The original idea for the patent came from a discussion at the Lunar Society in Birmingham in 1779. Up to that time a copy had to be made by a scribe. Erasmus Darwin, a poet, a physiologist, grandfather of Charles, and a fellow member of the Lunar Society, described what he called the "Bigrapher, a duplex pen, a pen with two or more quills, by the help of which one may write two copies of anything; which will thus, in a single operation produce both the original and a transcript." Darwin's "Bigrapher" seems to describe Mark Isambard Brunel's "Polygraph," patented in 1799. This is an early portable example of the Watts patent, and there seem to be more mechanisms for adjustment than any other examples I have seen. Benjamin Franklin commissioned French makers to make such boxes for his friends. This example is of an unusual form, in that it is longer from back to front. 15.5" back to front when closed. Ca. 1790. $?

During the latter part of the century, internal traveling began to increase as roads improved and journeys became less arduous. Coaches offered more comforts to passengers, including a pullout writing surface on which one could write, assuming the shaking was not too bad! Visiting friends became a much-indulged-in custom. Although men did go for long visits to each other's stately homes, it was mostly ladies who treated themselves to prolonged house parties, with the men excusing themselves with "business" in London.

Writing slopes must have accompanied many a Georgian lady on her social rounds. The slopes were suited to genteel, personal use, and although they were made in much fewer numbers, they were more varied in style than masculine "military" writing boxes. Their decoration also allowed for more personal and even idiosyncratic preferences than writing boxes of the same period.

The postal service had been pretty inefficient and chaotic up to about 1784, when armed guards were introduced on mail coaches, rendering them for the first time safe, fast, and efficient. Delivery of letters was much improved and so was the art of letter writing, which became an accomplishment in its own right. As the century was drawing to its close, more fine slopes that could easily be carried from room to room and fit

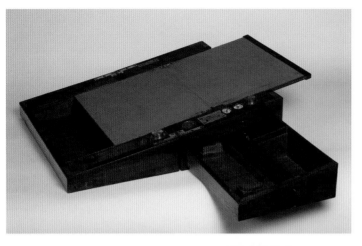

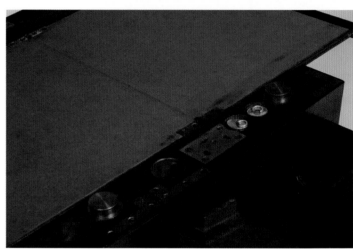

*This whole page:*
Figure 506. Rare polygraph by I. H. Farthing of Cornhill, London, to the patent design no. 129 of Marc Isambard Brunel (1769–1849) "for his Invention of a certain new and useful Writing and Drawing Machine, by which two or more Writings or Drawings, resembling each other may be made by the same Person at the same Time. Dated April 11, 1799." At the time of writing, only five examples are known. This has the earliest serial number and is the only example with secret drawers. The box is in the Campaign style, made of solid mahogany by using dovetail joints reinforced with brass corners, straps, and edges. The box has countersunk brass handles. There is a drawer designed to hold the polygraph mechanism when not in use. There are seven secret drawers concealed behind three sprung panels. The box retains its original paired inkwells. The polygraph mechanism that enabled the movements of one pen to be copied by another is now missing. The photo is of the surviving mechanism of machine no. 554, which is in the Science Museum London. Imagine a world before the copying machine. If you wanted a copy, it was necessary to write it again! Thomas Jefferson pronounced it "a most precious invention." The discussion at the Lunar Society in Birmingham inspired two inventions that changed the world. Both the Watts and the Brunel boxes seem to have played a pivotal part in the drafting of the US Declaration of Independence. 20" wide. Ca. 1803. *Photo of mechanism courtesy of the Science Museum London.* $?

comfortably within the interiors of fashionable drawing rooms and libraries were made to serve the need of private correspondence.

These boxes are smaller and of a more delicate structure than the solid mahogany, brassbound type. They are a development of the early sloping box shape, but now the slope is more gentle, the box shallower, and the construction much lighter. The front cover of the box opens back to reveal a sloping surface for writing. This consists of a flap, under which there is a space for paper. At the back there is a section for inkwells, pens, and other writing accoutrements.

Slopes were light and easy to carry. They were made mostly of pine—occasionally of mahogany or oak—and they were veneered in carefully selected saw-cut veneers of beautifully figured woods. Fruitwoods, yew, mahogany, satinwood, partridgewood, and many other timbers were combined in decorative patterns. The surface was often enhanced with stringing, crossbanding, and marquetry of the finest quality.

Some of the most exquisite writing slopes date from this period. A few betray work that can be attributed to the Tunbridge ware area. The partridgewood veneer combined with free-flowing floral inlays incorporating holly is a pointer to this region in its pre-"Tunbridge ware" classification.

By the end of the century, slopes of Tunbridge ware geometric inlay were also made.

Some of the most striking examples of penwork, painted, and chinoiserie slopes also date from this period. These were varnished to protect the pigments and inks, especially since the sloping front of the box could be used to prop up a book when the box was closed.

Small sloping boxes of the eighteenth century have the charm and period flavor of their era and are very much rarer than their "military" cousins.

Occasionally, boxes of this type combined sewing and writing elements; for example, a box could be made with a shallow drawer containing sewing tools. These are extremely rare. (See Fig. 20.)

*Above:*
Figure 507. A mahogany brassbound box with an extra section that opens up and remains in an upright position while the bottom part folds down to form the writing surface. Here it is not shown fully extended. The inside of the top is covered by a gold-embossed leather "envelope," which in turn folds down and offers extra space for documents. Note the small pockets on the leather section and the support half-round brass hinge. 20.2" wide. Early nineteenth century. $3,000–3,500.

Figure 508. A writing slope veneered in mahogany. The whole top is framed in pear wood; the center, with an oval of burr yew, crossbanded in mahogany. A symmetrical effect in the neoclassical tradition is achieved by the juxtaposition of timbers, grain, and figure. A subtle piece of inspired craftsmanship, the design belies the complexity of the work. Typical of the school of understated quality of the Georgian period. 14.5" wide. End of eighteenth century. $2,000–3,000.

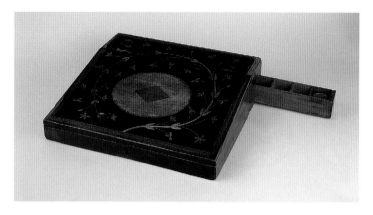

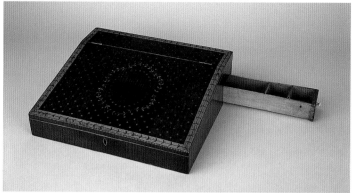

*Above:*

Figure 509. A harewood veneered writing slope. The top of the box is used as a writing surface, much in the manner of the portable desks of earlier centuries. There is no writing flap inside. When the lid is lifted, a space for writing paper is revealed. There are two small drawers at the back, under the top section of the box. The writing implements are stored in a small side drawer, which is placed under the internal drawers. The surface is inlaid in boxwood in a design of neoclassical inspiration blended with a degree of naturalism. The particular sweep of the inlay, the style of the design, and the choice of woods all point to early Tunbridge ware work. 14" wide. Ca. 1780. $?

*Above:*

Figure 510. A writing slope of delicate workmanship and finesse of design. It is veneered in harewood, with the banding in sycamore. The structure of the box is almost identical to the previous example, which makes me think that they were made in the same workshop, if not by the same hand. The inlay on this slope is exceptionally fine. It is very much within the neoclassical tradition, but the lightness of execution and the dot background design lighten the formality of the classical arrangement. The central oval-scalloped wreath design is elongated upward, which is contrary to tradition. The whole of the top is edged with a half-herringbone banding. There is a very thin line of half herringbone between the harewood and the sycamore surround. A truly delightful piece that has been allowed to age with grace. The inlay, especially the dots (which are executed in end grain), are slightly proud of the surface wood, which has settled with age. 13.4" wide. Ca. 1780–90. $?

## REGENCY WRITING BOXES AND SLOPES

Although George IV was Prince Regent only for the second decade of the nineteenth century, the term "Regency" typifies the period between the rigid neoclassicism of the Georgian era and the decorative style of the Victorians. In terms of portable desks, it is a period of strength combined with elegance and style.

### REGENCY WRITING BOXES

By the beginning of the nineteenth century, specialized cabinetmakers began to specifically offer "portable desks," copying machines, patent military traveling cases, and permutations within this theme.

Mahogany boxes with flat tops continued to be made with very slight modifications. The handles tended to be set in, and the escutcheons and top plates were often made in more-complex shapes.

It is difficult to generalize about exact dates, since styles overlapped and older features continued to be in use.

Customer preferences were considered, but although the rules were not rigid, we can detect a distinguishable trend toward more emphasis on refinement.

By the second decade of the nineteenth century, strengthening devices such as brass bindings, now often in the form of brass edgings, were enhanced with decorative features: extra stringing, circles, intricate escutcheons, ornamental top plates, and of course the Prince of Wales's favorite motif, the *fleur-de-lis*.

Instead of solid mahogany throughout, the boxes were made in plain mahogany for strength and stability and then veneered in figured mahogany, rosewood, or kingwood. The

*Above and left:*

Figure 511. A Rosewood veneered slope with corner and central inlays, the patterns of which are formed by combining and laying triangles of different woods separated by fine chequer stringing. Note the central star, which, although not very different overall in color from the background, gives a sharp and vital focus to the whole piece. The triangles of wood are skillfully juxtaposed to give bursts of light and darkness, without losing the subtlety of the whole composition. The work of a master who really loved his wood. Within the vandyke Tunbridge ware tradition, where each piece of inlay has to be specially selected. 13.75" wide. Ca. 1790. $4,000–5,000.

Figure 512. A writing slope in sycamore, the top with a parquetry design of exotic and native woods. Tunbridge ware. Note the wonderful selection and arrangement both of color and figure. 13" wide. Ca. 1800. $1,800–2,500.

Figure 513. A Rosewood veneered slope decorated in the neoclassical tradition. The top is decorated with a band of penwork, and a central oval cartouche of a hand-colored print depicting classical figures. This form of work is unusual on writing slopes. 9.5" wide. Ca. 1800. $1,500–2,500.

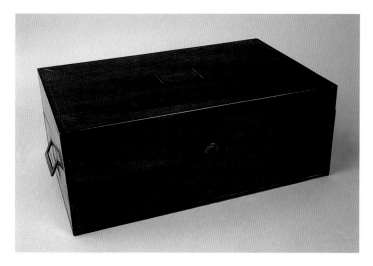

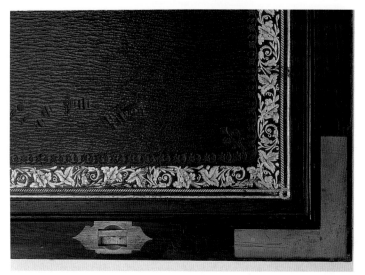

*Above:*

Figure 514. Writing box veneered in carefully selected Brazilian rosewood, edged in brass and ornamented with brass lines and spearhead-shaped brass ornaments in the four corners. The box has flat carrying handles and brass strengthening corners set into the interior facings. The original leather is finely tooled. The box bears the label of "David Edwards, at 21 King Str." (similar to sewing box in figure 440). It has all the characteristics of high-quality Regency work: the best rosewood, brass used both for beauty and strength, the ornament remaining subtle and unobtrusive, punctuating rather than embellishing. Original gold-embossed leather. 15" wide. Ca. 1815. $1,800–2,500.

veneers, which were saw cut and of a certain thickness, were carefully selected for their rich appearance. Rosewood and kingwood were the preferred woods. George Lawrence of Bond Street, London, billed George IV, in 1822, £3.13s.6d for an inlaid kingwood writing desk. Since this maker advertised himself as "pocket book, dressing case, and desk maker," the desks would have been of the portable kind.

During the second decade of the nineteenth century, French polishing gained ground as the preferred finish for wood. This enhanced the beauty of the dark striations within such woods as kingwood, rosewood, and figured mahogany. These were the most commonly used timbers for the veneering of boxes.

The writing surfaces of the boxes were covered in embossed velvet, or slightly later in gold-embossed leather. The interior wood was sometimes polished, especially after the second decade of the century. Secret drawers were becoming more popular than the side drawer. Occasionally, larger and deeper boxes had both secret drawers and side drawers.

The first boxes to depart from the military look still retained their robust qualities. Gradually, military features such as handles, thick brass edgings, and corners gave way to a more ornamental rather than strengthening use of brass. Dark rosewood or figured mahogany boxes were made with subtle brass stringing enhanced with circular small ornaments, stars, fleur-de-lis, or curvilinear escutcheons. Sometimes the basic structure was made of pine and not mahogany, rendering the box lighter and easier to carry.

Some boxes were more ambitiously ornamented in the manner promoted by Thomas Hope, with borders of inlaid brass ornaments. Hope, in his *Household Furniture* of 1807, described the benefit of such inlays on a flat surface: "enliven, without preventing it, by any raised ornaments, from being constantly rubbed and kept free from dust and dirt." Slightly later a box could be completely covered with inlays of leaves, flowers, and even grotesques in flowing combinations. Dark woods and bright brass are certainly mutually enhancing, and these high Regency boxes have an excellent period look.

More than any other type of box, the writing box does justice to this type of decoration, since its surface is large enough to testify to Sheraton's opinion in his 1803 *Cabinet Dictionary*: "the present mode of inlaying with brass is more durable and looks well into the black woods of any kind."

Bayley, Blew & Chapman, who described themselves as "dressing case makers and Perfumers to His Majesty and HRH Duke of York," are recorded in the accounts of George IV as having supplied (1828) a rosewood writing desk edged with brass and a buhl border, patent lock, and flaps covered with green velvet; interior glass mounted with silver, £15 12s. This included a solid leather traveling cover. This extra feature—the cover—was supplied with dressing boxes but not usually with writing boxes. The price for this box is very high indeed—at least five times what could be expected for a normal-quality

Figure 515. A solid-mahogany writing box in the military style, edged in brass and with countersunk brass handles. The lock is stamped Bramah with a crown. A Bramah lock immediately denotes high quality, and this box was definitely made for the top-quality end of the market. The woodwork is impeccable, using dovetailing to secure joints. When the flap is lifted, there is a surprise: not only does the box have a Bramah lock, but it was also made by Bramah. Bramah boxes are incredibly rare. This is the only labeled one I have ever handled, and I have seen only another one: a tea chest that is still in the hands of the Bramah family. I think Mr. Bramah was too busy thinking how to make his locks even more complicated. He became renowned for his locks, for which he was awarded a patent (1784). He was also responsible for

other ingenious inventions. The company still exists, offering modern security solutions. Joseph Bramah was obviously obsessive about security, which explains the next surprise: the skillfully concealed mechanism that allows for the secret drawers to be opened. First the lock has to be locked when the box is open. Then a rod has to be inserted into the lock, and the lever, which is hidden under the lock, must be pressed. The wooden panel springs open and the impeccably made small drawers are revealed under the pen-and-inkwell compartment. The whole structure is faultless, as one would expect from a perfectionist of Bramah's caliber. Bramah locks were used throughout the nineteenth century and later for high-quality boxes, especially dressing and jewelry boxes. 22" wide. Ca. 1815. $5,000–6,000.

*Above:*

Figure 516. A writing box that encapsulates the style of the Regency. The box is constructed in mahogany and veneered in well-figured Brazilian rosewood, strengthened and enhanced with brass surround and spaced brass ornaments. Note the fleur-de-lis motif in the four corners. The fleur-de-lis, being a symbol of the Bourbon kings of France, was a particular favorite of the Prince Regent. The box has a side drawer and secret drawers under the pen tray compartment. It also has a brass-hinged propping device, "a brass riser" as it was referred to in *The*

*Cabinet-Makers London Book of Prices*, for holding the box in a position that transforms it into a reading stand. A molded piece of wood is used to stop the books from sliding. This is stored inside the box, and it is held on to the outside by two prongs that fit into small brass-edged holes. When opened, candle sconces can be fixed just behind the pen tray, into similarly brass-edged small holes. A superb adaptation of strengthening elements to aesthetic consideration. 20" wide. Ca. 1815. $3,500–4,000.

Figure 517. Rosewood veneered box for carrying writing implements. The top has symmetrical brass inlaid ornaments. Ca. 1815–20. $800–1,000.

Figure 518. Rosewood veneered writing box, decorated on the top and front with a continuous band of brass inlay and a brass strip with cutout symmetrical ornament. This is the slightly later phase of brass inlay, when the ornament was no longer separate, but more in the style of boulle work. The gold-embossed leather is original. Note the unusual opening. The front of the box folds down to reveal the writing surface. The back, which covers the pen-and-inkwell sections, folds back in the manner of Regency writing slopes. However, unlike writing slopes, when closed the box has a flat surface, and the decoration forms a robust frame to the rich timber. There is space for storing papers under both flaps, as in a writing box. Ca. 1825. $5,000–6,500.

box—and reflects the appreciation of the intricate brasswork. Perhaps this was a writing/dressing box? (See Fig. 519.)

Another decorative device popular from the third decade of the nineteenth century was inlay in mother of pearl. This was very fine and usually consisted of stylized floral patterns. Birds and the occasional animal, such as deer, were sometimes incorporated within the design. If stringing was required, it was usually done in white metal.

Plainer rosewood boxes, with simple inlays of mother of pearl circles and metal stringing, were beginning to appear by the 1830s. This style continued to be made for a few decades, the veneers becoming thinner as the century progressed.

During the early part of the nineteenth century, a few striking Tunbridge ware boxes were made, making full use of the varieties of timber available to the makers at that particular period. Most of these were slopes, giving the opportunity to display the richness of the woods effectively on a slanting surface, although deeper boxes are not unknown. Parquetry, vandyke patterns, stringing, crossbanding, and inlays were skillfully combined and resulted in aesthetically pleasing pieces. The main body of the box was usually veneered in kingwood or rosewood, and sometimes in mahogany, yew wood, satinwood, or fruitwood. These boxes are often unique, idiosyncratic, and delightful, with a character all their own, and are very sought after by serious collectors.

### REGENCY WRITING BOXES: FEATURES

1. Thick veneers of mahogany, kingwood, rosewood, or occasionally yew or fruitwoods on a mahogany or pine base. Tunbridge ware makers preferred a pine base.

2. Brass inlay in fine lines, small ornaments, or floral swags

3. Fine mother of pearl inlay in controlled stylized designs

4. Marquetry of more naturalistic, neoclassical, or geometric designs

5. Secret drawers more prominent than side drawers. Leather and embossed velvet surfaces.

6. Robustness combined with refinement

Triple-opening writing boxes, captain's boxes, and combined writing and dressing boxes dating from this period are even rarer than eighteenth century examples. Dressing boxes were already offered by cabinetmakers and specialized box makers as separate items, and unlike earlier versions, most bottles and jars now had silver tops. This feature must have made it more important for the fittings to have their own separate containers.

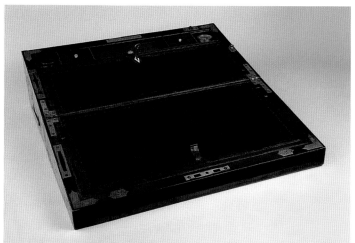

*This whole page:*

Figure 519. This is a box that needs a chapter to itself. It is both a writing and a dressing box. It has a screw-down mechanism, so that it can be secured to the floor or table. There are a plethora of tricks for revealing hidden sections and secret drawers. There are secret containers even in the back sections, the part that meets in the middle when the box is opened to the writing position. These fit very snugly in very precisely crafted spaces. The side drawer is fitted out as a dressing box. The tops of the glass jars are in silver, a most unusual feature in boxes of combined usage. The silver bears the design of a horse in a central cartouche, an indication that it belonged to an officer of the cavalry. It bears hallmarks for 1829. The maker's name is engraved on a brass strip inset into the inside front of the side drawer. The maker was George Palmer, who worked in St. James's London. He was a maker to the king and the royal family in the early 1830s, although it is not clear when he first attracted royal custom. A box of remarkable complexity and quality. 21.5" wide. $?

*Above:*

Figure 520. This is the earliest example of a box with a screw-down mechanism I have been able to find. It is also the only box I have ever seen that is covered in thick veneers, which are carved in contrasting ripple-effect patterns. I have seen similar work on frames used around seventeenth and early eighteenth century paintings from the Low Countries. The work on this box is finer than the carving on the frames, but it is compliant to the same aesthetic. The patterns are juxtaposed at angles that give a lively zigzag effect and catch the light at different angles. The brasswork is reminiscent of early Dutch snuff and tobacco boxes. The side lifts up in an ingenious way, not visible when the box is open, to reveal a secret compartment on the bottom of the box. This device was later used in English tea chests of the second half of the eighteenth century. There is also evidence of another secret space inside. The box has aged most gracefully. The raised parts have mellowed into a smooth honey patina. Is this a one-off example? It is very likely that the Dutch, who were pioneering seafarers and traders, first thought of the idea of the screw-down box. Such a box could be secured on the floor of a coach or a ship, or on a piece of furniture. This gave the contents additional protection both from movement and theft. An interesting piece of additional information about screw-down boxes: when Lord Thomas Clifford was sent by Charles the II to negotiate the Treaty of Dover in 1670, Lord Clifford carried the documents in a brass-strapped document box, probably made in Flanders, which also had a screw-down mechanism. There are a few known examples of this type of brass-strapped box. Seventeenth century. 16.6" wide. $?

Most of the decorative devices were the same as on the boxes. However, there are a few characteristics particular to slopes that help date such boxes more accurately. Sloping writing boxes made in the early part of the nineteenth century changed very little in style from those dating from the eighteenth century. The arrangement of the box was subtly modified so as to give more space for writing. They were no longer the direct descendants of the traveling desks of earlier centuries, but rather more compact versions of the writing box.

The introduction of a narrow flap at the back part of the top, which opened to reveal the pen-and-inkwell section, enabled the main flap to open downward, giving a longer writing surface. In addition to inlaid brass, mother of pearl, Tunbridge ware, and marquetry, there are very fine examples of penwork and painted slopes dating from this period. The decoration on these is of very high quality and artistic merit. They are now rare, but when seen they are a joy to behold.

## BOULLE

Another kind of writing slope that made its appearance in England at about this time was in the boulle style, in tortoiseshell and brass. Some of these were imported from France; others were made in England. The shapes of these slopes are elaborate versions of the wooden slopes. The back part is higher and often curved. The "apron" front is sometimes shaped, incorporating curves. The interiors are of polished rosewood, faux rosewood, or ebonized wood. The flaps are covered in velvet.

Before moving to the next section, a mention must be made of French boxes made at the time. Their shapes share certain characteristics with boulle-style boxes, in that they are more curvaceous than English boxes. They often feature intricate decoration in brass lines, and they make a feature of juxtaposing the figure of woods, such as kingwood, by placing pieces of veneer in opposing directions. The best of these boxes are very fine indeed.

## WRITING BOXES AND SLOPES AFTER 1830

The metamorphosis of English society that started in the middle of the eighteenth century culminated by the fourth decade of the nineteenth century in a social structure that would have been unrecognizable a hundred years earlier. Basically, what had been a mainly agricultural society had been transformed by land reforms, mechanical inventions, and expanding overseas trade into an industrial society of brisk trading and modified agricultural activity.

The greatly expanding population gravitated toward towns, with the result that many active commercial centers became established outside London. The necessity for goods to be transported gave great impetus to improved transport, which in turn facilitated a great boom in personal and business travel.

Figure 521. Veneered with a background of rosewood and a central panel of yew wood on the top. The front and sides of the box are veneered in a cube parquetry pattern in exotic and native woods. The top is inlaid with a bold star design. The cube design is larger than most Tunbridge ware of similar work, and the whole box has a slightly rustic appearance. The timbers used and the similarity to Tunbridge ware make it a good candidate for a very early example of this type of work. 14" wide. Late eighteenth to early nineteenth century. $2,800–3,300.

*Above:*
Figure 522. A combined writing box and printing machine. (See figure 505) The handle for turning the brass cylinder fits neatly into a specially prepared space in the box. When the cylinder turns, it propels a flat piece of wood, which is covered in baize, outward. The plate of what is to be printed was placed on this piece of flat wood, together with the paper. The pressure from the cylinder accomplished the printing. There are two side drawers for paper, both on the opposite side of the mechanism. This box must have seen some action. 18" wide. First quarter nineteenth century. *Courtesy of Kevin R. Kiernan.* $?

Education was encouraged in many levels of society to cope with new needs. Steam-driven presses (first used in 1814) lowered the cost of printing. Books, periodicals, journals, magazines, and so on became more plentiful, and mobility of ideas more possible. There was even a biweekly *Penny Cyclopedia*. Newspaper tax was reduced from 4d to 1d. Knowledge and awareness were becoming the prerogative of more and more people who had hitherto been excluded from anything except manual work.

In 1848, district schools were established by the government. By 1858, a Royal Commission had been set up that stated the aims of educating the people so that everyone would be able "to write a letter that was legible and intelligible, to make out or check a common bill . . . to know the position of the countries of the world." This was significantly more ambitious than merely being able to read the Bible.

The steel pen nib, which was first patented by Gillott in 1831, made the use of quills or rigid metal pens unnecessary. Blotting paper replaced sand and powder. Writing became simpler and cleaner. The Penny Post, introduced in 1840, enabled the sender to pay for letters at the sending end. Up to that time it was the recipient who had to carry the cost. This factor also contributed to an increase in correspondence. Within a decade the number of letters quadrupled. Christmas cards, greeting cards, and Valentines became a social necessity, since it was now so simple to remember one's friends with little notes. After 1870, new developments in photography encouraged the exchange of postcards from newly crowded holiday resorts.

Shops that appeared on London's Oxford Street as early as the eighteenth century and expanded into the fashionable Regent Street, Bond Street, and Burlington Arcade area during the Regency were now more widespread and accessible to most people. Many of these emporiums offered cabinetmakers' work "off the peg," or conveniently ordered through the shop. It is astonishing to look through shop catalogues of the mid-Victorian period and realize how many styles of boxes were readily available.

Easily portable writing boxes became a necessary personal accessory for anyone who transacted business, traveled, wrote letters from home, or simply went to the seaside for a week or two. Epistilography had joined the other virtues and accomplishments of every educated and fashionable person. Increases in wealth and improvements in sanitation and medical care all encouraged the growth of the Victorian family. Letter writing was the only way of keeping in touch with family members who had moved away.

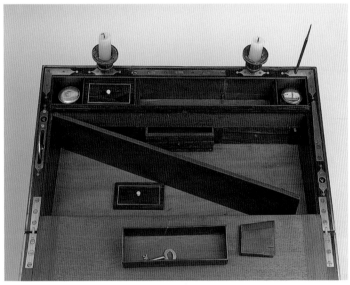

*This whole page:*

Figure 523. A Rosewood veneered box edged in brass, with a brass inlaid scrolling line pattern. This is a superb box that although constructed within the aesthetic vision of the Regency takes the style to its utmost limits. The proportions are pleasing, the workmanship impeccable, and the ornament bold and at the same time restrained. It is unusual in that the inlaid design is worked into the whole surface of the box as a complete composition. The interior of the box holds many surprises. It has the screw-down mechanism, a most unusual feature in an ornamented box. The key for turning the triangular-headed screw fits in the long slot behind the round hole where the spring-loaded screw is. It further has many tricks for revealing secret drawers and compartments, including a false base that, when the right spring is released, springs up to reveal a shallow secret compartment. There are more secret drawers even within this space! An ingenious and handsome box. Outstanding. Ca. 1820. $?

During the 1830s and 1840s, craftsmen making writing boxes continued to develop the structural and decorative possibilities of the earlier decades of the century. Machinery was increasingly used for cutting veneers, dovetailing, and other woodworking processes. At this stage the new operative possibilities were used as an aid to perfection and precision, rather than as a means to automatic mass production. Craftsmen still took pride in their work and exercised their own aesthetic criteria in the creation of their wares.

Mother of pearl inlay was still popular, and in the 1830s a few high quality boxes had acquired structural details, such as fielding and gadrooning, creating a sense of depth and perspective. Contrasting woods were also occasionally used for striking effects. By the 1830s, brass decoration was more in the design of a continuous Vitruvian scroll, rather than the more elaborate stylized flora of early Regency. By the middle of the nineteenth century, this style of decoration, which used large sheets of brass, went out of favor.

A new decorative style that became fashionable during the second half of the century was inlay in combinations of mother of pearl, abalone shell, and brass. Such inlays sometimes incorporated silver, ivory, bone, and wood. The style of this work was significantly different from earlier decoration. The brass was used mostly as thin lines, or if wider, it was engraved. The shell material, which was in different colors, suggested more-naturalistic representations, as well as light and shade. The designs were mostly floral, sometimes with a central vase motif. Even though the composition was stylized, it aspired to a more lively, rather than formal interpretation, and to a three-dimensional, fluid effect. This style was aesthetically more readily appreciated. Furthermore, technically it did not require the precision of execution necessary for controlled neoclassical designs.

This type of inlay was used mostly in conjunction with veneers of rosewood or coromandel wood on a few boxes of good quality. The basic box was often made in solid mahogany, or in pine veneered inside in thick mahogany, which made it heavier than other boxes of the period. In addition to designs of flowers, representations of birds, animals, and even humans were sometimes depicted in brass/shell combinations. Because both the materials and the work must have been very expensive, few boxes were decorated with this type of inlay. Lund of London and Austin of Dublin were two makers whose labels have been found attached to boxes with this type of work.

As the century progressed, brass surrounds or bandings were made of thinner brass and secured by small brass pins that, unlike the earlier screws, were invisible. Marquetry was usually executed in a combination of rosewood and bird's-eye maple, creating floral borders in a style aiming at some degree of naturalistic representation. Marquetry in the neoclassical style, or multitimber parquetry, was no longer fashionable.

After the first decade of Victoria's reign, writing boxes and slopes, like all categories of such work, seem to follow a dichotomous route. There were the majority of boxes made to a certain standard to sell to the increasingly wealthy middle classes. There were also the superbly crafted and finished boxes made with impeccable attention to detail. These were manufactured to high criteria of technical perfection. The achievement of this excellence was aided by new mechanized processes. A few makers straddled the period between the last years of the Georgian era through William IV to Victoria. These brought the consciousness of quality to bear on the new style trends. This strand of quality survived until the end of the century, albeit in increasingly fewer examples.

By the last quarter of the nineteenth century, brass inlay all but disappeared. Brass straps and corners became more popular than surrounds and decorative inlays. The brass bindings were made of thinner brass, and they were decorative rather than protective, although they did contribute some degree to the strengthening of the joints and corners. The veneers were by now cut quite thin. The basic structure of the box was made mostly of pine. The veneers were sometimes of rosewood and mahogany, but mostly of walnut, both in straight and burr figure. Dark, luxurious coromandel wood veneers were used on high quality boxes. Coromandel, amboyna, and veneers of other expensive woods were still cut quite thick.

Marquetry in wood also all but disappeared. The only wood inlay that featured on a significant number of writing boxes appeared in the last three decades of the century, in the form of pre-prepared geometric strips. (See Figure 102)

*Above:*

Figure 524. A triple-opening, Rosewood veneered box, edged and strung in brass. The box combines strength, elegance, and impeccable workmanship in the Regency tradition. Rosewood boxes of this form are more unusual that their mahogany cousins. Ca. 1825. $5,500–7,000.

Figure 525. Rosewood veneered writing slope with line and fleur-de-lis decoration in inlaid brass. The sloping surface is unusually edged with boxwood. The velvet is original and in keeping with the period. The understated elegance of such a piece is characteristic of the period. 14" wide. Ca. 1815. $1,000–1,500.

Figure 527. A French slope that typifies the best features of this particular type of work. The sloping front is gently undulating. This enhances the effect of the skillful veneering, which is done by laying pieces of kingwood with the grain following different directions so as to catch the light and create subtle patterns. The inlay is in brass and mother of pearl. The inside is similar to English slopes, except that in typical French fashion, the wood is stained and polished to look like rosewood. The writing surface is covered in velvet. Ca. 1835. *Courtesy of Mary Harris Russell.* $3,000–3,500.

*Above:*
Figure 526. A penwork decorated writing slope in chinoiserie designs. Note that the painting and drawing is flat, relying for its effect on the brush/pen strokes. The artist endeavored to encapsulate the magic of Cathay in a scene of calm and tranquility. Note the repartee between the central figures. Their facial expressions are interpreted with a few effective strokes. This is a departure from the eighteenth century oriental designs, in that it strives for more realism and consistency of perspective. A piece imbued with the spirit of its time. Original interior. 11" wide. Ca. 1800. $6,000–8,000.

*Above:*
Figure 528. A French slope in bird's-eye maple and ebonized wood decorated with fine inlay brasswork and colored composition. A later, lighter interpretation of boulle-type marquetry. 12" wide. Mid-nineteenth century. $2,000–2,500.

### CHARACTERISTICS

**1.** Basic box in mahogany or later in pine; the interior, if in pine, was usually veneered in mahogany.

**2.** Veneered in thin, knife-cut veneer, which was cut by mechanized processes, in walnut, bird's-eye maple, burr chestnut, or rosewood. In more expensive boxes the veneer was still quite thick, usually coromandel, rosewood, amboyna, or figured mahogany.

**3.** The brass bindings were either in the form of now-rounded brass surround or brass corners and straps. The brass was glued and secured by almost invisible small brass pins.

**4.** The outside and inside wood was French polished and glossy.

**5.** The flaps were covered mostly in leather, but velvet was still used.

**6.** Secret drawers invariably superseded the side drawer, although sometimes both were still used on very large boxes. The mechanism for opening the secret drawers was simplified and was the same on all boxes.

## WRITING SLOPES AFTER 1830

The form of writing slopes remained the same as the form of earlier periods, but decoration varied significantly.

Mother of pearl and brass inlay decoration was used most effectively on the slanting surface of slopes, creating some of the most effective Victorian boxes.

Slopes in beautifully figured walnut, amboyna, or coromandel with minimal decoration were also made. These relied simply on the beauty of the wood and were on the whole of very high quality.

## GOTHIC REVIVAL

Writing slopes and desk boxes were, in box terms, the main exponents of the Gothic Revival. Such boxes were made mostly in mahogany and veneered in coromandel or walnut. They were decorated with applied designs of perforated and engraved brass. Jasper medallions were sometimes inserted in the center of the brass motif. More rarely, costly *pietra dura* plaques were incorporated in the design. Occasionally, such boxes formed an integrated desk set, with the back part higher and more rounded, or even in the form of a domed envelope/card box. Sometimes they were part of a set, with blotter folder, inkstand, and separate envelope box. These boxes vary a great deal both in the quality of the woodwork and the brasswork. The best examples combine impeccable workmanship with glamour. They were obviously expensive to produce and looked good on new, massive Victorian desks.

*Above:*
Figure 529. A Rosewood veneered writing box that opens in three sections. It still has brass carrying handles, but the inlay is in mother of pearl. The design is very controlled and symmetrical, still very much in the neoclassical tradition. The pearl contrasts well with the rich tones of the wood and is inlaid with meticulous precision. The top is covered on the inside with a flap in gold-embossed leather. The box is of impeccable workmanship with fine detail. It is very unusual to find a box of this form dating from this period and with such decoration. 16" wide. Ca. 1835–40. *Courtesy of a private collection.* $3,500–4,000.

Figure 530. A writing box veneered in walnut, the top veneered with a parquetry pattern punctuated with Masonic symbols. Freemasonry enjoyed a period of popularity after the Napoleonic Wars, and it was considered a mark of distinction to join the fraternity of the people who were perceived to be distinguished. 15.25" wide. Difficult to date accurately. Ca. 1840 (?). $?

Figure 532. Rosewood veneered writing box inlaid in brass and mother of pearl. The inlay with flags and cannon under a pre-Imperial queen's crown is in the nature of a trophy of arms. An unusual design, it is likely to have been a special commission. 13.75" wide. Mid-nineteenth century. $?

Figure 531. The central panels of this box are veneered in amboyna, with the raised framing parts veneered in coromandel and inlaid with white metal lines and mother of pearl. This exceptional box is built using fielded panels to create a three-dimensional effect. The gadrooned framing bridges the difference in depth of the two surfaces. The inlay of mother of pearl is executed within very strict square patterns. The whole design is very controlled and gives the impression of an important structure. In this it succeeds in incorporating the Egyptian influence, which usually found expression only in boxes whose purpose did not limit their shape. The original leather too is of excellent quality, the embossed pattern echoing the square corner punctuation of the exterior. The interior, including the secret drawers, is veneered in satinwood. A fine example. 16" wide. Ca. 1840. *Courtesy of Mary Harris Russell.* $3,500–4,500.

*Above:*
Figure 533. A mahogany writing box veneered in coromandel and inlaid in mother of pearl, abalone shell, and brass. The exotic horsemen are an unusual theme. The work is executed skillfully, utilizing the color and light values of the shells to create a sense of movement. The box is immaculately finished inside, the coromandel facings punctuated with mother of pearl dots. High-quality work with a very smooth look that betrays dependence on mechanical processes. 15.8" wide. Mid-nineteenth century. $5,000–7,000.

Figure 534. A box veneered in rosewood and maple, forming a marquetry of leaves and birds. The birds are depicted more boldly than in similar earlier work. 14" wide. Mid-nineteenth century. $800–1,200.

Figure 535. Rosewood veneered writing slope with very fine inlay in engraved brass and ivory. The inlay is symmetrically placed, but there is more realism in the interpretation of the delicate floral bouquets than in Regency work. There is also clear influence of French craftsmanship in the engraved brass, which is now used as a purely decorative material. 13.5" wide. Ca. 1835. $2,500–3,500.

Figure 536. This is a very good example of a high quality writing box of this period in traditional design. Made of mahogany, it is veneered in Brazilian rosewood and edged in rounded brass. The interior is well fitted and polished, with secret drawers. This style of work could date from the 1830s to the end of the century and was done in a variety of woods. Earlier examples like this one are usually finished in thick rosewood veneers. Later examples are veneered in walnut or coromandel. 17.5" wide. $1,500–2,000.

*Right:*
Figure 537. A mahogany box veneered in thick coromandel veneer. A heavy, high quality mid-Victorian box that exemplifies the best practices of the time. The mechanically cut timber made for the immaculate fitting of the parts, such as secret drawers, pen trays, and flaps. The brass surround was still protective and looked striking against the dark wood. 19" wide. $2,000–3,000.

Figure 538. A very good example of a brass-edged, burr walnut–veneered writing box, of the second half of the nineteenth century. Note that no screws or pins are visible on the brass. The brass is thinner, and so are the veneers. It has the typical writing surface covered in leather, pen tray and inkwell arrangement, and secret drawers. By now, the mechanism for releasing the panel in front of the drawers was standard. The interior of the box is polished. 15.5" wide. $2,000–2,500.

Figure 540. A typical box dating from the second half of the nineteenth century. The brass, although affording some protection, was primarily used for decorative effect. Such boxes were still made with care, the veneers selected for figure and the surface usually covered in gold-embossed leather or embossed velvet. The customer was usually given a choice of veneering timber, lining material, and decoration, retaining some of the personalized quality of earlier times. 11.75" wide. Second half nineteenth century. *Courtesy of Mylissa Fitzsimmons-Grieve.* $600–800.

Figure 539. A burr walnut veneered box with mother of pearl escutcheon. A typical box made during the last three decades of the nineteenth century. The veneers were by now quite thin, but this enabled woods with very attractive figure to be used for covering a number of boxes. 11.75" wide. Second half nineteenth century. $600–800.

Figure 541. Rosewood veneered and crossbanded slope with white metal and mother of pearl decoration. An elegant box with well-constructed beautiful interior. 17.9" wide. Ca. 1835. $900–1,200.

Figure 542. A slope veneered in marquetry executed with rosewood and maple. Centrally it is inlaid with a design of birds among trees in wood and mother of pearl. The introduction of mother of pearl into this type of work is most unusual. The work is exceptionally fine. 13.8" wide. Ca. 1840. $2,000–2,800.

Figure 543. Rosewood veneered slope, with mother of pearl inlay. The inlay is arranged in formal strips around the box, with a central square motif of a horse and a bird. The large bird and especially the encircling plant are completely fantastical, but the horse is accurately executed. The outlines of the mother of pearl are engraved with fine lines, giving the pattern a sharp definition. Excellent-quality mother of pearl work. 14" wide. Ca. 1835–1840. $1,200–1,500.

Figure 544. A high-quality writing slope in burr chestnut, marked on a small plaque "Parkins and Gotto." Although nothing unexpected, the slope is superior to a standard example. The top part is gently rounded. The inside and the pen tray part are veneered in satinwood, which contrasts well with the coromandel facings of the writing surface. Inside it is impeccably finished and, unusually for a slope, it has secret drawers. 14" wide. Ca. 1840. *Courtesy of Naomi Moore.* $2,500–3,500.

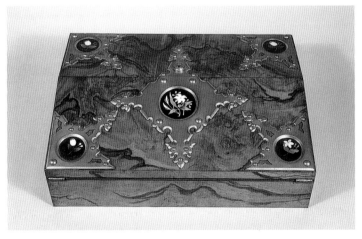

*Above and right:*
Figure 545. A box made by the firm of Betjemann's. Betjemann's was in the forefront of innovation and top quality, using machinery and skill in an effort to achieve very smooth finishes and stable structures. This box epitomizes the new fashion for the neo-Gothic. The brass shapes are punched with precision to achieve a certain depth. They are also gilded. The inserts are panels of *pietra dura*. Black slate is inlaid with marble in different colors in delicate designs of flowers. Inside, the slope is lined in gold-embossed blue velvet, which complements the design. The interior facings are in coromandel. The maker's mark is engraved on the lock plate, and the retailer's name is on a small strip of brass under the flap. 14" wide. Last quarter nineteenth century. $4,000–5,500.

able cabinets were made in Europe during the sixteenth and seventeenth centuries as miniature versions of large cabinets, or Spanish *vargueños*. Stylistically, they were not different from larger pieces of furniture, but instead of having their own stands, or standing directly on the floor, they were made to stand on a table, on a desk, or in an alcove.

The decorative techniques adopted for the decoration of boxes were naturally introduced by cabinetmakers who made furniture and also smaller, portable cabinets. During the eighteenth century, the table cabinet underwent a transformation. Instead of being a small replica of a piece of furniture, it became more like a box in the shape of a piece of furniture.

During the seventeenth and early eighteenth centuries, table cabinets were made throughout Europe and the European colonies. The stylistic influence of these small pieces of furniture is demonstrable in ivory and tortoiseshell work, as well as in chinoiserie and marquetry.

One kind of work that influenced English craftsmen to a great extent was the decoration on cabinets introduced from southern Germany and Flanders as early as the sixteenth century. These cabinets were inlaid with elaborate compositions representing mostly buildings endowed with a touch of Moorish fantasy. The inspiration for such designs was derived from Lorenz Stoer's *Geometria et Perspectiva*, which was published in 1567. The work was carried out by intarsia workers who had settled in Augsburg. One important cabinetmaker was known as Master H.S. His work was influential throughout Europe and even Italy, where elaborate marquetry had already been practiced for more than two centuries.

A particular characteristic of these cabinets was the extensive use of scorched woods to introduce light and shade within a very subtle range of color. This practice, on a smaller scale, was widely adopted for marquetry decoration on boxes during the second half of the eighteenth century.

Figure 546. A group of Regency table cabinets, which show the successful combination of different architectural elements and decorative techniques. The dark-green leather-covered cabinet at the front opens up to reveal yellow leather-covered drawers enhanced with gilt metal handles. The top lifts with a trick opening to reveal a concealed compartment. 10.6" wide. It dates from the second decade of the nineteenth century. Front cabinet: $5,000–6,000.

*This whole page:*
Figure 547. A South German cabinet dating from the end of the seventeenth century or the beginning of the eighteenth. Note the particular perspective and shading. The outside door panel is inlaid with birds and flowers. It was the usual practice to reserve the architectural scenes for the interior of such cabinets. Sometimes, especially in smaller pieces, the exterior was not decorated. 16.5" wide (closed). $16,000–20,000.

*Left and below:*
Figure 548. A Rosewood veneered and brass-inlaid table cabinet. This exemplifies the influence of Egyptian architectural prototypes on the work of cabinetmakers. The lines and decoration of the piece guide the vision upward to the superbly constructed top. Note the robustness of the carved elements, which reinforce the idea of monumental strength. The top panel is inlaid with a brass-mirror-matched anthemion. The front folds down to provide a writing surface and reveal a series of drawers. This is an unusual arrangement, which allows for unity of design at the front. A very curious feature is the central brass inlay, which depicts lambs under a tree. Although the tree and the animals are arranged in a symmetrical, still way, they introduce a rather romantic bucolic note, which is surprising but not discordant with the stylized borders. A very individual piece. 10.5" wide. Ca. 1815–20. $7,000–9,000.

Sometimes, southern German cabinets are described as "Nonsuch," referring to the name of one of the palaces of Henry VIII. This appears to be a nineteenth-century term that has no justification other than usage. The work on these pieces is extraordinary. They combine marquetry at its best with a feel of the antique world of arcane mystery.

In England, table cabinets made during the eighteenth century were constructed like miniature cupboards or presses, with doors opening outward to reveal a series of drawers. Since these pieces were regarded as something to be observed from close proximity, and therefore a style statement, they were made to be decorated in the fashion of the time.

Chinoiserie decoration was regarded as the most exotic new trend of the time. Table cabinets japanned and decorated with scenes of Cathay were often worked with more care and panache than many larger pieces of furniture. (See Fig. 38.)

A few very understated, elegant table cabinets were also made in figured mahogany with fine stringings. These were either in the form of cupboards with drawers, or arranged for carrying medical bottles and instruments.

The table cabinet was also the ideal object for the interpretation of neoclassicism. The proportions of the cabinet, unlike those of other boxes, allow for more height than width, a feature that prompts architectural design. The cabinetmakers of the period made full use of this characteristic and produced table cabinets in striking forms with the unmistakable flavor of the Regency.

Judging by the fact that during the Regency, table cabinets were decorated in the fashionable methods of the time and that the interior arrangements were more like boxes rather than furniture, it is reasonable to conclude that most were made by makers specializing in box making.

Penwork cabinets were decorated both on the outside doors and on the inside drawers. Some were even decorated on the flip side of the doors. The decoration was of chinoiserie, classical themes, fauna and flora, and rustic and Gothic themes. These cabinets were often made to contain sewing tools in the top section, which opened from the top, like a box. The other drawers were usually empty.

Tunbridge ware cabinets dating from the early part of the nineteenth century were decorated with parquetry and

Figure 549. A penwork cabinet, the top of which combines structured pyramid and scrolling elements, which together with the tall elegant form achieves a striking hybrid Regency style. 9.25" wide. Ca. 1810. $7,000–9,000.

vandyke patterns. The tops and doors were usually completely covered in parquetry. Such relatively large surfaces gave the maker the opportunity to show off not only his skill, but also the wonderful range of timbers he had at his disposal.

Wonderful Chinese lacquer cabinets were imported from the beginning of the nineteenth century and for the next few decades. These cabinets sometimes stand on a pedestal. Inside there are four, five, or six drawers with turned ivory knobs. The drawers are also decorated but are not fitted for any particular purpose.

Very rarely, a Chinese table cabinet was made with fitted drawers in the style of a series of English boxes. These compendium cabinets were probably the result of special commissions, and as such they are of the highest quality. (See Fig. 237.)

The time between George IV and Queen Victoria was an interesting period in terms of cabinetwork. The architectural forms and stylized decoration of the Regency had reached the zenith of robust beauty, with no element of sentimentality. The table cabinets dating from the short period of William IV are the epitome of the style of this brief moment of aesthetic history.

These table cabinets are veneered in figured rosewood and feature structured details emphasized with gadrooning. They stand on stepped pedestals, their tops are architecturally structured, and they are decorated with mother of pearl inlay. The inlay, which is usually very fine and precise, combines fluid and delicate elements within a neoclassical design tradition. The interior arrangements of such cabinets rendered them the perfect personal compendium.

Right:
Figure 550. A cabinet that combines more-rounded Regency elements, with its domed top and shaped apron. The chinoiserie design is well spaced and executed. 10" wide. Ca. 1820. $7,000–9,000.

Below left and right:
Figure 551. A superb quality example of a William IV compendium table cabinet. The form is structured so as to convey an architectural three-dimensional effect, with fielded panels and carefully orchestrated angles and concave lines. The handles and feet are turned and carved with extra detail. There are edgings and frames of gadrooning, giving strength and definition. The mother of pearl inlay is symmetrically arranged in the neoclassical tradition, although the central motif of a deer under a winding plant incorporates echoes of the Tree of Life design and looks forward to a more naturalistic interpretation of flora. The interior of the cabinet is arranged so that the top part provides a fitted sewing section; the middle drawers, a jewelry and storage section; and the bottom drawer, a folding-out writing slope. 14" wide. Ca. 1835. *Courtesy of Christodoulides Family Collection*. $6,500–7,000.

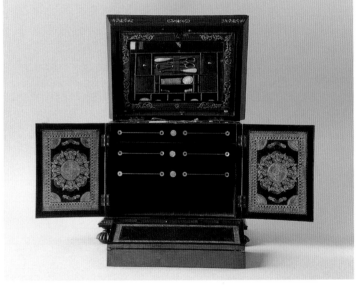

During the first decades of the Victorian period, a few table cabinets were made in rosewood and coromandel. These were decorated with inlays of brass and mother of pearl, in more fluid and naturalistic designs than the earlier examples.

As the second half of the nineteenth century progressed, table cabinets came full circle, abandoning the architectural form and returning to basic rectangular shapes. Straight doors enclosed brass-handled drawers. Sometimes the cabinets were edged in brass or had brass corners in the fashion of writing boxes of the period. The preferred woods for veneers were coromandel and walnut.

Tunbridge ware cabinets were now decorated with designs of castles, flowers, ruins, etc., in wood micro-mosaic. They were mostly smaller than earlier parquetry cabinets.

Papier-mâché was the only medium to be developed in more-ambitious forms at a time when everything else was returning to straight lines. Papier-mâché lent itself to being molded in plastic shapes, and this quality enabled makers to produce cabinets with rounded tops, bombe sides, molded pedestals and plinths, and generally shapes with few, if any, straight lines. The multiple large surfaces allowed for quite elaborate decoration, such as Gothic scenes, combinations of floral designs and birds, and generally free flowing asymmetrical painting.

Throughout the eighteenth and nineteenth centuries, collectors' cabinets were also made. These consisted of a series of drawers, sometimes enclosed by doors. At a time when specimen collecting reached epidemic proportions, these cabinets allowed collectors to display their "finds" for their own pleasure and to show them off to their friends

*Left:*
Figure 552. A hardwood- and shell-inlaid Chinese cabinet. The quality and color of the shell is used with extraordinary skill to define both the figures and the landscape. Very fine work. 15" wide. Mid-nineteenth century. $2,000–3,000.

*Above and left:*
Figure 553. Japanese-export-lacquer table cabinet of exceptional quality. The cherry blossoming trees and landscapes are rooted in the Japanese decorative tradition. Flat painting and raised lacquer create three-dimensional effects, giving the piece texture and depth. The treatment of the cockerel combines light strokes with robust patterns to suggest both the delicate nature of the feathers and the strength of the bird. 17.5" wide. Ca. 1865. $3,000–5,000.

In addition to the boxes covered in previous chapters, a variety of boxes were made for specific or nonspecific purposes. The second category is by far the largest. During the eighteenth century, and to a lesser degree during the nineteenth century, empty boxes, or boxes with trays not designed for particular requisites, were made in considerable numbers. These boxes were stylistically similar to boxes made for identifiable purposes.

One type of box worthy of mention is the "specimen" box. Specimen boxes appeared at the end of the eighteenth century and continued to be made during the early part of the nineteenth century. They were boxes that displayed to full advantage the different timbers available at the time and the various combinations of shapes in which they could be arranged. Sometimes one box was veneered with different parquetry designs on every side. Most of these boxes featured striking contrasts and sharp defining lines. The Tunbridge ware parquetry and vandyke-patterned boxes belong to this category.

Sometimes a box was made to demonstrate or explore a different decorative technique. Such boxes defy categorization and are more often than not unique.

Trick openings, such as the lining up of letters to make up words to open a box, were sometimes used to create teasingly amusing containers.

Boxes for specific purposes multiplied as the needs of the population became more defined. The interiors were arranged according to their contents. For example, decanter boxes for carrying bottles of spirits were made both for traveling and for domestic use. In the late nineteenth century, the decanter box was mostly superseded by the open-top tantalus, which survives to this day.

Another category was the paint box, which came in a variety of designs and was used both by professionals and amateurs. Many of these boxes were rather plain, but a few did feature inlays and decorative devices found on other types of boxes. The majority was fitted for watercolors, but other pigments were also accommodated. The watercolor boxes must have been taken on many a journey, judging by the proliferation of topographical watercolors dating from the eighteenth and nineteenth centuries.

From the eighteenth century onward, the changing social and economic landscape encouraged the flourishing of diverse professions and boosted the class position of many men whose status had hitherto been considered no higher than that of tradesmen. Doctors and apothecaries gained respect and wealth, and many furnished themselves with portable cabinets and boxes in which they could carry their medicines when visiting patients at home. (See Fig. 82.)

Some boxes were made for individual purposes, and as such are probably unique. The most acclaimed eighteenth century actor, David Garrick, was given the Freedom of the City of Stratford-on-Avon in 1768, in a casket bearing in relief the

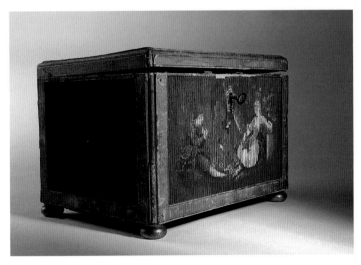

*Above:*
Figure 554. A box painted using the lenticular principle to reveal different images when viewed from different angles. The front is painted both with an image of two figures in eighteenth-century costume and a rococo floral design. All four sides and the top are similarly decorated, giving ten images in all. There is a stamp on the leather-covered surround that reads "K.K. Patent." Our research has not yet uncovered further information of the origins of this most extraordinary box. $?

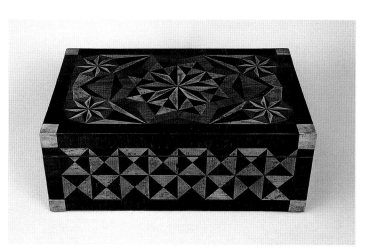

Figure 555. Veneered with bird's-eye maple contrasted with darker and midtone woods, the geometric patterns on this box utilize the qualities of the different timbers to create a sharp and striking design. 14" wide. Ca. 1800. $2,000–2,500.

Figure 556. This is an example of a more unusual but equally attractive veneering technique: it uses only a few specimens of wood, of similar color. These are combined in minutely varied patterns, exploiting the grain and pattern of the timber rather than its color. The appeal of such boxes was very subtle, since they were not as immediately dramatic as the boxes veneered in sharply contrasting patterns and woods. This explains their rarity, since their beauty could be appreciated only by patrons whose taste was quietly refined. The main woods in this box are yew and rosewood. 14" wide. Ca. 1790. $3,000–4,000.

Figure 557. A decanter box veneered with mahogany, inlaid in the Dutch style. 7" wide. Ca. 1840. $2,000–3,000.

Figure 558. A paint box of typical form with watercolor cakes, mixing palette, and other painting and drawing utensils. 10.7" wide. Mid-nineteenth century. $800–1,000.

portrait of Shakespeare surrounded by naked nymphs, rococo scrolls, trees, and a classical temple in the background. The wood of the box was reputed to have come from the mulberry tree in the Bard's garden.

Another unique box I have come across bears witness to its past both by its contents and the transfer decoration on the surface. Whether the owner was a professional, or even a competent witch, we will never know. One hopes that she/he was a benign practitioner of the occult.

This magical note is a good point with which to conclude; after all, every box has its magic.

Figure 561. Made to hold small watch parts, this most unusual watchmaker's box encloses ten welled compartments. The individual lids decorated with a layer of fine fretwork offer extra protection to the delicate watch parts. 6.25" wide. Ca. 1810. $1,500–2,000.

Figure 559. A label with "ROBERSON & COMPY." on the inside of a watercolor box, showing other boxes, painting equipment, and classical still-life props. 10" wide. Ca. 1835.

Figure 560. A paint box containing phials of powdered overglaze enameling colors for painting on ceramics. It was produced by Reeves and Son for Hancock and Son, who during the Victorian period were the owners of the Royal Worcester porcelain factory. The porcelain plaque illustrates samples of colors, after firing, contained in the box. 10.5" wide. Second half nineteenth century. $1,500–2,000.

*Above:*
Figure 562. A pine box decorated with scenes of the dark arts. The detail is from the inside of the lid: an old witch is prompted by the winged and horned devil, while she tutors two young women. 13.5" wide. Ca. 1840. $?

*Above and right:*
Figure 563. A Venetian wig box decorated in japanned work in the manner advocated in Stalker and Parker's *Treatise of Japanning and Varnishing* (see chapter 3). The decoration is unusual in that it depicts a vase of flowers in realistic perspective and not oriental scenes in the chinoiserie manner. This example demonstrates "japanning" as a technique rather than a combination of craft and theme. 11.75" wide. Ca. 1750. $3,500–4,000. *Wig courtesy of Thomas Kibling of Counsel.*

*Above and right:*

Figure 564. A straw workbox for the exchange of *billet-doux*. Because the activity that such boxes facilitated was delicate and often tantalizingly risqué, they were of exquisite taste, hinting at the superior aesthetic sensitivity of the would-be lover. This box is decorated in beautifully executed straw work, the romantic motifs hinting at its purpose. One side features a brightly feathered bird among forget-me-nots. On the other side a heart crowns an unfolding piece of paper, with red and blue Cupid arrows crossed with quiver and torch. Imagine receiving a *billet-doux* slipped surreptitiously in a box such as this. It could be life changing! Ca. 1770, France. 6.25" long when closed. $800–1,000.

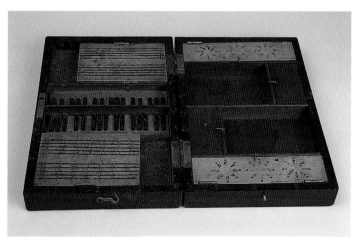

*Left:*

Figure 565. Mahogany veneered and symmetrically decorated. The inlay is a good example of a well-thought-out design. The central part is made up of a delicate floral inlay within a light oval background, set into the center of a sunflower, with only the outer leaves visible. The corners are inlaid with quarters of sunflower depicting marquetry. A good example of a characteristic arrangement. The inside of the box holds a special surprise in that it appears to contain a prototype for a musical tuition game that was patented by Ann(e) Young (married name Gunn) of Edinburgh in 1801 (patent no. 2485). "New invented apparatus, consisting of an oblong square box, which when opened presents two faces or tables, and of various dice, pins, counters, &c. . ." Patents were very costly to obtain at this date and are rare. Patents held by women are even rarer. Muir Wood and Co., Edinburgh, manufactured the game and also sold Miss Young's book, *An Introduction to Music*, printed by C. Stewart and Co. in 1803. 9.5" wide. $?

# Box Makers

Many craftsmen described themselves as makers of boxes during the nineteenth century, when most boxes were made by specialists and not general cabinetmakers. I will not list these unless I have handled their work myself and can point out special characteristics. Most antique boxes have lost their paper labels, so the record is of necessity incomplete. Many eighteenth-century boxes were individually commissioned and as such were not labeled. Certain eighteenth-century cabinetmakers branded their furniture, but this was seldom done with boxes. Labeling became more widespread when marketing consciousness took the place of the old ways of one-to-one business. Makers specializing in particular work have been mentioned in relevant chapters. The following are some additional notes to help complete the picture of the box-making story.

**AUSTIN:** Green label with black letters reads "GEO. AUSTIN cabinetmaker, 7 St. Andrews, One door from Wicklow St. Dublin, Man. of Portable Writing Desks, Dressing Cases, Workboxes &c. Canteens & Plate Chests."

> **Item 1.** Writing slope veneered in coromandel. Very good-quality work, with mother of pearl and brass inlay work in a flowing floral pattern. Immaculate and beautiful work. Ca. 1860—70.

> **Item 2.** Writing box in exceptionally well-figured flame mahogany with brass corners and set in brass handles. Shaped escutcheon and central plaque. Interesting brass catch on flap Three secret drawers veneered in rosewood, opening through lock mechanism, which is unusual. Blue-purple velvet lining on writing surface. Excellent quality. Ca. 1830—40.

> **Item 3.** Address given as Austin, Westmorland St. Dublin. Rosewood writing box with pewter stringing and mother of pearl circles. Good quality, modest appearance. Ca. 1830—40.

**BAGSHAW & SONS, J.:** Liverpool.

> **Item 1.** Envelope box, veneered in coromandel, and decorated with applied brass straps in the neo-Gothic manner. The interior is compartmented, with thin partitions covered in textured white paper and edged with blue silk. Good quality, solidly Victorian taste. Ca. 1870—80.

**BAYLEY'S:** As Bayley, Blew & Chapman they were "Dressing case makers and Perfumers to His Majesty and HRH Duke of York," 1829—35. The address is the same for when the name is given just as Bayley's, which is the only name on the box label. In the late eighteenth century they were Bayley, Son & Blew. Bayley's, 17 Cockspur St. Possibly a transitional form of label.

> **Item 1.** Small man's dressing box in mahogany, fitted with silver bottles. Early nineteenth century. Very fine.

**BETJEMANN:** The firm that embodies Victorian excellence. Their workshop was in Islington in North London, but much of their work was retailed through luxury shops in the fashionable West End. The firm was started by the great grandfather of Sir John Betjeman, who held the position of poet laureate from 1972 until his death in 1984. Sir John immortalized in verse his regrets about letting down his father in refusing to continue the family business, especially since it meant letting down the artists/craftsmen who worked for them. The origins of the family were Dutch. Betjemann's made full use of the machinery available to produce work of impeccable precision. They took out many patents and were masters of smooth and complex openings. Most of their work was executed in mahogany, veneered in coromandel or burr walnut. They favored either brass bandings and stringing or applied gilded-brass decoration. They made just about every type of box fashionable in the mid-Victorian and Edwardian periods. The visual impact is always of opulence. The quality is faultless. The pieces have a strength often lost in this type of Victorian work. One of their dressing boxes (figure 94) and a writing slope (figure 545) are illustrated. I have handled other items by them, including domed-top boxes with brass strap and handle decoration, and complete desk sets in the same style. I will give details of an unusual piece, which I sold long ago and can no longer trace and therefore cannot illustrate.

> **Item 1.** Writing slope veneered in coromandel on the outside and satinwood inside. The applied decoration is in silver, shaped in roundels of slightly Gothic design. The part of the box that usually houses the pen tray, etc. is rounded and slides out and up to form an envelope box. The writing surface is covered in blue velvet, embossed in gold with a Greek key pattern. Dated 1878.

**BIRLEY:** Oval label, George Birley & Company, Late Manning Worcester.

> **Item 1.** Jewelry box veneered in walnut. Lined in red satin, trimmed with red leather. Red padded satin on the inside of the lid. The front folds down to reveal another drawer. It has a rounded brass handle on the top. Ca. 1880.

**BRAMAH, J. & Sons, West End of Piccadilly London:** Although Joseph Bramah is most famous for the high-quality patented secure locks he supplied to other box makers, he originally trained as a cabinetmaker. In 1817–1823, Bramah supplied the Royal Household with traveling and dressing cases and writing boxes.

Item 1. Well-made writing box ca. 1815 with rare Bramah label.

**BRIGGS, T.:** (1819–35) "Manufacturer No. 27 Piccadilly."

Item 1. Letterbox shaped like a short, angular knife box in burr yew. Escutcheon and central plaque in mother of pearl. The interior is lined in yellow paper, the top in silk. Very well made and attractive in a quiet way. Ca. 1830.

**CADDEL, J & E:** 113 Leadenhall Street, London. Name written on an ivory plaque on the side drawer panel, in nice black flowing script.

Item 1. Writing box veneered in rosewood, with secret drawers and a side drawer. Brass corners. Good quality, and refined Regency look.

**CARTLAND, W.:** "Travelling & Dressing Case Desk & Workbox Manufacturer, 4 Old Bond Street Bath. Repairs Attended to."

Item 1. Coromandel-veneered dressing box. Lined in blue velvet, with gold-embossed leather trimmings. Good, solid Victorian quality.

**CHILDS, W., Jr.:** 56 King's Rd Brighton. "Desk & Dressing Case Makers, Toys Baskets Leather Work 'Glass' Papier Mache, Cutlery Brushes combs &c."

Item 1. Dressing box veneered in burr walnut, brass surround. Mid-Victorian.

Item 2. Papier-mâché workbox with typical mid-Victorian floral mother of pearl decoration.

**CLARK:** Exeter Change, Strand London. Writing desks and shaving cases, listed among other things.

Item 1. Small, solid-mahogany man's dressing case with brass corners. Early nineteenth century.

**CORFIELD, J.:** "J. Corfield Pocket Book, writing desk and dressing case makers."

Item 1. Writing box, veneered in rosewood. Brass inlay in wide bands of stylized flora, emanating symmetrically from a central motif, on top, front, and, unusually, sides. Distinctive quality of decoration ca. 1830.

**CORMACK:** "Cormack Brothers-Makers-37 Ludgate Hill, London." Name written on set-in ivory plaque.

Item 1. Man's dressing box veneered in burr walnut. Brass straps and corners. Round brass carrying handle set on top. The inside is fitted with perfume bottles on one side and two lift-out trays fitted for jewelry. The trays are covered in blue velvet and black leather. There is a fold-out mirror fitted into the inside of the lid, encased in gold-embossed leather. Very good quality. Ca. 1860.

**DALTON**: A firm of more than one address. Different addresses in Soho Bazaar, and also at 85 Quadrant, Regent St. London. Portable Writing Desk Fancy Cabinet Manufacturer. The work of the firm seems to have that special quality of the years between the Regency and the high Victorian periods, when mechanical refinement was introduced, but quality and structure were still very important. One characteristic item is illustrated in the Tea Caddy (figure 392). Other examples:

Item 1. Workbox veneered in coromandel. Mother of pearl inlay in a transitional style, of stylized curved foliage. The escutcheon appears to be "embraced" by two floral branches. The interior lined in green silk and gold-tooled leather. Very superior quality. Aesthetically pleasing. William IV or early Victorian.

Item 2. Another example identical to this, but lined in silver paper, with red velvet tops and ruche velvet back. A special detail is the edging on the surround of the tray and the pieces separating the sections. This is made of a thin red velvet strip, which finishes the interior with an edge of extra quality. Inside the box there is also the seller's label, which is "Sold at Mansfield's General Fancy Repository, 90 Grafton St. Dublin."

Item 3. Rosewood veneered workbox with simple inlay of star-shaped mother of pearl. Interior fitted with a tray with eight thread spools. The tray is covered in yellow paper, with maroon, gold-tooled leather covers. Very beautiful. Ca. 1830.

Item 4. Dressing box veneered in rosewood with brass surround and subtle inlay. Interior in velvet and tooled leather. Excellent quality.

**DILLER:** "Dressing Case Maker, 5 Chandos Street Covent Garden."

Item 1. Very fine small dressing box veneered in burr walnut. Interior covered in velvet and gold-tooled leather. The silver tops for the jars were made by V. Fisher of 188 Strand, an address near Diller's. Ca. 1838–40.

**DOBSON, W., or DOBSON, W. M.:** "Hardware man Stationer and Dealer in Fine Cutlery. Strand 162 London. Pocket Books, Writing Desks Shaving & Dressing Cases every article for fitting up the same on the Lower Terms possible." This firm traded from 1797 to 1847, from different numbers in the Strand. They had a very interesting label with quarter paterae designs in the four corners, listing some of their wares in each narrow section, in addition to the list in the center of the label, for which they were "manufacturers." The business must have sold associated items, since much of their stock required different disciplines. Two amusing items they list are "teeth instruments" and "Ear Wares"? (See label, figure 451.) Although they did trade into the Victorian era, all the items I have handled belonged to their earlier period. This of course could be that they continued to make older designs, using mahogany well into the nineteenth century.

Item 1. Fine flat gentleman's box. Oval inlay in the center. Four lines of stringing radiating from center to outer crossbanding. Opens from the narrower side, which makes the front of the box shorter than the sides. Four bottles arranged horizontally, two on each side. Razor space in between. The inside of the lid has a leather "envelope" attached. Most unusual arrangement. Fine work. Early nineteenth century (figure 471).

**Item 2.** Simple but well-constructed two-division tea caddy veneered in mahogany. Late eighteenth century.

**Item 3.** Brassbound mahogany "campaign" writing box, with side drawer fitted with silver-plated bottles and razors.

**Item 4.** Artist's box. Mahogany brass bound.

**Item 5.** Fitted sewing box (figure 444).

Other items, such as printing boxes, Reeves color cases, and Tunbridge ware items have been recorded.

**DOWN:** Down Bros. Ltd. London. Later retailers? Label of silver plate on the inside of the lid.

**Item 1.** Solid reddish mahogany flat box for instruments or guns. Brass straps.

**EDWARDS:** 21 King St. Holborn, also Bloomsbury, and for one year, 1813—14, at 84 St. James St. 1813—1848 d. A formidable maker of luxury boxes. David Edwards and Thomas Edwards (1832—39). Family connection established through bills. Made for the royal family. Used kingwood and rosewood extensively. Also mahogany for what he claimed to be "patent travelling cases." Writing boxes and dressing boxes mostly in Regency styles. All of impeccable quality.

**Item 1.** Mahogany strongbox with brass corners, straps, and flat side handles. Early nineteenth century.

**Item 2.** (St. James address) Rosewood man's dressing box. Edged in thick square brass. Sunk-in handles. Interior lined in red leather.

**Item 3.** Similar to 2, from Bloomsbury address.

**Item 4.** Rosewood man's dressing box. Brass surround and sunk-in handles. Interior with gold-embossed blue leather lining, and silver-topped fittings dated 1835.

**Item 5.** Rosewood lady's dressing box with brass stringing and fleur-de-lis decoration. Silver tops on heavy cut-glass bottles dated 1829. Gold leather-embossed interior. Full tray of silver-topped jars lifts out to expose second tray fitted with scissors, files, hooks, and other accessories.

**Item 6.** See illustration in the chapter on dressing boxes. The quality of the woodwork and brasswork is very typical of much of this firm's work. This is rather more subtle than most of their work, and most probably an early example (figure 473).

**Item 7.** Fitted sewing box (figure 440).

**Item 8.** Writing box (figure 514).

**Item 9.** Fitted dressing box.

**FARTHING, J. H.:** "Manufacturer of Dressing Cases Portable Russia Travelling & Writing Desks Ladies Work Boxes Fine Cutlery Needles &c 42 Cornhill London Near the Royal Exchange." Farthing manufactured the Polygraph for Mark Isambard Brunell and later ca. 1806 purchased the patent from Brunell.

**Item 1.** Brunell's Polygraph

**Item 2.** Rosewood veneered dressing box inlaid with two lines of brass stringing and sunk-in handles. Bramah lock. Lined in blue velvet and gold-embossed leather.

The drawer for jewelry is at the front with a separate lock. Excellent quality. Ca. 1830.

**FISHER:** 188 Strand, London.

**Item 1.** Small writing box, label embossed on the facing inside. Burr chestnut, good, predictable look and quality. Early Victorian.

**FROST:** "Made by G. Frost 143 Leadenhall St. Opp. the India House." Could also be 2 Manor St. Clapham in late 1830s.

**Item 1.** Dressing box in coromandel, with rounded brass surround. High-quality fittings and hardware. Bramah lock. Good-quality Victorian box with the smooth appearance and high polish characteristic of the period.

**FULLER, W. C. (Late Batley):** 1835—39, "Manufacturer 13 Brownlow Str. Holborn London."

**Item 1.** Rosewood veneered writing box with brass surround and sunk-in handles. Complicated arrangement of secret drawers, having an extra trap with a side drawer under the secret drawers. There is also a very unusual double bottom, with one layer constructed of narrow strips of mahogany, folding back like a rolled-top desk. Good quality and unique arrangement.

**GAINES or W. GAINNES:** (*The Dictionary of English Furniture Makers* records E. GAIMES at the same address—perhaps some old printing error can explain one or more wrong labels?) Cutler & Perfumer St. Paul's Church Place. No 56 Cornhill. Both addresses on the same label.

**Item 1.** Small, solid-mahogany writing box with side drawer. Good early-nineteenth-century solid quality.

**GILLOW, Lancaster and London:** Robert Gillow was the founder of Gillows and began cabinetmaking and finishing furniture from 1731 onward, after he had finished his apprenticeship as a joiner and cabinetmaker. He actually became a Freeman of Lancaster in the year 1728 and went into business partnership with George Haresnape. He had two sons who joined him in his business, Richard and Robert. These two sons expanded the business to London, where many of the wealthiest buyers lived, and this is where the firm quickly became recognized as one the best cabinetmakers of their time. Gillows chartered ships to import mahogany from the West Indies, Cuba, and Jamaica. The timber used was of such good quality because it was old, slowly grown solid woods, which record the stories of their growths. These woods are now almost unobtainable. See chapters 22—23.

**GREEN:** Label in the shape of a star with a cross on top. 168 Oxford St. London. Maker to the Royal Family.

**Item 1.** Dressing box in rosewood with brass stringing. Lined in green velvet and gold-embossed leather. Excellent quality. Ca. 1830.

**Item 2.** Similar to 1, but lined in red.

**HALSTAFF AND HANNAFORD:** "Manufacturers 228 Regent St." Another firm straddling the time between the Regency and the time of Victoria, making exceptional-quality glamorous boxes. Emphasis on strengthening with brass corners, brass surrounds, "T" hinges.

**Item 1.** Dressing box veneered in coromandel with brass round edging, and inlaid with a surround of a foliage design in brass. Sunk-in handles. The inside facings also inlaid with two thin lines of brass. Dark-blue velvet interior and gold-tooled leather. Embossed on the leather in the drop-down flat on the inside of the lid: "Robinson & Son 53 Queen St." Removable mirror behind the flap with gold-embossed surround. Bramah lock. The jewelry drawer also has a silk-covered lid. Fitted with exceptional-quality silver gilt-topped bottles and jars. Gilt and mother of pearl tools. 1835 date on silver items.

**Item 2.** Similar to 1 without the floral inlay. The drawer cover is attached on the sides and opens up from the middle. The mirror can "click" in place when the box is open, or stand. Silver-topped, high-quality bottles, 1840.

**Item 3.** Dressing box veneered in rosewood. Brass surround and inlay of lines and star patterns on the four corners. Escutcheon and central plaque in starlike daisy pattern. Bramah lock. Brass strengthening angles inlaid into the corners of the inside facings. Interior lined in navy-blue velvet and gold-embossed leather. "Pocket" on the inside of the lid lined in pale-blue silk. Mid- to late 1830s.

**Item 4.** Man's dressing box. Flat without a drawer. Veneered in coromandel. Brass surround. Lined in green velvet and leather. Brass corners inside. Heavy T-shaped hinges. Mordan & Co. lock. Freestanding mirror. Unusual in that the bottom and top of the box are of the same depth.

**Item 5.** See the chapter "Dressing Boxes" (figure 476).

**HANCOCK'S & CO.:** "38 & 39 Bruton St. London."

**Item 1.** Dressing box veneered in coromandel. Gilded-brass surround. Larger than average. Splendid interior with silver gilt tops with gold initials. Mid-Victorian.

Other excellent dressing boxes, all quite splendid.

**HANDFORDS:** "Improved W. D. Manufactury No 7 Strand London."

**Item 1.** Solid-mahogany writing box with carrying handles and side drawer. Unusual secret drawer under the pen tray. Early nineteenth century.

**HANSBURG:** "Manf. Liverpool."

**Item 1.** Very fine walnut veneered dressing box with velvet and leather-covered interior. Silver by Thomas Johnson, 1856.

**Item 2.** Good-quality coromandel dressing box. Silver T & J 1870. Side flat handles, in unusual shape, with the center stepped down in an inverted bell form.

**HARRISON Bros. & HOWSON:** "Cutlers to her Majesty, Shaving box-razors The Celebrated Sheffield Hollow Ground. Special Steel."

**Item 1.** Small mahogany box with brass straps fitted with razors.

Other razor or combination razor and small dressing boxes dating from the second quarter of the nineteenth century.

**HENRY, CHARLES:** 22 King St. Manchester.

**Item 1.** Mahogany box with brass surround, handles on the side. Leather lined. Three divisions. Possibly a stationery box. Ca. 1840.

**JONES & SONS:** "Castle S. Liverpool."

**Item 1.** Box veneered in coromandel with engraved brass straps ending in three points. Contains several games in ivory, ebony, and gilded brass.

**LEUCHARDS or LEUCHARS:** "Leuchards & Son Makers to the Queen 38 Piccadilly London."

**Item 1.** Dressing box veneered in rosewood with rounded brass surround and stringing. Side-opening jewelry drawer. When opened there is a continuous hinge at the back and brass reinforcements on all corners. Interior in green velvet and silk. Good, impressive quality. Fittings in engraved silver, marked 1841 FD London.

**Item 2.** Address given as "James Leuchars Fancy Head Dress Maker To Their Royal Highnesses The Duke of Sussex, The Duke of York AND THE PRINCESSES Ladies Hair Dresser, Perfumer &c Writing Desks, Dressing Cases, & Ladies Workboxes of all sorts 47 Piccadilly." Also two more addresses in small letters.

**Item 3.** Small writing box veneered in well-figured mahogany. Square brass edge and two lines of brass stringing. Secret drawer in satinwood, inlaid with stringing. Excellent quality. Second quarter of nineteenth century.

**LUND, WILLIAM:** 2 or 24 Fleet St., and **Thomas**, 56 or 57 Cornhill, London. Looking at the work, possibly a dynastic family firm, producing work of high quality, straddling the period between the Regency and the Victorian periods.

**Item 1.** High-quality writing box veneered in rosewood and inlaid with brass stringing. Thomas Lund, ca. 1825.

**Item 2.** Fine sewing box veneered in rosewood, brass stringing. Silk-covered interior. Thomas, ca. 1825.

**Item 3.** Dressing box veneered in coromandel with rounded brass surround and two thin lines of stringing. Side drawer for jewelry has silk cover. Interior fitted with velvet and gold-tooled leather. Nicely engraved silver tops on the bottles by Francis Douglas, London 1841. Thomas. Another almost identical box with maker's name on brass plaque.

**Item 4.** Burr chestnut—veneered sewing box. Label engraved on mother of pearl plaque inside. Blue watersilk and velvet interior. Silver-plated hinges. Bow-shaped lock. Meticulously finished, both inside and outside. William Lund. ca. 1840.

**Item 5.** Coromandel-veneered sewing box with fine inlay in brass and mother of pearl. Thomas. ca. 1835.

**Item 6.** Leather box. See "Regency" chapter (figure 54).

**Item 7.** Flat leather nécessaire, fitted with small scent bottles and dressing tools.

Many tortoiseshell and mother of pearl items. Caddies, letterboxes, and small boxes. See "Tortoiseshell" chapter (figure 209). An aside: makers of excellent chess sets in ivory.

Boxes from this firm seem to have this special quality that has a refinement without overelaboration. The interiors of their boxes are meticulously finished, with the fabrics coordinated with flair. Everything opens and shuts well, without strange tricks.

**MANSFIELD:** "Mansfield Dublin."

**Item 1.** "Mansfield Dublin" marked on the bottom drawer. Lady's dressing box veneered in burr walnut. Two drawers under the main tray, one opening from the side and one from the front. Side handles and hinges are silver plated. Silver-plated wavy ribbon inset on top with bird in center. Engraved motto *Deus Pascit Corvos*. Silver tops, London, 1871. Lined in velvet and silk. Mirror reverses and clicks on the back of the lid. Good Victorian quality.

**S. MAWSON & THOMPSON:** Aldergate St., London. Label engraved on bone small plaque on front inside facing.

**Item 1.** Empty box in solid mahogany with heavy brass corners and straps. Carrying handle on top in unusual construction in that the top bar protrudes from the supporting bars. Good, solid quality.

**MECHI, I. J.:** "Maker, 4 Leadenhall St. London."

**Item 1.** Small gentleman's dressing box veneered in coromandel. Very fine quality. Interior beautifully lined in blue velvet and leather. Silver tops dated 1851, engraved with flowers and central visor with feathers. Central plaque on top of the box, with engraved visor encircled by a belt, containing the motto *Nihil Sine Deo*.

**Item 2.** Lady's dressing box veneered in rosewood, with stylized floral inlay in mother of pearl. This is unusual, since most dressing boxes feature brass decoration. Sunk-in side handles in brass. The interior lined in green leather and bright-green silk. The internal mirror is edged in rosewood and can be removed from the lid and stand independently. Silver tops dating from the 1840s. Side jewelry drawer with separate lock. Very good, subtle quality.

**Item 3.** Sewing box veneered in rosewood. Mother of pearl escutcheon and fine pewter inlay. Tray inside lined with paper with a leafy gold pattern. Tops covered in soft blue taffeta silk. The inside of the lid is lined with an "envelope" covered in blue taffeta and opening with a silver catch. Very fine work. Regency period.

I have seen other boxes made by this firm, mostly in the style of the second and third quarter of the nineteenth century. All of very fine quality. Rather understated.

**(James) MIDDLETON:** "Middleton Manufacturer, King William Street, City."

**Item 1.** Solid-mahogany writing box with brass corners and sunk-in carrying handles. Steel screws. T-shaped hinge. Secret drawers and a side drawer. The flaps inside are held in place with engraved clips. Writing surface covered with purple velvet, embossed with a thick line of pattern. Very good, solid campaign box. Early-nineteenth-century style, although the *Dictionary of English Furniture Makers* records this address for 1837—39.

**(Nicholas) MIDDLETON:** 1801—10, 162 Strand, London. See the chapter "Writing Boxes and Slopes" (figure 501).

**MILLIKIN & DOWN:** "Opposite Guy's Hosp'l." Judging from the look of this item, this must be the same Millikin.

**Item 1.** Solid mahogany with brass straps going all around the box. Likely to have contained medical instruments.

**MILLIKIN & LAWLEY:** 165 Strand, London.

**Item 1.** Long, flat box in solid mahogany with two heavy brass straps for guns or instruments.

**MILNE, W. & J.:** "Makers 126 Princes St. Edinburgh."

**Item 1.** Dressing box veneered in rosewood. Three lines of fine brass stringing. Interior lined with blue velvet and gold-embossed leather. Tops of bottles in gilded silver, 1864. Excellent quality.

**MITCHELL, H.:** 168 Oxford St.

**Item 1.** Dressing box, larger than usual, veneered in coromandel with rounded brass edging. Fitted with silver-topped bottles dating from the 1820s and 1830s, of matching design. The box is of later date.

**MORDAN & Co., S.:** London.

**Item 1.** Lady's dressing box veneered in coromandel. Very thin brass stringing lines. Very good quality.

I have seen other boxes by this firm, all in the "dressing" line, in standard designs, all well made and aesthetically fine. They also made or supplied small items such as vinaigrettes, etc.

**PARKINS & GOTTO:** 24—25 Oxford St., London. A firm that believed in combining high-quality timbers. Marked their wares with small bone plaques, or on the brass hardware; sometimes both.

**Item 1.** Writing slope veneered in coromandel. Escutcheon, central plaque, and surround in engraved brass. The interior in satinwood. Unusually for slopes, it has secret drawers. The writing surface is covered in gold-embossed blue velvet. The drawers too are lined in blue velvet. The pen tray is covered in velvet with cutout places for mother of pearl writing tools. T-shaped hinges. At the back of the pen-and-well space there is a divided section for cards, envelopes, etc. This, as well as the pen tray, is a very unusual arrangement. Meticulous work. Glamorously beautiful. Mid-nineteenth century.

**Item 2.** Similar to 1. Elaborately engraved hinges.

**Item 3.** Small writing box veneered in burr walnut. Secret drawers. No decoration, but of exceptional quality. Bramah lock. Mid-nineteenth century.

**Item 4.** Writing box veneered in burr walnut with brass surround and straps. The facings and tops and pen tray inside are in coromandel. Secret drawers with (unusually for a Victorian box) push-down mechanism. Bramah lock. Writing surface lined with gold-embossed leather. Inkwells with screw on tops with an embossed crown, unusually bearing the name of Parkins & Gotto. Best of all mid-Victorian brassbound box features.

**Item 5.** Burr chestnut slope. See figure 544.

**Item 6.** Gentleman's dressing box veneered in burr walnut. Rounded brass edge and two lines of fine stringing. Interior lined in gold-embossed green leather. Fine mid-Victorian work.

**PEARCE:** "Sold by Pearce 77 Cornhill" marked on silver plaque.

**Item 1.** Writing slope veneered in coromandel. Fine quality, with no unusual features. 1870s.

**Item 2.** Dressing case veneered in rosewood, with very fine mother of pearl inlay, which is rare in this type of box. Interior lined in red velvet and leather.

**POWELL, T.:** "Lounge, Boar Lane, Leeds. Jeweller & Manufacturer of Desks Workboxes Dressing Cases &c."

**Item 1.** Tortoiseshell oblong nécessaire.

**Item 2.** Tortoiseshell flat sewing box made of four pieces of shell with central silver-plated square plaque. Late eighteenth—early nineteenth century.

**RIGGE, J. T.:** See the chapter "Dressing Boxes" (figure 468).

**RUSSELL & JACKSON:** "Sheffield, Manufacturers of Dressing Cases, Razor Strops." Mark pressed on back and bottom leather.

**Item 1.** Gentleman's dressing box veneered in burr walnut with brass surround. Interior covered in maroon leather. No drawer. Silver tops. Sheffield, 1875—1883. Nice quiet quality.

**SALTER, G.:** London.

**Item 1.** Mahogany man's box with shaving utensils. Ivory shaving brush with badger hair.

**SANGWINE:** "Sangwine & Sons, Shaving Case & Pocket Book Manufactory No 38 Strand, London."

**Item 1.** Writing box veneered in well-figured mahogany with brass bindings and drop carrying handles. Very unusual feature of crossbanding in kingwood around the top of the box. Very much in the Sheraton style. Another unusual feature is the two side drawers. Writing surface still retains the original "green cloth," as referred to in cabinetmakers' descriptions of the period. It also features a reading-stand device. Excellent example of late-eighteenth- to early-nineteenth-century traveling writing box.

**SCOTT:** Round label with drawing of an ark. "London, Birmingham & Sheffield Workshops. NOAH'S ARK BAZAAR E. Scott 45 Grainger St. Newcastle." Worth a mention because they seem to be everywhere. Labels seen on mid- and late Victorian boxes of average typical work, including Tunbridge ware.

**SEDDONS:** Late Georgian caddies described in the chapter "Tea Caddies." General cabinetmakers.

**SIMPSON, T. A.:** "T. A. Simpson & Co. 154 Regent St." Marked on Gothic Revival caddy. There was an earlier cabinetmaker operating from addresses in the same area. There could be a family connection, or it could be a retailer's mark.

**SIMPSON'S PICCADILLY:** Marked on Gothic Revival stationery box. More likely to be the retailer Simpsons.

**SMITH, J.:** See "Tortoiseshell and Ivory" chapter.

**SMITH, THOMAS:** "Carver Gilder Picture Frame Maker & Mount Cutter. Park Road Freemantle Southampton."

**Item 1.** Small box. A gem of high quality. Veneered in coromandel edged with brass, which is engraved on the four corners. Central handle also engraved. Long hinge and lock engraved too. Two lift-out trays inside, possibly for small stationery needs. Small matching stamp box enclosed. When open, it is held up by two half-round brass supports. Third quarter of nineteenth century.

**THOMAS, M.:** 54 Burlington Arcade.

**Item 1.** Rosewood veneered box with bands of brass inlay in *contre partie*. Same work for central plaque and escutcheon. Stylized floral design, of mid-Regency period. Very beautifully lined tray with maroon tooled leather. Ca. 1820.

**THOMAS, W. & F. B.** "Thomas Goldsmiths, Silversmiths 153 New Bond St." Brass plaque on box, perhaps bought in for presenting silver. Large burr walnut box painted with garlands, cornucopias, and mythical birds.

**THOMPSON & CAPPER:** "Homeopathic Chemists." Another case of buying-in for presenting own product. Burr walnut box with lower drawer, fitted to accommodate small medicine jars.

**TRUEFITT:** "Arcade & Brighton."

**Item 1.** Small, solid, rounded coromandel razor box with two folding razors.

**TURNBULL'S:** Exchange, 389 High Street, Cheltenham. Drawing of outside of emporium on small red label.

**Item 1.** Gentleman's dressing box. Unusual in that it is made of solid rosewood. Edged all around, including the base, with square brass. Sunk-in side handles and heavy double hinges. "GR" with crown engraved on lock. Space for only four bottles at the back. The arrangement inside is unique in that the flap that usually covers the inside of the lid starts from only a quarter of the way up in order to allow for more space for the tall bottles. Under this flap there is a rosewood-edged mirror. The flap and the rest of the interior are covered in beautifully embossed bright-red leather with no gold. Excellent quality and early-nineteenth-century period look.

**TURRILL:** "Turrill Maker 250 Regent Str." engraved on mother of pearl plaque.

**Item 1.** Workbox veneered in rosewood. Blue watersilk interior, fitted with mother of pearl spools and tools. Very understated, beautiful quality. Ca. 1840.

**Items 2, 3.** See the chapter "Sewing Boxes or Workboxes" (figures 459 and 460).

**Item 4.** 52 New Bond St. Lady's dressing box. Veneered in coromandel with round brass edging and side handles. Very opulent quality. The top tray is covered with silver-topped jars, and there is a second tray for scissors and other tools. The hinges are engraved with a rococo design. The maker's name is also engraved on the hinges. Silver dated 1849, concurrent with the box.

**WELLS:** "Portable Desk & Dressing Case Manufacturers, High Holborn."

**WELLS & LAMBE:** From 1815: Different addresses. One label with a crest with two lions reads: "5 Doors from Spring Garden, Pocket Book Portable Desk Dressing Case & Copying Machine Makers To His Royal Highness the Duke of York." This on Item 1. Dressing box veneered in rosewood. Edging in brass with an engraved line. Three lines of brass stringing, and sunk-in carrying handles. Good hinge, patent E. Wells & Cos. Interior in dark-red leather with silk tassels. Six bottles at the back, two of which are narrow. The tray is fitted with a long jar, two round jars, one small bottle, and one inkwell. The larger tops are pierced with a simple elegant design. The silver marked "CRO London 1824." Everything extremely fine and beautiful and yet strong. Superb Regency quality. This firm also seems to have operated from New Bond St. and Cockspur St. 1817—25 and also claimed the Duke of Cumberland as one of their patrons. They also stocked items that they did not make themselves. A Vizagapatam ivory-veneered writing box bearing their label sold at Sotheby's in 1976.

**WELSS'S:** "Welss's improved air tight case 62 Strand London." Engraved on brass plaque inside the box.

Item 1. Solid-mahogany box with brassbound corners and brass straps going all around.

**WEST:** "F. West, dressing & writing case manufacturers, 1 St. James Str. by appointment to Queen Victoria."

**Items:** Dressing boxes veneered in burr walnut and coromandel. Usually click on mirrors. Standard fittings. Ca. 1860s.

**WILLIAM & Co.:** "William & Co., 52 New Bond St. London."

Item 1. Gentleman's dressing box veneered in coromandel. Unusually, both edged in brass and also strapped. Silver 1857 with decoration of crown and phoenix crest.

**WILSON, WILLIAM:** "William Wilson, Pocket Book & Case Manufacturer 21 George Street, Edinburgh, Travelling & Dressing Cases, Portable Writing Desks etc. Every Article in the Fancy Wood & Leather Line."

Item 1. Workbox veneered in well-figured very beautiful mahogany. Sturdy construction with double hinge. The interior lined in olive-green paper and olive-green patterned silk. The fold-down silk-covered inside lid cover with silver-plated catch. Bottom lined in leather. Quietly beautiful, ca. 1820—25.

Item 2. Writing box veneered in rosewood. Escutcheon and top plaque in mother of pearl. A little very fine inlay of brass and mother of pearl. Discreetly beautiful. Ca. 1835.

Item 3. Second generation of Wilsons. "Wilson & Co, Late Wm Wilson Established 1817, 71 George Street Edinburgh, Manufacturers of Dressing Writing & Jewel Cases, Workboxes, Desks, Pocket Books & All Fancy Wood Shell & Leather Goods." Coromandel-veneered lady's dressing box with side handles and rounded brass edge. Larger than usual with jewelry drawer underneath with separate lock. Locks S. Mordan & Co. The interior lined in blue velvet and unusually arranged, with the flat jars in the middle of the tray and two cushions (one on each side) for scissors and other small dressing tools. Solid Victorian quality. Silver engraved, marked "J.V. London 1856." Impressive.

**WOOLFIELD:** "Made by S. Woolfield 28 Buckanan St. Glasgow."

Item 1. Writing slope veneered in rosewood. Very fine inlay in mother of pearl, abalone, brass, and pewter in flowing, yet-controlled floral design. Mid-Victorian.

**WRIGHT, R:** "R. Wright, Bond St, Hull." Cabinetmaker, made a stunning tea chest. See "Regency" chapter (figure 61). It is not always obvious who was the maker and who was the seller, especially when makers retailed the work of other firms, as well as their own. Some labels are quite explicitly retail labels, and I am giving a few examples just to give a flavor of the business.

1. A label under a small mahogany paint box reads "from SULMAN'S Jewellery, Perfumery, Toy, & Fancy Repository, GREENWICH." Inside the box we have another label: "Roger's superior London-made Water Colors Warranted soft & brilliant."

2. "'Alpin's' Emporium of Novelty, Strand." Found on a small rosewood box.

Sometimes both maker and retailer are recorded, especially later in the nineteenth century, when brand names of high quality acquired marketing kudos. For example, dressing boxes that are often referred to as "Asprey's" were actually made by Betjemann. See the chapters "Dressing Boxes" and "Writing Boxes and Slopes" (Victorian).

# Select Bibliography

This bibliography is by no means a complete record of all the works and sources I have consulted. I list here only the writings that have been of primary use in the making of this book. It indicates the substance and range of reading upon which I have formed my ideas, and I intend it to serve as a convenience for those who wish to further pursue the study of antique boxes and tea caddies and the societies that made them.

Ackermann, R. *The Repository of Arts, Literature, Commerce, Manufactures, Fashions, and Politics*. London (periodical publication): 1st ser., 14 vols., 1809–1815; 2nd ser., 14 vols., 1816–1822; 3rd ser., 12 vols., 1823–1828; 4th ser., 1829.

Adam, Robert, and James Adam. *The Works in Architecture*. London: Adam and Adam, 1778–1822.

Angerstein, R. R. *R. R. Angerstein's Illustrated Travel Diary, 1753–1755: Industry in England and Wales from a Swedish Perspective*. Translated by Torsten Berg and Peter Berg. London, Science Museum. 2001.

Archer, Mildred, Christopher Rowell, and Robert Skelton. *Treasures from India—the Clive collection at Powis Castle*. London: Herbert in association with the National Trust, 1987.

Armytage, Walter Harry Green. *Four Hundred Years of English Education*. Cambridge, UK: Cambridge University Press, 1964.

Ash, Douglas. *Dictionary of English Antique Furniture*. London: Muller, 1970.

Ashton, John. *Social England under the Regency*. London: Chatto & Windus, 1899a.

Ashton, John. *Florizel's Folly*. London: Chatto & Windus, 1899b.

Aslin, Elizabeth. *19th Century English Furniture*. London: Faber & Faber, 1962.

Austen, Brian. *Tunbridge Ware and Related European Decorative Woodwares*. London: W. F. Foulsham, 1989.

Backhouse, Sir Edmund Trelawny, and John Otway Percy Bland. *Annals & Memories of the Court of Peking from the 16th to 20th Century*. London: William Heinemann, 1914.

Bagshaw, Thomas W. "Straw Marquetry: Part I." *Apollo Magazine* 22 (1935): 283–86.

Bagshaw, Thomas W. "Straw Marquetry: Part II." *Apollo Magazine* 23 (1936): 332–35.

Barker, Felix, and Peter Jackson. *London: 2000 Years of a City & Its People*. London: Macmillan, 1983.

Barrow, Sir. John [Bart]. *Travels in China: Containing Descriptions, Observations and Comparisons Made and Collected in the Course of a Short Residence at the Imperial Palace of Yuen-min-yuen, and on a Subsequent Journey from Pekin to Canton*. London: T. Cadell & W. Davies, 1804.

Barton, Margaret, and Sir Osbert Sitwell [Bart]. *Brighton*. London: Faber & Faber, 1935.

Beard, Geoffrey. *Georgian Craftsmen and Their Work*. London: Country Life, 1966.

Beard, Geoffrey. *Craftsmen and Interior Decoration in England*. Edinburgh: Bartholomew, 1981.

Beard, Geoffrey. *The National Trust Book of English Furniture*. Harmondsworth, UK: Penguin in association with the National Trust, 1986.

Bédarida, François. *A Social History of England, 1851–1990*. Translated by A. S. Forster and Jeffrey Hodgkinson. London: Routledge, 1991.

Bedini, Silvio A. *Thomas Jefferson and His Copying Machines*. Monticellomonograph series. Charlottesville: University of Virginia Press, 1984.

Beevers, David. *Chinese Whispers: Chinoiserie in Britain, 1658–1930*. London: Royal Pavilion Libraries & Museums, 2009.

Bell, Robert Charles. *Board and Table Games from Many Civilizations*. New York: Dover, 1979.

Bennett-Oates, Phyllis, and Mary Seymour. *The Story of Western Furniture*. London: Herbert, 1980.

Birdwood, Sir George Christopher Molesworth. *Paris Universal Exhibition of 1878: Handbook to the British Indian Section*. London: Royal Commission, 1878.

Black, Jeremy. *An Illustrated History of Eighteenth-Century Britain, 1688–1793*. Manchester, UK: Manchester University Press, 1996.

Boswell, James. *Boswell's London Journal, 1762–63*. Harmondsworth, UK: Penguin, 1966.

Boswell, James. *Life of Johnson*. New ed. Edited by R. W. Chapman and G. D. Fleeman. London: Oxford University Press, 1970.

Bourne, Jonathan. *Lacquer: An International History and Collector's Guide*. London: Phillips Editions, 1984.

Bowden, Jean K. *Jane Austen's House*. Norwich, UK: Jarrold, 1990.

Brackett, Oliver. *Thomas Chippendale: A Study of His Life, Work and Influence*. London: Hodder and Stoughton, 1924.

Brackett, Oliver. *An Encyclopaedia of English Furniture: A Pictorial Review . . . from Gothic Times to the Mid-nineteenth Century*. London: Ernest Benn, 1927.

Brown, Ivor. *Dr. Johnson & His World*. London: Lutterworth, 1965.

Bryant, Arthur. *The Age of Elegance, 1812–1822*. London: Collins, 1950.

Buckley Ebrey, Patricia. *The Cambridge Illustrated History of China*. Cambridge, UK: Cambridge University Press, 1996.

Burnett, John. *A History of the Cost of Living*. Harmondsworth, UK: Penguin, 1969.

Bushell, Stephen W. *Chinese Art*. London: Victoria and Albert Museum Board of Education, 1924.

Calder-Marshall, Arthur. *The Two Duchesses*. London: Hutchinson, 1978.

Chippendale, Thomas. *The Gentleman and Cabinet-Maker's Director*. London, 1754.

Chippendale, Thomas. *The Gentleman and Cabinet-Maker's Director*. 3rd ed. London, 1762

Clarke, John. *The Life and Times of George III*. London: George Weidenfeld & Nicolson, 1972.

Coleridge, Anthony. *Chippendale Furniture: The Work of Thomas Chippendale and His Contemporaries in the Rococo Taste*. London: Faber & Faber, 1968.

Collard, Frances. *Regency Furniture*. Woodbridge, UK: Antique Collectors' Club, 1985.

Columbani, Placido. *A New Book of Ornaments*. London: Taylor, 1775.

Conner, Patrick. *Oriental Architecture in the West*. London: Thames & Hudson, 1979.

Cook, Olive. *The English Country House: An Art and a Way of Life*. London: Thames & Hudson, 1974.

Copper-Royer, Jacqueline. *La Marqueterie de paille*. Paris: Librairie Grund, 1954.

Crossman, Carl L. *The China Trade*. Woodbridge, UK: Antique Collectors' Club, 1991.

Davis, John R. *The Great Exhibition*. Gloucestershire, UK: Sutton, 1999.

Day, Angélique. *Letters from Georgian Ireland: The Correspondence of Mary Delany, 1731—68*. Belfast: Friar's Bush Press, 1991.

Defoe, Daniel. *Tour thro' the Whole Island of Great Britain*. Dublin: James Williams, 1779.

DeVoe, Shirley Spaulding. *English Papier-mâché of the Georgian and Victorian Periods*. London: Barrie & Jenkins, 1971.

Drury, Elizabeth. *Antiques: Traditional Techniques of the Master Craftsmen; Furniture, Glass, Ceramics, Gold, Silver and Much More*. London: Macmillan, 1986.

Du Halde, Jean Baptiste. *Description géographique, historique, chronologique et physique de l'Empire de la Chine et de la Tartarie Chinoise: Enrichies des cartes generales et particulières de ces pays, etc.* 4 vols. Paris: La Haye, 1736a.

Du Halde, Jean Baptiste. *The General History of China, Containing a Geographical . . . and Physical Description of the Empire of China, Chinese Tartary, Corea and Thibet . . . with Maps and Copper Plates: Done from the French of Du Halde [by R. Brookes]*. London: John Watts, 1736b.

Eberhard, Wolfram. *A Dictionary of Chinese Symbols*. London: Routledge & Kegan Paul, 1986.

Edwards, Amelia B. *Pharaohs, Fellahs and Explorers*. London: James R. Osgood, McIlvaine, 1892.

Edwards [engraver], and Matthias Darly. *A New Book of Chinese Designs: Calculated to Improve the Present Taste, Consisting of Figures, Buildings, & Furniture, etc.* London, 1754.

Edwards, Ralph, and Margaret Jourdain. *Georgian Cabinet Makers*. London: Country Life, 1944.

Elville, E. M. *English and Irish Cut Glass*. London: Country Life, 1953.

Fastnedge, Ralph. *English Furniture Styles from 1500 to 1830*. Harmondsworth, UK: Penguin Books, 1955.

Feder, Theodore. *Pompeii & Herculaneum*. New York: Abbeville, 1978.

Fleming, John. *Robert Adam and His Circle*. London: John Murray, 1962.

Foreman, Amanda. *Georgiana-Duchess of Devonshire*. London: Harper Collins, 1998.

Forrest Denys Mostyn. *Tea for the British*. London: Chatto & Windus, 1973.

Fraser, Lady Antonia. *Royal Charles, Charles II and the Restoration*. New York: Alfred A. Knopf, 1980.

Garner, Sir Harry. *Chinese Lacquer*. London: Faber, 1979.

Gascoigne, Bamber Arthur. *The Treasures and Dynasties of China*. London: Jonathan Cape, 1973.

George, Mary Dorothy. *Hogarth to Cruikshank: Social Change in Graphic Satire*. London: Penguin, 1967.

George, Mary Dorothy. *English Political Caricature, 1793—1832*. 2 vols. Oxford: Clarendon, 1959.

Gilbert, Christopher. *The Life and Works of Thomas Chippendale*. 2 vols. London: Studio Vista, Christie Manson & Woods, 1978.

Gilbert, Christopher. *Dictionary of English Furniture Makers, 1660—1840*. Edited by Geoffrey Beard and Christopher Gilbert, assisted by Brian Austen, Arthur Bond, and Angela Evans. London: W. S. Maney & Son in association with the Furniture Society, 1986.

Gilbert, Christopher. *Pictorial Dictionary of Marked London Furniture, 1700—1840*. London: W. S. Maney & Son in association with the Furniture Society, 1996.

Gill, Margaret. *Tunbridge Ware*. Aylesbury UK: Shire, 1985.

Goodman, William Louis. *History of Woodworking Tools*. London: G. Bell & Sons, 1964.

Goodwin, Jason. *The Gunpowder Gardens: Travels through India and China in Search of Tea*. London: Chatto & Windus, 1990.

Gregg, Pauline. *A Social and Economic History of Britain, 1760—1972*. London: Harrap, 1973.

Harris, Eileen. *The Furniture of Robert Adam*. London: Alec Tiranti, 1963.

Hayden, Ruth. *Mrs Delany, Her Life and Her flowers*. London: British Museum Press, 1980.

Hayward, Charles H. *English Period Furniture*. London: Evans Bros., 1957.

Hayward, Helena, ed. *World Furniture*. London: Hamlyn, 1965.

Heal, Ambrose. *London Tradesmen's Cards of the XVIII Century*. London: Batsford, 1925.

Heal, Ambrose. *The London Furniture Makers from the Restoration to the Victorian Era, 1660—1840 . . . A record of 2500 Cabinet-Makers, Upholsterers, Carvers and Gilders with Their Addresses and Working Dates, Illustrated by 165 Reproductions of Makers' Trade-Cards: With a Chapter by R. W. Symonds . . . on the Problem of Identification of the Furniture They Produced, etc.* London: Batsford, 1953.

Hepplewhite, George. *The Cabinet-Maker and Upholsterer's Guide; or, Repository of Designs for Every Article of Household Furniture . . . from Drawings by . . .* London: Alice. Hepplewhite, 1794.

Herberts, Kurt. *Oriental Lacquer: Art& Technique.* Translated by Brian Morgan. London: Thames & Hudson, 1962.

Hibbert, Christopher. *The Dragon Wakes: China and the West, 1793—1911.* London: Longman, 1970.

Hibbert, Christopher. *George IV Regent and King.* London: Allen Lane, 1973.

Hibbert, Christopher. *London: The Biography of a City.* Harmondsworth, UK: Penguin, 1980.

Hibbert, Christopher. *The English: A Social History, 1066—1945.* London: Harper Collins, 1994.

Hickey, William. *Memoirs of William Hickey, 1745—1809.* Edited by Peter Quennell. London: Routledge & Kegan Paul, 1975.

Hinckley, F. Lewis. *A Directory of Antique Furniture.* New York: Bonanza Books, 1953.

Holmes, Edwin F. *A History of Thimbles.* New York and London: Cornwall Books, 1985.

Honour, Hugh. *Chinoiserie: The Vision of Cathay.* London: John Murray, 1961.

Hope, Thomas. *Household Furniture and Interior Decoration Executed from Designs by Thomas Hope.* London, 1807.

How, George Evelyn Paget, and Jane Penrice How. *English and Scottish Silver Spoons, Mediaeval to Late Stuart, and Pre-Elizabethan Hall-Marks on English Plate.* London: Curwen, 1952.

Huggett, Frank E. *A Dictionary of British History, 1815—1973.* Oxford: Basil Blackwell, 1974.

Hughes, Bernard, and Therle Hughes. *Small Antique Furniture.* London: Lutterworth, 1958.

Hunter, William Wilson. *A Brief History of the Indian Peoples.* Oxford: Clarendon, 1907.

Hussey, Christopher Edward Clive. *English Country Houses: Early Georgian, 1715—1760.* London: Country Life Books, 1956a.

Hussey, Christopher Edward Clive. *English Country Houses: Mid Georgian, 1760—1800.* London: Country Life Books, 1956b.

Hussey, Christopher Edward Clive. *English Country Houses: Late Georgian, 1800—1840.* London: Country Life Books, 1958.

Huth, Hans. *Lacquer of the West: The History of a Craft and an Industry.* Chicago: University of Chicago Press, 1971.

Hutt, Julia. *Understanding Far Eastern Art.* Oxford: Phaidon, 1987.

Inglis, Brian. *The Opium War.* London: Hodder & Stoughton, 1976.

Jackson, Anna, and Amin Jaffer. *Encounters: The Meeting of Asia and Europe, 1500—1800.* London: V&A Publications, 2004.

Jacobson, Dawn. *Chinoiserie.* London: Phaidon, 1987.

Jaffer, Amin. *Furniture from British India and Ceylon.* London: V&A Publications, 2001.

Jarry, Madeleine. *Chinoiserie: Le rayonnement du gout chinois sur les arts decoratifs du XVIIe et XVIIIe siecles.* Fribourg, Switzerland: Office du Livre, 1981a.

Jarry, Madeleine. *Chinoiserie: Chinese Influence on European Decorative Art, 17th and 18th Centuries.* New York: Vendome, 1981b.

Johnson, Reginald Brimley. *Mrs. Delany at Court and among the Wits . . . Arranged from "The Autobiography and Correspondence of Mrs. Delany, with Interesting Remembrances of George III and Queen Charlotte."* London: Stanley Paul, 1925.

Jones, Mary Eirwen. *A History of Western Embroidery.* London: Studio Vista, 1969.

Jones, Owen. *The Grammar of Ornament.* London: Studio Editions, 1988. First published in 1856.

Jones, Yvonne. *Japanned Papier-mâché and Tinware.* Woodbridge, UK: Antique Collectors' Club, 2012.

Jourdain, Margaret. *Regency Furniture, 1795—1820.* Rev. ed. London: Country Life, 1948.

Jourdain, Margaret, and Herbert Cecil Ralph Edwards. *Georgian Cabinetmakers.* London: Country Life, 1944.

Jourdain, Margaret, and Fred Rose. *English Furniture: The Georgian Period, 1750—1830.* London: B. T. Batsford, 1953.

Joy, Edward T. *English Furniture, 1800—1851.* London: Ward Lock for Sotheby Parke Bernet, 1977.

Joy, Edward T. *Gaming.* London: H.M.S.O. for Victoria and Albert Museum, 1982.

Joyce, Ernest. *The Technique of Furniture Making.* London: Batsford, 1980.

Kirkham, Pat, Rodney Mace, and Julia Porter. *Furnishing the World: The East London Furniture Trade, 1830—1980.* London: Journeyman, 1987.

Lambert, Susan, ed. *Pattern and Design: Designs for the Decorative Arts, 1480—1980.* London: Victoria and Albert Museum, 1983.

Lane, Peter. *The Industrial Revolution: The Birth of the Modern Age.* London: Weidenfeld & Nicolson, 1978.

Lane, Richard. *Images from the Floating World: The Japanese Print.* Oxford: Oxford University Press, 1978.

Latham, Robert, comp. and ed. *The Illustrated Pepys.* London: Bell & Hyman, 1978.

Le Corbeiller, Clare. *European and American Snuff Boxes, 1730—1830.* New York: Viking, 1966.

Lever, Jill. *Architects' Designs for Furniture.* London: Trefoil Books, 1982.

Lewis, Philippa, and Gillian Darley. *Dictionary of Ornament.* London: Macmillan, 1986.

Lincoln, William Alexander. *The Art and Practice of Marquetry.* London: Thames & Hudson, 1971.

Llanover, Lady [Augusta]. *The Autobiography and Correspondence of Mary Granville, Mrs Delaney.* London: Richard Brntley, 1862.

Lloyd, Clive L. *The Arts and Crafts of Napoleonic and American Prisoners of War, 1756—1816.* Woodbridge, UK: Antique Collectors' Club, 2007.

Locke, Michael. *Bone, Ivory, and Horn: Identifying Natural Materials.* Atglen, PA: Schiffer, 2013.

Lockhead, Marion Cleland. *The Victorian Household.* London: John Murray, 1964.

Lofts, Norah. *Queens of Britain.* London: Hodder & Stoughton, 1977.

Low, Donald A. *That Sunny Dame: A Portrait of Regency Britain*. London: Dent, 1977.

Low, Donald A. *The Regency Underworld*. Stroud UK: Sutton, 1999.

Luzzato-Bilitz, Oscar. *Oriental Lacquer*. London: Cassell, 1988.

Macquoid, Percy, and Ralph Edwards. *The Dictionary of English Furniture from the Middle Ages to the Late Georgian Period*. London: Country Life, 1954.

Mayer, Ralph. *The Artist's Handbook of Materials and Techniques*. London and Boston: Faber & Faber, 1951.

Merriman, John M. *A History of Modern Europe from the Renaissance to the Present*. New York and London: W. W. Norton, 1996.

Meyer, Franz Sales. *Handbook of Ornament*. Translated from German. London: Omega Books, 1987. First published in English in 1894 (London: B. T. Batsford).

Mingay, Gordon Edmond. *The Gentry: The Rise and Fall of a Ruling Class*. London: Longman, 1976.

Mingay, Gordon Edmond. *A Social History of the English Countryside*. London: Routledge, 1990.

Morse, Hosea B. *The Chronicles of the East India Company Trading to China, 1635—1834*. 5 vols. Oxford: Clarendon, 1926—1929.

Murray, Venetia. *High Society in the Regency Period, 1788—1830*. London: Viking, 1998.

Musgrave, Clifford. *Regency Furniture, 1800—1830*. London: Faber & Faber, 1962.

Musgrave, Clifford. *Adam and Hepplewhite and other Neo-Classical Furniture*. London: Faber, 1966.

Newton, William. *The Antiquities of Athens Measured and Delineated by J. S. . . . and N. R.* 4 vols. Edited by William Newton, Willey Reveley, and Joseph Woods. London, 1762—1816.

Nicolson, Colin. *Strangers to England: Immigration to England, 1100—1952*. London: Wayland, 1974.

Oreskó, Robert. *The Works in Architecture of Robert and James Adam*. London: Academy Editions, 1975

Paladdio, Andrea. *The Four Books of Andrea Palladio's Architecture: Wherein, after a Short Treatise of the Five Orders, Those Observations That Are Most Necessary in Building, Private Houses, Streets, Bridges, Piazzas, Xisti, and Temples Are Treated of*. London: Isaac Ware, 1738.

Palmer, Alan. *The Life & Times of George IV*. London: George Weidenfeld & Nicolson, 1972.

Parissien, Steven. *Adam Style*. London: Phaidon, 1992a.

Parissien, Steven. *Regency Style*. London: Phaidon, 1992b.

Parissien, Steven. *Palladian Style*. London: Phaidon, 1994.

Parker E. H. *China: Her History, Diplomacy and Commerce, from the Earliest Times to the Present Day*. London: Murray, 1917.

Perkin, Harold. *The Origins of Modern English Society, 1780—1880*. London: Routledge & Kegan Paul, 1969.

Perry, Walter C. *Greek and Roman Sculpture*. London: Longmans, Green, 1882.

Pinto, Edward H., and Eva Pinto. *Treen and Other Wooden Bygones*. London: G. Bell & Sons, 1969.

Pinto, Edward H., and Eva Pinto. *Tunbridge and Scottish Souvenir Woodware*. London: G. Bell & Sons, 1970.

Plumb, J. H., and Huw Wheldon. *The Horizon Book of the Renaissance*. New York: American Heritage, 1961.

Plumb, J. H., and Huw Wheldon. *The First Four Georges*. London: Book Club Associates with Hamlyn Group, 1975.

Plumb, J. H., and Huw Wheldon. *Royal Heritage: The Story of Britain's Royal Builders and Collectors*. London: British Broadcasting Corporation, 1977.

Priestley, J. B. *The Prince of Pleasure and His Regency*. London: Heinemann, 1969.

Raynsford, Julia. *The Story of Furniture*. London: Hamlyn, 1975.

Reade, Alfred Arthur. *Tea and Tea Drinking*. London: Sampson Low, 1884.

Renton, Andrew. "Straw Marquetry Made in Lübeck, Leiden and London by the Hering Family." *Furniture History* 35 (1999): 51—86.

Richardson, Joanna. *George IV: A Portrait*. London: Sidwick & Jackson, 1966.

Riou, Stephen. *The Grecian Orders of Architecture, Delineated and Explained from the Antiquities of Athens: Also the Parallels of the Orders of Palladio, Scamozzi and Vignola, to Which Are Added Remarks . . . with Designs*. London, 1768.

Roberts, Henry D. *A History of the Royal Pavilion, Brighton*. London: Country Life, 1939.

Robinson, John Martin. *The Wyatts: An Architectural Dynasty*. Oxford: Oxford University Press, 1979.

Roe, Frederic Gordon. *Victorian Furniture*. London: Phoenix House, 1952.

Rykwert, Joseph, and Anne Rykwert. *The Brothers Adam: The Men and the Style*. London: Collins, 1985.

Salomonsky, Verna Cook. *Masterpieces of Furniture Design*. New York: Dover, 1953.

Saumarez Smith, Charles. *Eighteenth-Century Decoration*. London: Weidenfeld & Nicolson, 1993.

Sayer, Robert. *Genteel Household Furniture in the Present Taste by a Society of Upholsterers, Cabinet-Makers, etc*. London and Wakefield, UK: EP Publishing, 1978.

Selby, John. *The Paper Dragon: An Account of the China Wars*. London: Arthur Baker, 1968.

Shearer, Thomas. *The Cabinet-Makers London Book of Prices, and Designs of Cabinet-Work in Perspective, on Twenty Copper Plates: Containing above One Hundred Various Designs, by the London Society of Cabinet-makers; Fully Illustrating the Methods of Calculation Adopted in the Work, etc*. London: W. Brown & A. O'Neil for the London Society of Cabinet Makers, 1793.

Sheraton, Thomas. *The Cabinet-Maker and Upholsterer's Drawing Book*. London, 1793.

Silcock, Arnold. *Introduction to Chinese Art*. London: Oxford University Press, 1935.

Singleton, Esther. *French and English Furniture*. London: Hodder & Stoughton, 1904.

Smith, Nancy A. *Old Furniture: Understanding the Craftsman's Art*. New York: Dover, 1991.

Society of Dilettanti. *Ionian Antiquities*. 4 vols. London: Society of Dilettanti, 1769, 1797, 1840, 1881.

Somerset, Anne. *The Life and Times of William IV*. London: Weidenfeld & Nicolson, 1980.

Sparke, Cynthia Coleman. *Russian Decorative Arts*. Woodbridge, UK: Antique Collectors' Club, 2014.

Stalker, John, and [George] Parker of Oxford. *A Treatise of Japanning and Varnishing, Being a Compleat Discovery of Those Arts ... with ... Patterns for Japan-Work ... Engraven on 24 ... Copper-Plates*. Oxford, 1688.

Steiger, George Nye. *China and the Occident: The Origin and Development of the Boxer Movement*. New Haven, CT: Yale University Press, 1927.

Stillman, Damie. *The Decorative Work of Robert Adam*. London: Alec Tiranti, 1966.

Strange, Thomas Arthur. *English Furniture, Decoration Woodwork and Allied Arts*. London: Studio Editions, 1986.

Stroud, Dorothy. *Sir John Soane—Architect*. London: Faber & Faber, 1984.

Sullivan, Michael. *The Meeting of Eastern and Western Art, from the 16th Century to the Present Day*. New York: New York Graphic Society, 1973.

Swann, Peter Charles. *Art of China Korea and Japan*. London: Thames & Hudson, 1963.

Tatham, Charles Heathcote. *Etchings, Representing the Best Examples of Ancient Ornamental Architecture: Drawn from the Originals in Rome, and Other Parts of Italy, during the Years 1794, 1795, and 1796*. London: T. Gardiner, 1799.

Taunton, Nerylla. *Antique Needlework Tools and Embroideries*. Woodbridge, UK: Antique Collectors' Club, 1997.

Thomson, David. *England in the 19th Century*. London: Jonathan Cape, 1964.

Tillyard, Eustace M. *The Elizabethan World Picture*. Middlesex, UK: Penguin Books, 1963.

Toller, Jane. *Papier-mâché in Great Britain and America*. London: G. Bell & Sons, 1962.

Toller, Jane. *Prisoner of War Work, 1756—1815*. Cambridge, UK: Golden Head, 1965.

Tonge, Neil. *Industrialisation and Society, 1700—1914*. Surrey, UK: Thomas Nelson and Sons, 1993.

Trevelyan, George Macaulay. *British History in the Nineteenth Century and After (1782—1919)*. London: Longmans, 1937.

Trevelyan, George Macaulay. *A Shortened History of England*. Harmondsworth, UK: Penguin Books, 1959.

Trevelyan, George Macaulay. *English Social History*. London: Longman, 1978.

Truman, Nevil. *Historic Furnishing*. London: Sir Isaac Pitman & Sons, 1950.

Turk, F. A. *Japanese Objets d'Art*. London: Arco, 1962.

Vadgama, Kusoom. *India in Britain*. London: Robert Royce, 1982.

Wainwright, Clive. *The Romantic Interior: The British Collector at Home, 1750—1850*. New Haven, CT: Yale University Press, 1989.

Waley, Arthur David. *The Opium War through Chinese Eyes*. London: George Allen & Unwin, 1958.

Walker, Philip. *Woodworking Tools*. Aylesbury, UK: Shire, 1980.

Walker, Thomas James, and Alfred Rhodes. *The Depot for Prisoners of War at Norman Cross, Huntingdonshire, 1796 to 1816*. London: Constable, 1913.

Walkling, Gillian. *Tea Caddies*. London: Victoria and Albert Museum, 1985.

Ward-Jackson, Peter. *English Furniture Designers of the Eighteenth Century*. London: Victoria and Albert Museum, 1958.

Watkin, David. *The Buildings of Britain: Regency*. London: Barrie & Jenkins, 1982.

Watson, John Steven. *The Oxford History of England: The Reign of George III, 1760—1815*. Oxford: Oxford University Press, 1960.

White, Elizabeth, comp. *Pictorial Dictionary of British 18th Century Furniture Design: The Printed Sources*. Woodbridge, UK: Antique Collectors' Club, 2000.

White, R. J. *The Age of George III*. London: Heinemann, 1968.

Whittick, Arnold. *Symbols, Signs and Their Meaning and Uses in Design*. London: Leonard Hill, 1971.

Wild, Antony. *The East India Company: Trade & Conquest from 1600*. London: Harper Collins, 1999.

Williams, Ernest Neville. *Life in Georgian England*. London: B. T. Batsford, 1962.

Wills, Geoffrey. *English Furniture, 1760—1900*. Enfield, UK: Guinness Superlatives, 1971.

Wilson, Michael. *William Kent, Architect, Designer, Painter, Gardener, 1685—1748*. London: Routledge & Kegan Paul, 1984.

Winckelmann, Johann Joachim. *Geschichte der Kunst des Alterthums*. Dresden, 1764.

Winckelmann, Johann Joachim. *Monumenti antichi inediti spiegati ed illustrati*. 2 vols. Rome, 1767.

Winckelmann, Johann Joachim. *Reflections on the Imitation of Greek Works in Painting and Sculpture: Johann Joachim Winckelmann, Complete German Text, with a New English Translation by Elfriede Heyer and Roger C. Norton*. La Salle, IL: Open Court, 1987.

Wood, Anthony. *Nineteenth Century Britain, 1815—1914*. Essex, UK: Longman, 1982.

Woodham-Smith, Cecil. *Queen Victoria: Her Life and Times*. London: Hamish Hamilton, 1972.

Wright, Thomas, comp. *Caricature History of the Georges*. London: Chatto & Windus, 1904.

Wulff, Hans Eberhard. *The Traditional Crafts of Persia: Their Development, Technology, and Influence on Eastern and Western Civilizations*. Cambridge, MA: MIT Press, 1966.

Yglesias, John Roy Charles. *London Life and the Great Exhibition 1851*. London: Longmans, Green, 1964.

Young, Anne. *An Introduction to Music*. Edinburgh: Muir, Wood, 1803.

Young, George Malcolm. *Portrait of an Age: Early Victorian England, 1830—65*. London: Oxford University Press, 1936.

Younghusband, Ethel. *Mansions, Men and Tunbridge Ware*. Slough, UK: Windsor, 1949.

# Index

Hogarth, William, 220

Hollamby, Henry, **125**, **126**

Holland, Henry, 22, 47; commissioned by Prince of Wales, 34

honeysuckle: brass inlay, 47

Hong Kong, 67: China was forced to cede, 67

Hong merchants, 62—67; Co, 175

Hong Xiuquan, **61**

Hope, Thomas, 49, 50; advocated brass, 250; architect-designer, 48; brass ornament, 336; recommended poppy as a motif, 80; studying ruins of Greece, 47; tea chest, **255**; tea chest drawing, **247**

horn. *See* Anglo-Indian; segmented, 268

horn, Anglo-Indian, 186

Horniman, John: tea man, 268

*Household Furniture and Interior Decoration executed from Designs by Thomas Hope*, 47

How: Jane Penrice, silversmith, **217**

Hubball, Thomas, of Clerkenwell; patentpapier mâché, 109; hunting scenes, 163

Hyde Park, London, 72

Immortals, land of the, 24

Imperial Garden, 24

import duties, 58, 59; wallpaper, 64

Ince, William, 8

incised ivory, **188**, **189**, **194**, **204**; with porcupine quills, **192**

India: a land of immense culture, 187; colonizing large parts of, 61; Dutch and English factories, 188; influence of on chinoiserie, 40; Portuguese, 187; Indian and Chinese" designs, 32; artists, 189

Indian boxes, **186**—**203**

Indo-Portuguese, **131**

inlay: acanthus leaf, **229**; and carved elements, **248**; brass, **51**—**52**; brass with mother of pearl, **76**; chased silver, **75**; English rose. The thistle, **214**; festoon, **232**; fluted patterns, **18**; geometric bands, **75**, **269**; Grecian laurel or myrtle wreath, **216**; half human creature, **232**; holly and ivory, **232**; ivory in rosewood, **203**; leaf and berry, **18**; mahogany; with brass, 250; marquetry shell, **20**, **22**, **232**, **241**; metal, ivory, and shell, **72**; mother of pearl, **71**, **349**, **354**, **355**; mother of pearl and pewter lines, **47**; mother of pearl and silver, **76**; mother of pearl, classical figures, **303**; mother of pearl, Egyptian inspired, **53**; pewter and mother of pearl, **45**; *piqué*, **133**, **134**, **136**, **168**; stylized motifs, 19

innovation, 106, 163; age mad after, 6; stylistic Victorian, 70

Ireland: visit by George IV, 166

Irish boxes: **166**—**67**, 166—67; made caddy bowls, 230; tea caddy Dublin Hills, **215**; oak leaves, acorns, holly thistles, 166

Italian Renaissance, 13

Italian work: *piqué*, 131

ivory: and horn in boulle, 138; carved Chinese, 145; Catherine the Great, patron, 143; cutting, 143; early boxes, 142; English cabinet makers, 143; engraved, **146**; facings, 144; fixed with ivory pins, 189, 191, 195; incised, **186**, **187**; incised and lac filled, 187; Russia, **298**; sewing boxes, 296—300; sewing tools, 296; tea caddies, 143; tea caddy, **147**; turning, France, Russia, 142; walrus and mammoth, 142; working; Peter the Great, 143; Russia, 143

ivory and tortoiseshell: **130**—**48**; marquetry, **130**

ivory panels incised and lac filled, **192**

Japan: Dutch trading post (1609), 184; Portuguese expelled (1639), 184

Japanese: inspired silver, **317**; tea chest, **268**

Japanese design, 185

Japanese lacquer, 184—85, **186**; table cabinet, **185**, **355**

Japanese objects: Great Exhibition(1862), 184

Japanese Shogun, 208

japanned: blue, **35**; raised, **271**; seal wax red, **226**; writing slope, **325**

japanning, 64, 108; Chippendale, 10; Germany, The Low Countries, Russia, 96; ovens, 96; papier mâché, 95; patents, 33; preparation for, 87; raised, **27**, 32

Jardine and Matheson, 66

jasper medallions, 345

Java: Dutch trading base, 208

Jefferson, Thomas, **332**

Jehol, 34

Jennens and Bettridge, 102—**3**, 103, 104, **105**, 106, 108, 110; "sculptors", 106; Alsager, 111; Belgrave Square, 102; in association with Booth, Edwin, 111; Japanners, 102; Jennens, Theodore Hyla, 106; mold method, 106; papier mâché, 101; patent, 102; The Great Exhibition, 105; use of mother of pearl, 103; views of Oxford and Cambridge, 105; writing desk, 105

Jennens, Theodore Hyla: patent "gem laying", 104

Jesuits, 171; first to penetrate China, 23; in China, 24; pioneered far eastern exploration, 184

jewelry boxes, 180, 314

jewelry caskets, 314

Johnson, Dr. Samuel, 6; on tea, 212

Johnston, George: sewing box, **291**

Jones, Arthur, Son & Co, 166

Jones, Inigo, 6

Jones, Thomas, of Bilston, 106

K'ang Hsi, Emperor: garden, 24

Kauffmann, Angelica, 15, **16**, 111, 243; commissioned by Robert Adam, 16

Keats, John, 14

Kew: Menagerie Pavilion, 82; royal garden in Chinese taste, 26

Kholmogory: ivory work, 299

Killarney House, 166

Killarney Lakes, 166; Tunbridge ware, 166

Killarney ware, **167**; distinctive style, 167; Royal patronage, 166

kingwood, 50, 119, 288, 363

knife box, **320**—**23**, 362; urn shaped, 20

knife boxes, 319—22

Knight, Frederick, 102

krater, 49

lac, 51, 54, 64; decoration, 191; private trading in, forbidden, 33; used in incised ivory, 188; Vernis Martin, 96; Vincent Brixhe, 160

lacquer, 102, 185, *See* oriental lacquer, *See also* Oriental lacquer; applying, 169—71; box structure, 169; box types, 180; boxes, 65, 171, 178; condition, 183; feet, 180; Prince Regent, 174; shapes in eighteenth c., 173; Chinese export, 171—72; Chinese/Japanese, 172—73; decoration, 171; tea caddies, 268; export 18c. to 1820, 173—74; export 19c., 174—83; gathering, preparing, 169; inlaid in ivory and semi precious stones, **171**; mother of pearl, 184; polymerization, 169; quality of, 169; red, 171; restoration, 183; revered in China, 171; sewing boxes, 296, 307; workshops, 169

lacquer ovens, 32

*Ladies Amusement, or The Whole Art of Japanning Made Easy, The*, 32

*Ladies Amusement, The*, **36**, **211**, **260**; *inspired by*, **215**

Landseer: painter, 110

Lane, T., 105

Langlois, Pierre: active in London, 138

lap desks. *See* writing boxes

Lascelles family, 19

laudanum, 62, 64, **64**

Laurencekirk box, 159

Laurencekirk boxes: stamped, 161

Laurentini (*piqué*), 130

Le Gaigneur, Louis, 51

leaf and berry pattern, **236**

leaf and dot design, 12

Papworth, J. B., archchitect/designer, 70

Parker, Thomas, 51, 139

Parkesine, **306**

Parks, Alexander, **306**

parquetry, **18**, 50, **71**, 354; (1830), 122; cube patern, 258; French, **72**; no longer fashionable, 343; *sadeli* mosaic, **199**; sample, 286; specimen, 356; Tunbridge ware, 119, 120, **119—21**; vandyke, 338, 352

partridge wood, 268

pastoral scenes, 163, 243, **101**

Patch, Thomas, 14

patent: Ann(e) Young's musical game, **360**; Betjemann's dressing box, **73**; optical, lenticular, **356**; Playfairs shaving aparatus, **327**

patents: Bentham, woodworking machine, 6; Betjemann's, 74, 314, 361; cost of, 101; dressing box, 312; early nineteenth century, Brunel, 71; 332, Polygraph; Hubball, T., for painting with metals, 109; military traveling cases, 334; painting lines on tartanware, 165; papier mâché; Brindley, 110; Clay, 98; Haselar, 111; Jennens and Bettridge, 102; Lane's, 104; portable writing desks, 330; steel nib, 341; veneer cutting machine, 71

paterae, **14**, 20, 229, 238, **244**, 362, **285**

patina, 239, 242, 286

patinated: (18 c.) to a warm glow, **22**; beautifully, **287**

patination: aged with dignity, **214**; exceptionally fine, **13**, **42**; restoration, 330; value, 7

Paxton, Joseph, 72: architect of the Crystal Palace, 281

Peace of 1814, 51

Pearl Glass, inlaid, 104

pen box: papier-mâché, **96**

Penny Post, 341

penwork, **60**, **80—91**, 238; and filigree work, 150; and painted, 80—89; and transfer decorated, 165; categories, 84; chinoiserie, **260**; classical scene, **86**; cribbage and cards, **271**; exotic animals, 83; Gothic themes, 352; Greco-Roman, Egyptian, **17**; Indian, 87; Indian figures, **86**; Indian inspiration, 68; Indian life, **39**; *memento mori*, 87; neoclassical, 20; reminiscent of Anglo Indian work, **91**; reminiscent of engraved ivory work, 87; sewing boxes, 291; table cabinet, **37**, **353**, **354**; table cabinets, 352; tea caddies, 258; Tunbridge ware, **116**, 118, 291; very fine lines, **85**; with rosewood, **294**; woods, 163; writing slope, 333, 340, **344**

Pepys, Samuel, 270: mentioned chinoiserie, 30; tea, 209

Percier, French architect, 48

perfume, 302, 362

perfume bottles, 307

Perks, Frederick: papier mâché, 109

Perks, Henry: papier mâché, 109

Perry, Edward and Richard: papier mâché, 110

Persian: pen box, **96**

Persian design, 189

pet: goose of Sandy, James, 159; lion of Britannia, 69; pig of Gardenstone, Francis, Lord, 159

Peter the Great of Russia; ivory working, 143

Petersham, Lord, 219, 282; photography, 72, 341; age of no, 27

Physic Garden, Chelsea, 80

piano shaped boxes, 302

Piccadilly, 47, 82, 366; Egyptian Hall, 46, 51

*Pickwick Papers*, 264

picture, topographical on papier-mâché, **105**

*pietra dura*, 345, **349**

Pillement, Jean-Baptiste, 26, 32, 34

tradition, **38**, **100**

*piqué*, **133**, **134**, **136**, 143, **168**; Laurentini, 130; national styles, 130; tortoiseshell, 130

Piranesi, 18, 46; prints, 326

Pitt, William, 62, 211

planing, 6

playing cards, 270—81

Police, Metropolitan, established, 276

Polygraph, (Brunell) **332**

Pompadour, Mme. De, diva of style, 27

Pompeii, 13, 14, 174

Pontypool, 101

Pope Joan boxes, **278**

Pope, Alexander, 27, 324; gambling metaphors, 271

poppy , *See* opium, 54

porcupine quill, **190**, **192**, 191

Portuguese, 52, 208, 209; in India, 187; leased Macao, 55; trade supremacy, 55

Portuguese colonial tea box, **210**

Potter, William, maker, tea chest, **243**

Powell, T: maker, 146

prancing ponies; Chinese considered the English, 60

pressed tortoiseshell, **139**; price; toilette box (1814), 309; caddy (1832), 250; dressing box (1745), 308; refinishing detrimental, 7; Tea Chests (1788), 229; writing box (1822), 336; writing box (1828), 336; writing boxes (1798), **326**

price guide, 7; knife boxes, 322; straw work, 158

Prince of Wales, 41, 46, 47, 334, *See* also George IV; atbiter of taste, 34; frequented The Cocoa-Tree Club, 273; Killarney ware, 166; supplied small toilette box, 309; taste for French splendor, 139

Prince of Wales's feathers, 21, 238

Prince Regent; invited so many, 216; lacquer work, 174; *See also* Prince of Wales, 216

printed silk, **44**

printing box, **331**, **341**

prints, **48**, **150**; Brighton Pavilion, **42**, **219**; classical, **244**

decorated with classical scene, **15**; hand colored, **244**, 87; used by Edmund Nye, 117

prisoner of war work, **56**

Prussia, King of, 43

Pugin, Augustus Welby, 72

putti, 139, 216, 243; putti (Sheraton), 50; putti or angels; *piqué*, 131

pyramid tops, 48, 248

pyrography, 166

*Quarterly Magazine*, 54

quills: porcupine, 186, 190; for writing, 341

Raikes, Thomas; gold dressing case, 309

Ranelagh Gardens (print), **218**; (tea), 215

*Rape of the Lock, The*, 271

Rawlings, Charles: silver smith, **315**

reeded carving, 49

reeded segments, 191

refinishing is detrimental, 7

Regency, 41—54; "patent travelling cases", 363; Anglo Indian, 268; card boxes, 273, 270—76; crisis, 21; dressing boxes, 311; Egyptian elements, 45; forms; adopted in India, 201; Anglo Indian, 304; forms used later, 265; lacquer, 180; leather covered, 290; magnificent excess, 53; make up, 309; metal feet and handles, 84; moneylender, 275; rakes, 274; rise of the effete vain dandy, 309; sewing box, 288—304; shopping, 341; sparkle gone by 1820, 276; table cabinets, 352; tea, 264; tea caddies, 246; writing boxes, 334—38; Regency Bill, 21

Registration of Designs Act, 110

reliquaries, 142

Reni, Guido, 99

*Repository of Arts, Literature, Commerce, Manufacture, Fashions and Politics; See also* Ackermann, 50

restoration, 7, 270; impossible, 245; insensitive, 286; lacquer, 183

reverse painting (glass); Crystal Palace, **107;** St. Paul's Cathedral, **67**; Westminster Abbey, **104:** eighteenth century, **217**

Reynolds, Joshua, 14